OXFORD ENGLISH DRAMA

General Editor: MICHAEL CORDNER
Associate General Editors: PETER HOLLAND · MARTIN WIGGINS

PETER PAN
AND OTHER PLAYS

JAMES MATTHEW BARRIE was born at Kirriemuir in Angus, Scotland, in 1860. After attending Dumfries Academy and Edinburgh University, he joined the *Nottingham Journal* as leader writer in 1883. Two years later he went to London to seek a living as a freelance writer. Drawing on his mother's memories of her childhood years, he achieved early success with stories about his home town. The first such collection, *Auld Licht Idylls*, was published in 1888. His novel *The Little Minister* (1891) achieved great popularity, but from the 1890s onwards he turned most of his attention to the theatre. A succession of long-running plays brought Barrie wealth and critical acclaim. His most famous creation, Peter Pan, first appeared in the novel *The Little White Bird* (1902), and the play *Peter Pan* was first staged in 1904. *Peter and Wendy* followed seven years later. Barrie continued to enjoy great public recognition and success, but his private life was clouded by divorce and a series of bereavements, and he wrote less in his later years. His last play, *The Boy David*, was first performed in 1936, a few months before his death in 1937.

PETER HOLLINDALE is Reader in English and Educational Studies at the University of York. He has written widely on Shakespeare and on children's literature and children's theatre. For Oxford World's Classics he has also edited Barrie's *Peter Pan in Kensington Gardens* and *Peter and Wendy*, and his other publications include *Signs of Childness in Children's Books* (1997).

MICHAEL CORDNER is Reader in the Department of English and Related Literature at the University of York. His editions include George Farquhar's *The Beaux' Stratagem*, the *Complete Plays* of Sir George Etherege, *Four Comedies* of Sir John Vanbrugh, and *Four Restoration Marriage Comedies*. He is completing a book on *The Comedy of Marriage 1660–1737*.

PETER HOLLAND is Professor of Shakespeare Studies and Director of the Shakespeare Institute, University of Birmingham.

MARTIN WIGGINS is a Fellow of the Shakespeare Institute and Lecturer in English at the University of Birmingham.

OXFORD ENGLISH DRAMA

OXFORD WORLD'S CLASSICS

J. M. BARRIE

The Admirable Crichton
Peter Pan
When Wendy Grew Up
What Every Woman Knows
Mary Rose

Edited with an Introduction and Notes by
PETER HOLLINDALE

General Editor
MICHAEL CORDNER
Associate General Editors
PETER HOLLAND   MARTIN WIGGINS

OXFORD
UNIVERSITY PRESS

OXFORD
UNIVERSITY PRESS

Great Clarendon Street, Oxford OX2 6DP

Oxford University Press is a department of the University of Oxford.
It furthers the University's objective of excellence in research, scholarship,
and education by publishing worldwide in

Oxford New York

Athens Auckland Bangkok Bogotá Buenos Aires Calcutta
Cape Town Chennai Dar es Salaam Delhi Florence Hong Kong Istanbul
Karachi Kuala Lumpur Madrid Melbourne Mexico City Mumbai
Nairobi Paris São Paulo Singapore Taipei Tokyo Toronto Warsaw

with associated companies in Berlin Ibadan

Oxford is a registered trade mark of Oxford University Press
in the UK and in certain other countries

Published in the United States
by Oxford University Press Inc., New York

© Peter Hollindale 1995

The moral rights of the author have been asserted

Database right Oxford University Press (maker)

First published as a World's Classics paperback 1995
Reissued as an Oxford World's Classics paperback 1999

British Library Cataloguing in Publication Data

Data available

Library of Congress Cataloging in Publication Data
Barrie, J. M. (James Matthew), 1860–1937
Peter Pan; When Wendy grew up; The admirable Crichton;
What every woman knows; Mary Rose / J. M. Barrie;
edited with an introduction by Peter Hollindale; general editor, Michael Cordner.
p.   cm.—(Oxford world's classics)
I. Hollindale, Peter.   II. Title.   III. Title: Peter Pan.   IV. Series.
PR4072.H65   1995   822'.912—dc20   94–22791 CIP

ISBN 0–19–283919–5

5

Printed in Great Britain by
Clays Ltd, St Ives plc

CONTENTS

ACKNOWLEDGEMENTS

For assistance in the preparation of this edition I am grateful to John Rowlands Pritchard, Richard Shephard, Meg Ross, Jeffrey Lewis, Martin Phillips of Samuel French Ltd., and staff of the Victoria and Albert Museum. The General Editor, Michael Cordner, has been generous with encouragement, suggestions, and practical help throughout. My wife, *sine qua non*, has driven me to distant theatres, typed the manuscript, untangled knotty research problems, and generally kept the show on the road. My thanks to them all.

P. H.

INTRODUCTION

On 22 February 1908, the last night of the fourth London season of
Peter Pan, the audience was surprised by the unexpected insertion of
a new scene before the closing tableau of the Tree Tops. In the pause
which preceded it, as the play's historian Roger Lancelyn Green
records:

'a small nightgowned figure', according to a privileged reviewer present that
night, 'appeared before the curtain and made the following announcement:

'My friends, I am the Baby Mermaid. We are now going to do a new act,
the first and only time on any stage. Mr Barrie told us a story one day about
what happened to Peter when Wendy grew up, and we made it into an act,
and it will never be done again. You are to think that a lot of years have rolled
by, and that Wendy is an old married lady. You will be surprised to see what
I'm going to play . . .'[1]

The scene which followed is very close in dialogue to the last
chapter of Barrie's novelization of *Peter Pan*, *Peter and Wendy*,
published in 1911. This new scene was itself entitled *An Afterthought*.
The last night of the 1908 season was indeed its only performance in
Barrie's lifetime, and it remained unpublished until 1957. In 1982,
however, it was revived for the Royal Shakespeare Company production, and seems likely to find favour as the standard ending for a play
which has evolved through many possible conclusions. Despite its
sombre emphasis away from a child audience towards an audience of
adults, *An Afterthought* does seem an integral part of the play and one
that accords with modern tastes. Leonee Ormond notes that 'this
scene, with its stress on the eternal nature of Peter, makes a more
satisfying ending than the briefer episode with Wendy a year later
with which the play usually concludes'.[2] It is included in this edition
as perhaps the single most important instance of Barrie's variant
endings, and in the expectation that it will become the standard one.
Yet the circumstances of its first performance, which was followed by
'a glimpse of Mr Barrie'[3] at the curtain-call, were clearly extraordinary.

[1] Roger Lancelyn Green, *Fifty Years of 'Peter Pan'* (London, 1954), 110.
[2] Leonee Ormond, *J. M. Barrie*, (Edinburgh, 1987), 108.
[3] Lancelyn Green (n. 1 above), 112.

Extraordinary or not, it was not the last occasion in Barrie's career when a single audience found itself the chosen recipient of a one-performance afterthought. R. D. S. Jack records a 1931 performance of *The Admirable Crichton* in New York, observing that 'a single night and a single performance . . . witnessed the two extremes of the tonal spectrum' of the play. He continues:

The younger Gillette played Crichton in so tragic a fashion that *The New York Times* journalist commented: 'By the time the Third Act has ended you are likely to fly to the text to discover whether Barrie was writing comedy or a lucubration of the woes of the world'. The curtain fell. There stepped forward Gillette the elder (Crichton in the first American production) to read a 'happy ending' as provided by the author in a letter. Crichton, it seemed, wishes to stay where he was. A splash offstage interrupts the reading. 'Who can it be?' Gillette wonders aloud. The cast still being there after taking their bows begin to discuss the issue. Tweeny presumes it must be her. But no; it is in fact Lady Mary, Gillette informs them from the letter. He then, *in propria persona*, tells the audience that (if they are nice) a place on the Island remains for them.[4]

This additional variant to an already extensive list of possible endings for *The Admirable Crichton* (Jack has traced eighteen different conclusions, if minor variations are included) came from Barrie no less than twenty-nine years after the play was first produced. It shares with *An Afterthought* a set of disturbances to conventional audience expectations. Barrie himself is both retiringly and conspicuously present in the background, the 'onlie begetter' of these strange departures, yet also the 'ideas man' merely, the initiator who transfers responsibility and control to the characters and the actors. It is the Baby Mermaid and her friends (the personae or the players?) who have converted story into play; it is the actors in *The Admirable Crichton* who muse about the doings of their characters, and the characters who 'act', in response to the author's letter-as-story. In both cases the audience, overtly deprived of the consolations of illusionist theatre by having its attention drawn to eccentric theatricality, is paradoxically coaxed into intimate membership of the illusionist conspiracy which is theatre itself. As Jack correctly notes,

Here is one of the most ambitious extensions of Barrie's artistic views. The genre is being expanded in a whole variety of ways; the blockages between experience in word and theatre are being alternatively broken down and

[4] R. D. S. Jack, *The Road to the Never Land: A Reassessment of J. M. Barrie's Dramatic Art* (Aberdeen, 1991), 128.

re-established. The characters are not only in search of an author, they are discussing indirectly the nature of characterisation and authorship.[5]

Jack draws attention to yet another instance of an 'extreme movement of perspective . . . also suggested in a letter from the author; read aloud; at the end of only one performance'. This occasion came during the 1919 American production of *Dear Brutus*, the only one of Barrie's incontrovertibly major plays to be omitted from this edition. This revisionist episode, the most bizarre of all, is reported by Barrie's idiosyncratic and partisan biographer Denis Mackail, who in spite of his fierce loyalties seems here bemused by the perversities of genius:

Odd yet characteristic bit of Barrie-ism on January 23rd. Letter dated from the Athenaeum, to Dr Nicholas Murray Butler, President of Columbia University, and read four weeks later, from the stage of the Empire Theatre, to an audience assembled at a special performance of *Dear Brutus* . . . 'If I were there,' it begins, 'to appear in public for the first and only time . . .' And then it becomes even odder. *Dear Brutus*, it seems, is an allegory. Dearth is John Bull. Margaret, the might-have-been, is America. 'The play shows how on the fields of France this father and daughter get a second opportunity for coming together, and the nightingale is George Washington asking them to do it on his birthday. And so on. Astonishment of the distinguished audience . . . The magic from three thousand miles away isn't quite as powerful as all that, and the Declaration of Independence remains in force.[6]

Peculiar as this episode is, it is revealing about Barrie and his conviction of the multi-faceted, diversely interpretable nature of history, of personality, and of drama. As we shall see, *Dear Brutus* is a key statement of a recurrent Barrie theme, the impossibility of second chances. At this performance he attempted to unfix history from its course and to hypothesize a 'second chance' for two nations: 'Are now the two to make it up permanently or for ever to drift apart? A second chance comes to few. As for a third chance, who ever heard of it? It's now or never.' In order to promote this cause he reinterpreted potential history, and allegorized his characters and his play. Here, then, are three examples of a delayed authorial intervention in the script and meaning of a successful, well-established play, none of the three intended to be permanent or even to outlive a single unique performance. They alert us to several aspects of Barrie's dramatic practice and conception of theatre which must form the

---

[5] Ibid. 128–9.
[6] Denis Mackail, *The Story of J. M. B.* (London, 1941), 534.

starting-point for any evaluation of his work. Most important of all, we should notice his compulsion to revise. For Barrie none of his play-texts is ever fixed and stable. In successive preliminary drafts, then during rehearsal, then in the light of initial production experience, and as we have seen, even when a play is fully established in the repertoire, he is ceaselessly modifying, experimenting, refining, improvising possible variations, or simply changing his mind.

Some of the alterations were guided by practical experience of what worked or failed in the theatre. Barrie was a highly professional dramatist, for whom the collaborative nature of theatrical performance was one of the attractions which drew him to it from the novel. Leonee Ormond notes: 'An inveterate attender at rehearsals, he was always prepared to listen to the actors, and, if appropriate, to change his mind. A Barrie play was a collaboration between cast, director and playwright: never finally completed, the texts were always open to revision.'[7] But there were deeper reasons, too, which explained Barrie's restlessness with the provisional forms and closures which constituted his dramatic statements. Many of his plays can be seen as explorations of the tension between change and changelessness. It seems that in Barrie's thinking there was an unresolved contradiction between belief in the fixity of human personality and belief in the multiple possibilities opened up for every individual by roles and role-play.

In Barrie's novel *The Little White Bird*, the first episodes of the Peter Pan story (later extracted and published separately as *Peter Pan in Kensington Gardens*) reveal a sober insistence on the irreversibility of human choices and the impossibility of second chances. This became the theme of *Dear Brutus*, a tragic counterpart to *A Midsummer Night's Dream*, with its magician-figure, Lob, being a kind of Puck in old age. ('Lob' is another name for Puck.) Lob's guests, who mostly believe that their lives would be very different if they had a second chance, are given the opportunity they seek in a single night of midsummer woodland magic, only to repeat the errors and failings that have marred their first-time lives. Neither in time passing nor in time stilled do Barrie's people essentially change. In *The Admirable Crichton* Lord Loam and his family, restored to the indolent luxury of aristocratic London, at once revert to type and lose the alternative personalities they discovered on their island. And yet 'circumstances alter cases', and those alternative selves exist. Wendy is no more

[7] Ormond (n. 2 above), 87.

capable of permanent habitation of the Never Land than Peter is of growing up in Bloomsbury, but both are capable of multiple behaviour in imaginative play. Characters are caught between fixed personality in fixed circumstance and diverse potential if circumstances change. Inexhaustible adaptation within fixity is the paradoxical condition of human psychology, as Barrie perceives it, of his dramatic art, and, perhaps inseparable from either, of his own personality. Its consummate expression is Peter Pan, who, on one reading of his protean name, is everything in make-believe and role-play, but has a heart of stone.

Experiments with various logical progressions from a fixed idea, with various behaviour-patterns from a fixed persona, are expressed in Barrie's work by a corresponding dramatic practice which allows for various developments, and especially for various conclusions, from a fixed dramatic situation. In other words, Barrie's unending revisionism is not just the obsessive tinkering of a perfectionist or indecisive theatrical craftsman; it is the artistic projection of a philosophical stance which was sceptical of fixed and permanent truth, and convinced of relativity, of circumstantial change, seeing life and art alike as fluid and provisional. To assess his plays fairly we must see his compulsions to revise for what they are—a spectrum of decisions ranging from pragmatic choices about workable theatre to variant discoveries about the potential meanings of his texts.

The play which underwent the most comprehensive revisions was *Peter Pan*. The evolution of this play (which is still continuing) has been fully and helpfully discussed by Roger Lancelyn Green,[8] Jacqueline Rose,[9] and R. D. S. Jack.[10] One or two examples will suffice here to show the range of choices Barrie made in the process of revision, and the mixture of theatrical expediency and thematic self-discovery which conditioned them.

In the published text of 1928, and generally in the play's performance history, there are clear signals of sexual jealousy and rivalry for Peter's attentions on the part of Wendy and Tinker Bell, while Peter himself remains innocently unaware of and indifferent to such feelings. In the manuscript version of the play these suggestions are noticeably more pronounced, and Peter's would-be partners additionally include Tiger Lily. A brief passage of dialogue between Peter and

[8] Lancelyn Green (n. 1 above).

[9] Jacqueline Rose, *The Case of Peter Pan, or The Impossibility of Children's Fiction* (London, 1984).

[10] R. D. S. Jack, 'The Manuscript of *Peter Pan*', in *Children's Literature*, vol. 18 (New Haven, Conn., 1990).

Tiger Lily indicates the belligerent sexuality which Barrie originally included in his script:

TIGER LILY Suppose Tiger Lily runs into wood—Peter Paleface catch her—what then?

PETER (*bewildered*) Paleface can never catch Indian girl, they run so fast.

TIGER LILY If Peter Paleface chase Tiger Lily—she no run very fast—she tumble in a heap what then? (*Peter puzzled. She addresses Indians*) What then?

ALL INDIANS She him's squaw.

This passage was quickly removed from the production script, as was another scene, inserted later in the play's first drafting, where Tiger Lily comes to the house under the ground and makes a second effort to win Peter:

PETER Now, then, what is it you want?

TIGER LILY Want to be your squaw.

PETER Is that what you want, Wendy?

WENDY I suppose it is, Peter.

PETER Is that what you want, Tink?

  (*Bells answer*)

PETER You all three want that. Very well—that's really wishing to be my mother.

By removing Tiger Lily's advances, which are the most sexually explicit and most 'normal', and by giving more muted expression to the still childlike and part-playful sexuality of Wendy, and to the flirtatious asperity of disembodied Tinker Bell, Barrie succeeded in blurring the reality of the female figures' sexual drive and Peter's uncomprehending, sexually neuter state. His revision emphasized instead the mingled comedy and pathos of Peter's supposedly pre-sexual perception of the female, not as wife but as mother. As practical theatre this was a necessary adjustment to make *Peter Pan* more evidently a play for children. For adults in the audience it also sharpened the thematic focus and placed the emphasis squarely on the play's most disconcerting element of sexual comedy, namely its presentation of the male as child, and its investment of female gender attraction in the role of mother rather than wife.

Also excised before the first performance was a scene set in Kensington Gardens, where Wendy and Peter, playing mother and son, had set up house together. In this scene, derived from the nineteenth-century tradition of pantomime and harlequinade, Hook pursues Peter to London disguised as a schoolmaster, and hunts him in the Gardens. Peter is dressed as a clown, but for a long time escapes Hook's detection because Tinker Bell ('Tippy' in this version) turns *all* the children and grown-ups of the Gardens into clowns, columbines, and harlequins. This was dropped, no doubt in part because it was so difficult to stage, but also because it drew nostalgically on those very performance traditions from which Barrie's play was emancipating children's theatre. Another casualty of revision was the notorious 'Beautiful Mothers' scene, in which a group of London mothers claim possession of the lost boys and undergo sundry tests of maternal feeling. The scene was acutely embarrassing and was abandoned early in the play's first season. Other episodes familiar to us in both stage performance and printed scripts were added gradually after the opening run, notably Hook's famous soliloquy on death, 'How still the night is'.

Though virtually all the omissions and additions had a straightforward theatrical rationale, they also clarified Barrie's evolving sense of the work he had created. The downgrading of Tiger Lily, along with other changes, had the effect of making Wendy more important, and highlighting her situation as both child and incipient mother, acting out those true-life roles which the adult Wendy could eventually expect (as opposed to the melodramatic dream-heroics and pretence of Peter's various guises). Wendy is a citizen of reality rather than illusion and exists in time, contrasting with the frozen eternity of Peter's youthfulness. The evolving clarification of the play's form, therefore, sharpens the focal contrast between time and timelessness which Wendy's relationship with Peter represents. In Barrie's imagination this is the essential form of the contrast between change and changelessness. Therefore, one performance or no, *An Afterthought: When Wendy Grew Up* is a logical continuation from the choices made during the first few years of the play's existence. It darkens the play with a sense of tragedy (in the special meaning which must attach to Barrie's use of the word), and sits uneasily in a piece for children. Lancelyn Green notes that it 'would not quite do in the theatre, where a children's play must end happily'.[11] But nowadays it also defines the logic of the play even for children, living as they do in an age where they too are effectively schooled against finales of unambiguous happiness.

Barrie's lasting habits of revision, and his continuing preoccupations, are clear again in his last great stage success, *Mary Rose*, which

---

[11] Lancelyn Green (n. 1 above), 58.

like *Peter Pan* reflects a gradual darkening of vision in its movement from initial conception to performance script. Leonee Ormond gives a succinct and just account of this too-easily underestimated play. Part of her commentary, including as it does Barrie's initial plan for the play, is worth quoting at some length. Having noted the progressively more sinister staging of Mary Rose's disappearance at the end of Act 2, she goes on:

The darkening of Barrie's vision in the development of this passage can be paralleled in later scenes of the play. In the first manuscript the island is revealed as a place of perfect happiness, the Never Land, the home of Peter Pan. Behind a gauze curtain the audience was to see the trees through which Peter and the lost boys make their way underground:

> Peter himself emerges & sits on Joanna's [Mary Rose's] tree trunk playing his pipes. Joanna arrives (from a boat if this can be suggested) and the two meet. They don't kiss or shake hands—they double up with mirth at being together again on what we now realise to be Peter's island. They claw at each other like two inordinately gay children. He pulls down her hair & puts leaves in it, so that she looks like Wendy. 'The wood' is mysteriously lit up in the background, and exquisite music comes vaguely from it, including the laughter of unseen children. Peter signs jocularly that all is ready and dances off doubled with mirth and playing his pipes. In a similar ecstasy she dances after him. When they have gone we hear the plop, plop, plop, meaning that the island has got her again.

By originally locating Mary Rose's two absences on Peter's island, and by returning her to it at the end, Barrie relied on a direct theatrical reference. He was wise to change the ending, which an audience unfamiliar with *Peter Pan* would find inexplicable and bizarre ... The *Peter Pan* ending might seem to reduce the seriousness of *Mary Rose*, but there are other parallels between the Peter Pan story and *Mary Rose* ...[12]

Indeed there are, and they represent a continuing preoccupation in Barrie's work with the tragic interplay between time and timelessness, reality and fantasy-as-reality. In both plays these themes are represented by the figure of the child-mother and the death-in-life tragedy of perpetual youth. Mary Rose embodies features of both Peter and Wendy. Although the two plays are beset by ambiguities and multiple uncertainties characteristic of Barrie, R. D. S. Jack seems right in his view of the implied imaginative verdict: 'Barrie seems to have argued throughout his writings that escape from time and so from death, whether through the fantasy of Neverland or through various art

---

[12] Ormond (n. 2 above), 130–1.

forms, cannot be a wholly satisfactory solution to the human situation."[13] What needs to be added is that through the evolution of his plays, and the cumulative effect of his revision choices, he seems usually to have opted for the darker implications of his drama.

Faced with Barrie's unendingly self-renewing stagecraft, and his addiction to spontaneous refashioning of his plays' significance, historians and editors of his work have had difficulty in arriving at a stable text. We cannot say that the plays ever reached a final form, or that one text is more 'theatrical' than another. Some plays, of course, escaped any notable convulsions (as did *What Every Woman Knows*), and others had completed their important evolutions before they reached production (as had *Mary Rose*). Even here, however, there is a further stage of authorial working entailed by the preparation of the published script. The text which Barrie approved for printing may differ in major or minor ways from the production script, and those for which he approved publication are embellished by elaborate stage directions. The more obviously mobile texts, including *The Admirable Crichton* and above all *Peter Pan*, permit all manner of synthetic reconstructions but will not yield a single text which was verifiably used in the theatre and can also be shown to be more 'theatrical'. All we can do is to take a 'freeze-frame' of one stage in Barrie's thinking about a play. For this edition I have chosen to respect Barrie's own inclinations, and retain the texts in the form which he approved for printing. These are, in a sense, more 'literary' texts, but it does not follow, as is sometimes supposed, that they are for that reason less 'theatrical'. The essential question on which the editor must make a decision is the status of Barrie's published stage directions.

We get a revealing glimpse into his mind on this matter in the prefatory stage direction for *Alice-Sit-by-the-Fire*, as Barrie muses on the problem that he is unable to show us the diary of his character Amy, because the stage forbids him to lean over her shoulder and tell us what is in it:

Then why don't we do it? Is it because this would be a form of eavesdropping, and that we cannot be sure our hands are clean enough to turn the pages of a young girl's thoughts? It cannot be that, because the novelists do it. It is because in a play we must tell little that is not revealed by the spoken words; you must ferret out all you want to know from them, although of course now and then we may whisper a conjecture in brackets . . . we are expected merely

---

[13] Jack (n. 10 above).

to present our characters as they toe the mark; then the handkerchief falls, and off they go.[14]

What are we to make of Barrie's 'conjectures in brackets'? Certainly there are signs in these remarks of his envy of the novelist's freedoms. Here, after all, is a dramatist who began his career as a novelist, and who wrote two early plays, *Walker, London* and *The Little Minister*, which draw heavily on his previous fiction. We recall, too, that the Peter Pan story originated in a novel, and eventually found its way back into another one, *Peter and Wendy*. The negative view that one can take of Barrie's published texts is to see them as throwbacks to novelization, with the literary stage direction as a Trojan horse allowing covert reoccupation of the house of fiction. One can, therefore, argue that the printed texts of the Uniform, Collected, and Definitive editions should be abandoned as mere reading-texts, and replaced by a production script wherever this is recoverable.

It can certainly be contended that Barrie overdoes it. J. C. Trewin draws a comparison with Shaw, another devotee of didactic, interventionist stage directions:

Some scamper-comedies have no true place on paper; but the major theatre-men can always straddle with ease between book and stage. Barrie luxuriated in stage directions, even beyond Shaw. His plays in printed form are often a trickle of dialogue through a forest of commentary.[15]

My own view, however, is that Barrie's printed stage directions are not only one of the glories of his dramatic achievement but an indispensable key to its true nature. Considered in their primary, practical function, they contain direct instructions to the actor and director, prescriptive where necessary but also introducing areas of speculative openness which allow the players their own entitlement to participatory interpretative freedoms. That is, they reflect Barrie's customary practice in rehearsal, being both directive and technically self-effacing. At the same time, they allow the reading theatregoer, gifted with an amateur's theatrical imagination while not claiming professional skills, to stage performances in the mind. They liberate the printed script from enslavement to dialogue, and reproduce the truth that speech is only one of theatre's several languages, which include also silence, movement and stillness, mime and tableau, dance and music, and ritualized effect. We can note, as an example, the

[14] J. M. Barrie, *Alice Sit-by-the-Fire*, in A. E. Wilson (ed.), *The Definitive Edition of the Plays of J. M. Barrie* (London, 1942), 597.

[15] J. C. Trewin, *The Theatre Since* 1900 (London, 1951), 62.

ingenious reproduction through the prefatory stage directions of the long and daring silence which opens *What Every Woman Knows*—a novel and risky effect in its time, but one which Barrie himself repeated at the opening of *The Boy David* and which has since been much admired and adopted, for instance, in the opening of Peter Ustinov's *The Love of Four Colonels*.

If Barrie is accused of betraying the novelist *manqué* in his stage directions, it is surely enough in his defence to show him as a dramatist who, for his time, was singularly free of enslavement to the word and at home with other forms of dramatic language. Even in the more socially realistic of his plays, the never wholly absent element of fantasy is often expressed through non-verbal effects. One of the strongest moments in the brilliant first Act of *What Every Woman Knows* is John Shand's silent nocturnal exploit of burglarious scholarship. In the central phase of fantasy in *The Admirable Crichton*, an atmospherically vivid stage direction which concludes Act 2 reflects a superb theatrical *coup de silence*, as the aristocrats gather to the lure of Crichton's cooking-pot. Silences, ethereal voices, sound and music stage the eerie disappearances of Mary Rose, and they alone suggest the ambiguity of good and evil in the island's powers, and the way the balance falls. *Peter Pan*, of course, is full of such occasions. Barrie's stage directions do not obscure but recreate them. His commitment to non-verbal dramatic statement is confirmed again and again. Examples include his reworking of the dropped harlequinade from *Peter Pan* as the ruthless one-act play *Pantaloon*, and his projected film-scenario for *Peter Pan*, which reduces dialogue to a minimum. These episodes suggest a theatrical imagination in constant and successful quest for dramatic equivalents of the novelist's expressive freedoms.

Above all, however, the stage directions give printed testimony to another crucial Barrie paradox: the ostensibly self-obscuring dramatist and anonymous, self-cancelling writer who in truth is omnipresent in his own dramatic fictions. The Royal Shakespeare Company's production of *Peter Pan* in 1982 brought the narrator on stage, and, as Jacqueline Rose reports:

the narrator becomes Barrie himself, a sage and untroubled Edwardian commentator: the famous opening line of the 1911 novel 'All children, except one, grow up' is divided into two halves in the production's opening sequence with 'All children grow up' spoken by the narrator and 'Except one' as the first line and challenge to him by Peter Pan himself.[16]

[16] Rose (n. 9 above), 114.

Annie Castledine's 1991 production of *What Every Woman Knows* at the West Yorkshire Playhouse, Leeds, brought Barrie on to a balcony to eavesdrop on the opening scene and speak his stage directions as part of the script. The device was brilliantly successful, and points to the stage reality of Barrie's authorial presence. As Allardyce Nicoll observes: 'Barrie's genius gains its distinctive quality from his utter simplicity, from a frank acceptance of, and indeed emphasis upon, the fact that a play is no more than a figment, and on his ability to mingle with his characters on the boards, unseen yet omnipotent.'[17]

In bringing Barrie on the stage, as a character-narrator, these productions were recognizing a truth about his plays, that visibly and audibly they contain his own fictive presence. Yet, with what we can detect as characteristic paradox, Barrie made elaborate if unconvincing gestures of a public kind towards disclaiming authorship and achieving authorial invisibility. They were the disingenuous hide-and-seek games of an author who was never able to conceal himself. The strangest item in Barrie's bibliography is *The Boy Castaways of Black Lake Island*, a photographic record with mock adventure-story captions of Barrie's summer holiday with the Llewelyn Davies family, a holiday which supplied many of the imaginary incidents later immortalized in *Peter Pan*. Authorship is attributed on the title-page to Peter Llewelyn Davies, one of the children, but the book is 'Published by J. M. Barrie'. A comparable spoof was the attribution of *Peter Pan* on the first programme to Ela Q. May, the diminutive actress who played Liza; but Barrie's name was still printed in bigger letters. This mock self-abnegation was evident again in the statement in the 1928 Dedication of *Peter Pan* that the author had no recollection of having written it. Barrie's plays are of a piece with these external games of self-exclusion. He remains a strong, ostensibly self-denying, but actually conspicuous intermediate persona between his creations and their audience.

An instance of this persona which has proved controversial over the years lies in his jokes about Scotland and the Scots. For various reasons Barrie's reputation has not been high in Scotland; one accusation against him has been that he renounced his Scottishness for the sake of commercial success in England, while another has been that in pursuit of this success he ridiculed his countrymen in the plays. Alan Bold observes:

---

[17] Allardyce Nicoll, *English Drama 1900–1930: The Beginnings of the Modern Period* (Cambridge, 1973), 347.

The notion that he deserted his Scottish origins is refuted by *What Every Woman Knows* (1908) . . . Barrie may have valued success but he was able to appreciate the inhumanity that goes with the pursuit of success for its own sake. In John Shand he created a character who is familiar enough to his fellow countrymen: the arrogant boor whose antics may be comic but whose nature is far from funny.[18]

Not all Scottish critics have taken so generous a view of Barrie's jokes about the Scots, though it has to be said that several of the most famous examples, notably in *What Every Woman Knows*, are also indirectly jokes about the English. Several of these are conveyed through the ingenuous shrewdness of David: 'A young Scotsman of your ability let loose upon the world with £300, what could he not do? It's almost appalling to think of; especially if he went among the English.' (Act 1); 'My lady, there are few more impressive sights in the world than a Scotsman on the make.' (Act 2). There is a difference between these two examples. The first is plausibly in character; as a sub-persona for Barrie, David is speaking with naïvely serious national superiority and the dramatic context makes it funny. The second is almost choric, resting on a dispassionate satiric objectivity (and concealed authorial self-mockery) which cuts from David's voice to Barrie's. The most blatant example comes in the comic revelation of John Shand's humourlessness:

JOHN I remember reading of someone that said it needed a surgical operation to get a joke into a Scotsman's head.
MAGGIE Yes, that's been said.
JOHN What beats me, Maggie, is how you could insert a joke with an operation.

In this exchange, all pretence of realistic characterization is dropped in order to admit the audible stage presence of Barrie the surreptitious satirist. It is Barrie's own Peter Pan-like fluidity of roles and perspectives, comprising at once a detached, objective coldness and a double-agent's gift for infiltrating both national cultures, that permits and guides the insidious, satiric on-stage presence of the author.

Scottish indignation at Barrie's nationalist calumnies might well be muted by the realization that this is his customary practice on other topics besides nationhood. We see a comparable example of his interventionist satire in *The Admirable Crichton*, in Lady Mary's spirited tomboy relation of her victorious solitary hunting in Act 3.

[18] Alan Bold, *Modern Scottish Literature* (London, 1983), 282.

Her physical feats, the ultimate apotheosis of Outward Bound philosophy, are marginally plausible in the play's comic convention of circumstances radically altering cases, but they are also extravagantly over the top, a satiric *jeu d'esprit* on Barrie's part at the expense of great white hunters and their counterparts in popular literature. The speech depends for its brilliant comic effect on Barrie's combination of detached amusement at absurd conventions, and simultaneous imaginative relish of them.

The interventionist on-stage voice is, therefore, a multiple and complex one, an indication of the many levels at which Barrie's dramas operate. *Peter Pan* is full of such voices. Barrie can be at once Scot and Englishman, mother and child, Pan and Hook, aristocrat and democrat, romantic endorser and satiric detractor of literary convention and heroic commonplace. He moves in cold detachment and conspiratorial involvement among the voices and actions of his creatures, both intimate and remote. The special idiosyncrasy of his drama lies in an interventionist persona which is almost invariably pushing the plays towards satire and pulling them towards tragedy. This is the contradiction which, it seems to me, explains both his complexity and his greatness.

What Every Woman Knows is in many respects the most conventionally successful and cohesive of the plays included here, the most standard instance of the well-made play. Not devoid of fantasy through its masterly first act, it is chiefly a dexterous blend of nationalist, social, and political comedy. Yet characteristic Barrie ambiguities sustain it, notably, of course, through its treatment of the position of women. In the background is the movement for women's suffrage. But who bears the brunt of Barrie's comedy? Is it the women's movement, or the male politician's ham-fisted efforts, part-principled, part-cynical, to exploit it? The ambiguities cluster on the figure of Maggie Wylie, and whilst the feminist theme has given the play a new topicality, its uncertainties are evident in the continuing difficulty of deciding whether it is a feminist or anti-feminist play. The whole of Barrie's career, and especially the proximity in time of his overtly feminist one-acter, *The Twelve Pound Look*, predisposes one to see it as a feminist text, but its chosen practice makes this a contentious view. Maggie is used, and underrated, and condescended to. She is penalized for lack of beauty and 'charm'. Wylie by name and wily by nature, she must always fight her cause by stealth. In this socio-politico-sexual wrestling match, she uses her opponents' strengths against them and wins submissions by submitting. In acceding (on her own terms) to the preposterous marriage-contract, in releasing John Shand from his bargain, in masking her political acumen, in 'giving up' her husband to his idiotic English mistress, she succeeds throughout by acts of intelligent surrender. Although her plight, her means, and her ends can all be plausibly adduced in support of anti-feminist readings, the play seems primarily to be an unpatronizing celebration of covert female power.

All the other plays included here show the structure which Barrie found most congenial for his purposes: a first act or opening section more or less 'realistic' in nature or domestic in setting, to which the play eventually returns after a middle act or phase of fantasy. *Mary Rose* reveals a double structure of this kind. Its two 'realistic' scenes at beginning and end, enacting Harry's return to his boyhood home, enclose the two pre-war scenes of mingled domestic comedy and supernatural unease, which in turn contain the central episode on 'the island that likes to be visited'.

'To be born', wrote Barrie in his Preface to R. M. Ballantyne's *The Coral Island*, 'is to be wrecked on an island', and it cannot escape our notice that the central episode of fantasy in *The Admirable Crichton*, *Peter Pan*, and *Mary Rose* takes place on an island. Barrie was a lover of islands, both real and imaginary. Stories of 'wrecked islands' had been his favourite reading as a boy, and these same 'wrecked islands' were the subject of his summer games with the Llewelyn Davies children which directly inspired *Peter Pan*. The Never Land is an island, waiting to be called into activity by the imagination of a child. Children relish tales of redskins, pirates, mermaids, fairies, and if the fairies are a little past their sell-by date for the young men who want pirates or young women who want underground houses, they can still be enjoyed with nostalgia armour-plated by amusement. And adult playwrights, or the parents of young theatregoers, can also protect their maturity with verbal comedy and satire, whilst happily regressing under cover of the laughter to more primitive satisfactions. Barrie the participant observer is able to indulge the undiscarded child in himself and in his audience, whilst satirizing the very conventions of narrative which allow these childhood pleasures to exist. *Peter Pan* is a great play in part because of its multiple dramatic voice. It speaks for and to the child in the audience directly, never allowing its brilliant verbal games to smother the immediate life of action and adventure; but its layering of tones, its variety of perspectives on events, make its world of fantasy accessible for audiences of every age and level of sophistication.

The 'wrecked islands', with their residual trace of childhood games-playing, are there in the other plays too. Crichton's island is in part a literary place, a creation of affectionate satire glancing back to *Robinson Crusoe*, *The Swiss Family Robinson*, *Masterman Ready*, and *The Coral Island*. The butler's genius for technical improvisation and his delight in do-it-yourself gadgetry (this last being, characteristically, the eventual cause of his downfall) are genuine boyhood fantasies in Barrie's mind as well as literary spoofs and props in comedy. In one way everything that happens on the island is a game, which Crichton and Tweeny are good at from the start and all the others learn to play. The happiness which they achieve on the island is partly the happiness of rediscovered childhood play, and they enjoy it as children do—more than they enjoy real life, but only until real life and thoughts of home return to mind. Like the Never Land for all but Peter, so Crichton's island for all except (perhaps) Crichton, has a time limit on it.

Mary Rose's island is also, for her at least, a place for play. Certainly it is in a spirit of fond childhood memory that she begs Simon to take her back there. As we have seen, Mary Rose's island was first conceived as a re-creation of the Never Land, but it fast outgrew this early form and became an altogether more menacing and sinister locale. This island too has a time limit on it, but in Mary Rose's case it is not time on the island itself that runs out, for there is Peter Pan's eternity in its hold on her; it is unstoppable time in the world outside that makes for Mary Rose's tragedy, and she, even more than Peter Pan, is a disturbing version of Barrie's lifelong obsession with the child-in-adult and adult-in-child.

Different as the three plays are, therefore, they all make audible the more sombre and pessimistic echoes of 'to be born is to be wrecked on an island'. Full of comedy and wit as they all are, drawing as they all do on the world of adventure, romance and folklore, they 'are subjects all | To envious and calumniating time'. When Barrie came to write *Mary Rose*, in the aftermath of the First World War, his own awareness of a tragic tension between time and timelessness had become a nation's. The sense of lost, eternal youth had been implanted in him irreversibly at the age of 6, when his elder brother David (his mother's favourite child) was killed in a skating accident on the eve of his fourteenth birthday. 'When I became a man', he wrote later in *Margaret Ogilvy*, 'he was still a boy of thirteen'.[19]

---

[19] *Margaret Ogilvy* (London, 1896), 15.

David's death was undoubtedly the origin of *Peter Pan*, but its persistence in his consciousness was carried through into his writing during the war. Barrie's one-act play *The New Word* (1915) presents the last evening together of a middle-class family before their surviving son goes off to the Front, and on this proud, embarrassed, difficult occasion the mother, Mrs Torrance, remembers her other son, who died in childhood: 'He would be twenty-one now; but though you and Emma grew up I have always gone on seeing him as just seven. Always till the war broke out. And now I see him as a man of twenty-one, dressed in khaki, fighting for his country, same as you.'[20]

It would seem that somehow the division between time stilled and time continuing, and the awareness of painfully unsurrendered childhood, which had preoccupied Barrie for so many years was at last transcended in some measure by the war—partly perhaps by the death in action of his adopted son George Llewelyn Davies, and partly by the universality of equivalent bereavement. Barrie found himself in a tragic country full of parents who, like his own mother, had outlived a beloved child, full of the brothers and sisters of dead siblings, full of those who had cause to say with Kipling, 'But who shall return us the children?' It is in this comprehensive post-war mood that we might account for the writing of *Mary Rose*, and for its outstanding popular success.

There are some embarrassing passages in the play, some fits of fanciful childlikeness in the heroine which are hard to take, and a self-indulgent cult of naïvety which leads Barrie to depend on shallow, easily won effects, but awkward as they are they do not submerge its power, even for modern audiences. J. C. Trewin observes:

There are uncomfortable passages, when Barrie lets his whimsicality wander, but there are others of a queer, delicate beauty and one at least in which we feel the same helpless terror as at the end of the second act of *Dear Brutus*. The play, in its 1920 production, was an immense success: there was something in it to console many who had been bereaved during the war.[21]

Patrick Chalmers, in a panegyric of Barrie published soon after the playwright's death, concurred as to its capturing the mood of its time: 'I will only say of [*Mary Rose*] that this lovely and spiritual conception was staged in the ugly and uneasy period that followed immediately

[20] *The New Word*, in A. E. Wilson (ed.), *The Definitive Edition of the Plays of J. M. Barrie* (London, 1942), 863.
[21] Trewin (n. 15 above), 92.

upon the War . . . It brought . . . joy and peace and a tear or two to thousands, weary of the War and the War's aftermath, during the years of its run.'[22] What was there in this curious mixture of social comedy and fey, ambiguous enchantment to console a bereaved generation? There was the portrait of naïve, idyllic, precarious, and endangered romance in a world all too aware of relationships that were over before the lovers had properly ceased to be children; an enigmatic spiritual realm, part hoped-for and part feared, but finally presented as benign; the loss of children, remembered as if stilled in youth for ever, like Barrie's David and like all too real Peter Pans; the universal shared awareness of that least-desired condition, surviving one's own children; the affectionate, satirical enactment of a vanished social world; the painful depiction of tragic return, with its reminder of a contrary brutal kindness in the fact that 'gone is gone'; and the guilty consolation of discovery that life does indeed go on. In Barrie's late-war one-act play, *A Well-Remembered Voice*, continuing life's pleasures and routines is a courageous effort in the wake of loss, but two years later, in *Mary Rose*, it is shown as the natural order of things. Mr Morland asks: 'Why is my heart not broken?' and his wife's reply is a reply to guilt: 'What better encouragement to the young than to be able to tell them that happiness keeps breaking through?' In part social comedy, in part romantic fantasy, in part supernatural thriller, and only at the margins a play about wartime, *Mary Rose* is accidentally a subtle psychological diagnosis of the crisis of survival and the happy anguish of peace.

Critics recognize the play's absence of 'philosophy'. Roger Lancelyn Green admits that it lacks 'the underlying philosophy'[23] of *Dear Brutus*, and Leonee Ormond notes that 'no satisfactory philosophical outcome can be deduced from it'.[24] It is hard to disagree, but as William Golding said in the Foreword to his Sea Trilogy *To The Ends of the Earth*: 'there are higher languages than that of the toiling mind, deeper intuitions than can be overtaken by the microscope or telescope, even a space one. They require metaphors, and mixed ones at that.'[25] *Mary Rose* is a dramatic mixed metaphor. As the alternative to life and time and ageing, Mary Rose's island is both good and evil, and her fate in being exempted from time is both innocent and tragic. For a bereaved generation the play repeats more sombrely the central

[22] Patrick Chalmers, *The Barrie Inspiration* (London, 1938), 191–2.
[23] Roger Lancelyn Green, *J. M. Barrie* (London, 1960), 54.
[24] Ormond (n. 2 above), 135.
[25] William Golding, *To The Ends of the Earth* (London, 1991), p. xi.

Barrie contradiction at the heart of *Peter Pan*: you cannot win, Peter and Wendy are both losers, because each part of the equation invalidates the other. Consolation lies in human tenderness and love, and in the gradual recession of pain which is the healing nature of accepted time. Beyond that, the enigma and the ambiguity remain, and Barrie's attitude is best summed up by Allardyce Nicoll's comment on the portrait which formed the frontispiece to the 1928 *Collected Plays*: 'The photograph shows Barrie steadily staring out as if in quiet resignation at something which lies beyond our view, but which from his plays we realise was the entire mummery show of life.'[26]

[26] Nicoll (n. 17 above), 350.

NOTE ON THE TEXT

The history of Barrie's texts, especially that of *Peter Pan*, is long and complicated. For this edition the simplest of solutions has been adopted, but for reasons which are not simple and fall into various categories of choice. The background is set out below, with some illustrative examples.

The copy-text is *The Definitive Edition of the Plays of J. M. Barrie*, edited by A. E. Wilson (1942). This volume was an expanded version of Barrie's *Collected Plays* (1928), in which all but one of the plays in this collection were included. The exception, *When Wendy Grew Up*, was first printed in 1957. The 1942 text retains that of 1928 and the volume adds those plays which had originally been excluded. (By 1928 only one substantial dramatic text by Barrie, *The Boy David*, had yet to be written.)

The 1928 text in turn reproduces, with corrections, the plays as they had been individually printed in the Uniform Edition, at various dates in the preceding years. *Peter Pan* appeared in print for the first time in 1928 in the two formats of the single-play Uniform Edition and the *Collected Plays*, but other works were substantially revised for the collected edition. A notable instance is *What Every Woman Knows*, which in the Uniform Edition lapses into novelized form for substantial sections, abandoning speech-prefixes and other conventions of the printed play. This extreme example illustrates the main feature of the printed texts, namely that they were prepared by Barrie (not usually with such non-dramatic abandon) for publication in the form he preferred, which commonly entailed minor or even major departures from production texts and pronounced intervention in the form of dramatic commentary through stage directions. This practice, which might seem to generate a less 'theatrical' text, is fully endorsed in the present edition.

In his Introduction to the *Definitive Edition* A. E. Wilson gave what is in fact the negative case for retaining Barrie's chosen printed text:

The plays of Barrie's maturity are given with his own introductions as they have appeared in previous editions. In editing the first four plays I have taken the liberty of slightly amending the stage directions in order that the pleasure of the reader should not be hindered by the constant repetition of such technical phrases as '*exit* L.C.', '*Enter* R.', '*Crosses* R. C.', and such other guides to the actor's movements as irritatingly besprinkle the pages of 'prompt copies'. I have made only slight changes in the wording and have allowed such directions to remain as will enable the reader to follow the action clearly. Would that we could have had Barrie's own introductions to these plays and that linking together of the scenes, those explanations of the motives of his characters, which give such added charm and *narrative interest* [my italics] in the reading of his later plays. (p. ix)

The proposition on which this edition is based is that Barrie's stage directions in the printed text do not add 'narrative interest' in the sense intended by Wilson—that is, they do not convert the plays into something resembling novels—but rather that they constantly illuminate the plays' theatrical nature and constitute subtle and demanding instructions to directors and actors. Many instances of the theatricality of Barrie's stage directions are suggested in the Explanatory Notes. The directions also clarify Barrie's true nature and originality as a dramatist, and the reality of his presence in his own dramatic texts; this, which is primarily a question of critical interpretation, is discussed in the Introduction. The point can, however, be briefly illustrated by a comparison between the following passage from the standard acting edition of *The Admirable Crichton*, the surviving form of various production scripts, and the equivalent in the *Definitive Edition*, the preferred text in this volume (p. 35). Crichton and Ernest have just returned from Ernest's first immersion:

> (*Enter Ernest with the bucket from up R., at C., leaves it by the hut, crosses up and sits on the rocks L. Lady Agatha follows him on and sits beside him, below him, and helps to dry his head with palm leaves, etc.*)

LADY AGATHA It's infamous!

LORD LOAM *My* orders, Agatha!

LADY MARY (*encouraging him*) Father!

LORD LOAM Before I give you further orders, Crichton—

CRICHTON Yes, my lord. (*He rises, moves L., picking up twigs for the fire.*)

LORD LOAM (*delighted—to the others*) Pooh! It's all right.

LADY MARY No.

LORD LOAM (*crossing to L. C. followed by LADY MARY, on his R.*) Well, well! This question of leadership—what do you think now?

CRICHTON My lord, I feel it is a matter with which I have nothing to do. (*He moves down L. for more wood.*)

LORD LOAM Excellent! Mary! That settles it, I think.

LADY MARY It seems to, but—

CRICHTON (*below the rocks L., picking up twigs*) It will settle itself naturally, my lord, without any interference from us.

> (*The others exchange disturbed glances, turning to each other, very concerned.*)

Although the differences are slight, it will be seen that the 1942 (previously 1928) text is not significantly less 'theatrical'. However, its minor changes emphasize the role of Lady Mary in anxiously insisting on the clarification of a situation she perceives to be threatening. The individual relationship which most sharply articulates the play's theme is nudged into the foreground. Similarly, the closing stage direction in the 1942 text highlights a thematic keyword. The 1942 text is less prescriptive of acting detail, substituting a clearer thematic rationale. As such it gives not only the reader but the intelligent actor (here, the actress playing Lady Mary especially) a greater purchase on the play. This is a small but fully representative example of Barrie's interventions in his printed text.

Such considerations as these accord with the choice of the 1928 and 1942 texts for quite separate reasons of textual necessity—namely, that they supply the only form in which Barrie's texts achieved stability. The production scripts of Barrie's plays show a process of evolution and revision which, while it may help to clarify Barrie's developing dramatic interests and intentions, makes it impossible to 'freeze' any text in a form which could be called definitive or final. The 1928 and 1942 texts are the nearest we can get to a fixed choice of the form in which Barrie wished the plays to be known, and the only alternative to concurring with him is to make an arbitrary choice of a script we happen to prefer, presumably on the grounds—the only defensible ones—that we consider it more 'theatrical'. This edition argues strongly for the theatricality of the 1928 and 1942 texts.

Some instances of the plays at different points in their evolution are discussed in the Introduction. The special case of *Peter Pan* is summarized below.

The earliest known text of *Peter Pan* is a manuscript in six scenes entitled *Anon*. This manuscript (the existence of which Barrie disingenuously questioned in the 1928 Dedication) dates from 1903–4. It was given by Barrie to the actress Maude Adams (who played Peter in the first American production of the play), was rediscovered in 1964, and is now in the possession of the Lilly Library of the University of Indiana. Along with the most important collection of Barrie manuscripts, the typescript of the 1904–5 initial production of *Peter Pan* is in the Walter Beinecke Jnr. Collection at the Beinecke Rare Book and Manuscript Library at Yale University (Beinecke p. 45, 1904–5B). The production text for the play's second season (1905–6) was substantially revised from 1904–5. The development of this initial series of texts has been widely discussed, notably by Roger Lancelyn

Green,[1] Jacqueline Rose,[2] and R. D. S. Jack.[3] Important features of the sequence include the initial adoption and subsequent discarding of figures and incidents derived from pantomime, in particular the presence of Harlequin and Columbine; successive versions of the ending, including the abandonment of closing scenes in Kensington Gardens, and Hook's survival from the Pirate Ship scene; the inclusion, and discarding during the first season, of the 'Beautiful Mothers' scene, in which the Lost Boys were adopted after their would-be parents had been subjected to tests of their maternal suitability; the conversion of the play from three to five acts; and the introduction in 1905 of Act 3, 'The Mermaid's Lagoon', which allowed a generally disliked front-cloth scene to be removed. By 1905–6 the play had largely reached the form in which it was subsequently performed, but further revisions were introduced for the 1928 text as Barrie finally determined it.

Although the other plays included in this volume have less complex textual histories, both *The Admirable Crichton* and *Mary Rose* were substantially revised before or after production, and provide evidence of Barrie's reluctance to allow his texts a fixed and permanent form.

---

[1] *Fifty Years of 'Peter Pan'* (London, 1954).
[2] *The Case of Peter Pan, or The Impossibility of Children's Fiction* (London, 1984).
[3] 'The Manuscript of *Peter Pan*', *Children's Literature*, 18 (1990).

SELECT BIBLIOGRAPHY

The position regarding criticism of Barrie is admirably summarized in a note in R. D. S. Jack's recent study *The Road to the Never Land: A Reassessment of J. M. Barrie's Dramatic Art* (Aberdeen, 1991), which is itself considered below. Jack's note (p. 266) reads:

W. M. Parker in *Modern Scottish Writers* . . . warns that Barrie is difficult to pin down critically. 'Alas! quite a number of us have tried to catch hold of him, but he invariably slips away.' Nor are his antagonists the only guilty ones. Enthusiasm may also sweep away precision. Patrick Braybrooke, commenting on *The Little Minister*, finds it a work which 'just escapes being futile and the reason that it escapes such a fate, is to be found in the fact that its writer happened to be a genius.'

This indicates several points which quickly become apparent to readers of Barrie criticism. First, he is an elusive writer, characteristically engaged in layered composition, offsetting mode against mode and genre against genre, and one authorial persona against another, in a complex game which makes it very difficult for critics to confront either the dramatic corpus or the single work *whole*; Barrie positively invites distorting choices of emphasis. Perhaps in response to this problem, critics have tended towards large-scale and dogmatic vagueness, either defending his work with the vapid passionate assertiveness of Braybrooke in the passage quoted by Jack, or else attacking him, often with barely concealed irritation and anger, and either with a vagueness to equal that of his admirers or with selectively precise assaults on particular aspects of his work. The multiple perspectives which Barrie calls for, across the whole range of his work and in each individual novel, story, or play, have yet to find their way into criticism, though Jack's own book, over-ambitious as it is, establishes a level and directs a way for future work.

Early studies of Barrie tended very much towards hagiographic assertions of his genius. Examples of the devout critical reception he gained during and just after his own lifetime can be found in studies such as those by H. M. Walbrook, *J. M. Barrie and the Theatre* (London, 1922); Thomas Moult, *Barrie* (London, 1928); J. A. Hammerton, *Barrie: the Story of a Genius* (London, 1929); and by the immensely experienced *Daily Telegraph* theatre critic W. A. Darlington in *Barrie* (London, 1938). These can be taken as representative examples of Barrie's reputation during his life, and especially of its twin bases—first as the celebrator, at once sentimental and satirical, of Scottish domestic life in the 'Thrums' stories and the plays derived from them, such as *The Little Minister*, and secondly as the metropolitan dramatist dealing characteristically in enigmatic blends of comedy and fantasy.

The admiration, akin to reverence, in which Barrie was widely held up to and beyond his death is best exemplified by Patrick Chalmers's study *The Barrie Inspiration* (London, 1938), which typifies other early studies in using the scenes and events of Barrie's life as supportive vindication of the extravagant critical judgements proposed, and this points to the difficulty of detaching Barrie the writer from Barrie the man in the existing critical literature.

The man has, in fact, been much better served than the writer. The first full biography was Denis Mackail's *The Story of J. M. B.* (London, 1941), a massive, intimate, anecdotal, detailed life distinguished for its dedication, inexhaustible abrupt energy, and verbless sentences. It remains an indispensable archive of material on Barrie, but it is essentially accumulative rather than evaluative. Janet Dunbar's *J. M. Barrie: The Man Behind the Image* (London, 1970) has not entirely superseded Mackail (for nothing could), but it is a more dependable, orthodox, carefully researched biography which is a model of temperate judgement. Also indispensable is Andrew Birkin's *J. M. Barrie and the Lost Boys* (London, 1979). As the title suggests, this is above all a history of Barrie's relations with the Llewelyn Davies family, a story which is essential to the proper understanding of *Peter Pan*, but the book goes far beyond the particular relationships and contains many acute insights into Barrie's life and plays. The central biographical account of the Llewelyn Davies story was successfully dramatized by Birkin in his three-part television serial, *The Lost Boys*.

To the group of biographical studies should be added Cynthia Asquith's memoir *Portrait of Barrie* (London, 1954), which gives a subjective and often moving account of the dramatist's later years.

The directly biographical works are usefully augmented by examples of 'Barrie topography'—books which trace the origins of Barrie's work in his real and imaginary Scottish background and thus combine regional and cultural context with biographical data and critical comment. Two works exemplifying this strain of writing are J. A. Hammerton's *Barrieland: A Thrums Pilgrimage* (London, 1931) and John Kennedy's *Thrums and the Barrie Country* (London, 1930).

In recent years critical attention to Barrie has been sparse. What might be termed the 'hagiographic tradition' produced probably its final, and certainly its best, work in two books by Roger Lancelyn Green, a very short, succinct essay *J. M. Barrie*, in the Bodley Head Monograph series (London, 1960), and, most importantly, a comprehensive, scholarly, and extremely entertaining stage history of *Peter Pan, Fifty Years of 'Peter Pan'* (London, 1954), which follows the history of the play from its initial conception through to the brilliant scenario prepared by Barrie for a film of the play which, in the event, was never produced. This book remains an indispensable source of information.

More recently, the relatively few significant books and major articles on Barrie have in the main been ideologically biased or hostile interpretations, sometimes persuasive, well-researched, and convincing on specific aspects of the work, but too heavily governed in their emphases by the ideological predilections of the critic. Although such work is far more sophisticated than the earlier naïve encomia, it has no greater claims to success in accounting for the complexity and elusive distinction of Barrie's drama. Harry M. Geduld's *James Barrie* (New York, 1971) is a psychoanalytical study primarily concerned with Barrie's intense relationship with his mother, which he himself described with painful openness in *Margaret Ogilvy*. The book entirely ignores the theatrical dimension of the plays. A number of other Freudian interpretations of article length have since appeared. Barrie at once invites this approach and pre-empts it by his own cold, self-examining precision. The mysteries which critics seek to expose and tabulate in terms of psychological orthodoxies (themselves now objects of historical rather than clinical interest) were not mysteries to Barrie himself.

A hostile socio-political account of the 'Thrums' stories and their theatrical aftermath can be found in George Blake's *Barrie and the Kailyard School* (London, 1951).

One of the two most important modern studies of Barrie is Jacqueline Rose's *The Case of Peter Pan or The Impossibility of Children's Fiction* (London, 1984). This is the first serious study to use the ideas and vocabulary of current literary theory in a systematic consideration of Barrie, and it is rooted in much exemplary and valuable research into the origin and proliferation of the *Peter Pan* texts. Unfortunately the study is guided by some questionable premises about the psychology of childhood and the vulnerability of children, and appears to be influenced by anxieties about relationships between children and adults, with the consequence that critical balance is adversely affected, and the critique of Barrie himself is too emotively expressed. As a study in cultural production the book is highly intelligent and thorough, and the sociological dimension in the second half is excellent, but Barrie and *Peter Pan* are in a sense merely incidental and illustrative for the purposes of its main argument, and as a contribution to Barrie studies the book is disappointing.

In the critical articles of recent decades commentators have continued to confuse psychological analysis with literary evaluation, and criticism of Barrie will not itself reach the maturity which it habitually questions in Barrie until it begins to keep the distinction clear. Characteristic essays, interesting in themselves but typifying the problem, are those by David Daiches, ('The Sexless Sentimentalist', in the *Listener*, 12 May 1960), which speaks of Barrie's resentment of life for 'daring to pose adult problems'; by Martin Green ('The Charm of *Peter Pan*', *Children's Literature*, 9 (1981)), which accuses Barrie of exhibiting the 'senile whimsy of English Imperial culture at the end of its tether'; and by Catherine Storr ('Peter Pan', *Children's Literature in Education*, 23:1 (1992)), who finds the work to be of only psychiatric interest.

Occasional competent and useful surveys have continued to appear, notably Leonee Ormond's *J. M. Barrie* (Edinburgh, 1987), but by far the most substantial study of Barrie ever published is R. D. S. Jack's *The Road to the Never Land* (see above). This is a highly original and ambitious study which makes intellectual claims for Barrie going far beyond anything previously suggested. Jack presents Barrie as the proponent of the literary theory which accounts for his own work, and therefore as an artistically self-conscious and subtle dramatist who stands at least on equal terms with Ibsen, Shaw, and the other major writers of his time. Jack's most challenging claims rest on the relationship he discovers between Barrie and the ideas of Darwin and Nietzsche. His reading is highly controversial and calls for further serious debate, but it has crucially raised the stakes for the estimation of Barrie's achievement and the level on which criticism should be conducted. The book goes no later than *Peter Pan* in its chronological treatment of Barrie, but it contains full and theatrically sensitive studies of the earlier plays, including a brilliant innovatory critique of *Little Mary*.

Barrie is frequently regarded as an outdated dramatist, and *Peter Pan* as being of very limited interest to modern children. Against this should be set Humphrey Carpenter's argument for it as a durable yet deeply self-questioning new myth, in _Secret Gardens_ (London, 1985). The durability, continuing attraction, and adaptability of the myth have become freshly apparent in Steven Spielberg's film _Hook_ (1991). Like _Peter Pan_ itself, _Hook_ has produced prose retellings graded for different levels of maturity and reading competence, notable amongst which is Geary Gravel's _Hook_ (New York and London, 1991 and 1992). The relationship between Barrie's play and Spielberg's film is discussed by Peter Hollindale in 'Peter Pan, Captain Hook, and the book of the video', in _Signal_ 72 (1993).

A CHRONOLOGY OF J. M. BARRIE

1860 Born, 9 May, at Kirriemuir in Angus, Scotland.

1868 Attends Glasgow Academy.

1871 Attends Forfar Academy.

1873 Attends Dumfries Academy.

1878 Enters Edinburgh University.

1882 MA, Edinburgh.

1885 Leaves Kirriemuir to seek his living in London as a freelance writer.

1888 Publication of *Auld Licht Idylls* and *When a Man's Single*.

1889 Publication of *A Window in Thrums*.

1890 Publication of *My Lady Nicotine*.

1891 Publication of *The Little Minister*; *Ibsen's Ghost* first performed (Toole's Theatre, 30 May).

1892 *Walker, London* first performed (Toole's Theatre, 25 February).

1892 *The Professor's Love Story* first performed (Star Theatre, New York, 19 December).

1894 Marries the actress Mary Ansell.

1895 Death of his mother, Margaret Ogilvy.

1896 Publication of *Margaret Ogilvy* and *Sentimental Tommy*; visits the USA for the first time, and is entertained by Charles Frohman, eventual producer of *Peter Pan*.

1897 First meeting with the Llewelyn Davies family. The five children of George and Sylvia Llewelyn Davies were very important to the evolution of *Peter Pan*, and Barrie eventually adopted them in 1910 after both parents had died from cancer.

1900 Publication of *Tommy and Grizel*; *The Wedding Guest* first performed (Garrick Theatre, 27 September).

1902 Death of his father, David Barrie; publication of *The Little White Bird*; *Quality Street* first performed (Vaudeville Theatre, 17 September); *The Admirable Crichton* first performed (Duke of York's Theatre, 4 November).

1903 *Little Mary* first performed (Wyndham's Theatre, 24 September).

1904 *Peter Pan* first performed (Duke of York's Theatre, 27 December).

1905 *Alice-Sit-by-the-Fire* first performed (Duke of York's Theatre, 5 April).

1906 Publication of *Peter Pan in Kensington Gardens* (extracted from *The Little White Bird*).

1907 Death of Arthur Llewelyn Davies.

1907 Involved in campaign for the reform of theatre censorship, after Harley Granville-Barker's *Waste* was refused a licence by the Lord Chamberlain.

1908 Sole performance in Barrie's lifetime of *When Wendy Grew Up: An Afterthought* (22 February).

1908 *What Every Woman Knows* first performed (Duke of York's Theatre, 3 September).

1909 Divorces Mary Barrie on the grounds of her adultery with Gilbert Cannan; receives Hon. LL D (Edinburgh).

1910 Death of Sylvia Llewelyn Davies.

1911 Publication of *Peter and Wendy*.

1913 Receives baronetcy in the Birthday Honours, 14 June.

1913 *The Adored One* first performed (Duke of York's Theatre, 4 September).

1914 Visits USA on diplomatically contentious mission to raise support for the allied war effort.

1915 George Llewelyn Davies, eldest of the five boys, killed in action in France.

1917 *Dear Brutus* first performed (Wyndham's Theatre, 17 October).

1919 Elected Rector of St Andrews University.

1920 *Mary Rose* first performed (Haymarket Theatre, 22 April).

1921 Death by drowning of Michael Llewelyn Davies, fourth son of Arthur and Sylvia Llewelyn Davies, and Barrie's favourite; *Shall We Join the Ladies?* first performed (RADA, 27 May).

1922 Receives the Order of Merit.

1928 First publication of *Peter Pan*; publication of *The Plays of J. M. Barrie* (first single-volume collection, Barrie determining which plays were to be included and which omitted).

1930 Receives Hon. LL D (Cambridge); installed as Chancellor of Edinburgh University.

1931 Publication in *The Times* of *Farewell, Miss Julia Logan* (book publication 1932).

1936 *The Boy David* first performed (His Majesty's Theatre, 21 November).

1937 Dies, 19 June; buried at Kirriemuir.

THE ADMIRABLE CRICHTON

CHARACTERS
(in order of appearance)

Crichton
The Hon. Ernest Woolley
Lady Agatha Lasenby
Lady Catherine Lasenby
Lady Mary Lasenby
The Revd John Treherne
The Earl of Loam
Lord Brocklehurst
Mrs Perkins
Monsieur Fleury
Mr Rolleston
Mr Tompsett
Miss Fisher

Miss Simmons
Mademoiselle Jeanne
Thomas
John
Jane
Gladys
Eliza ('Tweeny')
Stable-Boy
A Kitchen Wench
A Page-Boy
A Naval Officer
The Countess of Brocklehurst

Act 1

AT LOAM HOUSE, MAYFAIR

A moment before the curtain rises, the Hon. Ernest Woolley drives up to the door of Loam House in Mayfair. There is a happy smile on his pleasant, insignificant face, and this presumably means that he is thinking of himself. He is too busy over nothing, this man about town, to be always thinking of himself, but, on the other hand, he almost never thinks of any other person. Probably Ernest's great moment is when he wakes of a morning and realises that he really is Ernest, for we must all wish to be that which is our ideal. We can conceive him springing out of bed light-heartedly and waiting for his man to do the rest. He is dressed in excellent taste, with just the little bit more which shows that he is not without a sense of humour: the dandiacal are often saved by carrying a smile at the whole thing in their spats,° let us say. Ernest left Cambridge the other day, a member of the Athenaeum° (which he would be sorry to have you confound with a club in London of the same name). He is a bachelor, but not of arts, no mean epigrammatist (as you shall see), and a favourite of the ladies. He is almost a celebrity in restaurants, where he dines frequently, returning to sup;° and during this last year he has probably paid as much in them for the privilege of handing his hat to an attendant as the rent of a working-man's flat. He complains brightly that he is hard up, and that if somebody or other at Westminster° does not look out the country will go to the dogs. He is no fool. He has the shrewdness to float with the current because it is a labour-saving process, but he has sufficient pluck to fight, if fight he must (a brief contest, for he would soon be toppled over). He has a light nature, which would enable him to bob up cheerily in new conditions and return unaltered to the old ones. His selfishness is his most endearing quality. If he has his way he will spend his life like a cat in pushing his betters out of the soft places, and until he is old he will be fondled in the process.

He gives his hat to one footman and his cane to another, and mounts the great staircase unassisted and undirected. As a nephew of the house he need show no credentials even to Crichton, who is guarding a door above.

It would not be good taste to describe Crichton, who is only a servant; if to the scandal of all good houses° he is to stand out as a figure in the play, he must do it on his own, as they say in the pantry and the boudoir.° We are not going to help him. We° have had misgivings ever since we found his name in the title, and we shall keep him out of his rights as long as we can. Even though we softened to him he would not be a hero in these clothes of servitude; and he loves his clothes. How to get him out of them? It would require a cataclysm. To be an indoor servant at all is to Crichton a badge of honour; to be a butler at thirty is the realisation of his proudest ambitions. He is devotedly attached to his master, who, in his opinion, has but one fault, he is not sufficiently contemptuous of his inferiors. We are immediately to be introduced to this solitary failing of a great English peer.

This perfect butler, then, opens a door, and ushers Ernest into a certain room. At the same moment the curtain rises on this room, and the play begins.

It is one of several reception-rooms in Loam House, not the most magnificent but quite the softest; and of a warm afternoon all that those who are anybody° crave for is the softest. The larger rooms are magnificent and bare, carpetless, so that it is an accomplishment to keep one's feet on them; they are sometimes lent for charitable purposes; they are also all in use on the night of a dinner-party, when you may find yourself alone in one, having taken a wrong turning; or alone, save for two others who are within hailing distance. This room, however, is comparatively small and very soft. There are so many cushions in it that you wonder why, if you are an outsider and don't know that it needs six cushions to make one fair head comfy. The couches themselves are cushions as large as beds, and there is an art of sinking into them and of waiting to be helped out of them. There are several famous paintings on the walls, of which you may say 'Jolly thing that,' without losing caste° as knowing too much; and in cases there are glorious miniatures, but the daughters of the house cannot tell you of whom; 'there is a catalogue somewhere.' There are a thousand or so of roses in basins, several library novels, and a row of weekly illustrated newspapers lying against each other like fallen soldiers. If any one disturbs this row Crichton seems to know of it from afar and appears noiselessly and replaces the wanderer. One thing unexpected in such a room is a great array of tea-things. Ernest spots them with a twinkle, and has his epigram at once unsheathed. He dallies, however, before delivering the thrust.

ERNEST I perceive, from the tea-cups, Crichton, that the great function is to take place here.

CRICHTON (*with a respectful sigh*) Yes, sir.

ERNEST (*chuckling heartlessly*) The servants' hall° coming up to have tea in the drawing-room! (*With terrible sarcasm*) No wonder you look happy, Crichton.

CRICHTON (*under the knife*) No, sir.   80

ERNEST Do you know, Crichton, I think that with an effort you might look even happier. (*Crichton smiles wanly*) You don't approve of his lordship's compelling his servants to be his equals—once a month?

CRICHTON It is not for me, sir, to disapprove of his lordship's   85
Radical views.°

ERNEST Certainly not. And, after all, it is only once a month that he is affable to you.

CRICHTON On all other days of the month, sir, his lordship's treatment of us is everything that could be desired.   90

ERNEST (*This is the epigram*) Tea-cups! Life, Crichton, is like a cup of tea; the more heartily we drink, the sooner we reach the dregs.

CRICHTON (*obediently*) Thank you, sir.

ERNEST (*becoming confidential, as we do when we have need of an ally*) Crichton, in case I should be asked to say a few words to the   95
servants, I have strung together a little speech. (*His hand strays to his pocket*) I was wondering where I should stand.

> (*He tries various places and postures, and comes to rest leaning over a high chair, whence, in dumb show, he addresses a gathering. Crichton, with the best intentions, gives him a footstool to stand on, and departs, happily unconscious that Ernest in some dudgeon has kicked the footstool across the room*)

ERNEST (*addressing an imaginary audience, and desirous of startling them at once*) Suppose you were all little fishes at the bottom of the
sea—   100

> (*He is not quite satisfied with his position, though sure that the fault must lie with the chair for being too high, not with him for being too short. Crichton's suggestion was not perhaps a bad one after all. He lifts the stool, but hastily conceals it behind him on the entrance of the Ladies Catherine and Agatha, two daughters of the house. Catherine is twenty, and Agatha two years younger. They are very fashionable young women indeed, who might wake up for a dance, but they are very lazy, Catherine being two years lazier than Agatha*)

ERNEST (*uneasily jocular, because he is concealing the footstool*) And how are my little friends to-day?

5

AGATHA (*contriving to reach a settee*) Don't be silly, Ernest. If you want to know how we are, we are dead. Even to think of entertaining the servants is so exhausting.   105

CATHERINE (*subsiding nearer the door*) Besides which, we have had to decide what frocks to take with us on the yacht, and that is such a mental strain.

ERNEST You poor overworked things. (*Evidently Agatha is his favourite, for he helps her to put her feet on the settee, while Catherine*   110 *has to dispose of her own feet*) Rest your weary limbs.

CATHERINE (*perhaps in revenge*) But why have you a footstool in your hand?

AGATHA Yes?

ERNEST Why? (*Brilliantly; but to be sure he has had time to think it*   115 *out*) You see, as the servants are to be the guests I must be butler. I was practising. This is a tray, observe.

> (*Holding the footstool as a tray, he minces across the room like an accomplished footman. The gods favour him, for just here Lady Mary enters, and he holds out the footstool to her*)

Tea, my lady?

> (*Lady Mary is a beautiful creature of twenty-two, and is of a natural hauteur which is at once the fury and the envy of her sisters. If she chooses she can make you seem so insignificant that you feel you might be swept away with the crumb-brush.° She seldom chooses, because of the trouble of preening herself as she does it; she is usually content to show that you merely tire her eyes. She often seems to be about to go to sleep in the middle of a remark: there is quite a long and anxious pause, and then she continues, like a clock that hesitates, bored in the middle of its strike*)

LADY MARY (*arching her brows*) It is only you, Ernest; I thought there was some one here. (*She also bestows herself on cushions*)   120

ERNEST (*a little piqued, and deserting the footstool*) Had a very tiring day also, Mary?

LADY MARY (*yawning*) Dreadfully. Been trying on engagement-rings all the morning.

ERNEST (*who is as fond of gossip as the oldest club member°*) What's   125 that? (*To Agatha*) Is it Brocklehurst?

> (*The energetic Agatha nods*)

You have given your warm young heart to Brocky?

> (*Lady Mary is impervious to his humour, but he continues bravely*)

6

I don't wish to fatigue you, Mary, by insisting on a verbal answer, but if, without straining yourself, you can signify Yes or No, won't you make the effort?   130
>   (*She indolently flashes a ring on her most important finger, and he starts back melodramatically*)

The ring! Then I am too late, too late! (*Fixing Lady Mary sternly, like a prosecuting counsel*) May I ask, Mary, does Brocky know? Of course, it was that terrible mother of his who pulled this through. Mother does everything for Brocky. Still, in the eyes of the law you will be, not her wife, but his, and, therefore, I hold that   135 Brocky ought to be informed. Now——
>   (*He discovers that their languorous eyes have closed*)

If you girls are shamming sleep in the expectation that I shall awaken you in the manner beloved of ladies, abandon all such hopes.
>   (*Catherine and Agatha look up without speaking*)

LADY MARY (*speaking without looking up*) You impertinent boy.   140

ERNEST (*eagerly plucking another epigram from his quiver*) I knew that was it, though I don't know everything. Agatha, I'm not young enough to know everything.
>   (*He looks hopefully from one to another, but though they try to grasp this, his brilliance baffles them*)

AGATHA (*his secret admirer*) Young enough?

ERNEST (*encouragingly*) Don't you see? I'm not young enough to   145 know everything.

AGATHA I'm sure it's awfully clever, but it's so puzzling.
>   (*Here Crichton ushers in an athletic, pleasant-faced young clergyman, Mr Treherne, who greets the company*)

CATHERINE Ernest, say it to Mr Treherne.

ERNEST Look here, Treherne, I'm not young enough to know everything.   150

TREHERNE How do you mean, Ernest?

ERNEST (*a little nettled*) I mean what I say.

LADY MARY Say it again; say it more slowly.

ERNEST I'm—not—young—enough—to—know—everything.

TREHERNE *I* see. What you really mean, my boy, is that you are not   155 old enough to know everything.

ERNEST No, I don't.

TREHERNE I assure you that's it.

LADY MARY Of course it is.

CATHERINE Yes, Ernest, that's it.   160

7

(*Ernest, in desperation, appeals to Crichton*)

ERNEST I am not young enough, Crichton, to know everything.

(*It is an anxious moment, but a smile is at length extorted from Crichton as with a corkscrew*)

CRICHTON Thank you, sir. (*He goes*)

ERNEST (*relieved*) Ah, if you had that fellow's head, Treherne, you would find something better to do with it than play cricket. I hear you bowl with your head.°   165

TREHERNE (*with proper humility*) I'm afraid cricket is all I'm good for, Ernest.

CATHERINE (*who thinks he has a heavenly nose*) Indeed, it isn't. You are sure to get on, Mr Treherne.

TREHERNE Thank you, Lady Catherine.   170

CATHERINE But it was the bishop who told me so. He said a clergyman who breaks both ways° is sure to get on in England.

TREHERNE I'm jolly glad.

(*The master of the house comes in, accompanied by Lord Brocklehurst. The Earl of Loam is a widower, a philanthropist, and a peer of advanced ideas. As a widower he is at least able to interfere in the domestic concerns of his house—to rummage in the drawers, so to speak, for which he has felt an itching all his blameless life; his philanthropy has opened quite a number of other drawers to him; and his advanced ideas have blown out his figure. He takes in all the weightiest monthly reviews, and prefers those that are uncut,° because he perhaps never looks better than when cutting them; but he does not read them, and save for the cutting it would suit him as well merely to take in the covers. He writes letters to the papers, which are printed in a type to scale with himself, and he is very jealous of those other correspondents who get his type. Let laws and learning, art and commerce die,° but leave the big type to an intellectual aristocracy. He is really the reformed House of Lords which will come some day.*

Young Lord Brocklehurst is nothing save for his rank. You could pick him up by the handful any day in Piccadilly or Holborn,° buying socks—or selling them)

LORD LOAM (*expansively*) You are here, Ernest. Feeling fit for the voyage, Treherne?   175

TREHERNE Looking forward to it enormously.

LORD LOAM That's right. (*He chases his children about as if they were chickens*) Now then, Mary, up and doing, up and doing. Time we had the servants in. They enjoy it so much.

LADY MARY They hate it.   180

LORD LOAM Mary, to your duties. (*And he points severely to the tea-table*)

ERNEST (*twinkling*) Congratulations, Brocky.

LORD BROCKLEHURST (*who detests humour*) Thanks.

ERNEST Mother pleased?   185

LORD BROCKLEHURST (*with dignity*) Mother is very pleased.

ERNEST That's good. Do you go on the yacht with us?

LORD BROCKLEHURST Sorry I can't. And look here, Ernest, I will *not* be called Brocky.

ERNEST Mother don't like it?°   190

LORD BROCKLEHURST She does not. (*He leaves Ernest, who forgives him and begins to think about his speech. Crichton enters*)

LORD LOAM (*speaking as one man to another*) We are quite ready, Crichton. (*Crichton is distressed*)

LADY MARY (*sarcastically*) How Crichton enjoys it!   195

LORD LOAM (*frowning*) He is the only one who doesn't; pitiful creature.

CRICHTON (*shuddering under his lord's displeasure*) I can't help being a Conservative, my lord.

LORD LOAM Be a man, Crichton. You are the same flesh and blood   200
as myself.°

CRICHTON (*in pain*) Oh, my lord!

LORD LOAM (*sharply*) Show them in; and, by the way, they were not all here last time.

CRICHTON All, my lord, except the merest trifles.   205

LORD LOAM It must be every one. (*Lowering*°) And remember this, Crichton, for the time being you are my equal. (*Testily*) I shall soon show you whether you are not my equal. Do as you are told.

> (*Crichton departs to obey, and his lordship is now a general. He has no pity for his daughters, and uses a terrible threat*)

And girls, remember, no condescension. The first who conde-
scends recites. (*This sends them scurrying to their labours*) By the   210
way, Brocklehurst, can you do anything?°

LORD BROCKLEHURST How do you mean?

LORD LOAM Can you do anything—with a penny or a handkerchief, make them disappear, for instance?

LORD BROCKLEHURST Good heavens, no.   215

LORD LOAM It's a pity. Every one in our position ought to be able to do something. Ernest, I shall probably ask you to say a few words; something bright and sparkling.

9

ERNEST But, my dear uncle, I have prepared nothing.

LORD LOAM Anything impromptu will do.   220

ERNEST Oh—well—if anything strikes me.

> (*He unostentatiously gets the footstool into position behind the chair. Crichton reappears to announce the guests, of whom the first is the housekeeper. They should be well-mannered. Nothing farcical, please*)

CRICHTON (*reluctantly*) Mrs Perkins.

LORD LOAM (*shaking hands*) Very delighted, Mrs Perkins. Mary, our friend, Mrs Perkins.

LADY MARY How do you do, Mrs Perkins? Won't you sit here?   225

LORD LOAM (*threateningly*) Agatha!

AGATHA (*hastily*) How do you do? Won't you sit down?

LORD LOAM (*introducing*) Lord Brocklehurst—my valued friend, Mrs Perkins.

> (*Lord Brocklehurst bows and escapes. He has to fall back on Ernest*)

LORD BROCKLEHURST For heaven's sake, Ernest, don't leave me   230
for a moment; this sort of thing is utterly opposed to all my principles.

ERNEST (*airily*) You stick to me, Brocky, and I'll pull you through.

CRICHTON Monsieur Fleury.

ERNEST The chef.   235

LORD LOAM (*shaking hands with the chef*) Very charmed to see you, Monsieur Fleury.

FLEURY Thank you very much.

> (*Fleury bows to Agatha, who is not effusive*)

LORD LOAM (*warningly*) Agatha—recitation!

> (*She tosses her head, but immediately finds a seat and tea for M. Fleury. Treherne and Ernest move about, making themselves amiable. Lady Mary is presiding at the tea-tray*)

CRICHTON Mr Rolleston.   240

LORD LOAM (*shaking hands with his valet*) How do you do, Rolleston?

> (*Catherine looks after the wants of Rolleston*)

CRICHTON Mr Tompsett.

> (*Tompsett, the coachman, is received with honours, from which he shrinks, but with quiet dignity*)

CRICHTON Miss Fisher.

> (*This superb creature is no less than Lady Mary's maid, and even Lord Loam is a little nervous*)

LORD LOAM This is a pleasure, Miss Fisher.

ERNEST (*unabashed*) If I might venture, Miss Fisher—(*And he takes   245
her unto himself*)

CRICHTON Miss Simmons.

LORD LOAM (*to Catherine's maid*) You are always welcome, Miss
Simmons.

ERNEST (*perhaps to kindle jealousy in Miss Fisher*) At last we meet.   250
Won't you sit down?

CRICHTON Mademoiselle Jeanne.

LORD LOAM Charmed to see you, Mademoiselle Jeanne.
(*A place is found for Agatha's maid, and the scene is now an
animated one; but still our host thinks his girls are not sufficiently
sociable. He frowns on Lady Mary*)

LADY MARY (*in alarm*) Mr Treherne, this is Fisher, my maid.

LORD LOAM (*sharply*) Your what, Mary?   255

LADY MARY My friend.

CRICHTON Thomas.

LORD LOAM How do you do, Thomas?
(*The first footman gives him a reluctant hand*)

CRICHTON John.

LORD LOAM How do you do, John?   260
(*Ernest signs to Lord Brocklehurst, who hastens to him*)

ERNEST (*introducing*) Brocklehurst, this is John. I think you have
already met on the door-step.

CRICHTON Jane.
(*She comes, wrapping her hands miserably in her apron*)

LORD LOAM (*doggedly*) Give me your hand, Jane.

CRICHTON Gladys.   265

ERNEST How do you do, Gladys? You know my uncle?

LORD LOAM Your hand, Gladys.
(*He bestows her on Agatha*)

CRICHTON Tweeny.
(*She is a very humble and frightened kitchen-maid, of whom we
are to see more*)

LORD LOAM So happy to see you.

FISHER John, I saw you talking to Lord Brocklehurst just now;   270
introduce me.

LORD BROCKLEHURST (*who is really a second-rate John*) That is an
uncommon pretty girl; if I must feed one of them, Ernest, that is
the one.
(*But Ernest tries to part him and Fisher as they are about to
shake hands*)

ERNEST No you don't, it won't do, Brocky. (*To Miss Fisher*) You are   275
too pretty, my dear. Mother wouldn't like it. (*Discovering Tweeny*)
Here is something safer. Charming girl, Brocky, dying to know
you; let me introduce you. Tweeny, Lord Brocklehurst—Lord
Brocklehurst, Tweeny.
> (*Brocklehurst accepts his fate; but he still has an eye for Fisher,
> and something may come of this*)

LORD LOAM (*severely*) They are not all here, Crichton.   280

CRICHTON (*with a sigh*) Odds and ends.
> (*A Stable-Boy and a Page are shown in, and for a moment no
> daughter of the house advances to them*)

LORD LOAM (*with a roving eye on his children*) Which is to recite?
> (*The last of the company are, so to say, embraced*)

LORD LOAM (*to Tompsett, as they partake of tea together*) And how
are all at home?

TOMPSETT Fairish, my lord, if 'tis the horses you are inquiring for?   285

LORD LOAM No, no, the family. How's the baby?

TOMPSETT Blooming, your lordship.

LORD LOAM A very fine boy. I remember saying so when I saw him;
nice little fellow.

TOMPSETT (*not quite knowing whether to let it pass*) Beg pardon, my   290
lord, it's a girl.

LORD LOAM A girl? Aha! ha! ha! exactly what I said. I distinctly
remember saying, If it's spared° it will be a girl.
> (*Crichton now comes down*)

LORD LOAM Very delighted to see you, Crichton.
> (*Crichton has to shake hands*)

Mary, you know Mr Crichton?   295
> (*He wanders off in search of other prey*)

LADY MARY Milk and sugar, Crichton?

CRICHTON I'm ashamed to be seen talking to you,° my lady.

LADY MARY To such a perfect servant as you all this must be most
distasteful. (*Crichton is too respectful to answer*) Oh, please to speak,
or I shall have to recite. You do hate it, don't you?   300

CRICHTON It pains me, your ladyship. It disturbs the etiquette of the
servants' hall. After last month's meeting the page-boy, in a burst
of equality, called me Crichton. He was dismissed.

LADY MARY I wonder—I really do—how you can remain with us.

CRICHTON I should have felt compelled to give notice, my lady,   305
if the master had not had a seat in the Upper House.° I cling to
that.

LADY MARY Do go on speaking. Tell me, what did Mr Ernest mean
by saying he was not young enough to know everything?

CRICHTON I have no idea, my lady.   310

LADY MARY But you laughed.

CRICHTON My lady, he is the second son of a peer.

LADY MARY Very proper sentiments. You are a good soul, Crichton.

LORD BROCKLEHURST (*desperately to Tweeny*) And now tell me,
have you been to the Opera? What sort of weather have you been   315
having in the kitchen? (*Tweeny gurgles*) For Heaven's sake, woman,
be articulate.

CRICHTON (*still talking to Lady Mary*) No, my lady; his lordship may
compel us to be equal upstairs, but there will never be equality in
the servants' hall.   320

LORD LOAM (*overhearing this*) What's that? No equality? Can't you
see, Crichton, that our divisions into classes are artificial, that if we
were to return to Nature,° which is the aspiration of my life, all
would be equal?

CRICHTON If I may make so bold as to contradict your lordship——   325

LORD LOAM (*with an effort*) Go on.

CRICHTON The divisions into classes, my lord, are not artificial. They
are the natural outcome of a civilised society. (*To Lady Mary*) There
must always be a master and servants in all civilised communities, my
lady, for it is natural, and whatever is natural is right.   330

LORD LOAM (*wincing*) It is very unnatural for me to stand here and
allow you to talk such nonsense.

CRICHTON (*eagerly*) Yes, my lord, it is. That is what I have been
striving to point out to your lordship.

AGATHA (*to Catherine*) What is the matter with Fisher? She is   335
looking daggers.°

CATHERINE The tedious creature; some question of etiquette, I
suppose.
    (*She sails across to Fisher*)
How are you, Fisher?

FISHER (*with a toss of her head*) I am nothing, my lady, I am nothing   340
at all.

AGATHA Oh dear, who says so?

FISHER (*affronted*) His lordship has asked that kitchen wench to have
a second cup of tea.

CATHERINE But why not?   345

FISHER If it pleases his lordship to offer it to *her* before offering it to
me——

AGATHA So that is it. Do you want another cup of tea, Fisher?

FISHER No, my lady—but my position—I should have been asked first.   350

AGATHA Oh dear.

> (*All this has taken some time, and by now the feeble appetites of the uncomfortable guests have been satiated. But they know there is still another ordeal to face—his lordship's monthly speech. Every one awaits it with misgiving—the servants lest they should applaud, as last time, in the wrong place, and the daughters because he may be personal about them, as the time before. Ernest is annoyed that there should be this speech at all when there is such a much better one coming, and Brocklehurst foresees the degradation of the peerage. All are thinking of themselves alone save Crichton, who knows his master's weakness, and fears he may stick in the middle. Lord Loam, however, advances cheerfully to his doom. He sees Ernest's stool, and artfully stands on it, to his nephew's natural indignation. The three ladies knit their lips, the servants look down their noses, and the address begins*)

LORD LOAM My friends, I am glad to see you all looking so happy. It used to be predicted by the scoffer that these meetings would prove distasteful to you. Are they distasteful? I hear you laughing° at the question.   355

> (*He has not heard them, but he hears them now, the watchful Crichton giving them a lead*)

No harm in saying that among us to-day is one who was formerly hostile to the movement, but who to-day has been won over. I refer to Lord Brocklehurst, who, I am sure, will presently say to me that if the charming lady now by his side has derived as much pleasure from his company as he has derived from hers, he will be   360
more than satisfied.

> (*All look at Tweeny, who trembles*)

For the time being the artificial and unnatural—I say unnatural (*glaring at Crichton, who bows slightly*)—barriers of society are swept away. Would that they could be swept away for ever.

> (*The Page-Boy cheers, and has the one moment of prominence in his life. He grows up, marries and has children, but is never really heard of again*)

But that is entirely and utterly out of the question.° And now for   365
a few months we are to be separated. As you know, my daughters
and Mr Ernest and Mr Treherne are to accompany me on my

yacht, on a voyage to distant parts of the earth. In less than forty-eight hours we shall be under way.°

(*But for Crichton's eye the reckless Page-Boy would repeat his success*)

Do not think our life on the yacht is to be one long idle holiday.   370
My views on the excessive luxury of the day are well known, and what I preach I am resolved to practise. I have therefore decided that my daughters, instead of having one maid each as at present, shall on this voyage have but one maid between them.

(*Three maids rise; also three mistresses*)

CRICHTON My lord!   375

LORD LOAM My mind is made up.

ERNEST I cordially agree.

LORD LOAM And now, my friends, I should like to think that there is some piece of advice I might give you, some thought, some noble saying over which you might ponder in my absence. In this   380
connection I remember a proverb, which has had a great effect on my own life. I first heard it many years ago. I have never forgotten it. It constantly cheers and guides me. That proverb is—that proverb was—the proverb I speak of——

(*He grows pale and taps his forehead*)

LADY MARY Oh dear, I believe he has forgotten it.   385

LORD LOAM (*desperately*) The proverb—that proverb to which I refer——

(*Alas, it has gone. The distress is general. He has not even the sense to sit down. He gropes for the proverb in the air. They try applause, but it is no help*)

I have it now—(*not he*)

LADY MARY (*with confidence*) Crichton.°

(*He does not fail her. As quietly as if he were in goloshes, mind as well as feet, he dismisses the domestics; they go according to precedence but without servility, and there must be no attempt at 'comic effect.' Then he signs to Mr Treherne, and they conduct Lord Loam with dignity from the room. His hands are still catching flies; he still mutters, 'The proverb—'; but he continues, owing to Crichton's treatment, to look every inch a peer. The ladies have now an opportunity to air their indignation*)

LADY MARY One maid among three grown women!   390

LORD BROCKLEHURST Mary, I think I had better go. That dreadful kitchen-maid——

LADY MARY I can't blame you, George.

(*He salutes her*)

LORD BROCKLEHURST Your father's views are shocking to me, and
I am glad I am not to be one of the party on the yacht. My respect   395
for myself, Mary, my natural anxiety as to what mother will say.
I shall see you, darling, before you sail.
     (*He bows to the others and goes*)

ERNEST Selfish brute, only thinking of himself. What about my speech?

LADY MARY One maid among three of us. What's to be done?

ERNEST Pooh! You must do for yourselves, that's all.   400

LADY MARY Do for ourselves. How can we know where our things
are kept?

AGATHA Are you aware that dresses button up the back?

CATHERINE How are we to get into our shoes and be prepared for
the carriage?   405

LADY MARY Who is to put us to bed, and who is to get us up, and
how shall we ever know it's morning if there is no one to pull up
the blinds?
     (*Crichton crosses on his way out*)

ERNEST How is his lordship now?

CRICHTON A little easier, sir.   410

LADY MARY Crichton, send Fisher to me. (*He goes*)

ERNEST I have no pity for you girls, I——

LADY MARY Ernest, go away, and don't insult the broken-hearted.

ERNEST And uncommon glad I am to go. Ta-ta, all of you. He asked
me to say a few words. I came here to say a few words, and I'm   415
not at all sure that I couldn't bring an action against him.
     (*He departs, feeling that he has left a dart behind him. The girls
     are alone with their tragic thoughts°*)

LADY MARY (*become a mother to the younger ones at last*) My poor
sisters, come here. (*They go to her doubtfully*) We must make this
draw us closer together. I shall do my best to help you in every
way. Just now I cannot think of myself at all.   420

AGATHA But how unlike you, Mary.

LADY MARY It is my duty to protect my sisters.

CATHERINE I never knew her so sweet before, Agatha. (*Cautiously*)
What do you propose to do, Mary?

LADY MARY I propose when we are on the yacht to lend Fisher to   425
you when I don't need her myself.

AGATHA Fisher?

LADY MARY (*who has the most character of the three*) Of course, as the
eldest, I have decided that it is *my* maid we shall take with us.

CATHERINE (*speaking also for Agatha*) Mary, you toad.   430
AGATHA Nothing on earth would induce Fisher to lift her hand for
either me or Catherine.
LADY MARY I was afraid of it, Agatha. That is why I am so sorry for
you.
     (*The further exchange of pleasantries is interrupted by the
     arrival of Fisher*)
LADY MARY Fisher, you heard what his lordship said?   435
FISHER Yes, my lady.
LADY MARY (*coldly, though the others would have tried blandishment*)
You have given me some satisfaction of late, Fisher, and to mark
my approval I have decided that you shall be the maid who
accompanies us.   440
FISHER (*acidly*) I thank you, my lady.
LADY MARY That is all; you may go.
FISHER (*rapping it out*) If you please, my lady, I wish to give notice.
     (*Catherine and Agatha gleam, but Lady Mary is of sterner stuff*)
LADY MARY (*taking up a book*) Oh, certainly—you may go.
CATHERINE But why, Fisher?   445
FISHER I could not undertake, my lady, to wait upon three. *We* don't
do it.° (*In an indignant outburst to Lady Mary*) Oh, my lady, to
think that this affront——
LADY MARY (*looking up*) I thought I told you to go, Fisher.
     (*Fisher stands for a moment irresolute; then goes. As soon as she
     has gone Lady Mary puts down her book and weeps.° She is a
     pretty woman, but this is the only pretty thing we have seen her
     do yet*)
AGATHA (*succinctly*) Serves you right.   450
     (*Crichton comes*)
CATHERINE It will be Simmons after all. Send Simmons to me.
CRICHTON (*after hesitating*) My lady, might I venture to speak?
CATHERINE What is it?
CRICHTON I happen to know, your ladyship, that Simmons desires
to give notice for the same reason as Fisher.   455
CATHERINE Oh!
AGATHA (*triumphant*) Then, Catherine, we take Jeanne.
CRICHTON And Jeanne also, my lady.
     (*Lady Mary is reading, indifferent though the heavens fall, but
     her sisters are not ashamed to show their despair to Crichton*)
AGATHA We can't blame them. Could any maid who respected
herself be got to wait upon three?   460

LADY MARY (*with languid interest*) I suppose there are such persons, Crichton?

CRICHTON (*guardedly*) I have heard, my lady, that there are such.

LADY MARY (*a little desperate*) Crichton, what's to be done? We sail in two days; could one be discovered in the time?   465

AGATHA (*frankly a supplicant*) Surely you can think of some one?

CRICHTON (*after hesitating*) There is in this establishment, your ladyship, a young woman——

LADY MARY Yes?

CRICHTON A young woman, on whom I have for some time cast an   470 eye.

CATHERINE (*eagerly*) Do you mean as a possible lady's-maid?

CRICHTON I had thought of her, my lady, in another connection.

LADY MARY Ah!

CRICHTON But I believe she is quite the young person you require.   475 Perhaps if you could see her, my lady——

LADY MARY I shall certainly see her. Bring her to me. (*He goes*) You two needn't wait.

CATHERINE Needn't we? We see your little game, Mary.

AGATHA We shall certainly remain and have our two-thirds of her.   480
        (*They sit there doggedly until Crichton returns with Tweeny,
        who looks scared*)

CRICHTON This, my lady, is the young person.

CATHERINE (*frankly*) Oh dear!
        (*It is evident that all three consider her quite unsuitable*)

LADY MARY Come here, girl. Don't be afraid.
        (*Tweeny looks imploringly at her idol*)

CRICHTON Her appearance, my lady, is homely, and her manners, as you may have observed, deplorable, but she has a heart of gold.   485

LADY MARY What is your position downstairs?

TWEENY (*bobbing*) I'm a tweeny, your ladyship.

CATHERINE A what?

CRICHTON A tweeny; that is to say, my lady, she is not at present, strictly speaking, anything; a *between* maid; she helps the vegetable   490 maid. It is she, my lady, who conveys the dishes from the one end of the kitchen table, where they are placed by the cook, to the other end, where they enter into the charge of Thomas and John.

LADY MARY I see. And you and Crichton are—ah—keeping company?°
                                                                        495
        (*Crichton draws himself up*)

TWEENY (*aghast*) A butler don't keep company, my lady.

LADY MARY (*indifferently*) Does he not?

CRICHTON No, your ladyship, we butlers may—(*he makes a gesture with his arms*)—but we do not keep company.

AGATHA I know what it is; you are engaged?   500
        (*Tweeny looks longingly at Crichton*)

CRICHTON Certainly not, my lady. The utmost I can say at present is that I have cast a favourable eye.
        (*Even this is much to Tweeny*)

LADY MARY As you choose. But I am afraid, Crichton, she will not suit us.

CRICHTON My lady, beneath this simple exterior are concealed a 505
very sweet nature and rare womanly gifts.

AGATHA Unfortunately, that is not what we want.

CRICHTON And it is she, my lady, who dresses the hair of the ladies'-maids for our evening meals.
        (*The ladies are interested at last*)

LADY MARY She dresses Fisher's hair?   510

TWEENY Yes, my lady, and I does them up when they goes to parties.

CRICHTON (*pained, but not scolding*) Does!

TWEENY Doos. And it's me what alters your gowns to fit them.

CRICHTON *What* alters!   515

TWEENY Which alters.

AGATHA Mary?

LADY MARY I shall certainly have her.

CATHERINE *We* shall certainly have her. Tweeny, we have decided to make a lady's-maid of you.   520

TWEENY Oh lawks!°

AGATHA We are doing this for you so that your position socially may be more nearly akin to that of Crichton.

CRICHTON (*gravely*) It will undoubtedly increase the young person's chances.   525

LADY MARY Then if I get a good character° for you from Mrs Perkins, she will make the necessary arrangements.
        (*She resumes reading*)

TWEENY (*elated*) My lady!

LADY MARY By the way, I hope you are a good sailor.

TWEENY (*startled*) You don't mean, my lady, I'm to go on the ship? 530

LADY MARY Certainly.

TWEENY But——(*To Crichton*) You ain't going, sir?

CRICHTON No.

TWEENY (*firm at last*) Then neither ain't I.

AGATHA You must.   535

TWEENY Leave him! Not me.

LADY MARY Girl, don't be silly. Crichton will be—considered in
your wages.°

TWEENY I ain't going.

CRICHTON I feared this, my lady.   540

TWEENY Nothing'll budge me.

LADY MARY Leave the room.

(*Crichton shows Tweeny out with marked politeness*)

AGATHA Crichton, I think you might have shown more displeasure
with her.

CRICHTON (*contrite*) I was touched, my lady. I see, my lady, that to   545
part from her would be a wrench to me, though I could not well
say so in her presence, not having yet decided how far I shall go
with her.

(*He is about to go when Lord Loam returns, fuming*)

LORD LOAM The ingrate! The smug! The fop!°

CATHERINE What is it now, father?   550

LORD LOAM That man of mine, Rolleston, refuses to accompany us
because you are to have but one maid.

AGATHA Hurrah!

LADY MARY (*in better taste*) Darling father, rather than you should
lose Rolleston, we will consent to take all the three of them.   555

LORD LOAM Pooh, nonsense! Crichton, find me a valet who can do
without three maids.

CRICHTON Yes, my lord. (*Troubled*) In the time—the more suitable
the party,° my lord, the less willing will he be to come without
the—the usual perquisites.   560

LORD LOAM Any one will do.

CRICHTON (*shocked*) My lord!

LORD LOAM The ingrate! The puppy!

(*Agatha has an idea, and whispers to Lady Mary*)

LADY MARY I ask a favour of a servant?—never!

AGATHA Then I will. Crichton, would it not be very distressing to   565
you to let his lordship go, attended by a valet who might prove
unworthy? It is only for three months; don't you think that
you—you yourself—you——

(*As Crichton sees what she wants he pulls himself up with noble,
offended dignity, and she is appalled°*)

I beg your pardon.

(*He bows stiffly*)

CATHERINE (*to Crichton*) But think of the joy to Tweeny. 570
    (*Crichton is moved, but he shakes his head*)

LADY MARY (*so much the cleverest*) Crichton, do you think it safe to let the master you love go so far away without you while he has these dangerous views about equality?
    (*Crichton is profoundly stirred. After a struggle he goes to his master, who has been pacing the room*)

CRICHTON My lord, I have found a man.

LORD LOAM Already? Who is he? 575
    (*Crichton presents himself with a gesture*)
Yourself?

CATHERINE Father, how good of him.

LORD LOAM (*pleased, but thinking it a small thing*) Uncommon good. Thank you, Crichton. This helps me nicely out of a hole; and how it will annoy Rolleston! Come with me, and we shall tell him. Not 580 that I think you have lowered yourself in any way. Come along.
    (*He goes, and Crichton is to follow him, but is stopped by Agatha impulsively offering him her hand*)

CRICHTON (*who is much shaken*) My lady—a valet's hand!°

AGATHA I had no idea you would feel it so deeply; why did you do it?
    (*Crichton is too respectful to reply*)

LADY MARY (*regarding him*) Crichton, I am curious. I insist upon an answer. 585

CRICHTON My lady, I am the son of a butler and a lady's-maid—perhaps the happiest of all combinations; and to me the most beautiful thing in the world is a haughty, aristocratic English house, with every one kept in his place. Though I were equal to your ladyship, where would be the pleasure to me? It would be 590 counterbalanced by the pain of feeling that Thomas and John were equal to me.

CATHERINE But father says if we were to return to Nature——

CRICHTON If we did, my lady, the first thing we should do would be to elect a head. Circumstances might alter cases;° the same person 595 might not be master; the same persons might not be servants. I can't say as to that, nor should we have the deciding of it. Nature would decide for us.

LADY MARY You seem to have thought it all out carefully, Crichton.

CRICHTON Yes, my lady. 600

CATHERINE And you have done this for us, Crichton, because you thought that—that father needed to be kept in his place?°

CRICHTON I should prefer you to say, my lady, that I have done it for the house.°

AGATHA Thank you, Crichton. Mary, be nicer to him. (*But Lady* 605
Mary has begun to read again) If there was any way in which we could show our gratitude?

CRICHTON If I might venture, my lady, would you kindly show it by becoming more like Lady Mary? That disdain is what we like from our superiors. Even so do we, the upper servants, disdain the lower 610
servants, while they take it out of the odds and ends.

  (*He goes, and they bury themselves in cushions*)

AGATHA Oh dear, what a tiring day.

CATHERINE I feel dead. Tuck in your feet, you selfish thing.

  (*Lady Mary is lying reading on another couch*)

LADY MARY I wonder what he meant by circumstances might alter cases. 615

AGATHA (*yawning*) Don't talk, Mary, I was nearly asleep.

LADY MARY I wonder what he meant by the same person might not be master, and the same persons might not be servants.

CATHERINE Do be quiet, Mary, and leave it to Nature; he said Nature would decide. 620

LADY MARY I wonder——

  (*But she does not wonder very much. She would wonder more if
  she knew what was coming. Her book slips unregarded to the
  floor. The ladies are at rest until it is time to dress*°)

Act 2
THE ISLAND

Two months have elapsed, and the scene is a desert island in the Pacific, on which our adventurers have been wrecked.

The curtain rises on a sea of bamboo, which shuts out all view save the foliage of palm trees and some gaunt rocks. Occasionally Crichton and Treherne come momentarily into sight, hacking and hewing the bamboo, through which they are making a clearing between the ladies and the shore; and by and by, owing to their efforts, we shall have an unrestricted outlook on to a sullen sea that is at present hidden. Then we shall also be able to note a mast standing out of the water—all that is left, saving floating wreckage, of the ill-fated yacht the *Bluebell*. The beginnings of a hut will also be seen, with Crichton driving its walls into the ground or astride its roof of saplings, for at present he is doing more than one thing at a time. In a red shirt, with the ends of his sailor's breeches thrust into wading-boots, he looks a man for the moment; we suddenly remember some one's saying—perhaps it was ourselves°—that a cataclysm would be needed to get him out of his servant's clothes, and apparently it has been forthcoming. It is no longer beneath our dignity to cast an inquiring eye on his appearance. His features are not distinguished, but he has a strong jaw and green eyes, in which a yellow light burns that we have not seen before. His dark hair, hitherto so decorously sleek, has been ruffled this way and that by wind and weather, as if they were part of the cataclysm and wanted to help his chance. His muscles must be soft and flabby still, but though they shriek aloud to him to desist, he rains lusty blows with his axe, like one who has come upon the open for the first time in his life, and likes it. He is as yet far from being an expert woodsman—mark the blood on his hands at places where he has hit them instead of the tree; but note also that he does not waste time in bandaging them—he rubs them in the earth and goes on. His face is still of the discreet pallor that befits a butler, and he carries the smaller logs as if they were a salver; not in a day or a month will he shake off the badge of servitude, but without knowing it he has begun.

But for the hatchets at work, and an occasional something horrible falling from a tree into the ladies' laps, they hear nothing save the mournful surf breaking on a coral shore.

They sit or recline huddled together against a rock, and they are farther from home, in every sense of the word, than ever before. Thirty-six hours ago, they were given three minutes in which to dress, without a maid, and reach the boats, and they have not made the best of that valuable time.° None of them has boots, and had they   40
known this prickly island they would have thought first of boots. They have a sufficiency of garments, but some of them were gifts dropped into the boat—Lady Mary's tarpaulin coat and hat, for instance, and Catherine's blue jersey and red cap, which certify that the two ladies were lately before the mast.° Agatha is too gay in   45
Ernest's dressing-gown, and clutches it to her person with both hands as if afraid that it may be claimed by its rightful owner. There are two pairs of bath slippers between the three of them, and their hair cries aloud and in vain for hairpins.

By their side, on an inverted bucket, sits Ernest, clothed neatly in   50
the garments of day and night, but, alas, bare-footed. He is the only cheerful member of this company of four, but his brightness is due less to a manly desire to succour the helpless than to his having been lately in the throes of composition, and to his modest satisfaction with the result. He reads to the ladies, and they listen, each with one scared   55
eye to the things that fall from trees.

ERNEST (*who has written on the fly-leaf of the only book saved from the wreck*) This is what I have written. 'Wrecked, wrecked, wrecked! on an island in the Tropics, the following: the Hon. Ernest Woolley, the Rev John Treherne, the Ladies, Mary, Catherine,   60
and Agatha Lasenby, with two servants. We are the sole survivors of Lord Loam's steam yacht *Bluebell*, which encountered a fearful gale in these seas, and soon became a total wreck. The crew behaved gallantly, putting us all into the first boat. What became of them I cannot tell, but we, after dreadful sufferings, and   65
insufficiently clad, in whatever garments we could lay hold of in the dark'—

LADY MARY Please don't describe our garments.

ERNEST —'succeeded in reaching this island, with the loss of only one of our party, namely, Lord Loam, who flung away his life in   70
a gallant attempt to save a servant who had fallen overboard.'

  (*The ladies have wept long and sore for their father, but there is something in this last utterance that makes them look up*)

AGATHA But, Ernest, it was Crichton who jumped overboard trying to save father.

ERNEST (*with the candour that is one of his most engaging qualities*)
Well, you know, it was rather silly of uncle to fling away his life   75
by trying to get into the boat first; and as this document may be
printed in the English papers, it struck me, an English peer, you
know——

LADY MARY (*every inch an English peer's daughter*) Ernest, that is
very thoughtful of you.   80

ERNEST (*continuing, well pleased*) —'By night the cries of wild cats
and the hissing of snakes terrify us extremely'—(*This does not
satisfy him so well, and he makes a correction*)—'terrify the ladies
extremely. Against these we have no weapons except one cutlass
and a hatchet. A bucket washed ashore is at present our only   85
comfortable seat'—

LADY MARY (*with some spirit*) And Ernest is sitting on it.

ERNEST H'sh! Oh, do be quiet.—'To add to our horrors, night falls
suddenly in these parts, and it is then that savage animals begin to
prowl and roar.'   90

LADY MARY Have you said that vampire bats suck the blood from
our toes as we sleep?

ERNEST No, that's all. I end up, 'Rescue us or we perish. Rich
reward. Signed Ernest Woolley, in command of our little party.'
This is written on a leaf taken out of a book of poems that Crichton   95
found in his pocket. Fancy Crichton being a reader of poetry! Now
I shall put it into the bottle and fling it into the sea.
     (*He pushes the precious document into a soda-water bottle, and
     rams the cork home. At the same moment, and without effort, he
     gives birth to one of his most characteristic epigrams*)
The tide is going out, we mustn't miss the post.
     (*They are so unhappy that they fail to grasp it, and a little
     petulantly he calls for Crichton, ever his stand-by in the hour of
     epigram. Crichton breaks through the undergrowth quickly,
     thinking the ladies are in danger*)

CRICHTON Anything wrong, sir?

ERNEST (*with fine confidence*) The tide, Crichton, is a postman who   100
calls at our island twice a day for letters.

CRICHTON (*after a pause*) Thank you, sir.
     (*He returns to his labours, however, without giving the smile
     which is the epigrammatist's right, and Ernest is a little
     disappointed in him*)

ERNEST Poor Crichton! I sometimes think he is losing his sense of
humour. Come along, Agatha.

(*He helps his favourite up the rocks, and they disappear gingerly from view*)

CATHERINE How horribly still it is.   105

LADY MARY (*remembering some recent sounds*) It is best when it is still.

CATHERINE (*drawing closer to her*) Mary, I have heard that they are always very still just before they jump.

LADY MARY Don't.

(*A distinct chopping is heard, and they are startled*)   110
(*controlling herself*) It is only Crichton knocking down trees.

CATHERINE (*almost imploringly*) Mary, let us go and stand beside him.

LADY MARY (*coldly*) Let a servant see that I am afraid!

CATHERINE Don't, then; but remember this, dear, they often drop   115
on one from above.

(*She moves away, nearer to the friendly sound of the axe, and Lady Mary is left alone. She is the most courageous of them as well as the haughtiest, but when something she had thought to be a stick glides toward her, she forgets her dignity and screams*)

LADY MARY (*calling*) Crichton, Crichton!

(*It must have been Treherne who was tree-felling, for Crichton comes to her from the hut, drawing his cutlass*)

CRICHTON (*anxious*) Did you call, my lady?

LADY MARY (*herself again, now that he is there*) I! Why should I?

CRICHTON I made a mistake, your ladyship. (*Hesitating*) If you are   120
afraid of being alone, my lady——

LADY MARY Afraid! Certainly not. (*Doggedly*) You may go.

(*But she does not complain when he remains within eyesight cutting the bamboo. It is heavy work, and she watches him silently*)

LADY MARY I wish, Crichton, you could work without getting so hot.

CRICHTON (*mopping his face*) I wish I could, my lady.   125

(*He continues his labours*)

LADY MARY (*taking off her oilskins*) It makes me hot to look at you.

CRICHTON It almost makes me cool to look at your ladyship.

LADY MARY (*who perhaps thinks he is presuming*) Anything I can do for you in that way, Crichton, I shall do with pleasure.

CRICHTON (*quite humbly*) Thank you, my lady.   130

(*By this time most of the bamboo has been cut, and the shore and sea are visible, except where they are hidden by the half completed hut. The mast rising solitary from the water adds to*

26

*the desolation of the scene, and at last tears run down Lady
Mary's face)*

CRICHTON Don't give way, my lady, things might be worse.

LADY MARY My poor father!

CRICHTON If I could have given my life for his——

LADY MARY You did all a man could do. Indeed I thank you,
Crichton. (*With some admiration and more wonder*) You are a   135
man.°

CRICHTON Thank you, my lady.

LADY MARY But it is all so awful. Crichton, is there any hope of a
ship coming?

CRICHTON (*after hesitation*) Of course there is, my lady.   140

LADY MARY (*facing him bravely*) Don't treat me as a child. I have
got to know the worst, and to face it. Crichton, the truth.

CRICHTON (*reluctantly*) We were driven out of our course, my lady;
I fear far from the track of commerce.°

LADY MARY Thank you; I understand.   145

(*For a moment, however, she breaks down. Then she clenches her
hands and stands erect*)

CRICHTON (*watching her,° and forgetting perhaps for the moment that
they are not just a man and woman*) You're a good pluckt 'un,° my
lady.

LADY MARY (*falling into the same error*) I shall try to be. (*Extricating
herself*) Crichton, you presume!   150

CRICHTON I beg your ladyship's pardon; but you are.

(*She smiles, as if it were a comfort to be told this even by
Crichton*)

And until a ship comes we are three men who are going to do our
best for you ladies.

LADY MARY (*with a curl of the lip*) Mr Ernest does no work.

CRICHTON (*cheerily*) But he will, my lady.   155

LADY MARY I doubt it.

CRICHTON (*confidently, but perhaps thoughtlessly*) No work—no dinner—will make a great change in Mr Ernest.

LADY MARY No work—no dinner. When did you invent that rule,
Crichton?   160

CRICHTON (*loaded with bamboo*) I didn't invent it, my lady. I seem
to see it growing all over the island.

LADY MARY (*disquieted*) Crichton, your manner strikes me as curious.

CRICHTON (*pained*) I hope not, your ladyship.   165

LADY MARY (*determined to have it out with him*) You are not implying anything so unnatural,° I hope, as that if I and my sisters don't work there will be no dinner for *us*?

CRICHTON (*brightly*) If it is unnatural, my lady, that is the end of it.

LADY MARY If? Now I understand. The perfect servant at home 170 holds that we are all equal now. I see.

CRICHTON (*wounded to the quick*) My lady, can you think me so inconsistent?

LADY MARY That is it.

CRICHTON (*earnestly*) My lady, I disbelieved in equality at home 175 because it was against nature, and for that same reason I as utterly disbelieve in it on an island.

LADY MARY (*relieved by his obvious sincerity*) I apologise.

CRICHTON (*continuing unfortunately*) There must always, my lady, be one to command and others to obey.   180

LADY MARY (*satisfied*) One to command, others to obey. Yes. (*Then suddenly she realises that there may be a dire meaning in his confident words*) Crichton!

CRICHTON (*who has intended no dire meaning*) What is it, my lady?
(*But she only stares into his face and then hurries from him. Left alone he is puzzled,° but being a practical man he busies himself gathering firewood, until Tweeny appears excitedly carrying cocoa-nuts in her skirt. She has made better use than the ladies of her three minutes' grace for dressing*)

TWEENY (*who can be happy even on an island if Crichton is with her*) 185 Look what I found!

CRICHTON Cocoa-nuts. Bravo!

TWEENY They grows on trees with this round them.

CRICHTON Where did you think they grew?

TWEENY I thought as how they grew in rows on top of little 190 sticks.°

CRICHTON (*wrinkling his brows*) Oh, Tweeny, Tweeny!

TWEENY (*anxiously*) Have I offended of your feelings again, sir?

CRICHTON A little.

TWEENY (*in a despairing outburst*) I'm full o' vulgar words and ways; 195 and though I may keep them in their holes when you are by, as soon as I'm by myself out they comes in a rush like beetles when the house is dark. I says them gloating-like, in my head—'Bloom-ing,' I says, and 'All my eye,'° and 'Ginger,'° and 'Nothink';° and all the time we was being wrecked I was praying to myself, 'Please 200 the Lord it may be an island as it's natural to be vulgar on.'

(*A shudder passes through Crichton, and she is abject*)
That's the kind I am, sir. I'm 'opeless. You'd better give me up.
(*She is a pathetic, forlorn creature, and his manhood is stirred*)

CRICHTON (*wondering a little at himself for saying it*) I won't give you up. It is strange that one so common should attract one so fastidious; but so it is. (*Thoughtfully*) There is something about you, Tweeny, there is a *je ne sais quoi* about you. 205

TWEENY (*knowing only that he has found something in her to commend*) Is there, is there? Oh, I am glad.

CRICHTON (*putting his hand on her shoulder like a protector*) We shall fight your vulgarity together. (*All this time he has been arranging sticks for his fire*) Now get some dry grass. 210
(*She brings him grass, and he puts it under the sticks. He produces an odd lens from his pocket, and tries to focus the sun's rays*)

TWEENY Why, what's that?

CRICHTON (*the ingenious creature*) That's the glass from my watch and one from Mr Treherne's, with a little water between them. I'm hoping to kindle a fire with it. 215

TWEENY (*properly impressed*) Oh, sir!
(*After one failure the grass takes fire, and they are blowing on it when excited cries near by bring them sharply to their feet. Agatha runs to them, white of face, followed by Ernest*)

ERNEST Danger! Crichton, a tiger-cat!

CRICHTON (*getting his cutlass*) Where?

AGATHA It is at our heels.

ERNEST Look out, Crichton. 220

CRICHTON H'sh!
(*Treherne comes to his assistance, while Lady Mary and Catherine join Agatha in the hut*)

ERNEST It will be on us in a moment.
(*He seizes the hatchet and guards the hut. It is pleasing to see that Ernest is no coward°*)

TREHERNE Listen!

ERNEST The grass is moving. It's coming.
(*It comes. But it is no tiger-cat; it is Lord Loam crawling on his hands and knees, a very exhausted and dishevelled peer, wondrously attired in rags. The girls see him, and with glad cries rush into his arms*)

LADY MARY Father! 225

LORD LOAM Mary—Catherine—Agatha! Oh dear, my dears, my dears, oh dear!

LADY MARY Darling.

AGATHA Sweetest.

CATHERINE Love.   230

TREHERNE Glad to see you, sir.

ERNEST Uncle, uncle, dear old uncle.
>   (*For a time such happy cries fill the air, but presently Treherne is thoughtless*)

TREHERNE Ernest thought you were a tiger-cat.

LORD LOAM (*stung somehow to the quick*) Oh, did you? I knew you at once, Ernest; I knew you by the way you ran.   235
>   (*Ernest smiles forgivingly*)

CRICHTON (*venturing forward at last*) My lord, I am glad.

ERNEST (*with upraised finger*) But you are also idling, Crichton. (*Making himself comfortable on the ground*) We mustn't waste time. To work, to work.

CRICHTON (*after contemplating him without rancour*) Yes, sir.   240
>   (*He gets a pot from the hut and hangs it on a tripod over the fire, which is now burning brightly*)

TREHERNE Ernest, you be a little more civil. Crichton, let me help.
>   (*He is soon busy helping Crichton to add to the strength of the hut*)°

LORD LOAM (*gazing at the pot as ladies are said to gaze on precious stones*) Is that—but I suppose I'm dreaming again. (*Timidly*) It isn't by any chance a pot on top of a fire, is it?

LADY MARY Indeed, it is, dearest. It is our supper.   245

LORD LOAM I have been dreaming of a pot on a fire for two days. (*Quivering*) There's nothing in it, is there?

ERNEST Sniff, uncle. (*Lord Loam sniffs*)

LORD LOAM (*reverently*) It smells of onions!
>   (*There is a sudden diversion*)

CATHERINE Father, you have boots!   250

LADY MARY So he has.

LORD LOAM Of course I have.

ERNEST (*with greedy cunning*) You are actually wearing boots, uncle. It's very unsafe, you know, in this climate.

LORD LOAM Is it?   255

ERNEST We have all abandoned them, you observe. The blood, the arteries, you know.

LORD LOAM I hadn't a notion.
>   (*He holds out his feet, and Ernest kneels*)

ERNEST Oh Lord, yes.

(*In another moment those boots will be his*)

LADY MARY (*quickly*) Father, he is trying to get your boots from 260
you. There is nothing in the world we wouldn't give for boots.

ERNEST (*rising haughtily, a proud spirit misunderstood*) I only wanted
the loan of them.

AGATHA (*running her fingers along them lovingly*) If you lend them to
any one, it will be to us, won't it, father? 265

LORD LOAM Certainly, my child.

ERNEST Oh, very well. (*He is leaving these selfish ones*) I don't want
your old boots. (*He gives his uncle a last chance*) You don't think
you could spare me *one* boot?

LORD LOAM (*tartly*) I do not. 270

ERNEST Quite so. Well, all I can say is I'm sorry for you.
(*He departs to recline elsewhere*)

LADY MARY Father, we thought we should never see you again.

LORD LOAM I was washed ashore, my dear, clinging to a hencoop.
How awful that first night was.

LADY MARY Poor father. 275

LORD LOAM When I woke, I wept. Then I began to feel extremely
hungry. There was a large turtle on the beach. I remembered from
the *Swiss Family Robinson°* that if you turn a turtle over he is
helpless. My dears, I crawled towards him, I flung myself upon
him—(*here he pauses to rub his leg*)—the nasty, spiteful brute. 280

LADY MARY You didn't turn him over?

LORD LOAM (*vindictively, though he is a kindly man*) Mary, the
senseless thing wouldn't wait; I found that none of them would
wait.

CATHERINE We should have been as badly off if Crichton hadn't— 285

LADY MARY (*quickly*) Don't praise Crichton.

LORD LOAM And then those beastly monkeys. I always understood
that if you flung stones at them they would retaliate by flinging
cocoa-nuts at you. Would you believe it, I flung a hundred stones,
and not one monkey had sufficient intelligence to grasp my 290
meaning. How I longed for Crichton.

LADY MARY (*wincing*) For us also, father?

LORD LOAM For you also. I tried for hours to make a fire. The
authors say that when wrecked on an island you can obtain a
light by rubbing two pieces of stick together. (*With feeling*) The 295
liars!

LADY MARY And all this time you thought there was no one on the
island but yourself?

31

LORD LOAM I thought so until this morning. I was searching the pools for little fishes, which I caught in my hat, when suddenly I saw before me—on the sand—

CATHERINE What?

LORD LOAM A hairpin.

LADY MARY A hairpin! It must be one of ours. (*Greedily*) Give it me, father.

AGATHA No, it's mine.

LORD LOAM I didn't keep it.

LADY MARY (*speaking for all three*) Didn't keep it? Found a hairpin on an island, and didn't keep it?

LORD LOAM (*humbly*) My dears.

AGATHA (*scarcely to be placated*) Oh, father, we have returned to Nature more than you bargained for.

LADY MARY For shame, Agatha. (*She has something on her mind*) Father, there is something I want you to do at once—I mean to assert your position as the chief person on the island.

(*They are all surprised*)

LORD LOAM But who would presume to question it?

CATHERINE She must mean Ernest.

LADY MARY Must I?

AGATHA It is cruel to say anything against Ernest.

LORD LOAM (*firmly*) If any one presumes to challenge my position, I shall make short work of him.

AGATHA Here comes Ernest; now see if you can say these horrid things to his face.

LORD LOAM I shall teach him his place at once.

LADY MARY (*anxiously*) But how?

LORD LOAM (*chuckling*) I have just thought of an extremely amusing way of doing it. (*As Ernest approaches*) Ernest.

ERNEST (*loftily*) Excuse me, uncle, I'm thinking. I'm planning out the building of this hut.

LORD LOAM I also have been thinking.

ERNEST That don't matter.

LORD LOAM Eh?

ERNEST Please, please, this is important.

LORD LOAM I have been thinking that I ought to give you my boots.

ERNEST What!

LADY MARY Father.

LORD LOAM (*genially*) Take them, my boy. (*With a rapidity we had not thought him capable of, Ernest becomes the wearer of the boots*)

And now I dare say you want to know why I give them to you, Ernest?   340

ERNEST (*moving up and down in them deliciously*) Not at all. The great thing is, 'I've got 'em, I've got 'em.'

LORD LOAM (*majestically, but with a knowing look at his daughters*) My reason is that, as head of our little party, you, Ernest, shall be our hunter, you shall clear the forests of these savage beasts that   345
make them so dangerous. (*Pleasantly*) And now you know, my dear nephew, why I have given you my boots.

ERNEST This is my answer.
         (*He kicks off the boots*)

LADY MARY (*still anxious*) Father, assert yourself.

LORD LOAM I shall now assert myself. (*But how to do it? He has a*   350
happy thought) Call Crichton.

LADY MARY Oh, father!
         (*Crichton comes in answer to a summons,° and is followed by*
         Treherne)

ERNEST (*wondering a little at Lady Mary's grave face*) Crichton, look here.

LORD LOAM (*sturdily*) Silence! Crichton, I want your advice as to   355
what I ought to do with Mr Ernest. He has defied me.

ERNEST Pooh!

CRICHTON (*after considering*) May I speak openly, my lord?

LADY MARY (*keeping her eyes fixed on him*) That is what we desire.

CRICHTON (*quite humbly*) Then I may say, your lordship, that I have   360
been considering Mr Ernest's case at odd moments ever since we were wrecked.

ERNEST My case?

LORD LOAM (*sternly*) Hush.

CRICHTON Since we landed on the island, my lord, it seems to me   365
that Mr Ernest's epigrams have been particularly brilliant.

ERNEST (*gratified*) Thank you, Crichton.

CRICHTON But I find—I seem to find it growing wild, my lord, in the woods, that sayings which would be justly admired in England are not much use on an island. I would therefore most respectfully   370
propose that henceforth every time Mr Ernest favours us with an epigram his head should be immersed in a bucket of cold spring water.
         (*There is a terrible silence*)

LORD LOAM (*uneasily*) Serve him right.

ERNEST I should like to see you try to do it, uncle.   375

CRICHTON (*ever ready to come to the succour of his lordship*) My feeling, my lord, is that at the next offence I should convey him to a retired spot, where I shall carry out the undertaking in as respectful a manner as is consistent with a thorough immersion.

> (*Though his manner is most respectful, he is resolute; he evidently means what he says*)

LADY MARY (*a ramrod*) Father, you must not permit this; Ernest is 380
your nephew.

LORD LOAM (*with his hand to his brow*) After all, he is my nephew, Crichton; and, as I am sure, he now sees that I am a strong man——

ERNEST (*foolishly in the circumstances*) A strong man. You mean a stout man. You are one of mind to two of matter. 385

> (*He looks round in the old way for approval. No one has smiled, and to his consternation he sees that Crichton is quietly turning up his sleeves. Ernest makes an appealing gesture to his uncle; then he turns defiantly to Crichton*)

CRICHTON Is it to be before the ladies, Mr Ernest, or in the privacy of the wood? (*He fixes Ernest with his eye. Ernest is cowed*) Come.

ERNEST (*after a long time*) Oh, all right.

CRICHTON (*succinctly*) Bring the bucket.

> (*Ernest hesitates. He then lifts the bucket and follows Crichton to the nearest spring*)

LORD LOAM (*rather white*) I'm sorry for him, but I had to be firm. 390

LADY MARY Oh, father, it wasn't you who was firm. Crichton did it himself.

LORD LOAM Bless me, so he did.

LADY MARY Father, be strong.

LORD LOAM (*bewildered*) You can't mean that my faithful Crich- 395
ton——

LADY MARY Yes, I do.

TREHERNE Lady Mary, I stake my word that Crichton is incapable of acting dishonourably.

LADY MARY I know that; I know it as well as you. Don't you see, 400
that is what makes him so dangerous?

TREHERNE By Jove, I—I believe I catch your meaning.

CATHERINE He is coming back.

LORD LOAM (*who has always known himself to be a man of ideas*) Let us all go into the hut, just to show him at once that it is *our* hut. 405

LADY MARY (*as they go*) Father, I implore you, assert yourself now and for ever.

LORD LOAM I will.

LADY MARY And, please, don't ask him how you are to do it.
(*Crichton returns with sticks to mend the fire*)

LORD LOAM (*loftily, from the door of the hut*) Have you carried out   410
my instructions, Crichton?

CRICHTON (*deferentially*) Yes, my lord.
(*Ernest appears, mopping his hair, which has become very wet
since we last saw him. He is not bearing malice, he is too busy
drying, but Agatha is specially his champion*)

AGATHA It's infamous, infamous.

LORD LOAM (*strongly*) *My* orders, Agatha.

LADY MARY Now, father, please.   415

LORD LOAM (*striking an attitude*) Before I give you any further
orders, Crichton——

CRICHTON Yes, my lord.

LORD LOAM (*delighted*) Pooh! It's all right.

LADY MARY No. Please go on.   420

LORD LOAM Well, well. This question of the leadership; what do
you think now, Crichton?

CRICHTON My lord, I feel it is a matter with which *I* have nothing
to do.

LORD LOAM Excellent. Ha, Mary? That settles it, I think.   425

LADY MARY It seems to, but—I'm not sure.

CRICHTON It will settle itself naturally, my lord, without any
interference from us.
(*The reference to Nature gives general dissatisfaction*)

LADY MARY Father.

LORD LOAM (*a little severely*) It settled itself long ago, Crich-   430
ton, when I was born a peer, and you, for instance, were born a
servant.

CRICHTON (*acquiescing*) Yes, my lord, that was how it all came about
quite naturally in England. We had nothing to do with it there,
and we shall have as little to do with it here.   435

TREHERNE (*relieved*) That's all right.

LADY MARY (*determined to clinch the matter*) One moment. In short,
Crichton, his lordship will continue to be our natural head.

CRICHTON I dare say, my lady, I dare say.

CATHERINE But you must *know*.   440

CRICHTON Asking your pardon, my lady, one can't be sure—on an
island.
(*They look at each other uneasily*)

LORD LOAM (*warningly*) Crichton, I don't like this.

CRICHTON (*harassed*) The more I think of it, your lordship, the more uneasy I become myself. When I heard, my lord, that you had left 445
that hairpin behind——
    (*He is pained*)

LORD LOAM (*feebly*) One hairpin among so many would only have caused dissension.

CRICHTON (*very sorry to have to contradict him*) Not so, my lord. From that hairpin we could have made a needle; with that needle 450
we could, out of skins, have sewn trousers—of which your lordship is in need; indeed, we are all in need of them.

LADY MARY (*suddenly self-conscious*) All?

CRICHTON On an island, my lady.

LADY MARY Father. 455

CRICHTON (*really more distressed by the prospect than she*) My lady, if Nature does not think them necessary, you may be sure she will not ask you to wear them. (*Shaking his head*) But among all this undergrowth——

LADY MARY Now you see this man in his true colours. 460

LORD LOAM (*violently*) Crichton, you will either this moment say, 'Down with Nature,' or—

CRICHTON (*scandalised*) My lord!

LORD LOAM (*loftily*) Then this is my last word to you; take a month's notice. 465
    (*If the hut had a door he would now shut it to indicate that the interview is closed*)

CRICHTON (*in great distress*) Your lordship, the disgrace——

LORD LOAM (*swelling*) Not another word: you may go.

LADY MARY (*adamant*) And don't come to me, Crichton, for a character.

ERNEST (*whose immersion has cleared his brain*) Aren't you all forget- 470
ting that this is an island?
    (*This brings them to earth with a bump. Lord Loam looks to his eldest daughter for the fitting response*)

LADY MARY (*equal to the occasion*) It makes only this difference—that you may go at once, Crichton, to some other part of the island.
    (*The faithful servant has been true to his superiors ever since he was created, and never more true than at this moment; but his fidelity is founded on trust in Nature, and to be untrue to it would be to be untrue to them. He lets the wood he has been gathering slip to the ground, and bows his sorrowful head. He turns to obey. Then affection for these great ones wells up in him*)

CRICHTON My lady, let me work for you.

LADY MARY Go.   475

CRICHTON You need me so sorely; I can't desert you; I won't.

LADY MARY (*in alarm, lest the others may yield*) Then, father, there is but one alternative, *we* must leave him.

> (*Lord Loam is looking yearningly at Crichton*)

TREHERNE It seems a pity.

CATHERINE (*forlornly*) *You* will work for us?   480

TREHERNE Most willingly. But I must warn you all that, so far, Crichton has done nine-tenths of the scoring.°

LADY MARY The question is, are we to leave this man?

LORD LOAM (*wrapping himself in his dignity*) Come, my dears.

CRICHTON My lord!   485

LORD LOAM Treherne—Ernest—get our things.

ERNEST We don't have any, uncle. They all belong to Crichton.

TREHERNE Everything we have he brought from the wreck—he went back to it before it sank. He risked his life.

CRICHTON My lord, anything you would care to take is yours.   490

LADY MARY (*quickly*) Nothing.

ERNEST Rot! If I could have your socks, Crichton——

LADY MARY Come, father; we are ready.

> (*Followed by the others, she and Lord Loam pick their way up the rocks. In their indignation they scarcely notice that daylight is coming to a sudden end*)

CRICHTON My lord, I implore you—*I* am not desirous of being head. Do you have a try at it, my lord.   495

LORD LOAM (*outraged*) A try at it!

CRICHTON (*eagerly*) It may be that you will prove to be the best man.

LORD LOAM *May* be! My children, come.

> (*They disappear proudly but gingerly up those splintered rocks*)

TREHERNE Crichton, I'm sorry; but of course I must go with them.

CRICHTON Certainly, sir.   500

> (*He calls to Tweeny, and she comes from behind the hut, where she has been watching breathlessly*)

Will you be so kind, sir, as to take her to the others.°

TREHERNE Assuredly.

TWEENY But what do it all mean?

CRICHTON Does, Tweeny, does. (*He passes her up the rocks to Treherne*) We shall meet again soon, Tweeny. Good-night, sir.   505

TREHERNE Good-night. I dare say they are not far away.

CRICHTON (*thoughtfully*) They went westward, sir, and the wind is blowing in that direction. That may mean, sir, that Nature is already taking the matter into her own hands. They are all hungry, sir, and the pot has come a-boil. (*He takes off the lid*) The smell   510
will be borne westward. That pot is full of Nature, Mr Treherne. Good-night, sir.

TREHERNE Good-night.

(*He mounts the rocks with Tweeny, and they are heard for a little time after their figures are swallowed up in the fast growing darkness. Crichton stands motionless, the lid in his hand, though he has forgotten it and his reason for taking it off the pot. He is deeply stirred, but presently is ashamed of his dejection, for it is as if he doubted his principles. Bravely true to his faith that Nature will decide now as ever before, he proceeds manfully with his preparations for the night. He lights a ship's lantern, one of several treasures he has brought ashore, and is filling his pipe with crumbs of tobacco from various pockets, when the stealthy movement of some animal in the grass startles him. With the lantern in one hand and his cutlass in the other, he searches the ground around the hut. He returns, lights his pipe, and sits down by the fire, which casts weird moving shadows. There is a red gleam on his face; in the darkness he is a strong and perhaps rather sinister figure. In the great stillness that has fallen over the land, the wash of the surf seems to have increased in volume. The sound is indescribably mournful. Except where the fire is, desolation has fallen on the island like a pall.*

Once or twice, as Nature dictates, Crichton leans forward to stir the pot, and the smell is borne westward. He then resumes his silent vigil.

Shadows other than those cast by the fire begin to descend the rocks. They are the adventurers returning. One by one they steal nearer to the pot until they are squatted round it, with their hands out to the blaze. Lady Mary only is absent. Presently she comes within sight of the others, then stands against a tree with her teeth clenched. One wonders, perhaps, what Nature is to make of her)

Act 3

THE HAPPY HOME

The scene is the hall of their island home two years later. This sturdy log-house is no mere extension of the hut we have seen in process of erection, but has been built a mile or less to the west of it, on higher ground and near a stream. When the master chose this site, the others thought that all he expected from the stream was a sufficiency of drinking water. They know better now every time they go down to the mill or turn on the electric light.

This hall is the living-room of the house, and walls and roof are of stout logs. Across the joists supporting the roof are laid many home-made implements, such as spades, saws, fishing-rods, and from hooks in the joists are suspended cured foods, of which hams are specially in evidence. Deep recesses half-way up the walls contain various provender in barrels and sacks. There are some skins, trophies of the chase, on the floor, which is otherwise bare. The chairs and tables are in some cases hewn out of the solid wood, and in others the result of rough but efficient carpentering. Various pieces of wreckage from the yacht have been turned to novel uses: thus the steering-wheel now hangs from the centre of the roof, with electric lights attached to it encased in bladders. A lifebuoy has become the back of a chair. Two barrels have been halved and turn coyly from each other as a settee.

The farther end of the room is more strictly the kitchen, and is a great recess, which can be shut off from the hall by folding-doors. There is a large open fire on it. The chimney is half of one of the boats of the yacht. On the walls of the kitchen proper are many plate-racks, containing shells; there are rows of these of one size and shape, which mark them off as dinner plates or bowls; others are as obviously tureens. They are arranged primly as in a well-conducted kitchen; indeed, neatness and cleanliness are the note struck everywhere, yet the effect of the whole is romantic and barbaric.

The outer door into this hall is a little peculiar on an island. It is covered with skins and is in four leaves, like the swing-doors of fashionable restaurants, which allow you to enter without allowing the hot air to escape. During the winter season our castaways have found this contrivance useful, but Crichton's brain was perhaps a little

39

lordly when he conceived it. Another door leads by a passage to the sleeping-rooms of the house, which are all on the ground-floor, and to Crichton's work-room, where he is at this moment, and whither we should like to follow him, but in a play we may not,° as it is out of sight. There is a large window space without a window, which, however, can be shuttered, and through this we have a view of cattle-sheds, fowl-pens, and a field of grain. It is a fine summer evening.

Tweeny is sitting there, very busy plucking the feathers off a bird and dropping them on a sheet placed for that purpose on the floor. She is trilling to herself in the lightness of her heart. We may remember that Tweeny, alone among the women, had dressed wisely for an island when they fled the yacht, and her going-away gown° still adheres to her, though in fragments. A score of pieces have been added here and there as necessity compelled, and these have been patched and repatched in incongruous colours; but, when all is said and done, it can still be maintained that Tweeny wears a skirt. She is deservedly proud of her skirt, and sometimes lends it on important occasions when approached in the proper spirit.

Some one outside has been whistling to Tweeny; the guarded whistle which, on a less savage island, is sometimes assumed to be an indication to cook that the constable is willing, if the coast be clear. Tweeny, however, is engrossed, or perhaps she is not in the mood for a follower, so he climbs in at the window undaunted, to take her willy-nilly. He is a jolly-looking labouring man, who answers to the name of Daddy, and——But though that may be his island name, we recognise him at once. He is Lord Loam, settled down to the new conditions, and enjoying life heartily as handy-man about the happy home. He is comfortably attired in skins. He is still stout, but all the flabbiness has dropped from him; gone too is his pomposity; his eye is clear, brown his skin; he could leap a gate.

In his hands he carries an island-made concertina, and such is the exuberance of his spirits that, as he alights on the floor, he bursts into music and song, something about his being a chickety chickety chick chick, and will Tweeny please to tell him whose chickety chick is she. Retribution follows sharp. We hear a whir, as if from insufficiently oiled machinery, and over the passage door appears a placard showing the one word 'Silence.' His lordship stops, and steals to Tweeny on his tiptoes.

LORD LOAM I thought the Gov. was out.

TWEENY Well, you see he ain't. And if he were to catch you here idling——

> (*Lord Loam pales. He lays aside his musical instrument and hurriedly dons an apron. Tweeny gives him the bird to pluck, and busies herself laying the table for dinner*)

LORD LOAM (*softly*) What is he doing now?

TWEENY I think he is working out that plan for laying on hot and cold.

LORD LOAM (*proud of his master*) And he'll manage it too. The man who could build a blacksmith's forge without tools——

TWEENY (*not less proud*) He made the tools.

LORD LOAM Out of half a dozen rusty nails. The sawmill, Tweeny; the speaking-tube; the electric lighting; and look at the use he has made of the bits of the yacht that were washed ashore. And all in two years. He is a master I'm proud to pluck for.

> (*He chirps happily at his work, and she regards him curiously*)

TWEENY Daddy, you're of little use, but you're a bright, cheerful creature to have about the house. (*He beams at this commendation*) Do you ever think of old times now? We was a bit different.

LORD LOAM (*pausing*) Circumstances alter cases.

> (*He resumes his plucking contentedly*)

TWEENY But, Daddy, if the chance was to come of getting back?

LORD LOAM I have given up bothering about it.

TWEENY You bothered that day long ago when we saw a ship passing the island. How we all ran like crazy folk into the water, Daddy, and screamed and held out our arms. (*They are both a little agitated*) But it sailed away, and we've never seen another.

LORD LOAM If the electrical contrivance had been made then that we have now we could have attracted that ship's notice. (*Their eyes rest on a mysterious apparatus that fills a corner of the hall*) A touch on that lever, Tweeny, and in a few moments bonfires would be blazing all round the shore.

TWEENY (*backing from the lever as if it might spring at her*) It's the most wonderful thing he has done.

LORD LOAM (*in a reverie*) And then—England—home!

TWEENY (*also seeing visions*) London of a Saturday night!

LORD LOAM My lords, in rising once more to address this historic chamber——

TWEENY There was a little ham and beef shop off the Edgware Road——

> (*The visions fade; they return to the practical*)

LORD LOAM Tweeny, do you think I could have an egg to my tea? (*At this moment a wiry, athletic figure in skins darkens the window. He is carrying two pails, which are suspended from a pole on his shoulder, and he is Ernest. We should say that he is Ernest completely changed if we were of those who hold that people change. As he enters by the window he has heard Lord Loam's appeal, and is perhaps justifiably indignant*)

ERNEST What is that about an egg? Why should you have an egg?

LORD LOAM (*with hauteur*) That is my affair, sir. (*With a Parthian shot° as he withdraws stiffly from the room*) The Gov. has never put *my* head in a bucket.   115

ERNEST (*coming to rest on one of his buckets, and speaking with excusable pride*) Nor mine for nearly three months. It was only last week, Tweeny, that he said to me, 'Ernest, the water cure has worked marvels in you, and I question whether I shall require to dip you any more.' (*Complacently*) Of course that sort of thing encourages   120
a fellow.

TWEENY (*who has now arranged the dinner-table to her satisfaction*) I will say, Erny, I never seen a young chap more improved.

ERNEST (*gratified*) Thank you, Tweeny; that's very precious to me. (*She retires to the fire to work the great bellows with her foot, and Ernest turns to Treherne, who has come in looking more like a cow-boy than a clergyman. He has a small box in his hand which he tries to conceal*)
What have you got there, John?   125

TREHERNE Don't tell anybody. It is a little present for the Gov.; a set of razors. One for each day in the week.

ERNEST (*opening the box and examining its contents*) Shells! He'll like that. He likes sets of things.

TREHERNE (*in a guarded voice*) Have you noticed that?   130

ERNEST Rather.

TREHERNE He is becoming a bit magnificent in his ideas.

ERNEST (*huskily*) John, it sometimes gives me the creeps.

TREHERNE (*making sure that Tweeny is out of hearing*) What do you think of that brilliant robe he got the girls to make for him?   135

ERNEST (*uncomfortably*) I think he looks too regal in it.

TREHERNE Regal! I sometimes fancy that is why he is so fond of wearing it. (*Practically*) Well, I must take these down to the grindstone and put an edge on them.

ERNEST (*button-holing him*) I say, John, I want a word with you.   140

TREHERNE Well?

ERNEST (*become suddenly diffident*) Dash it all, you know, you're a clergyman.

TREHERNE One of the best things the Gov. has done is to insist that none of you forget it.   145

ERNEST (*taking his courage in his hands*) Then—would you, John?

TREHERNE What?

ERNEST (*wistfully*) Officiate at a marriage ceremony, John?

TREHERNE (*slowly*) Now, that is really odd.

ERNEST Odd? Seems to me it's natural. And whatever is natural, 150 John, is right.

TREHERNE I mean that same question has been put to me to-day already.

ERNEST (*eagerly*) By one of the women?

TREHERNE Oh no; they all put it to me long ago. This was by the 155 Gov. himself.

ERNEST By Jove! (*Admiringly*) I say, John, what an observant beggar he is.

TREHERNE Ah! You fancy he was thinking of you?

ERNEST I do not hesitate to affirm, John, that he has seen the 160 love-light in my eyes. You answered——

TREHERNE I said Yes, I thought it would be my duty to officiate if called upon.

ERNEST You're a brick.

TREHERNE (*still pondering*) But I wonder whether he *was* thinking of 165 you?

ERNEST Make your mind easy about that.

TREHERNE Well, my best wishes. Agatha is a very fine girl.

ERNEST Agatha? What made you think it was Agatha?

TREHERNE Man alive, you told me all about it soon after we were 170 wrecked.

ERNEST Pooh! Agatha is all very well in her way, John, but I am flying at bigger game.°

TREHERNE Ernest, which is it?

ERNEST Tweeny, of course.   175

TREHERNE Tweeny? (*Reprovingly*) Ernest, I hope her cooking has nothing to do with this.

ERNEST (*with dignity*) Her cooking has very little to do with it.

TREHERNE But does she return your affection?

ERNEST (*simply*) Yes, John, I believe I may say so. I am unworthy of 180 her, but I think I have touched her heart.

TREHERNE (*with a sigh*) Some people seem to have all the luck. As you know, Catherine won't look at me.

ERNEST I'm sorry, John.

TREHERNE It's my deserts; I'm a second eleven sort of chap.° Well, 185
my heartiest good wishes, Ernest.

ERNEST Thank you, John. How is the little black pig to-day?

TREHERNE (*departing*) He has begun to eat again.

(*After a moment's reflection Ernest calls to Tweeny*)

ERNEST Are you very busy, Tweeny?

TWEENY (*coming to him good-naturedly*) There is always work to do; 190
but if you want me, Ernest——

ERNEST There is something I should like to say to you if you could
spare me a moment.

TWEENY Willingly. What is it?

ERNEST What an ass I used to be, Tweeny. 195

TWEENY (*tolerantly*) Oh, let bygones be bygones.

ERNEST (*sincerely, and at his very best*) I'm no great shakes even now.
But listen to this, Tweeny; I have known many women, but until
I knew you I never knew any woman.

TWEENY (*to whose uneducated ears this sounds dangerously like an* 200
epigram) Take care—the bucket.

ERNEST (*hurriedly*) I didn't mean it in that way. (*He goes chivalrously
on his knees*) Ah, Tweeny, I don't undervalue the bucket, but what
I want to say now is that the sweet refinement of a dear girl has
done more for me than any bucket could do. 205

TWEENY (*with large eyes*) Are you offering to walk out with me,°
Erny?

ERNEST (*passionately*) More than that. I want to build a little house
for you—in the sunny glade down by Porcupine Creek. I want to
make chairs for you and tables; and knives and forks, and a 210
sideboard for you.

TWEENY (*who is fond of language*) I like to hear you. (*Eyeing him*)
Would there be any one in the house except myself, Ernest?

ERNEST (*humbly*) Not often; but just occasionally there would be
your adoring husband. 215

TWEENY (*decisively*) It won't do, Ernest.

ERNEST (*pleading*) It isn't as if I should be much there.

TWEENY I know, I know; but I don't love you, Ernest, I'm that sorry.

ERNEST (*putting his case cleverly*) Twice a week I should be away
altogether—at the dam. On the other days you would never see me 220
from breakfast time to supper.

(With the self-abnegation of the true lover)
If you like I'll even go fishing on Sundays.

TWEENY It's no use, Erny.

ERNEST *(rising manfully)* Thank you, Tweeny; it can't be helped.
(Then he remembers) Tweeny, we shall be disappointing the Gov.   225

TWEENY *(quaking)* What's that?

ERNEST He wanted us to marry.

TWEENY *(blankly)* You and me? the Gov.! *(Her head droops woefully.
From without is heard the whistling of a happier spirit, and Tweeny
draws herself up fiercely.)* That's her; that's the thing what has stole   230
his heart from me.

> *(A stalwart youth° appears at the window, so handsome and
> tingling with vitality that, glad to depose Crichton, we cry
> thankfully, 'The hero at last.' But it is not the hero; it is the
> heroine. This splendid boy, clad in skins, is what Nature has
> done for Lady Mary. She carries bow and arrows and a
> blow-pipe, and over her shoulder is a fat buck, which she drops
> with a cry of triumph. Forgetting to enter demurely, she leaps
> through the window)*

(Sourly) Drat you, Polly, why don't you wipe your feet?

LADY MARY *(good-naturedly)* Come, Tweeny, be nice to me. It's a
splendid buck.

> *(But Tweeny shakes her off, and retires to the kitchen fire)*

ERNEST Where did you get it?   235

LADY MARY *(gaily)* I sighted a herd near Penguin's Creek, but had
to creep round Silver Lake to get to windward of them. However,
they spotted me and then the fun began. There was nothing for it
but to try and run them down, so I singled out a fat buck and away
we went down the shore of the lake, up the valley of rolling stones;   240
he doubled into Brawling River and took to the water, but I swam
after him; the river is only half a mile broad there, but it runs
strong. He went spinning down the rapids, down I went in pursuit;
he clambered ashore, I clambered ashore; away we tore helter-
skelter up the hill and down again. I lost him in the marshes, got   245
on his track again near Bread Fruit Wood, and brought him down
with an arrow in Firefly Grove.°

TWEENY *(staring at her)* Aren't you tired?

LADY MARY Tired! It was gorgeous.

> *(She runs up a ladder and deposits her weapons on the joists. She
> is whistling again)*

TWEENY *(snapping)* I can't abide a woman whistling.   250

LADY MARY (*indifferently*) I like it.

TWEENY (*stamping her foot*) Drop it, Polly, I tell you.

LADY MARY I won't. I'm as good as you are.
> (*They are facing each other defiantly*)

ERNEST (*shocked*) Is this necessary? Think how it would pain *him*.
> (*Lady Mary's eyes take a new expression. We see them soft for the first time*)

LADY MARY (*contritely*) Tweeny, I beg your pardon. If my whistling   255
annoys you, I shall try to cure myself of it.
> (*Instead of calming Tweeny, this floods her face in tears*)
Why, how can that hurt you, Tweeny dear?

TWEENY Because I can't make you lose your temper.

LADY MARY (*divinely*) Indeed, I often do. Would that I were nicer
to everybody.   260

TWEENY There you are again. (*Large-eyed*) What makes you want to
be so nice, Polly?

LADY MARY (*with fervour*) Only thankfulness, Tweeny. (*She exults*)
It is such fun to be alive.
> (*So also seem to think Catherine and Agatha, who bounce in
> with fishing-rods and creel. They, too, are in manly attire*)

CATHERINE We've got some ripping fish for the Gov.'s dinner. Are   265
we in time? We ran all the way.°

TWEENY (*tartly*) You'll please to cook them yourself, Kitty, and look
sharp about it.
> (*She retires to her hearth, where Agatha follows her*)

AGATHA (*yearning*) Has the Gov. decided who is to wait upon him
to-day?   270

CATHERINE (*who is cleaning her fish*) It's my turn.

AGATHA (*hotly*) I don't see that.

TWEENY (*with bitterness*) It's to be neither of you, Aggy; he wants
Polly again.
> (*Lady Mary is unable to resist a joyous whistle*)

AGATHA (*jealously*) Polly, you toad.   275
> (*But they cannot make Lady Mary angry*)

TWEENY (*storming*) How dare you look so happy?

LADY MARY (*willing to embrace her*) I wish, Tweeny, there was
anything I could do to make you happy also.

TWEENY Me! Oh, I'm happy. (*She remembers Ernest, whom it is easy
to forget on an island*) I've just had a proposal, I tell you.   280
> (*Lady Mary is shaken at last, and her sisters with her*)

AGATHA A proposal?

CATHERINE (*going white*) Not—not—
     (*She dare not say his name*)
ERNEST (*with singular modesty*) You needn't be alarmed; it was only
    me.
LADY MARY (*relieved*) Oh, you!   285
AGATHA (*happy again*) Ernest, you dear, I got such a shock.
CATHERINE It was only Ernest (*showing him her fish in thankfulness*)
    They are beautifully fresh; come and help me to cook them.
ERNEST (*with simple dignity*) Do you mind if I don't cook fish
    to-night? (*She does not mind in the least. They have all forgotten him.* 290
    A lark is singing in three hearts) I think you might all be a little sorry
    for a chap. (*But they are not even sorry, and he addresses Agatha in*
    these winged words) I'm particularly disappointed in you, Aggy;
    seeing that I was half engaged to you, I think you might have had
    the good feeling to be a little more hurt.   295
AGATHA Oh, bother.
ERNEST (*summing up the situation in so far as it affects himself*) I shall
    now go and lie down for a bit.
        (*He retires coldly but unregretted. Lady Mary approaches*
        Tweeny with her most insinuating smile)
LADY MARY Tweeny, as the Gov. has chosen me to wait on him,
    please may I have the loan of *it* again?   300
        (*The reference made with such charming delicacy is evidently to*
        Tweeny's skirt)
TWEENY (*doggedly*) No, you mayn't.
AGATHA (*supporting Tweeny*) Don't you give it to her.
LADY MARY (*still trying sweet persuasion*) You know quite well that
    he prefers to be waited on in a skirt.
TWEENY I don't care. Get one for yourself.   305
LADY MARY It is the only one on the island.
TWEENY And it's mine.
LADY MARY (*an aristocrat after all*) Tweeny, give me that skirt
    directly.
CATHERINE Don't.   310
TWEENY I won't.
LADY MARY (*clearing for action*) I shall make you.
TWEENY I should like to see you try.
        (*An unseemly fracas appears to be inevitable, but something*
    happens. The whir is again heard, and the notice is displayed
    'Dogs delight to bark and bite.' ° *Its effect is instantaneous and*
    cheering. The ladies look at each other guiltily and immediately

proceed on tiptoe to their duties. These are all concerned with the master's dinner. Catherine attends to his fish. Agatha fills a quaint toast-rack and brings the menu, which is written on a shell. Lady Mary twists a wreath of green leaves around her head, and places a flower beside the master's plate. Tweeny signs that all is ready, and she and the younger sisters retire into the kitchen, closing the screen that separates it from the rest of the room. Lady Mary beats a tom-tom,° which is the dinner-bell. She then gently works a punkah,° which we have not hitherto observed, and stands at attention. No doubt she is in hopes that the Gov. will enter into conversation with her, but she is too good a parlour-maid to let her hopes appear in her face. We may watch her manner with complete approval. There is not one of us who would not give her £26 a year.°

The master comes in quietly, a book in his hand, still the only book on the island, for he has not thought it worth while to build a printing-press. His dress is not noticeably different from that of the others, the skins are similar, but perhaps these are a trifle more carefully cut or he carries them better. One sees somehow that he has changed for his evening meal. There is an odd suggestion of a dinner jacket about his doeskin coat. It is, perhaps, too grave a face for a man of thirty-two, as if he were overmuch immersed in affairs, yet there is a sunny smile left to lighten it at times and bring back its youth; perhaps too intellectual a face to pass as strictly handsome, not sufficiently suggestive of oats.° His tall figure is very straight, slight rather than thick-set, but nobly muscular. His big hands, firm and hard with labour though they be, are finely shaped—note the fingers so much more tapered, the nails better tended than those of his domestics; they are one of many indications that he is of a superior breed. Such signs, as has often been pointed out, are infallible. A romantic figure, too. One can easily see why the women-folks of this strong man's house both adore and fear him.

He does not seem to notice who is waiting on him to-night, but inclines his head slightly to whoever it is, as she takes her place at the back of his chair. Lady Mary respectfully places the menu-shell before him, and he glances at it.)

CRICHTON Clear,° please.

(Lady Mary knocks on the screen, and a serving hatch in it opens, through which Tweeny offers two soup plates. Lady Mary

selects the cleat, and the aperture is closed. She works the punkah while the master partakes of the soup)

CRICHTON (*who always gives praise where it is due*) An excellent soup, 315
  Polly, but still a trifle too rich.

LADY MARY Thank *you*.
    (*The next course is the fish, and while it is being passed through the hatch we have a glimpse of three jealous women. Lady Mary's movements are so deft and noiseless that any observant spectator can see that she was born to wait at table)*

CRICHTON (*unbending as he eats*) Polly, you are a very smart girl.

LADY MARY (*bridling, but naturally gratified*) La!

CRICHTON (*smiling*) And I'm not the first you've heard it from, I'll 320
  swear.

LADY MARY (*wriggling*) Oh Gov.!

CRICHTON Got any followers on the island, Polly?

LADY MARY (*tossing her head*) Certainly not.

CRICHTON I thought that perhaps John or Ernest—— 325

LADY MARY (*tilting her nose*) I don't say that it's for want of asking.

CRICHTON (*emphatically*) I'm sure it isn't.
    (*Perhaps he thinks he has gone too far)*
  You may clear.
    (*Flushed with pleasure, she puts before him a bird and vegetables, sees that his beaker is filled with wine, and returns to the punkah. She would love to continue their conversation, but it is for him to decide. For a time he seems to have forgotten her)*

CRICHTON (*presently*) Did you lose any arrows to-day?

LADY MARY Only one in Firefly Grove. 330

CRICHTON You were as far as that? How did you get across the Black
  Gorge?

LADY MARY I went across on the rope.°

CRICHTON Hand over hand?

LADY MARY (*swelling at the implied praise*) I wasn't in the least dizzy. 335

CRICHTON (*moved*) You brave girl! (*He sits back in his chair a little agitated*) But never do that again.

LADY MARY (*pouting*) It is such fun, Gov.

CRICHTON (*decisively*) I forbid it.

LADY MARY (*the little rebel*) I shall. 340

CRICHTON (*surprised*) Polly!
    (*He signs to her sharply to step forward, but for a moment she holds back petulantly, and even when she does come it is less obediently than like a naughty, sulky child. Nevertheless, with*

*the forbearance that is characteristic of the man, he addresses her
with grave gentleness rather than severely*)

You must do as I tell you, you know.

LADY MARY (*strangely passionate*) I won't.

CRICHTON (*smiling at her fury*) We shall see. Frown at me, Polly;
there, you do it at once. Clench your little fists, stamp your feet,   345
bite your ribbons——

(*A student of women, or at least of this woman, he knows that
she is about to do those things, and thus she seems to do them to
order. Lady Mary screws up her face like a baby and cries. He
is immediately kind*)

You child of Nature; was it cruel of me to wish to save you from
harm?

LADY MARY (*drying her eyes*) I'm an ungracious wretch. Oh Gov., I
don't try half hard enough to please you. I'm even wearing—(*she   350
looks down sadly*)—when I know you prefer *it*.

CRICHTON (*thoughtfully*) I admit I do prefer *it*. Perhaps I am a little
old-fashioned in these matters.

(*Her tears again threaten*)

Ah, don't, Polly; that's nothing.

LADY MARY If I could only please you, Gov.   355

CRICHTON (*slowly*) You do please me, child, very much—(*he half
rises*)—very much indeed. (*If he meant to say more he checks himself.
He looks at his plate*) No more, thank you.

(*The simple island meal is soon ended, save for the walnuts and
the wine, and Crichton is too busy a man to linger long over
them. But he is a stickler for etiquette, and the table is cleared
charmingly, though with dispatch, before they are placed before
him. Lady Mary is an artist with the crumb-brush, and there
are few arts more delightful to watch. Dusk has come sharply,
and she turns on the electric light. It awakens Crichton from a
reverie in which he has been regarding her*)

CRICHTON Polly, there is only one thing about you that I don't quite
like.   360

(*She looks up, making a moue,° if that can be said of one who
so well knows her place. He explains*)

That action of the hands.

LADY MARY What do I do?

CRICHTON This—like one washing them.° I have noticed that the
others tend to do it also. It seems odd.

LADY MARY (*archly*) Oh Gov., have you forgotten?   365

CRICHTON What?

LADY MARY That once upon a time a certain other person did that?

CRICHTON (*groping*) You mean myself? (*She nods, and he shudders*)
Horrible!

LADY MARY (*afraid she has hurt him*) You haven't for a very long   370
time. Perhaps it is natural to servants.

CRICHTON That must be it. (*He rises*) Polly! (*She looks up expectantly,
but he only sighs and turns away*)

LADY MARY (*gently*) You sighed, Gov.

CRICHTON Did I? I was thinking. (*He paces the room and then turns   375
to her agitatedly, yet with control over his agitation. There is some
mournfulness in his voice*) I have always tried to do the right thing
on this island. Above all, Polly, I want to do the right thing by
you.

LADY MARY (*with shining eyes*) How we all trust you. That is your   380
reward, Gov.

CRICHTON (*who is having a fight with himself*) And now I want a
greater reward. Is it fair to you? Am I playing the game?° Bill
Crichton would like always to play the game. If we were in
England——   385

     (*He pauses so long that she breaks in softly*)

LADY MARY We know now that we shall never see England again.

CRICHTON I am thinking of two people whom neither of us has
seen for a long time—Lady Mary Lasenby, and one Crichton, a
butler.

     (*He says the last word bravely, a word he once loved, though it
     is the most horrible of all words to him now*)

LADY MARY That cold, haughty, insolent girl. Gov., look around   390
you and forget them both.

CRICHTON I had nigh forgotten them. He has had a chance, Polly—
that butler—in these two years of becoming a man, and he has
tried to take it. There have been many failures, but there has been
some success, and with it I have let the past drop off me, and   395
turned my back on it. That butler seems a far-away figure to me
now, and not myself. I hail him, but we scarce know each other.
If I am to bring him back it can only be done by force, for in my
soul he is now abhorrent to me. But if I thought it best for you
I'd haul him back; I swear as an honest man, I would bring him   400
back with all his obsequious ways and deferential airs, and let you
see the man you call your Gov. melt for ever into him who was
your servant.

LADY MARY (*shivering*) You hurt me. You say these things, but you
    say them like a king. To me it is the past that was not real.   405
CRICHTON (*too grandly*) A king! I sometimes feel——
        (*For a moment the yellow light gleams in his green eyes. We
        remember suddenly what Treherne and Ernest said about his
        regal look. He checks himself*)
    I say it harshly, it is so hard to say, and all the time there is another
    voice within me crying—— (*He stops*)
LADY MARY (*trembling but not afraid*) If it is the voice of Nature——
CRICHTON (*strongly*) I know it to be the voice of Nature.   410
LADY MARY (*in a whisper*) Then, if you want to say it very much,
    Gov., please say it to Polly Lasenby.
CRICHTON (*again in the grip of an idea*) A king! Polly, some people
    hold that the soul but leaves one human tenement for another, and
    so lives on through all the ages. I have occasionally thought of late   415
    that, in some past existence, I may have been a king. It has all come
    to me so naturally, not as if I had to work it out, but—as—if—I—
    remembered.
            'Or ever the knightly years were gone,
                With the old world to the grave,
                I was a *king* in Babylon,   420
                And you were a Christian slave.'°
    It may have been; you hear me, it may have been.
LADY MARY (*who is as one fascinated*) It may have been.
CRICHTON I am lord over all. They are but hewers of wood and   425
    drawers of water° for me. These shores are mine. Why should I
    hesitate; I have no longer any doubt. I do believe I am doing
    the right thing. Dear Polly, I have grown to love you; are you
    afraid to mate with me? (*She rocks her arms; no words will come from
    her*)   430
            'I was a king in Babylon,
            And you were a Christian slave.'
LADY MARY (*bewitched*) You are the most wonderful man I have ever
    known, and I am not afraid.
        (*He takes her to him with mastership. Presently he is seated, and
        she is at his feet looking up adoringly in his face. As the tension
        relaxes she speaks with a smile*)
    I want you to tell me—every woman likes to know—when was the   435
    first time you thought me nicer than the others?
CRICHTON (*stroking her hair*) I think a year ago. We were chasing
    goats on the Big Slopes, and you out-distanced us all; you were

the first of our party to run a goat down;° I was proud of you that day.

LADY MARY (*blushing with pleasure*) Oh Gov., I only did it to please you. Everything I have done has been out of the desire to please you. (*Suddenly anxious*) If I thought that in taking a wife from among us you were imperilling your dignity——

CRICHTON (*decisively*) Have no fear of that, dear. I have thought it all out. The wife, Polly, always takes the same position as the husband.

LADY MARY But I am so unworthy. It was sufficient to me that I should be allowed to wait on you at that table.

CRICHTON You shall wait on me no longer. At whatever table I sit, Polly, you shall soon sit there also. (*Boyishly*) Come, let us try what it will be like.

LADY MARY As your servant at your feet.

CRICHTON No, as my consort by my side.

> (*They are sitting thus when the hatch is again opened and coffee offered. But Lady Mary is no longer there to receive it. Her sisters peep through in consternation. In vain they rattle the cup and saucer. Agatha brings the coffee to Crichton*)

CRICHTON (*forgetting for the moment that it is not a month hence*) Help your mistress first, girl. (*Three women are bereft of speech, but he does not notice it. He addresses Catherine vaguely*) Are you a good girl, Kitty?

CATHERINE (*when she finds her tongue*) I try to be, Gov.

CRICHTON (*still more vaguely*) That's right.

> (*He takes command of himself again, and signs to them to sit down. Ernest comes in cheerily, but finding Crichton here is suddenly weak. He subsides on a chair, wondering what has happened*)

CRICHTON (*surveying him*) Ernest. (*Ernest rises*) You are becoming a little slovenly in your dress, Ernest; I don't like it.

ERNEST (*respectfully*) Thank you. (*Ernest sits again. Daddy and Treherne arrive*)

CRICHTON Daddy, I want you.

LORD LOAM (*gloomily*) Is it because I forgot to clean out the dam?

CRICHTON (*encouragingly*) No, no. (*He pours some wine into a goblet*) A glass of wine with you, Daddy.

LORD LOAM (*hastily*) Your health, Gov.

> (*He is about to drink, but the master checks him*)

CRICHTON And hers. Daddy, this lady has done me the honour to promise to be my wife.

LORD LOAM (*astounded*) Polly!

CRICHTON (*a little perturbed*) I ought first to have asked your consent. I deeply regret—but Nature; may I hope I have your approval? 475

LORD LOAM May you, Gov.? (*Delighted*) Rather! Polly!
(*He puts his proud arms round her*)

TREHERNE We all congratulate you, Gov., most heartily.

ERNEST Long life to you both, sir.
(*There is much shaking of hands, all of which is sincere*)

TREHERNE When will it be, Gov.?

CRICHTON (*after turning to Lady Mary, who whispers to him*) As soon 480 as the bridal skirt can be prepared. (*His manner has been most indulgent, and without the slightest suggestion of patronage. But he knows it is best for all that he should keep his place, and that his presence hampers them*) My friends, I thank you for your good wishes, I thank you all. And now, perhaps you would like me to leave you to 485 yourselves. Be joyous. Let there be song and dance to-night. Polly, I shall take my coffee in the parlour—you understand.
(*He retires with pleasant dignity. Immediately there is a rush of two girls at Lady Mary*)

LADY MARY Oh, oh! Father, they are pinching me.

LORD LOAM (*taking her under his protection*) Agatha, Catherine, never presume to pinch your sister again. On the other hand, she may 490 pinch you henceforth as much as ever she chooses.
(*In the meantime Tweeny is weeping softly, and the two are not above using her as a weapon*)

CATHERINE Poor Tweeny, it's a shame.

AGATHA After he had almost promised *you*.

TWEENY (*loyally turning on them*) No, he never did. He was always honourable as could be. 'Twas me as was too vulgar. Don't you 495 dare say a word agin that man.

ERNEST (*to Lord Loam*) You'll get a lot of tit-bits out of this, Daddy.

LORD LOAM That's what I was thinking.

ERNEST (*plunged in thought*) I dare say *I* shall have to clean out the dam now. 500

LORD LOAM (*heartlessly*) I dare say.
(*His gay old heart makes him again proclaim that he is a chickety chick. He seizes the concertina*)

TREHERNE (*eagerly*) That's the proper spirit.
(*He puts his arm round Catherine, and in another moment they are all dancing to Daddy's music. Never were people happier on*

an island. A moment's pause is presently created by the return of Crichton, wearing the wonderful robe of which we have already had dark mention. Never has he looked more regal, never perhaps felt so regal. We need not grudge him the one foible of his rule, for it is all coming to an end)

CRICHTON (*graciously, seeing them hesitate*) No, no; I am delighted to see you all so happy. Go on.

TREHERNE We don't like to before you, Gov. 505

CRICHTON (*his last order*) It is my wish.
(*The merrymaking is resumed, and soon Crichton himself joins in the dance. It is when the fun is at its fastest and most furious that all stop abruptly as if turned to stone. They have heard the boom of a gun. Presently they are alive again. Ernest leaps to the window*)

TREHERNE (*huskily*) It was a ship's gun! (*They turn to Crichton for confirmation; even in that hour they turn to Crichton*) Gov.?

CRICHTON Yes.
(*In another moment Lady Mary and Lord Loam are alone*)

LADY MARY (*seeing that her father is unconcerned*) Father, you heard. 510

LORD LOAM (*placidly*) Yes, my child.

LADY MARY (*alarmed by his unnatural calmness*) But it was a gun, father.

LORD LOAM (*looking an old man now, and shuddering a little*) Yes—a gun—I have often heard it. It's only a dream, you know; why don't 515
we go on dancing?
(*She takes his hands, which have gone cold*)

LADY MARY Father. Don't you see, they have all rushed down to the beach? Come.

LORD LOAM Rushed down to the beach; yes, always that—I often dream it. 520

LADY MARY Come, father, come.

LORD LOAM Only a dream, my poor girl.
(*Crichton presently returns. He is pale but firm*)

CRICHTON We can see lights within a mile of the shore—a great ship.

LORD LOAM A ship—always a ship. 525

LADY MARY Father, this is no dream.

LORD LOAM (*looking timidly at Crichton*) It's a dream, isn't it? There's no ship?

CRICHTON (*soothing him with a touch*) You are awake, Daddy, and there is a ship. 530

LORD LOAM (*clutching him*) You are not deceiving me?

CRICHTON It is the truth.

LORD LOAM (*reeling*) True?—a ship—at last!
>   (*He goes after the others pitifully*)

CRICHTON (*quietly*) There is a small boat between it and the island; they must have sent it ashore for water.   535

LADY MARY Coming in?

CRICHTON No. That gun must have been a signal to recall it. It is going back. They can't hear our cries.

LADY MARY (*pressing her temples*) Going away! So near—so near. (*Almost to herself*) I think I'm glad.   540

CRICHTON (*cheerily*) Have no fear. I shall bring them back.
>   (*He goes towards the table on which is the electrical apparatus*)

LADY MARY (*standing on guard as it were between him and the table*) What are you going to do?

CRICHTON To fire the beacons.

LADY MARY Stop! (*She faces him*) Don't you see what it means?   545

CRICHTON (*firmly*) It means that our life on the island has come to a natural end.

LADY MARY (*huskily*) Gov., let the ship go.

CRICHTON The old man—you saw what it means to him.

LADY MARY But I am afraid.   550

CRICHTON (*adoringly*) Dear Polly.

LADY MARY Gov., let the ship go. (*She clings to him, but though it is his death sentence he loosens her hold*)

CRICHTON Bill Crichton has got to play the game.
>   (*He pulls the levers. Soon through the window one of the beacons is seen flaring red. There is a long pause. Alarms and excursions outside. Ernest is the first to reappear*)

ERNEST Polly, Gov., the boat has turned back. (*He is gone. There is more disturbance. He returns*) They are English sailors; they have landed! We are rescued, I tell you, rescued!   555

LADY MARY (*wanly*) Is it anything to make so great a to-do about?

ERNEST (*staring*) Eh?

LADY MARY Have we not been happy here?   560

ERNEST Happy? Lord, yes.

LADY MARY (*catching hold of his sleeve*) Ernest, we must never forget all that the Gov. has done for us.

ERNEST (*stoutly*) Forget it? The man who could forget it would be a selfish wretch and a——But I say, this makes a difference!   565

LADY MARY (*quickly*) No, it doesn't.

ERNEST (*his mind tottering*) A mighty difference!
>(*The others come running in, some weeping with joy, others boisterous. For some time dementia rules. Soon we see blue-jackets° gazing through the window at the curious scene. Lord Loam comes accompanied by a naval officer, whom he is continually shaking by the hand*)

LORD LOAM And here, sir, is our little home. Let me thank you in the name of us all, again and again and again.

OFFICER Very proud, my lord. It is indeed an honour to have been able to assist so distinguished a gentleman as Lord Loam.   570

LORD LOAM A glorious, glorious day. I shall show you our other rooms. Come, my pets. Come, Crichton.
>(*He has not meant to be cruel. He does not know he has said it. It is the old life that has come back to him. They all go. All leave Crichton except Lady Mary*)

LADY MARY (*stretching out her arms to him*) Dear Gov., I will never give you up.   575
>(*There is a salt° smile on his face as he shakes his head to her. He lets the cloak slip to the ground. She will not take this for an answer; again her arms go out to him. Then comes the great renunciation. By an effort of will he ceases to be an erect figure;° he has the humble bearing of a servant. His hands come together as if he were washing them*)

CRICHTON (*it is the speech of his life*) My lady.
>(*She goes away. There is none to salute him now, unless we do it*)

Act 4

THE OTHER ISLAND

Some months have elapsed, and we have again the honour of waiting upon Lord Loam in his London home. It is the room of the first act,° but with a new scheme of decoration, for on the walls are exhibited many interesting trophies from the island, such as skins, stuffed birds, and weapons of the chase, labelled 'Shot by Lord Loam,' 'Hon. Ernest Woolley's Blowpipe,' etc. There are also two large glass cases containing other odds and ends, including, curiously enough, the bucket in which Ernest was first dipped, but there is no label calling attention to the incident.

It is not yet time to dress for dinner, and his lordship is on a couch, hastily yet furtively cutting the pages of a new book. With him are his two younger daughters and his nephew, and they also are engaged in literary pursuits; that is to say, the ladies are eagerly but furtively reading the evening papers, on copies of which Ernest is sitting complacently but furtively, doling them out as called for. Note the frequent use of the word 'furtive.'° It implies that they are very reluctant to be discovered by their butler, say, at their otherwise delightful task.

AGATHA (*reading aloud, with emphasis on the wrong words*) 'In conclusion, we most heartily congratulate the Hon. Ernest Woolley. This book of his, regarding the adventures of himself and his brave companions on a desert isle, stirs the heart like a trumpet.'

> (*Evidently the book referred to is the one in Lord Loam's hands*)

ERNEST Here is another.

CATHERINE (*reading*) 'From the first to the last of Mr Woolley's engrossing pages it is evident that he was an ideal man to be wrecked with, and a true hero.' (*Half-admiringly*) Ernest!

ERNEST (*calmly*) That's how it strikes *them*, you know. Here's another one.

AGATHA (*reading*) 'There are many kindly references to the two servants who were wrecked with the family, and Mr Woolley pays the butler a glowing tribute in a footnote.'

> (*Some one coughs uncomfortably*)

58

LORD LOAM (*who has been searching the index for the letter L*) Excellent, excellent. At the same time I must say, Ernest, that the whole book is about yourself.

ERNEST (*genially*) As the author—— 35

LORD LOAM Certainly, certainly. Still, you know, as a peer of the realm—(*with dignity*)—I think, Ernest, you might have given me one of your adventures.

ERNEST I say it was you who taught us how to obtain a fire by rubbing two pieces of stick together. 40

LORD LOAM (*beaming*) Do you, do you? I call that very handsome. What page?

> (*Here the door opens, and the well-bred Crichton enters with the evening papers as subscribed for by the house. Those we have already seen have perhaps been introduced by Ernest 'furtively.' Everyone except the intruder is immediately self-conscious, and when he withdraws there is a general sigh of relief. They pounce on the new papers. Ernest evidently gets a shock from one, which he casts contemptuously on the floor*)

AGATHA (*more fortunate*) Father, see page 81. 'It was a tiger-cat,' says Mr Woolley, 'of the largest size. Death stared Lord Loam in the face, but he never flinched.' 45

LORD LOAM (*searching his book eagerly*) Page 81.

AGATHA 'With presence of mind only equalled by his courage, he fixed an arrow in his bow.'

LORD LOAM Thank you, Ernest; thank you, my boy.

AGATHA 'Unfortunately he missed.' 50

LORD LOAM Eh?

AGATHA 'But by great good luck I heard his cries'—

LORD LOAM My cries?

AGATHA —'and rushing forward with drawn knife, I stabbed the monster to the heart.' 55

> (*Lord Loam shuts his book with a pettish slam. There might be a scene here were it not that Crichton reappears and goes to one of the glass cases. All are at once on the alert, and his lordship is particularly sly*)

LORD LOAM Anything in the papers, Catherine?

CATHERINE No, father, nothing—nothing at all.

ERNEST (*it pops out as of yore*) The papers! The papers are guides that tell us what we ought to do, and then we don't do it.

> (*Crichton having opened the glass case has taken out the bucket, and Ernest, looking round for applause, sees him carrying it off,*

and is undone. For a moment of time he forgets that he is no longer on the island, and with a sigh he is about to follow Crichton and the bucket to a retired spot.° The door closes, and Ernest comes to himself)

LORD LOAM (*uncomfortably*) I told him to take it away.   60

ERNEST I thought—(*he wipes his brow*)—I shall go and dress.
(*He goes*)

CATHERINE Father, it's awful having Crichton here. It's like living on tiptoe.

LORD LOAM (*gloomily*) While he is here we are sitting on a volcano.

AGATHA How mean of you! I am sure he has only stayed on with us   65
to—to help us through. It would have looked so suspicious if he had gone at once.

CATHERINE (*revelling in the worst*) But suppose Lady Brocklehurst were to get at him and pump him. She is the most terrifying, suspicious old creature in England; and Crichton simply can't tell   70
a lie.

LORD LOAM My dear, that is the volcano to which I was referring.
(*He has evidently something to communicate*) It is all Mary's fault. She said to me yesterday that she would break her engagement with Brocklehurst unless I told him about—you know what.   75
(*All conjure up the vision of Crichton*)

AGATHA Is she mad?

LORD LOAM She calls it common honesty.

CATHERINE Father, have you told him?

LORD LOAM (*heavily*) She thinks I have, but I couldn't. She is sure to find out to-night.   80
(*Unconsciously he leans on the island concertina, which he has perhaps been lately showing to an interviewer as something made for Tweeny. It squeaks, and they all jump*)

CATHERINE It is like a bird of ill-omen.

LORD LOAM (*vindictively*) I must have it taken away; it has done that twice.
(*Lady Mary comes in. She is in evening dress. Undoubtedly she meant to sail in, but she forgets, and despite her garments it is a manly entrance. She is properly ashamed of herself. She tries again, and has an encouraging success. She indicates to her sisters that she wishes to be alone with papa*)

AGATHA All right, but we know what it's about. Come along, Kit.
(*They go. Lady Mary thoughtlessly sits like a boy, and again corrects herself. She addresses her father, but he is in a brown*)

study,° and she seeks to draw his attention by whistling. This troubles them both)

LADY MARY How horrid of me!   85

LORD LOAM (*depressed*) If you would try to remember——

LADY MARY (*sighing*) I do; but there are so many things to remember.

LORD LOAM (*sympathetically*) There are——(*In a whisper*) Do you know, Mary, I constantly find myself secreting hairpins.   90

LADY MARY I find it so difficult to go up steps one at a time.

LORD LOAM I was dining with half a dozen members of our party last Thursday, Mary, and they were so eloquent that I couldn't help wondering all the time how many of their heads *he* would have put in the bucket.   95

LADY MARY I use so many of his phrases. And my appetite is so scandalous. Father, I usually have a chop before we sit down to dinner.

LORD LOAM As for my clothes——(*wriggling*). My dear, you can't think how irksome collars are to me nowadays.   100

LADY MARY They can't be half such an annoyance, father, as—— (*She looks dolefully at her skirt*)

LORD LOAM (*hurriedly*) Quite so—quite so. You have dressed early to-night, Mary.

LADY MARY That reminds me; I had a note from Brocklehurst saying that he would come a few minutes before his mother as—as   105 he wanted to have a talk with me. He didn't say what about, but of course we know.

(*His lordship fidgets*)

(*With feeling*) It was good of you to tell him, father. Oh, it is horrible to me——(*covering her face*) It seemed so natural at the time.   110

LORD LOAM (*petulantly*) Never again make use of that word in this house, Mary.

LADY MARY (*with an effort*) Father, Brocklehurst has been so loyal to me for these two years that I should despise myself were I to keep my—my extraordinary lapse from him. Had Brocklehurst   115 been a little less good, then you need not have told him my strange little secret.

LORD LOAM (*weakly*) Polly—I mean Mary—it was all Crichton's fault, he——

LADY MARY (*with decision*) No, father, no; not a word against him,   120 though I haven't the pluck to go on with it; I can't even understand how it ever was. Father, do you not still hear the surf? Do you see the curve of the beach?

LORD LOAM I have begun to forget——(*In a low voice*) But they were happy days; there was something magical about them. 125

LADY MARY It was glamour. Father, I have lived Arabian nights. I have sat out a dance with the evening star. But it was all in a past existence, in the days of Babylon, and I am myself again. But he has been chivalrous always. If the slothful, indolent creature I used to be has improved in any way, I owe it all to him. I am slipping 130 back in many ways, but I am determined not to slip back altogether—in memory of him and his island. That is why I insisted on your telling Brocklehurst. He can break our engagement if he chooses. (*Proudly*) Mary Lasenby is going to play the game.

LORD LOAM But my dear—— 135
(*Lord Brocklehurst is announced*)

LADY MARY (*meaningly*) Father, dear, oughtn't you to be dressing?

LORD LOAM (*very unhappy*) The fact is—before I go—I want to say——

LORD BROCKLEHURST Loam, if you don't mind, I wish very specially to have a word with Mary before dinner. 140

LORD LOAM But——

LADY MARY Yes, father.
(*She induces him to go, and thus courageously faces Lord Brocklehurst to hear her fate*)
I am ready, George.

LORD BROCKLEHURST (*who is so agitated that she ought to see he is thinking not of her but of himself*) It is a painful matter—I wish I 145 could have spared you this, Mary.

LADY MARY Please go on.

LORD BROCKLEHURST In common fairness, of course, this should be remembered, that two years had elapsed. You and I had no reason to believe that we should ever meet again. 150
(*This is more considerate than she had expected*)

LADY MARY (*softening*) I was so lost to the world, George.

LORD BROCKLEHURST (*with a groan*) At the same time, the thing is utterly and absolutely inexcusable——

LADY MARY (*recovering her hauteur*) Oh!

LORD BROCKLEHURST And so I have already said to mother. 155

LADY MARY (*disdaining him*) You have told her?

LORD BROCKLEHURST Certainly, Mary, certainly; I tell mother everything.

LADY MARY (*curling her lip*) And what did she say?

LORD BROCKLEHURST To tell the truth, mother rather pooh-   160
poohed the whole affair.

LADY MARY (*incredulous*) Lady Brocklehurst pooh-poohed the whole
affair!

LORD BROCKLEHURST She said, 'Mary and I will have a good laugh
over this.'   165

LADY MARY (*outraged*) George, your mother is a hateful, depraved
old woman.

LORD BROCKLEHURST Mary!

LADY MARY (*turning away*) Laugh indeed, when it will always be
such a pain to me.   170

LORD BROCKLEHURST (*with strange humility*) If only you would let
me bear all the pain, Mary.

LADY MARY (*who is taken aback*) George, I think you are the noblest
man——

    (*She is touched, and gives him both her hands. Unfortunately he
    simpers*)

LORD BROCKLEHURST She was a pretty little thing.   175

    (*She stares, but he marches to his doom*)

Ah, not beautiful like you. I assure you it was the merest folly;
there were a few letters, but we have got them back. It was all
owing to the boat being so late at Calais. You see she had such
large, helpless eyes.

LADY MARY (*fixing him*) George, when you lunched with father   180
to-day at the club——

LORD BROCKLEHURST I didn't. He wired me that he couldn't come.

LADY MARY (*with a tremor*) But he wrote you?

LORD BROCKLEHURST No.

LADY MARY (*a bird singing in her breast*) You haven't seen him since?   185

LORD BROCKLEHURST No.

    (*She is saved. Is he to be let off also? Not at all. She bears down
    on him like a ship of war*)

LADY MARY George, who and what is this woman?

LORD BROCKLEHURST (*cowering*) She was—she is—the shame of
it—a lady's-maid.

LADY MARY (*properly horrified*) A what?   190

LORD BROCKLEHURST A lady's-maid. A mere servant,° Mary.
(*Lady Mary whirls round so that he shall not see her face*) I first met
her at this house when you were entertaining the servants; so you
see it was largely your father's fault.

LADY MARY (*looking him up and down*) A lady's-maid?   195

LORD BROCKLEHURST (*degraded*) Her name was Fisher.

LADY MARY My maid!

LORD BROCKLEHURST (*with open hands*) Can you forgive me, Mary?

LADY MARY Oh George, George!

LORD BROCKLEHURST Mother urged me not to tell you anything   200
about it; but——

LADY MARY (*from her heart*) I am so glad you told me.

LORD BROCKLEHURST You see there was nothing catastrophic in it.

LADY MARY (*thinking perhaps of another incident*) No, indeed.

LORD BROCKLEHURST (*inclined to simper again*) And she behaved   205
awfully well.° She quite saw that it was because the boat was late.
I suppose the glamour to a girl in service of a man in high
position——

LADY MARY Glamour!—yes, yes, that was it.

LORD BROCKLEHURST Mother says that a girl in such circumstances 210
is to be excused if she loses her head.

LADY MARY (*impulsively*) George, I am so sorry if I said anything
against your mother. I am sure she is the dearest old thing.

LORD BROCKLEHURST (*in calm waters at last*) Of course for women
of our class she has a very different standard.   215

LADY MARY (*grown tiny*) Of course.

LORD BROCKLEHURST You see, knowing how good a woman she is
herself, she was naturally anxious that I should marry some one
like her. That is what has made her watch your conduct so
jealously, Mary.   220

LADY MARY (*hurriedly thinking things out*) I know. I—I think,
George, that before your mother comes I should like to say a word
to father.

LORD BROCKLEHURST (*nervously*) About this?

LADY MARY Oh no; I shan't tell him of this. About something else. 225

LORD BROCKLEHURST And you do forgive me, Mary?

LADY MARY (*smiling on him*) Yes, yes. I—I am sure the boat was *very*
late, George.

LORD BROCKLEHURST (*earnestly*) It really was.

LADY MARY I am even relieved to know that you are not quite   230
perfect, dear. (*She rests her hands on his shoulders. She has a moment
of contrition*) George, when we are married, we shall try to be not
an entirely frivolous couple, won't we? We must endeavour to be
of some little use, dear.

LORD BROCKLEHURST (*the ass*) Noblesse oblige.   235

LADY MARY (*haunted by the phrases of a better man*°) Mary Lasenby is determined to play the game, George.

> (*Perhaps she adds to herself, 'Except just this once.' A kiss closes this episode of the two lovers; and soon after the departure of Lady Mary the Countess of Brocklehurst is announced. She is a very formidable old lady*)

LADY BROCKLEHURST Alone, George?

LORD BROCKLEHURST Mother, I told her all; she has behaved magnificently.   240

LADY BROCKLEHURST (*who has not shared his fears*) Silly boy. (*She casts a supercilious eye on the island trophies*) So these are the wonders they brought back with them. Gone away to dry her eyes, I suppose?

LORD BROCKLEHURST (*proud of his mate*) She didn't cry, mother.   245

LADY BROCKLEHURST No? (*She reflects*) You're quite right. I wouldn't have cried. Cold, icy. Yes, that was it.

LORD BROCKLEHURST (*who has not often contradicted her*) I assure you, mother, that wasn't it at all. She forgave me at once.

LADY BROCKLEHURST (*opening her eyes sharply to the full*) Oh!   250

LORD BROCKLEHURST She was awfully nice about the boat being late; she even said she was relieved to find that I wasn't quite perfect.

LADY BROCKLEHURST (*pouncing*) She said that?

LORD BROCKLEHURST She really did.   255

LADY BROCKLEHURST I mean *I* wouldn't. Now if *I* had said that, what would have made me say it? (*Suspiciously*) George, is Mary all we think her?

LORD BROCKLEHURST (*with unexpected spirit*) If she wasn't, mother, you would know it.   260

LADY BROCKLEHURST Hold your tongue, boy. We don't really know what happened on that island.

LORD BROCKLEHURST You were reading the book all the morning.

LADY BROCKLEHURST How can I be sure that the book is true?

LORD BROCKLEHURST They all talk of it as true.   265

LADY BROCKLEHURST How do I know that they are not lying?

LORD BROCKLEHURST Why should they lie?

LADY BROCKLEHURST Why shouldn't they? (*She reflects again*) If I had been wrecked on an island, I think it highly probable that I should have lied when I came back. Weren't some servants with   270
them?

LORD BROCKLEHURST Crichton, the butler.

(*He is surprised to see her ring the bell*)
Why, mother, you are not going to——

LADY BROCKLEHURST   Yes, I am. (*Pointedly*) George, watch whether
Crichton begins any of his answers to my questions with 'The fact   275
is.'

LORD BROCKLEHURST   Why?

LADY BROCKLEHURST   Because that is usually the beginning of a lie.

LORD BROCKLEHURST (*as Crichton opens the door*) Mother, you can't
do these things in other people's houses.   280

LADY BROCKLEHURST (*coolly, to Crichton*) It was I who rang.
(*Surveying him through her eyeglass*) So you were one of the
castaways, Crichton?

CRICHTON   Yes, my lady.

LADY BROCKLEHURST   Delightful book Mr Woolley has written   285
about your adventures. (*Crichton bows*) Don't you think so?

CRICHTON   I have not read it, my lady.

LADY BROCKLEHURST   Odd that they should not have presented you
with a copy.

LORD BROCKLEHURST   Presumably Crichton is no reader.   290

LADY BROCKLEHURST   By the way, Crichton, were there any books
on the island?

CRICHTON   I had one, my lady—Henley's poems.

LORD BROCKLEHURST   Never heard of him.
(*Crichton again bows.*)

LADY BROCKLEHURST (*who has not heard of him either*) I think you   295
were not the only servant wrecked?

CRICHTON   There was a young woman, my lady.

LADY BROCKLEHURST   I want to see her. (*Crichton bows, but remains*)° Fetch her up.
(*He goes*)

LORD BROCKLEHURST (*almost standing up to his mother*) This is   300
scandalous.

LADY BROCKLEHURST (*defining her position*) I am a mother.
(*Catherine and Agatha enter in dazzling confections, and quake
in secret to find themselves practically alone with Lady Brocklehurst*)
(*Even as she greets them*) How d'you do, Catherine—Agatha? You
didn't dress like this on the island, I expect! By the way, how did
you dress?   305
(*They have thought themselves prepared, but——*)

AGATHA   Not—not so well, of course, but quite the same idea.

(They are relieved by the arrival of Treherne, who is in clerical dress)

LADY BROCKLEHURST How do you do, Mr Treherne? There is not so much of you in the book as I had hoped.

TREHERNE *(modestly)* There wasn't very much of me on the island, Lady Brocklehurst.   310

LADY BROCKLEHURST How d'ye mean?

(He shrugs his honest shoulders)

LORD BROCKLEHURST I hear you have got a living,° Treherne. Congratulations.

TREHERNE Thanks.

LORD BROCKLEHURST Is it a good one?   315

TREHERNE So-so. They are rather weak in bowling, but it's a good bit of turf.°

(Confidence is restored by the entrance of Ernest, who takes in the situation promptly, and, of course, knows he is a match for any old lady)

ERNEST *(with ease)* How do you do, Lady Brocklehurst.

LADY BROCKLEHURST Our brilliant author!

ERNEST *(impervious to satire)* Oh, I don't know.   320

LADY BROCKLEHURST It is as engrossing, Mr Woolley, as if it were a work of fiction.

ERNEST *(suddenly uncomfortable)* Thanks, awfully. *(Recovering)* The fact is——

(He is puzzled by seeing the Brocklehurst family exchange meaning looks)

CATHERINE *(to the rescue)* Lady Brocklehurst, Mr Treherne and   325
I—we are engaged.

AGATHA And Ernest and I.

LADY BROCKLEHURST *(grimly)* I see, my dears; thought it wise to keep the island in the family.

(An awkward moment this for the entrance of Lord Loam and Lady Mary, who, after a private talk upstairs, are feeling happy and secure)

LORD LOAM *(with two hands for his distinguished guest)* Aha! Ha, ha!   330
Younger than any of them, Emily.

LADY BROCKLEHURST Flatterer. *(To Lady Mary)* You seem in high spirits, Mary.

LADY MARY *(gaily)* I am.

LADY BROCKLEHURST *(with a significant glance at Lord Brocklehurst)*   335
After——

LADY MARY I—I mean. The fact is——
> (*Again that disconcerting glance between the Countess and her son*)

LORD LOAM (*humorously*) She hears wedding bells, Emily, ha, ha!

LADY BROCKLEHURST (*coldly*) Do you, Mary? Can't say I do; but I'm hard of hearing.

LADY MARY (*instantly her match*) If you don't, Lady Brocklehurst, I'm sure I don't.

LORD LOAM (*nervously*) Tut, tut. Seen our curios from the island, Emily? I should like you to examine them.

LADY BROCKLEHURST Thank you, Henry. I am glad you say that, for I have just taken the liberty of asking two of them° to step upstairs.
> (*There is an uncomfortable silence, which the entrance of Crichton° with Tweeny does not seem to dissipate. Crichton is impenetrable, but Tweeny hangs back in fear*)

LORD BROCKLEHURST (*stoutly*) Loam, I have no hand in this.

LADY BROCKLEHURST (*undisturbed*) Pooh, what have I done? You always begged me to speak to the servants, Henry, and I merely wanted to discover whether the views you used to hold about equality were adopted on the island; it seemed a splendid opportunity, but Mr Woolley has not a word on the subject.
> (*All eyes turn to Ernest*)

ERNEST (*with confidence*) The fact is——
> (*The fatal words again*)

LORD LOAM (*not quite certain what he is to assure her of*) I assure you, Emily——

LADY MARY (*as cold as steel*) Father, nothing whatever happened on the island of which I, for one, am ashamed, and I hope Crichton will be allowed to answer Lady Brocklehurst's questions.

LADY BROCKLEHURST To be sure. There's nothing to make a fuss about, and we're a family party. (*To Crichton*) Now, truthfully, my man.

CRICHTON (*calmly*) I promise that, my lady.
> (*Some hearts sink, the hearts that could never understand a Crichton*)

LADY BROCKLEHURST (*sharply*) Well, were you all equal on the island?

CRICHTON No, my lady. I think I may say there was as little equality there as elsewhere.

LADY BROCKLEHURST All the social distinctions were preserved?

CRICHTON As at home, my lady.

LADY BROCKLEHURST The servants?   370

CRICHTON They had to keep their place.°

LADY BROCKLEHURST Wonderful. How was it managed? (*With an inspiration*) You, girl, tell me that.

(*Can there be a more critical moment?*)

TWEENY (*in agony*) If you please, my lady, it was all the Gov.'s doing.

(*They give themselves up for lost. Lord Loam tries to sink out of sight*)

CRICHTON In the regrettable slang of the servants' hall, my lady, the   375
master is usually referred to as the Gov.

LADY BROCKLEHURST I see. (*She turns to Lord Loam*) You——

LORD LOAM (*reappearing*) Yes, I understand that is what they called me.

LADY BROCKLEHURST (*to Crichton*) You didn't even take your meals
with the family?   380

CRICHTON No, my lady, I dined apart.

(*Is all safe?*)

LADY BROCKLEHURST (*alas*) You, girl, also? Did you dine with
Crichton?

TWEENY (*scared*) No, your ladyship.

LADY BROCKLEHURST (*fastening on her*) With whom?   385

TWEENY I took my bit of supper with—with Daddy and Polly and
the rest.

(*Vae victis*)°

ERNEST (*leaping into the breach*) Dear old Daddy—he was our
monkey. You remember our monkey, Agatha?

AGATHA Rather! What a funny old darling he was.   390

CATHERINE (*thus encouraged*) And don't you think Polly was the
sweetest little parrot, Mary?

LADY BROCKLEHURST Ah! I understand; animals you had domestic-
ated?

LORD LOAM (*heavily*) Quite so—quite so.   395

LADY BROCKLEHURST The servants' teas that used to take place
here once a month——

CRICHTON They did not seem natural on the island, my lady, and
were discontinued by the Gov.'s orders.

LORD BROCKLEHURST A clear proof, Loam, that they were a   400
mistake here.

LORD LOAM (*seeing the opportunity for a diversion*) I admit it frankly.
I abandon them. Emily, as the result of our experiences on the
island, I think of going over to the Tories.

LADY BROCKLEHURST I am delighted to hear it.   405

LORD LOAM (*expanding*) Thank you, Crichton, thank you; that is all.
   (*He motions to them to go, but the time is not yet*)

LADY BROCKLEHURST One moment. (*There is a universal but stifled
   groan*) Young people, Crichton, will be young people, even on an
   island; now, I suppose there was a certain amount of—shall we say
   sentimentalising, going on?   410

CRICHTON Yes, my lady, there was.

LORD BROCKLEHURST (*ashamed*) Mother!

LADY BROCKLEHURST (*disregarding him*) Which gentleman? (*To
   Tweeny*) You, girl, tell me.

TWEENY (*confused*) If you please, my lady——   415

ERNEST (*hurriedly*) The fact is——
   (*He is checked as before, and probably says 'D——n' to himself,
   but he has saved the situation*)

TWEENY (*gasping*) It was him—Mr Ernest, your ladyship.

LADY BROCKLEHURST (*counsel for the prosecution*) With which lady?

AGATHA I have already told you, Lady Brocklehurst, that Ernest and
   I——   420

LADY BROCKLEHURST Yes, *now*; but you were two years on the
   island. (*Looking at Lady Mary*) Was it this lady?

TWEENY No, your ladyship.

LADY BROCKLEHURST Then I don't care which of the others it was.
   (*Tweeny gurgles*) Well, I suppose that will do.   425

LORD BROCKLEHURST Do! I hope you are ashamed of yourself,
   mother. (*To Crichton, who is going*) You are an excellent fellow,
   Crichton; and if, after we are married, you ever wish to change
   your place, come to us.

LADY MARY (*losing her head for the only time*) Oh no, impossible.   430

LADY BROCKLEHURST (*at once suspicious*) Why impossible? (*Lady
   Mary cannot answer, or perhaps she is too proud*) Do you see why it
   should be impossible, my man?
     (*He can make or mar his unworthy Mary now. Have you any
     doubt of him?*)

CRICHTON Yes, my lady. I had not told you, my lord, but as soon
   as your lordship is suited° I wish to leave service.   435
     (*They are all immensely relieved, except poor Tweeny*)

TREHERNE (*the only curious one*) What will you do, Crichton?
     (*Crichton shrugs his shoulders*)

CRICHTON Shall I withdraw, my lord?
     (*He withdraws with Tweeny; the thunderstorm is over*)

LADY BROCKLEHURST (*thankful to have made herself unpleasant*)
Horrid of me, wasn't it? But if one wasn't disagreeable now and
again, it would be horribly tedious to be an old woman. He will   440
soon be yours, Mary, and then—think of the opportunities you will
have of being disagreeable to me. On that understanding, my dear,
don't you think we might——?
> (*Their cold lips meet*)

LORD LOAM (*vaguely*) Quite so—quite so.
> (*Crichton announces dinner, and they file out. Lady Mary stays
> behind a moment and impulsively holds out her hand*)

LADY MARY To wish you every dear happiness.   445

CRICHTON (*an enigma to the last*) The same to you, my lady.

LADY MARY Do you despise me, Crichton? (*The man who could never
tell a lie makes no answer*) I am ashamed of myself, but I am the
sort of woman on whom shame sits lightly. (*He does not contradict
her*) You are the best man among us.   450

CRICHTON On an island, my lady, perhaps; but in England, no.

LADY MARY (*not inexcusably*) Then there is something wrong with
England.

CRICHTON My lady, not even from you can I listen to a word against
England.   455

LADY MARY Tell me one thing: you have not lost your courage?

CRICHTON No, my lady.
> (*She goes. He turns out the lights*)

PETER PAN

or
The Boy Who Would
Not Grow Up

CHARACTERS
(in order of appearance)

Nana (a dog and the
   children's nursemaid)
Michael
Mrs Darling
John
Wendy
Mr Darling
Peter Pan
Liza
Tinker Bell
Slightly
Tootles
Nibs
Curly
First Twin

Second Twin
Captain Hook
Cecco
Bill Jukes
Cookson
Gentleman Starkey
Skylights
Mullins
Noodler
Smee
Tiger Lily
Panther
Cabby and Friend
Animals and Fairies, Pirates,
   Indians, Mermaids, Birds

TO THE FIVE°
A Dedication

Some disquieting confessions must be made in printing at last° the
play of *Peter Pan*; among them this, that I have no recollection of
having written it.° Of that, however, anon. What I want to do first is
to give Peter to the Five without whom he never would have existed.
I hope, my dear sirs, that in memory of what we have been to each   5
other you will accept this dedication with your friend's love. The play
of Peter is streaky with you still,° though none may see this save
ourselves. A score of Acts had to be left out, and you were in them
all. We first brought Peter down, didn't we, with a blunt-headed
arrow in Kensington Gardens?° I seem to remember that we believed   10
we had killed him, though he was only winded,° and that after a
spasm of exultation in our prowess the more soft-hearted among us
wept and all of us thought of the police. There was not one of you
who would not have sworn as an eye-witness to this occurrence; no
doubt I was abetting, but you used to provide corroboration that was   15
never given to you by me. As for myself, I suppose I always knew
that I made Peter by rubbing the five of you violently together, as
savages with two sticks produce a flame. That is all he is, the spark I
got from you.

We had good sport of him before we clipped him small to make   20
him fit the boards.° Some of you were not born when the story began
and yet were hefty figures before we saw that the game was up. Do
you remember a garden at Burpham° and the initiation there of
No. 4° when he was six weeks old, and three of you grudged letting
him in so young? Have you, No. 3, forgotten the white violets at the   25
Cistercian abbey in which we cassocked our first fairies (all little
friends of St Benedict), or your cry to the Gods, 'Do I just kill one
pirate all the time?' Do you remember Marooners' Hut in the haunted
groves of Waverley, and the St Bernard dog° in a tiger's mask who
so frequently attacked you, and the literary record of that summer,   30
The Boy Castaways,° which is so much the best and the rarest of this
author's works? What was it that made us eventually give to the
public in the thin form of a play that which had been woven for
ourselves alone? Alas, I know what it was, I was losing my grip. One
by one as you swung monkey-wise from branch to branch in the wood   35

of make-believe you reached the tree of knowledge. Sometimes you swung back into the wood, as the unthinking may at a cross-road take a familiar path that no longer leads to home; or you perched ostentatiously on its boughs to please me, pretending that you still belonged; soon you knew it only as the vanished wood, for it vanishes if one needs to look for it. A time came when I saw that No. 1, the most gallant of you all, ceased to believe that he was ploughing woods incarnadine,° and with an apologetic eye for me derided the lingering faith of No. 2; when even No. 3 questioned gloomily whether he did not really spend his nights in bed. There were still two who knew no better, but their day was dawning. In these circumstances, I suppose, was begun the writing of the play of Peter.° That was a quarter of a century ago, and I clutch my brows in vain to remember whether it was a last desperate throw to retain the five of you for a little longer, or merely a cold decision to turn you into bread and butter.

This brings us back to my uncomfortable admission that I have no recollection of writing the play of *Peter Pan*, now being published for the first time so long after he made his bow upon the stage. You had played it until you tired of it, and tossed it in the air and gored it and left it derelict in the mud and went on your way singing other songs; and then I stole back and sewed some of the gory fragments together with a pen-nib. That is what must have happened, but I cannot remember doing it. I remember writing the story of *Peter and Wendy*° many years after the production of the play, but I might have cribbed that from some typed copy. I can haul back to mind the writing of almost every other assay° of mine, however forgotten by the pretty public; but this play of Peter, no. Even my beginning as an amateur playwright, that noble mouthful, *Bandelero the Bandit*,° I remember every detail of its composition in my school days at Dumfries. Not less vivid is my first little piece, produced by Mr Toole.° It was called *Ibsen's Ghost*,° and was a parody of the mightiest craftsman that ever wrote for our kind friends in front.° To save the management the cost of typing I wrote out the 'parts,'° after being told what parts were, and I can still recall my first words, spoken so plaintively by a now famous actress,—'To run away from my second husband just as I ran away from my first, it feels quite like old times.' On the first night a man in the pit found *Ibsen's Ghost* so diverting that he had to be removed in hysterics. After that no one seems to have thought of it at all. But what a man to carry about with one! How odd, too, that these trifles should adhere to the mind that cannot remember the long job of writing Peter. It does seem almost suspicious, especially as I

have not the original MS of *Peter Pan* (except a few stray pages) with
which to support my claim. I have indeed another MS, lately
made,° but that 'proves nothing.' I know not whether I lost that
original MS or destroyed it or happily gave it away. I talk of   80
dedicating the play to you, but how can I prove it is mine? How ought
I to act if some other hand, who could also have made a copy, thinks
it worth while to contest the cold rights? Cold they are to me now as
that laughter of yours in which Peter came into being long before he
was caught and written down. There is Peter still, but to me he lies   85
sunk in the gay Black Lake.

Any one of you five brothers has a better claim to the authorship
than most, and I would not fight you for it, but you should have
launched your case long ago in the days when you most admired me,°
which were in the first year of the play, owing to a rumour's reaching 90
you that my spoils were one-and-sixpence° a night. This was untrue,
but it did give me a standing among you. You watched for my next
play with peeled eyes, not for entertainment but lest it contained some
chance witticism of yours that could be challenged as collaboration;°
indeed I believe there still exists a legal document, full of the   95
Aforesaid and Henceforward to be called Part-Author, in which for
some such snatching I was tied down to pay No. 2 one halfpenny daily
throughout the run of the piece.

During the rehearsals of Peter (and it is evidence in my favour that
I was admitted to them) a depressed man in overalls, carrying a mug   100
of tea or a paint-pot, used often to appear by my side in the shadowy
stalls and say to me, 'The gallery boys° won't stand it.' He then
mysteriously faded away as if he were the theatre ghost. This
hopelessness of his is what all dramatists are said to feel at such times,
so perhaps he was the author. Again, a large number of children   105
whom I have seen playing Peter in their homes with careless
mastership, constantly putting in better words, could have thrown it
off with ease. It was for such as they that after the first production I
had to add something to the play at the request of parents (who thus
showed that they thought me the responsible person) about no one   110
being able to fly until the fairy dust had been blown on him; so many
children having gone home and tried it from their beds and needed
surgical attention.

Notwithstanding other possibilities, I think I wrote Peter, and if so
it must have been in the usual inky way. Some of it, I like to think, 115
was done in that native place° which is the dearest spot on earth to
me, though my last heart-beats shall be with my beloved solitary

London that was so hard to reach.° I must have sat at a table with
that great dog° waiting for me to stop, not complaining, for he knew
it was thus we made our living, but giving me a look when he found   120
he was to be in the play, with his sex changed. In after years when
the actor who was Nana had to go to the wars he first taught his wife
how to take his place as the dog till he came back, and I am glad that
I see nothing funny in this; it seems to me to belong to the play. I
offer this obtuseness on my part as my first proof that I am the author.   125

Some say that we are different people at different periods of our
lives, changing not through effort of will, which is a brave affair, but
in the easy course of nature every ten years or so. I suppose this
theory might explain my present trouble, but I don't hold with it; I
think one remains the same person throughout, merely passing, as it   130
were, in these lapses of time from one room to another, but all in the
same house. If we unlock the rooms of the far past we can peer in
and see ourselves, busily occupied in beginning to become you and
me. Thus, if I am the author in question the way he is to go should
already be showing in the occupant of my first compartment, at whom   135
I now take the liberty to peep. Here he is at the age of seven or so
with his fellow-conspirator Robb,° both in glengarry bonnets.° They
are giving an entertainment in a tiny old washing-house that still
stands. The charge for admission is preens, a bool, or a peerie° (I
taught you a good deal of Scotch, so possibly you can follow that),   140
and apparently the culminating Act consists in our trying to put each
other into the boiler, though some say that I also addressed the
spell-bound audience. This washing-house is not only the theatre of
my first play, but has a still closer connection with Peter. It is the
original of the little house the Lost Boys built in the Never Land for   145
Wendy, the chief difference being that it never wore John's tall hat as
a chimney. If Robb had owned a lum hat° I have no doubt that it
would have been placed on the washing-house.

Here is that boy again some four years older, and the reading he is
munching feverishly is about desert islands; he calls them wrecked   150
islands.° He buys his sanguinary tales surreptitiously in penny
numbers.° I see a change coming over him; he is blanching as he reads
in the high-class magazine, *Chatterbox*,° a fulmination against such
literature, and sees that unless his greed for islands is quenched he is
for ever lost. With gloaming° he steals out of the house, his library   155
bulging beneath his palpitating waistcoat. I follow like his shadow, as
indeed I am, and watch him dig a hole in a field at Pathhead farm°
and bury his islands in it; it was ages ago, but I could walk straight

to that hole in the field now and delve for the remains. I peep into the next compartment. There he is again, ten years older, an undergraduate now and craving to be a real explorer, one of those who do things instead of prating of them, but otherwise unaltered; he might be painted at twenty on top of a mast, in his hand a spy-glass through which he rakes the horizon for an elusive strand. I go from room to room, and he is now a man, real exploration abandoned (though only because no one would have him). Soon he is even concocting other plays, and quaking a little lest some low person counts how many islands there are in them. I note that with the years the islands grow more sinister, but it is only because he has now to write with the left hand,° the right having given out; evidently one thinks more darkly down the left arm. Go to the keyhole of the compartment where he and I join up, and you may see us wondering whether they would stand one more island. This journey through the house may not convince any one that I wrote Peter, but it does suggest me as a likely person. I pause to ask myself whether I read *Chatterbox* again, suffered the old agony, and buried that MS of the play in a hole in a field.

Of course this is over-charged. Perhaps we do change; except a little something in us which is no larger than a mote in the eye, and that, like it, dances in front of us beguiling us all our days. I cannot cut the hair by which it hangs.

The strongest evidence that I am the author is to be found, I think, in a now melancholy volume, the aforementioned *The Boy Castaways*; so you must excuse me for parading that work here. Officer of the Court, call *The Boy Castaways*. The witness steps forward and proves to be a book you remember well though you have not glanced at it these many years. I pulled it out of a bookcase just now not without difficulty, for its recent occupation has been to support the shelf above. I suppose, though I am uncertain, that it was I and not you who hammered it into that place of utility. It is a little battered and bent after the manner of those who shoulder burdens, and ought (to our shame) to remind us of the witnesses who sometimes get an hour off from the cells to give evidence before his Lordship. I have said that it is the rarest of my printed works, as it must be, for the only edition was limited to two copies, of which one (there was always some devilry in any matter connected with Peter) instantly lost itself in a railway carriage. This is the survivor. The idlers in court may have assumed that it is a handwritten screed, and are impressed by its bulk. It is printed by Constable's (how handsomely you did us, dear

Blaikie°), it contains thirty-five illustrations and is bound in cloth with   200
a picture stamped on the cover of the three eldest of you 'setting out
to be wrecked.' This record is supposed to be edited by the youngest
of the three, and I must have granted him that honour to make up
for his being so often lifted bodily out of our adventures by his nurse,
who kept breaking into them for the fell purpose of giving him a   205
midday rest. No. 4 rested so much at this period that he was merely
an honorary member of the band, waving his foot to you for luck
when you set off with bow and arrow to shoot his dinner for him; and
one may rummage the book in vain for any trace of No. 5. Here is
the title-page, except that you are numbered instead of named—   210

THE BOY

CASTAWAYS

OF BLACK LAKE ISLAND

Being a record of the Terrible
Adventures of Three Brothers   215
in the summer of 1901
faithfully set forth
by No. 3.

LONDON
Published by J. M. Barrie   220
in the Gloucester Road
1901

There is a long preface by No. 3 in which we gather your ages at
this first flight. 'No. 1 was eight and a month, No. 2 was approaching
his seventh lustrum,° and I was a good bit past four.' Of his two   225
elders, while commending their fearless dispositions, the editor
complains that they wanted to do all the shooting and carried the
whole equipment of arrows inside their shirts. He is attractively
modest about himself, 'Of No. 3 I prefer to say nothing, hoping that
the tale as it is unwound will show that he was a boy of deeds rather   230
than of words,' a quality which he hints did not unduly protrude upon
the brows of Nos. 1 and 2. His preface ends on a high note, 'I should
say that the work was in the first instance compiled as a record simply
at which we could whet our memories, and that it is now published

for No. 4's benefit. If it teaches him by example lessons in fortitude   235
and manly endurance we shall consider that we were not wrecked in
vain.'

Published to whet your memories. Does it whet them? Do you hear
once more, like some long-forgotten whistle beneath your window
(Robb at dawn calling me to the fishing!) the not quite mortal blows   240
that still echo in some of the chapter headings?—'Chapter II, No. 1
teaches Wilkinson (his master)° a Stern Lesson—We Run away to
Sea. Chapter III, A Fearful Hurricane—Wreck of the "Anna Pink"—
We go crazy from Want of Food—Proposal to eat No. 3—Land
Ahoy.' Such are two chapters out of sixteen. Are these again your   245
javelins cutting tunes in the blue haze of the pines; do you sweat as
you scale the dreadful Valley of Rolling Stones, and cleanse your
hands of pirate blood by scouring them carelessly in Mother Earth?
Can you still make a fire (you could do it once, Mr Seton-
Thompson° taught us in, surely an odd place, the Reform Club°) by   250
rubbing those sticks together? Was it the travail of hut-building that
subsequently advised Peter to find a 'home under the ground'? The
bottle and mugs in that lurid picture, 'Last night on the Island,' seem
to suggest that you had changed from Lost Boys into pirates, which
was probably also a tendency of Peter's. Listen again to our stolen   255
saw-mill, man's proudest invention; when he made the saw-mill he
beat the birds for music in a wood.

The illustrations (full-paged) in *The Boy Castaways* are all photographs taken by myself; some of them indeed of phenomena that had
to be invented afterwards, for you were always off doing the wrong   260
things when I pressed the button. I see that we combined instruction
with amusement; perhaps we had given our kingly word to that effect.
How otherwise account for such wording to the pictures as these: 'It
is undoubtedly,' says No. 1 in a fir tree that is bearing unwonted fruit,
recently tied to it, 'the *Cocos nucifera*,° for observe the slender   265
columns supporting the crown of leaves which fall with a grace that
no art can imitate.' 'Truly,' continues No. 1 under the same tree in
another forest as he leans upon his trusty gun, 'though the perils of
these happenings are great, yet would I rejoice to endure still greater
privations to be thus rewarded by such wondrous studies of Nature.'   270
He is soon back to the practical, however, 'recognising the Mango
(*Magnifera indica*) by its lancet-shaped leaves and the cucumber-
shaped fruit.' No. 1 was certainly the right sort of voyager to be
wrecked with, though if my memory fails me not, No. 2, to whom
these strutting observations were addressed, sometimes protested   275

because none of them was given to him. No. 3 being the author is in
surprisingly few of the pictures, but this, you may remember, was
because the lady already darkly referred to used to pluck him from
our midst for his siesta at 12 o'clock, which was the hour that best
suited the camera.° With a skill on which he has never been   280
complimented the photographer sometimes got No. 3 nominally
included in a wild-life picture when he was really in a humdrum
house kicking on the sofa. Thus in a scene representing Nos. 1 and 2
sitting scowling outside the hut it is untruly written that they scowled
because 'their brother was within singing and playing on a barbaric   285
instrument. The music,' the unseen No. 3 is represented as saying
(obviously forestalling No. 1), 'is rude and to a cultured ear discord-
ant, but the songs like those of the Arabs are full of poetic imagery.'
He was perhaps allowed to say this sulkily on the sofa.

   Though *The Boy Castaways* has sixteen chapter-headings, there is   290
no other letterpress;° an absence which possible purchasers might
complain of, though there are surely worse ways of writing a book
than this. These headings anticipate much of the play of *Peter Pan*,
but there were many incidents of our Kensington Gardens days that
never got into the book, such as our Antarctic exploits when we   295
reached the Pole in advance of our friend Captain Scott° and cut our
initials on it for him to find, a strange foreshadowing of what was
really to happen. In *The Boy Castaways* Captain Hook has arrived but
is called Captain Swarthy, and he seems from the pictures to have
been a black man. This character, as you do not need to be told, is   300
held by those in the know to be autobiographical. You had many
tussles with him (though you never, I think, got his right arm) before
you reached the terrible chapter (which might be taken from the play)
entitled 'We Board the Pirate Ship at Dawn—A Rakish Craft—No. 1
Hew-them-Down and No. 2 of the Red Hatchet—A Holocaust of   305
Pirates—Rescue of Peter.' (Hullo, Peter rescued instead of rescuing
others? I know what that means and so do you, but we are not going
to give away all our secrets.) The scene of the Holocaust is the Black
Lake (afterwards, when we let women in, the Mermaids' Lagoon).
The pirate captain's end was not in the mouth of a crocodile though   310
we had crocodiles on the spot ('while No. 2 was removing the
crocodiles from the stream No. 1 shot a few parrots, *Psittacidae*,° for
our evening meal'). I think our captain had divers deaths owing to
unseemly competition among you, each wanting to slay him single-
handed. On a special occasion, such as when No. 3 pulled out the   315
tooth himself, you gave the deed to him, but took it from him while

he rested. The only pictorial representation in the book of Swarthy's fate is in two parts. In one, called briefly 'We string him up,' Nos. 1 and 2, stern as Athos,° are hauling him up a tree by a rope, his face snarling as if it were a grinning mask (which indeed it was), and his garments very like some of my own stuffed with bracken. The other, the same scene next day, is called 'The Vultures had Picked him Clean,' and tells its own tale.

The dog in *The Boy Castaways* seems never to have been called Nana but was evidently in training for that post. He originally belonged to Swarthy (or to Captain Marryat?°), and the first picture of him, lean, skulking, and hunched (how did I get that effect?), 'patrolling the island' in that monster's interests, gives little indication of the domestic paragon he was to become. We lured him away to the better life, and there is, later, a touching picture, a clear forecast of the Darling nursery, entitled 'We trained the dog to watch over us while we slept.' In this he also is sleeping, in a position that is a careful copy of his charges; indeed any trouble we had with him was because, once he knew he was in a story, he thought his safest course was to imitate you in everything you did. How anxious he was to show that he understood the game, and more generous than you, he never pretended that he was the one who killed Captain Swarthy. I must not imply that he was entirely without initiative, for it was his own idea to bark warningly a minute or two before twelve o'clock as a signal to No. 3 that his keeper was probably on her way for him (Disappearance of No. 3); and he became so used to living in the world of Pretend that when we reached the hut of a morning he was often there waiting for us, looking, it is true, rather idiotic, but with a new bark he had invented which puzzled us until we decided that he was demanding the password. He was always willing to do any extra jobs, such as becoming the tiger in mask, and when after a fierce engagement you carried home that mask in triumph, he joined in the procession proudly and never let on that the trophy had ever been part of him. Long afterwards he saw the play from a box in the theatre, and as familiar scenes were unrolled before his eyes I have never seen a dog so bothered. At one matinee we even let him for a moment take the place of the actor who played Nana, and I don't know that any members of the audience ever noticed the change, though he introduced some 'business' that was new to them but old to you and me. Heigh-ho, I suspect that in this reminiscence I am mixing him up with his successor, for such a one there had to be, the loyal Newfoundland who, perhaps in the following year, applied, so to say, for the part by bringing hedgehogs to the hut in his mouth as offerings for our evening repasts. The head and coat of him were copied for the Nana of the play.   360

They do seem to be emerging out of our island, don't they, the little people of the play, all except that sly one, the chief figure,° who draws farther and farther into the wood as we advance upon him? He so dislikes being tracked, as if there were something odd about him, that when he dies he means to get up and blow away the particle that   365 will be his ashes.

Wendy has not yet appeared, but she has been trying to come ever since that loyal nurse° cast the humorous shadow of woman upon the scene and made us feel that it might be fun to let in a disturbing element. Perhaps she would have bored her way in at last whether we   370 wanted her or not. It may be that even Peter did not really bring her to the Never Land of his free will, but merely pretended to do so because she would not stay away. Even Tinker Bell had reached our island before we left it. It was one evening when we climbed the wood carrying No. 4 to show him what the trail was like by twilight. As our   375 lanterns twinkled among the leaves No. 4 saw a twinkle stand still for a moment and he waved his foot gaily to it, thus creating Tink. It must not be thought, however, that there were any other sentimental passages between No. 4 and Tink; indeed, as he got to know her better he suspected her of frequenting the hut to see what we had   380 been having for supper, and to partake of the same, and he pursued her with malignancy.

A safe but sometimes chilly way of recalling the past is to force open a crammed drawer. If you are searching for anything in particular you don't find it, but something falls out at the back that   385 is often more interesting. It is in this way that I get my desultory reading, which includes the few stray leaves of the original MS of Peter that I have said I do possess, though even they, when returned to the drawer, are gone again, as if that touch of devilry lurked in them still. They show that in early days I hacked at and added to the   390 play. In the drawer I find some scraps of Mr Crook's delightful music,° and other incomplete matter relating to Peter. Here is the reply of a boy whom I favoured° with a seat in my box and injudiciously asked at the end what he had liked best. 'What I think I liked best,' he said, 'was tearing up the programme and dropping   395 the bits on people's heads.' Thus am I often laid low. A copy of my favourite programme of the play is still in the drawer. In the first or second year of Peter No. 4 could not attend through illness, so we

took the play to his nursery, far away in the country, an array of
vehicles almost as glorious as a travelling circus; the leading parts   400
were played by the youngest children° in the London company, and
No. 4, aged five, looked on solemnly at the performance from his bed
and never smiled once. That was my first and only appearance on the
real stage, and this copy of the programme shows I was thought so
meanly of as an actor that they printed my name in smaller letters   405
than the others.

I have said little here of Nos. 4 and 5, and it is high time I had
finished. They had a long summer day, and I turn round twice and
now they are off to school. On Monday, as it seems, I was escorting
No. 5 to a children's party and brushing his hair in the ante-room;   410
and by Thursday he is placing me against the wall of an underground
station and saying, 'Now I am going to get the tickets; don't move till
I come back for you or you'll lose yourself.' No. 4 jumps from being
astride my shoulders fishing, I knee-deep in the stream, to becoming,
while still a schoolboy, the sternest of my literary critics. Anything he   415
shook his head over I abandoned, and conceivably the world has thus
been deprived of masterpieces. There was for instance an unfortunate
little tragedy which I liked until I foolishly told No. 4 its subject,
when he frowned and said he had better have a look at it. He read it,
and then, patting me on the back, as only he and No. 1 could touch   420
me,° said, 'You know you can't do this sort of thing.' End of a
tragedian. Sometimes, however, No. 4 liked my efforts, and I walked
in the azure that day when he returned *Dear Brutus* to me with the
comment 'Not so bad.' In earlier days, when he was ten, I offered him
the MS of my book *Margaret Ogilvy*. 'Oh, thanks,' he said almost   425
immediately, and added, 'Of course my desk is awfully full.' I
reminded him that he could take out some of its more ridiculous
contents. He said, 'I have read it already in the book.' This I had not
known, and I was secretly elated, but I said that people sometimes
liked to preserve this kind of thing as a curiosity. He said 'Oh' again.   430
I said tartly that he was not compelled to take it if he didn't want it.
He said, 'Of course I want it, but my desk——' Then he wriggled
out of the room and came back in a few minutes dragging in No. 5
and announcing triumphantly, 'No. 5 will have it.'

The rebuffs I have got from all of you! They were especially   435
crushing in those early days when one by one you came out of your
belief in fairies and lowered on me as the deceiver. My grandest
triumph, the best thing in the play of *Peter Pan* (though it is not in
it), is that long after No. 4 had ceased to believe, I brought him back

to the faith for at least two minutes. We were on our way in a boat   440
to fish the Outer Hebrides (where we caught *Mary Rose*), and though
it was a journey of days he wore his fishing basket on his back all the
time, so as to be able to begin at once. His one pain was the absence
of Johnny Mackay, for Johnny was the loved gillie° of the previous
summer who had taught him everything that is worth knowing (which   445
is a matter of flies) but could not be with us this time as he would
have had to cross and re-cross Scotland to reach us. As the boat drew
near the Kyle of Lochalsh pier I told Nos. 4 and 5 it was such a
famous wishing pier that they had now but to wish and they should
have. No. 5 believed at once and expressed a wish to meet himself (I   450
afterwards found him on the pier searching faces confidently), but
No. 4 thought it more of my untimely nonsense and doggedly
declined to humour me. 'Whom do you want to see most, No. 4?' 'Of
course I would like most to see Johnny Mackay.' 'Well, then, wish for
him.' 'Oh, rot.' 'It can't do any harm to wish.' Contemptuously he   455
wished, and as the ropes were thrown on the pier he saw Johnny
waiting for him, loaded with angling paraphernalia. I know no one
less like a fairy than Johnny Mackay, but for two minutes No. 4 was
quivering in another world than ours. When he came to he gave me
a smile which meant that we understood each other, and thereafter   460
neglected me for a month, being always with Johnny. As I have said,
this episode is not in the play; so though I dedicate *Peter Pan* to you
I keep the smile, with the few other broken fragments of immortality
that have come my way.

Act 1

THE NURSERY

The night nursery of the Darling family, which is the scene of our opening Act, is at the top of a rather depressed street in Bloomsbury. We have a right to place it where we will, and the reason Bloomsbury is chosen is that Mr Roget° once lived there. So did we in days when his *Thesaurus* was our only companion in London; and we whom he has helped to wend our way through life have always wanted to pay him a little compliment. The Darlings therefore lived in Bloomsbury. 5

It is a corner house whose top window, the important one, looks upon a leafy square from which Peter used to fly up to it, to the delight of three children and no doubt the irritation of passers-by. 10 The street is still there, though the steaming sausage shop has gone; and apparently the same cards perch now as then over the doors, inviting homeless ones to come and stay with the hospitable inhabitants. Since the days of the Darlings, however, a lick of paint has been applied; and our corner house in particular, which has swallowed its 15 neighbour, blooms with awful freshness as if the colours had been discharged upon it through a hose. Its card now says 'No children,' meaning maybe that the goings-on of Wendy and her brothers have given the house a bad name. As for ourselves, we have not been in it since we went back to reclaim our old *Thesaurus*. 20

That is what we call the Darling house, but you may dump it down anywhere you like, and if you think it was your house you are very probably right. It wanders about London looking for anybody in need of it, like the little house in the Never Land.°

The blind (which is what Peter would have called the theatre 25 curtain if he had ever seen one) rises on that top room, a shabby little room if Mrs Darling had not made it the hub of creation by her certainty that such it was, and adorned it to match with a loving heart and all the scrapings of her purse. The door on the right leads into the day nursery, which she has no right to have, but she made it 30 herself with nails in her mouth and a paste-pot in her hand. This is the door the children will come in by. There are three beds and (rather oddly) a large dog-kennel; two of these beds, with the kennel, being on the left and the other on the right. The coverlets of the beds (if visitors are expected) are made out of Mrs Darling's 35 wedding-gown, which was such a grand affair that it still keeps them pinched.° Over each bed is a china house, the size of a linnet's nest, containing a night-light. The fire, which is on our right, is burning as discreetly as if it were in custody, which in a sense it is, for supporting the mantelshelf are two wooden soldiers, home-made, begun by Mr Darling, finished by Mrs Darling, repainted (unfortunately) by John Darling. On the fire-guard hang incomplete parts of children's night attire. The door the parents will come in by is on the left. At the back is the bathroom door, with a cuckoo clock over it; and in the centre is the window, which is at present ever so staid and respectable, but half an hour hence (namely at 6.30 p.m.) will be able to tell a very strange tale to the police.

The only occupant of the room at present is Nana the nurse, reclining, not as you might expect on the one soft chair, but on the floor. She is a Newfoundland dog, and though this may shock the grandiose, the not exactly affluent will make allowances. The Darlings could not afford to have a nurse, they could not afford indeed to have children; and now you are beginning to understand how they did it. Of course Nana has been trained by Mrs Darling, but like all treasures° she was born to it. In this play we shall see her chiefly inside the house, but she was just as exemplary outside, escorting the two elders to school with an umbrella in her mouth, for instance, and butting them back into line if they strayed.

The cuckoo clock strikes six, and Nana springs into life. This first moment in the play is tremendously important, for if the actor playing Nana does not spring properly we are undone. She will probably be played by a boy, if one clever enough can be found, and must never be on two legs except on those rare occasions when an ordinary nurse would be on four. This Nana must go about all her duties in a most ordinary manner, so that you know in your bones that she performs them just so every evening at six; naturalness must be her passion;° indeed, it should be the aim of every one in the play, for which she is now setting the pace. All the characters, whether grown-ups or babes, must wear a child's outlook on life as their only important adornment. If they cannot help being funny they are begged to go away. A good motto for all would be 'The little less, and how much it is.'°

Nana, making much use of her mouth, 'turns down' the beds, and carries the various articles on the fire-guard across to them. Then pushing the bathroom door open, she is seen at work on the taps preparing Michael's bath; after which she enters from the day nursery with the youngest of the family on her back.

MICHAEL (*obstreperous*) I won't go to bed, I won't, I won't. Nana, it isn't six o'clock yet. Two minutes more, please, one minute more? Nana, I won't be bathed, I tell you I will not be bathed.

> (*Here the bathroom door closes on them, and Mrs Darling, who has perhaps heard his cry, enters the nursery. She is the loveliest lady in Bloomsbury, with a sweet mocking mouth, and as she is going out to dinner to-night she is already wearing her evening gown because she knows her children like to see her in it. It is a delicious confection made by herself out of nothing and other people's mistakes. She does not often go out to dinner, preferring when the children are in bed to sit beside them tidying up their minds,° just as if they were drawers. If Wendy and the boys could keep awake they might see her repacking into their proper places the many articles of the mind that have strayed during the day, lingering humorously over some of their contents, wondering where on earth they picked this thing up, making discoveries sweet and not so sweet, pressing this to her cheek and hurriedly stowing that out of sight. When they wake in the morning the naughtinesses with which they went to bed are not, alas, blown away, but they are placed at the bottom of the drawer; and on the top, beautifully aired, are their prettier thoughts ready for the new day.* ·*

> *As she enters the room she is startled to see a strange little face outside the window and a hand groping as if it wanted to come in*)

MRS DARLING Who are you? (*The unknown disappears; she hurries to the window*) No one there. And yet I feel sure I saw a face. My children! (*She throws open the bathroom door and Michael's head appears gaily over the bath. He splashes; she throws kisses to him and closes the door. 'Wendy, John,' she cries, and gets reassuring answers from the day nursery. She sits down, relieved, on Wendy's bed; and Wendy and John come in, looking their smallest size, as children tend to do to a mother suddenly in fear for them*)   80   85

JOHN (*histrionically*) We are doing an act; we are playing at being you and father.° (*He imitates the only father who has come under his special notice*) A little less noise there.   90

WENDY Now let us pretend we have a baby.

JOHN (*good-naturedly*) I am happy to inform you, Mrs Darling, that you are now a mother. (*Wendy gives way to ecstasy*) You have missed the chief thing; you haven't asked, 'boy or girl?'

WENDY I am so glad to have one at all, I don't care which it is.   95

JOHN (*crushingly*) That is just the difference between gentlemen and ladies. Now you tell me.

WENDY I am happy to acquaint you, Mr Darling, you are now a father.

JOHN Boy or girl?   100

WENDY (*presenting herself*) Girl.

JOHN Tuts.

WENDY You horrid.

JOHN Go on.

WENDY I am happy to acquaint you, Mr Darling, you are again a   105
father.

JOHN Boy or girl?

WENDY Boy. (*John beams*) Mummy, it's hateful of him.

(*Michael emerges from the bathroom in John's old pyjamas and giving his face a last wipe with the towel*)

MICHAEL (*expanding*) Now, John, have me.

JOHN We don't want any more.   110

MICHAEL (*contracting*) Am I not to be born at all?

JOHN Two is enough.

MICHAEL (*wheedling*) Come, John: boy, John. (*Appalled*) Nobody wants me!

MRS DARLING I do.   115

MICHAEL (*with a glimmer of hope*) Boy or girl?

MRS DARLING (*with one of those happy thoughts of hers*) Boy.

(*Triumph of Michael; discomfiture of John. Mr Darling arrives, in no mood unfortunately to gloat over this domestic scene. He is really a good man as breadwinners go, and it is hard luck for him to be propelled into the room now, when if we had brought him in a few minutes earlier or later he might have made a fairer impression. In the city where he sits on a stool all day, as fixed as a postage stamp, he is so like all the others on stools that you recognise him not by his face but by his stool, but at home the way to gratify him is to say that he has a distinct personality. He is very conscientious, and in the days when Mrs Darling gave up keeping the house books correctly and drew pictures instead (which he called her guesses), he did all the totting up for her, holding her hand while he calculated whether they could have Wendy or not, and coming down on the right side. It is with regret, therefore, that we introduce him as a tornado, rushing into the nursery in evening dress, but without his coat, and brandishing in his hand a recalcitrant white tie*)

MR DARLING (*implying that he has searched for her everywhere and that the nursery is a strange place in which to find her*) Oh, here you are, Mary.   120

MRS DARLING (*knowing at once what is the matter*) What is the matter, George dear?

MR DARLING (*as if the word were monstrous*) Matter! This tie, it will not tie. (*He waxes sarcastic*) Not round my neck. Round the bed-post, oh yes; twenty times have I made it up round the bed-post, but   125 round my neck, oh dear no; begs to be excused.

MICHAEL (*in a joyous transport*) Say it again, father, say it again!

MR DARLING (*witheringly*) Thank you. (*Goaded by a suspiciously crooked smile on Mrs Darling's face*) I warn you, Mary, that unless this tie is round my neck we don't go out to dinner to-night, and   130 if I don't go out to dinner to-night I never go to the office again, and if I don't go to the office again you and I starve, and our children will be thrown into the streets.

   (*The children blanch as they grasp the gravity of the situation*)

MRS DARLING Let me try, dear.

   (*In a terrible silence their progeny cluster round them. Will she succeed? Their fate depends on it. She fails—no, she succeeds. In another moment they are wildly gay, romping round the room on each other's shoulders. Father is even a better horse than mother. Michael is dropped upon his bed, Wendy retires to prepare for hers, John runs from Nana, who has reappeared with the bath towel*)

JOHN (*rebellious*) I won't be bathed. You needn't think it.   135

MR DARLING (*in the grand manner*) Go and be bathed at once, sir.

   (*With bent head John follows Nana into the bathroom. Mr Darling swells*)

MICHAEL (*as he is put between the sheets*) Mother, how did you get to know me?

MR DARLING A little less noise there.°

MICHAEL (*growing solemn*) At what time was I born, mother?   140

MRS DARLING At two o'clock in the night-time, dearest.

MICHAEL Oh, mother, I hope I didn't wake you.

MRS DARLING They are rather sweet, don't you think, George?

MR DARLING (*doting*) There is not their equal on earth, and they are ours, ours!   145

   (*Unfortunately Nana has come from the bathroom for a sponge and she collides with his trousers, the first pair he has ever had with braid on them*)

MR DARLING Mary, it is too bad; just look at this; covered with hairs. Clumsy, clumsy!

(*Nana goes, a drooping figure*)

MRS DARLING Let me brush you, dear.

(*Once more she is successful. They are now by the fire, and Michael is in bed doing idiotic things with a teddy bear*)

MR DARLING (*depressed*) I sometimes think, Mary, that it is a mistake to have a dog for a nurse.   150

MRS DARLING George, Nana is a treasure.

MR DARLING No doubt; but I have an uneasy feeling at times that she looks upon the children as puppies.

MRS DARLING (*rather faintly*) Oh no, dear one, I am sure she knows they have souls.   155

MR DARLING (*profoundly*) I wonder, I wonder.

(*The opportunity has come for her to tell him of something that is on her mind*)

MRS DARLING George, we must keep Nana, I will tell you why. (*Her seriousness impresses him*) My dear, when I came into this room to-night I saw a face at the window.

MR DARLING (*incredulous*) A face at the window, three floors up?   160
Pooh!

MRS DARLING It was the face of a little boy; he was trying to get in. George, this is not the first time I have seen that boy.

MR DARLING (*beginning to think that this may be a man's job*) Oho!

MRS DARLING (*making sure that Michael does not hear*) The first time   165
was a week ago. It was Nana's night out, and I had been drowsing here by the fire when suddenly I felt a draught, as if the window were open. I looked round and I saw that boy—in the room.

MR DARLING In the room?

MRS DARLING I screamed. Just then Nana came back and she at once   170
sprang at him. The boy leapt for the window. She pulled down the sash quickly, but was too late to catch him.

MR DARLING (*who knows he would not have been too late*) I thought so!

MRS DARLING Wait. The boy escaped, but his shadow° had not time   175
to get out; down came the window and cut it clean off.

MR DARLING (*heavily*) Mary, Mary, why didn't you keep that shadow?

MRS DARLING (*scoring*) I did. I rolled it up, George; and here it is.

(*She produces it from a drawer. They unroll and examine the flimsy thing, which is not more material than a puff of smoke, and if let go would probably float into the ceiling without discolouring it. Yet it has human shape. As they nod their heads over it they present the most satisfying picture on earth, two happy parents conspiring cosily by the fire for the good of their children*)

MR DARLING It is nobody I know, but he does look a scoundrel.   180

MRS DARLING I think he comes back to get his shadow, George.

MR DARLING (*meaning that the miscreant has now a father to deal with*) I dare say. (*He sees himself telling the story to the other stools at the office*) There is money in this, my love. I shall take it to the British Museum to-morrow and have it priced.   185

   (*The shadow is rolled up and replaced in the drawer*)

MRS DARLING (*like a guilty person*) George, I have not told you all; I am afraid to.

MR DARLING (*who knows exactly the right moment to treat a woman as a beloved child*) Cowardy, cowardy custard.

MRS DARLING (*pouting*) No, I'm not.   190

MR DARLING Oh yes, you are.

MRS DARLING George, I'm not.

MR DARLING Then why not tell? (*Thus cleverly soothed she goes on*)

MRS DARLING The boy was not alone that first time. He was accompanied by—I don't know how to describe it; by a ball of   195 light, not as big as my fist, but it darted about the room like a living thing.

MR DARLING (*though open-minded*) That is very unusual. It escaped with the boy?

MRS DARLING Yes. (*Sliding her hand into his*) George, what can all   200 this mean?

MR DARLING (*ever ready*) What indeed!

   (*This intimate scene is broken by the return of Nana with a bottle in her mouth*)

MRS DARLING (*at once dissembling*) What is that, Nana? Ah, of course; Michael, it is your medicine.

MICHAEL (*promptly*) Won't take it.   205

MR DARLING (*recalling his youth*) Be a man, Michael.

MICHAEL Won't.

MRS DARLING (*weakly*) I'll get you a lovely chocky to take after it. (*She leaves the room, though her husband calls after her*)

MR DARLING Mary, don't pamper him. When I was your age, Michael, I took medicine without a murmur. I said 'Thank you,   210 kind parents, for giving me bottles to make me well.'

(*Wendy, who has appeared in her night-gown, hears this and believes*)

WENDY That medicine you sometimes take is much nastier, isn't it, father?

MR DARLING (*valuing her support*) Ever so much nastier. And as an example to you, Michael, I would take it now (*thankfully*) if I 215 hadn't lost the bottle.

WENDY (*always glad to be of service*) I know where it is, father. I'll fetch it.

(*She is gone before he can stop her. He turns for help to John, who has come from the bathroom attired for bed*)

MR DARLING John, it is the most beastly stuff. It is that sticky sweet kind. 220

JOHN (*who is perhaps still playing at parents*) Never mind, father,° it will soon be over.

(*A spasm of ill-will to John cuts through Mr Darling, and is gone. Wendy returns panting*)

WENDY Here it is, father; I have been as quick as I could.

MR DARLING (*with a sarcasm that is completely thrown away on her*) You have been wonderfully quick, precious quick! 225

(*He is now at the foot of Michael's bed, Nana is by its side, holding the medicine spoon insinuatingly in her mouth*)

WENDY (*proudly, as she pours out Mr Darling's medicine*) Michael, now you will see how father takes it.

MR DARLING (*hedging*) Michael first.

MICHAEL (*full of unworthy suspicions*) Father first.

MR DARLING It will make me sick, you know. 230

JOHN (*lightly*) Come on, father.

MR DARLING Hold your tongue, sir.

WENDY (*disturbed*) I thought you took it quite easily, father, saying 'Thank you, kind parents, for——'

MR DARLING That is not the point; the point is that there is more 235 in my glass than in Michael's spoon. It isn't fair, I swear though it were with my last breath, it is not fair.

MICHAEL (*coldly*) Father, I'm waiting.

MR DARLING It's all very well to say you are waiting; so am I waiting. 240

MICHAEL Father's a cowardy custard.

MR DARLING So are you a cowardy custard.

(*They are now glaring at each other*)

MICHAEL I am not frightened.

MR DARLING Neither am I frightened.

MICHAEL Well, then, take it.   245

MR DARLING Well, then, you take it.

WENDY (*butting in again*) Why not take it at the same time?

MR DARLING (*haughtily*) Certainly. Are you ready, Michael?

WENDY (*as nothing has happened*) One—two—three.

   (*Michael partakes, but Mr Darling resorts to hanky-panky*)

JOHN Father hasn't taken his!   250

   (*Michael howls*)

WENDY (*inexpressibly pained*) Oh father!

MR DARLING (*who has been hiding the glass behind him*) What do you
 mean by 'oh father'? Stop that row, Michael. I meant to take mine
 but I—missed it. (*Nana shakes her head sadly over him, and goes into*
 the bathroom. They are all looking as if they did not admire him, and   255
 nothing so dashes a temperamental man) I say, I have just thought of
 a splendid joke. (*They brighten*) I shall pour my medicine into
 Nana's bowl, and she will drink it thinking it is milk! (*The*
 pleasantry does not appeal, but he prepares the joke, listening for
 appreciation)   260

WENDY Poor darling Nana!

MR DARLING You silly little things; to your beds every one of you;
 I am ashamed of you.

   (*They steal to their beds as Mrs Darling returns with the*
   chocolate)

MRS DARLING Well, is it all over?

MICHAEL Father didn't——(*Father glares*)   265

MR DARLING All over, dear, quite satisfactorily. (*Nana comes back*)
 Nana, good dog, good girl; I have put a little milk into your bowl.
 (*The bowl is by the kennel, and Nana begins to lap, only begins. She*
 retreats into the kennel)

MRS DARLING What is the matter, Nana?   270

MR DARLING (*uneasily*) Nothing, nothing.

MRS DARLING (*smelling the bowl*) George, it is your medicine!

   (*The children break into lamentation. He gives his wife an*
   imploring look; he is begging for one smile, but does not get it.
   In consequence he goes from bad to worse)

MR DARLING It was only a joke. Much good my wearing myself to
 the bone trying to be funny in this house.

WENDY (*on her knees by the kennel*) Father, Nana is crying.   275

MR DARLING Coddle her; nobody coddles me. Oh dear no. I am only
 the breadwinner, why should I be coddled? Why, why, why?

MRS DARLING George, not so loud; the servants will hear you.

> (*There is only one maid, absurdly small too, but they have got into the way of calling her the servants*)

MR DARLING (*defiant*) Let them hear me; bring in the whole world. (*The desperate man, who has not been in fresh air for days, has now lost all self-control*) I refuse to allow that dog to lord it in my nursery for one hour longer. (*Nana supplicates him*) In vain, in vain, the proper place for you is the yard, and there you go to be tied up this instant.

> (*Nana again retreats into the kennel, and the children add their prayers to hers*)

MRS DARLING (*who knows how contrite he will be for this presently*) George, George, remember what I told you about that boy.

MR DARLING Am I master in this house or is she? (*To Nana fiercely*) Come along. (*He thunders at her, but she indicates that she has reasons not worth troubling him with for remaining where she is. He resorts to a false bonhomie*) There, there, did she think he was angry with her, poor Nana? (*She wriggles a response in the affirmative*) Good Nana, pretty Nana. (*She has seldom been called pretty, and it has the old effect. She plays rub-a-dub with her paws, which is how a dog blushes*) She will come to her kind master, won't she? won't she? (*She advances, retreats, waggles her head, her tail, and eventually goes to him. He seizes her collar in an iron grip and amid the cries of his progeny drags her from the room They listen, for her remonstrances are not inaudible*)

MRS DARLING Be brave, my dears.

WENDY He is chaining Nana up!

> (*This unfortunately is what he is doing, though we cannot see him. Let us hope that he then retires to his study, looks up the word 'temper' in his Thesaurus, and under the influence of those benign pages becomes a better man. In the meantime the children have been put to bed in unwonted silence, and Mrs Darling lights the night-lights over the beds*)

JOHN (*as the barking below goes on*) She is awfully unhappy.

WENDY That is not Nana's unhappy bark. That is her bark when she smells danger.

MRS DARLING (*remembering that boy*) Danger! Are you sure, Wendy?

WENDY (*the one of the family, for there is one in every family, who can be trusted to know or not to know*) Oh yes.

> (*Her mother looks this way and that from the window*)

JOHN Is anything there?

MRS DARLING All quite quiet and still. Oh, how I wish I was not going out to dinner to-night.

MICHAEL Can anything harm us, mother, after the night-lights are lit? 310

MRS DARLING Nothing, precious. They are the eyes a mother leaves behind her to guard her children.

> (*Nevertheless we may be sure she means to tell Liza, the little maid, to look in on them frequently till she comes home. She goes from bed to bed, after her custom, tucking them in and crooning a lullaby*)

MICHAEL (*drowsily*) Mother, I'm glad of you.

MRS DARLING (*with a last look round, her hand on the switch*) Dear 315 night-lights that protect my sleeping babes, burn clear and steadfast to-night.

> (*The nursery darkens° and she is gone, intentionally leaving the door ajar. Something uncanny is going to happen, we expect, for a quiver has passed through the room, just sufficient to touch the night-lights. They blink three times one after the other and go out, precisely as children (whom familiarity has made them resemble) fall asleep. There is another light in the room now, no larger than Mrs Darling's fist, and in the time we have taken to say this it has been into the drawers and wardrobe and searched pockets, as it darts about looking for a certain shadow. Then the window is blown open, probably by the smallest and therefore most mischievous star, and Peter Pan flies into the room. In so far as he is dressed at all it is in autumn leaves and cobwebs*)

PETER (*in a whisper*) Tinker Bell, Tink, are you there? (*A jug lights up*) Oh, do come out of that jug. (*Tink flashes hither and thither*) Do you know where they put it? (*The answer comes as of a tinkle of* 320 *bells; it is the fairy language. Peter can speak it, but it bores him*) Which big box? This one? But which drawer? Yes, do show me.° (*Tink pops into the drawer where the shadow is, but before Peter can reach it, Wendy moves in her sleep. He flies on to the mantelshelf as a hiding-place. Then, as she has not waked, he flutters over the beds as* 325 *an easy way to observe the occupants, closes the window softly, wafts himself to the drawer and scatters its contents to the floor, as kings on their wedding day toss ha'pence to the crowd. In his joy at finding his shadow he forgets that he has shut up Tink in the drawer. He sits on the floor with the shadow, confident that he and it will join like drops* 330 *of water. Then he tries to stick it on with soap from the bathroom, and*

*this failing also, he subsides dejectedly on the floor. This wakens
Wendy, who sits up, and is pleasantly interested to see a stranger)*

WENDY (*courteously*) Boy, why are you crying?

    (*He jumps up, and crossing to the foot of the bed bows to her in
the fairy way. Wendy, impressed, bows to him from the bed*)

PETER What is your name?   335

WENDY (*well satisfied*) Wendy Moira Angela Darling.° What is yours?

PETER (*finding it lamentably brief*) Peter Pan.°

WENDY Is that all?

PETER (*biting his lip*) Yes.

WENDY (*politely*) I am so sorry.   340

PETER It doesn't matter.

WENDY Where do you live?

PETER Second to the right and then straight on till morning.

WENDY What a funny address!

PETER No, it isn't.   345

WENDY I mean, is that what they put on the letters?

PETER Don't get any letters.

WENDY But your mother gets letters?

PETER Don't have a mother.

WENDY Peter!   350

    (*She leaps out of bed to put her arms round him, but he draws
back; he does not know why, but he knows he must draw back*)

PETER You mustn't touch me.°

WENDY Why?

PETER No one must ever touch me.

WENDY Why?

PETER I don't know.   355

    (*He is never touched by any one in the play*)

WENDY No wonder you were crying.

PETER I wasn't crying. But I can't get my shadow to stick on.

WENDY It has come off! How awful. (*Looking at the spot where he had
lain*) Peter, you have been trying to stick it on with soap!

PETER (*snappily*) Well then?   360

WENDY It must be sewn on.

PETER What is 'sewn'?

WENDY You are dreadfully ignorant.

PETER No, I'm not.

WENDY I will sew it on for you, my little man. But we must have   365
more light. (*She touches something, and to his astonishment the room
is illuminated*) Sit here. I dare say it will hurt a little.

PETER (*a recent remark of hers rankling*) I never cry. (*She seems to attach the shadow. He tests the combination*) It isn't quite itself yet.

WENDY Perhaps I should have ironed it. (*It awakes and is as glad to be back with him as he to have it. He and his shadow dance together. He is showing off now. He crows like a cock. He would fly in order to impress Wendy further if he knew that there is anything unusual in that*) 370

PETER Wendy, look, look; oh the cleverness of me! 375

WENDY You conceit; of course I did nothing!

PETER You did a little.

WENDY (*wounded*) A little! If I am no use I can at least withdraw.
  (*With one haughty leap she is again in bed with the sheet over her face. Popping on to the end of the bed the artful one appeals*)

PETER Wendy, don't withdraw. I can't help crowing, Wendy, when I'm pleased with myself. Wendy, one girl is worth more than twenty boys. 380

WENDY (*peeping over the sheet*) You really think so, Peter?

PETER Yes, I do.

WENDY I think it's perfectly sweet of you, and I shall get up again.
  (*They sit together on the side of the bed*) I shall give you a kiss if you like. 385

PETER Thank you. (*He holds out his hand*)

WENDY (*aghast*) Don't you know what a kiss is?

PETER I shall know when you give it me. (*Not to hurt his feelings she gives him her thimble°*) Now shall I give you a kiss? 390

WENDY (*primly*) If you please. (*He pulls an acorn button off his person and bestows it on her. She is shocked but considerate*) I will wear it on this chain round my neck. Peter, how old are you?

PETER (*blithely*) I don't know, but quite young, Wendy. I ran away the day I was born. 395

WENDY Ran away, why?

PETER Because I heard father and mother talking of what I was to be when I became a man. I want always to be a little boy and to have fun;° so I ran away to Kensington Gardens and lived a long time among the fairies. 400

WENDY (*with great eyes*) You know fairies, Peter!

PETER (*surprised that this should be a recommendation*) Yes, but they are nearly all dead now.° (*Baldly*) You see, Wendy, when the first baby laughed for the first time, the laugh broke into a thousand pieces and they all went skipping about, and that was the beginning of fairies. And now when every new baby is born its first 405

laugh becomes a fairy. So there ought to be one fairy for every boy
or girl.

WENDY (*breathlessly*) Ought to be? Isn't there?

PETER Oh no. Children know such a lot now. Soon they don't believe   410
in fairies, and every time a child says 'I don't believe in fairies' there
is a fairy somewhere that falls down dead. (*He skips about heartlessly*)

WENDY Poor things!

PETER (*to whom this statement recalls a forgotten friend*) I can't think
where she has gone. Tinker Bell, Tink, where are you?   415

WENDY (*thrilling*) Peter, you don't mean to tell me that there is a
fairy in this room!

PETER (*flitting about in search*) She came with me. You don't hear
anything, do you?

WENDY I hear—the only sound I hear is like a tinkle of bells.   420

PETER That is the fairy language. I hear it too.

WENDY It seems to come from over there.

PETER (*with shameless glee*) Wendy, I believe I shut her up in that
drawer!

> (*He releases Tink, who darts about in a fury using language it
> is perhaps as well we don't understand*)

You needn't say that; I'm very sorry, but how could I know you   425
were in the drawer?

WENDY (*her eyes dancing in pursuit of the delicious creature*) Oh, Peter,
if only she would stand still and let me scc her!

PETER (*indifferently*) They hardly ever stand still.

> (*To show that she can do even this Tink pauses between two ticks
> of the cuckoo clock.*)

WENDY I see her, the lovely! where is she now?   430

PETER She is behind the clock. Tink, this lady wishes you were her
fairy. (*The answer comes immediately*)

WENDY What does she say?

PETER She is not very polite. She says you are a great ugly girl, and
that she is my fairy. You know, Tink, you can't be my fairy   435
because I am a gentleman and you are a lady.°

> (*Tink replies*)

WENDY What did she say?

PETER She said 'You silly ass.' She is quite a common girl, you
know. She is called Tinker Bell because she mends the fairy pots
and kettles.   440

> (*They have reached a chair, Wendy in the ordinary way and
> Peter through a hole in the back*)

WENDY Where do you live now?

PETER With the lost boys.

WENDY Who are they?

PETER They are the children who fall out of their prams° when the
nurse is looking the other way. If they are not claimed in seven   445
days they are sent far away to the Never Land. I'm captain.

WENDY What fun it must be.

PETER (*craftily*) Yes, but we are rather lonely. You see, Wendy, we
have no female companionship.

WENDY Are none of the other children girls?   450

PETER Oh no; girls, you know, are much too clever to fall out of their
prams.

WENDY Peter, it is perfectly lovely the way you talk about girls. John
there just despises us.

> (*Peter, for the first time, has a good look at John. He then neatly
> tumbles him out of bed*)

You wicked! you are not captain here. (*She bends over her brother*   455
who is prone on the floor) After all he hasn't wakened, and you
meant to be kind. (*Having now done her duty she forgets John, who
blissfully sleeps on*) Peter, you may give me a kiss.

PETER (*cynically*) I thought you would want it back.

> (*He offers her the thimble*)

WENDY (*artfully*) Oh dear, I didn't mean a kiss, Peter. I meant a   460
thimble.

PETER (*only half placated*) What is that?

WENDY It is like this. (*She leans forward to give a demonstration, but
something prevents the meeting of their faces*)

PETER (*satisfied*) Now shall I give you a thimble?   465

WENDY If you please. (*Before he can even draw near she screams*)

PETER What is it?

WENDY It was exactly as if some one were pulling my hair!

PETER That must have been Tink. I never knew her so naughty
before.   470

> (*Tink speaks. She is in the jug again*)

WENDY What does she say?

PETER She says she will do that every time I give you a thimble.

WENDY But why?

PETER (*equally nonplussed*) Why, Tink? (*He has to translate the
answer*) She said 'You silly ass' again.   475

WENDY She is very impertinent. (*They are sitting on the floor now*)
Peter, why did you come to our nursery window?

PETER To try to hear stories. None of us knows any stories.

WENDY How perfectly awful!

PETER Do you know why swallows build in the eaves of houses? It 480
is to listen to the stories. Wendy, your mother was telling you such
a lovely story.°

WENDY Which story was it?

PETER About the prince, and he couldn't find the lady who wore the
glass slipper. 485

WENDY That was Cinderella. Peter, he found her and they were
happy ever after.

PETER I am glad. (*They have worked their way along the floor close to
each other, but he now jumps up*)

WENDY Where are you going? 490

PETER (*already on his way to the window*) To tell the other boys.

WENDY Don't go, Peter. I know lots of stories. The stories I could
tell to the boys!

PETER (*gleaming*) Come on! We'll fly.

WENDY Fly? You can fly! 495
     (*How he would like to rip those stories out of her; he is dangerous
     now*)

PETER Wendy, come with me.

WENDY Oh dear, I mustn't. Think of mother. Besides, I can't fly.

PETER I'll teach you.

WENDY How lovely to fly!

PETER I'll teach you how to jump on the wind's back and then away 500
we go. Wendy, when you are sleeping in your silly bed you might
be flying about with me, saying funny things to the stars. There
are mermaids, Wendy, with long tails. (*She just succeeds in remaining on the nursery floor*) Wendy, how we should all respect you.
     (*At this she strikes her colours°*)

WENDY Of course it's awfully fas–cin–a–ting! Would you teach John 505
and Michael to fly too?

PETER (*indifferently*) If you like.

WENDY (*playing rum–tum on John*) John, wake up; there is a boy here
who is to teach us to fly.

JOHN Is there? Then I shall get up. (*He raises his head from the floor*) 510
Hullo, I am up!

WENDY Michael, open your eyes. This boy is to teach us to fly.
     (*The sleepers are at once as awake as their father's razor; but
     before a question can be asked Nana's bark is heard*)

JOHN Out with the light, quick, hide!

(*When the maid Liza,° who is so small that when she says she will never see ten again one can scarcely believe her, enters with a firm hand on the troubled Nana's chain the room is in comparative darkness*)

LIZA There, you suspicious brute, they are perfectly safe, aren't they? Every one of the little angels sound asleep in bed. Listen to their gentle breathing. (*Nana's sense of smell here helps to her undoing instead of hindering it. She knows that they are in the room. Michael, who is behind the curtain window, is so encouraged by Liza's last remark that he breathes too loudly. Nana knows that kind of breathing and tries to break from her keeper's control*) No more of it, Nana. (*Wagging a finger at her*) I warn you if you bark again I shall go straight for master and missus and bring them home from the party, and then won't master whip you just! Come along, you naughty dog.

(*The unhappy Nana is led away. The children emerge exulting from their various hiding-places. In their brief absence from the scene strange things have been done to them;° but it is not for us to reveal a mysterious secret of the stage. They look just the same*)

JOHN I say, can you really fly?

PETER Look! (*He is now over their heads*)

WENDY Oh, how sweet!

PETER I'm sweet, oh, I am sweet!

(*It looks so easy that they try it first from the floor and then from their beds, without encouraging results*)

JOHN (*rubbing his knees*) How do you do it?

PETER (*descending*) You just think lovely wonderful thoughts and they lift you up in the air. (*He is off again*)

JOHN You are so nippy at it; couldn't you do it very slowly once? (*Peter does it slowly*) I've got it now, Wendy. (*He tries; no, he has not got it, poor stay-at-home, though he knows the names of all the counties in England and Peter does not know one*)

PETER I must blow the fairy dust on you first. (*Fortunately his garments are smeared with it and he blows some dust on each*) Now, try; try from the bed. Just wriggle your shoulders this way, and then let go.

(*The gallant Michael is the first to let go, and is borne across the room*)

MICHAEL (*with a yell that should have disturbed Liza*) I flewed!

(*John lets go, and meets Wendy near the bathroom door though they had both aimed in an opposite direction*)

WENDY Oh, lovely!

JOHN (*tending to be upside down*) How ripping!

MICHAEL (*playing whack on a chair*) I do like it!

THE THREE Look at me, look at me, look at me!

> (*They are not nearly so elegant in the air as Peter, but their heads have bumped the ceiling, and there is nothing more delicious than that*)

JOHN (*who can even go backwards*) I say, why shouldn't we go out?   545

PETER There are pirates.

JOHN Pirates! (*He grabs his tall Sunday hat*) Let us go at once!

> (*Tink does not like it. She darts at their hair. From down below in the street the lighted window must present an unwonted spectacle; the shadows of children revolving in the room like a merry-go-round. This is perhaps what Mr and Mrs Darling see as they come hurrying home from the party, brought by Nana who, you may be sure, has broken her chain. Peter's accomplice, the little star, has seen them coming, and again the window blows open*)

PETER (*as if he had heard the star whisper 'Cave'°*) Now come!

> (*Breaking the circle he flies out of the window over the trees of the square and over the house-tops, and the others follow like a flight of birds. The broken-hearted father and mother arrive just in time to get a nip from Tink as she too sets out for the Never Land*)

Act 2

THE NEVER LAND

When the blind goes up all is so dark that you scarcely know it has gone up. This is because if you were to see the island bang (as Peter would say) the wonders of it might hurt your eyes. If you all came in spectacles perhaps you could see it bang, but to make a rule of that kind would be a pity. The first thing seen is merely some whitish dots trudging along the sward, and you can guess from their tinkling that they are probably fairies of the commoner sort going home afoot from some party and having a cheery tiff by the way. Then Peter's star wakes up, and in the blink of it, which is much stronger than in our stars, you can make out masses of trees, and you think you see wild beasts stealing past to drink, though what you see is not the beasts themselves but only the shadows of them. They are really out pictorially to greet Peter° in the way they think he would like them to greet him; and for the same reason the mermaids basking in the lagoon beyond the trees are carefully combing their hair; and for the same reason the pirates are landing invisibly from the longboat, invisibly to you but not to the redskins, whom none can see or hear because they are on the war-path. The whole island, in short, which has been having a slack time in Peter's absence, is now in a ferment because the tidings has leaked out that he is on his way back; and everybody and everything know that they will catch it from him if they don't give satisfaction. While you have been told this the sun (another of his servants) has been bestirring himself. Those of you who may have thought it wiser after all to begin this Act in spectacles may now take them off.

What you see is the Never Land. You have often half seen it before, or even three-quarters, after the night-lights were lit, and you might then have beached your coracle° on it if you had not always at the great moment fallen asleep. I dare say you have chucked things on to it, the things you can't find in the morning. In the daytime you think the Never Land is only make-believe, and so it is to the likes of you, but this is the Never Land come true. It is an open-air scene, a forest, with a beautiful lagoon beyond but not really far away, for the Never Land is very compact, not large and sprawly with tedious distances between one adventure and another, but nicely crammed. It is

5

10

15

20

25

30

35

summer time on the trees and on the lagoon but winter on the river, which is not remarkable on Peter's island where all the four seasons may pass while you are filling a jug at the well. Peter's home is at this very spot, but you could not point out the way into it even if you were told which is the entrance, not even if you were told that there   40
are seven of them. You know now because you have just seen one of the lost boys emerge. The holes in these seven great hollow trees are the 'doors' down to Peter's home, and he made seven because, despite his cleverness, he thought seven boys must need seven doors.

The boy who has emerged from his tree is Slightly, who has   45
perhaps been driven from the abode below by companions less musical than himself. Quite possibly a genius, Slightly has with him his home-made whistle to which he capers entrancingly, with no audience save a Never ostrich which is also musically inclined. Unable to imitate Slightly's graces the bird falls so low as to burlesque them   50
and is driven from the entertainment. Other lost boys climb up the trunks or drop from branches, and now we see the six of them, all in the skins of animals they think they have shot, and so round and furry in them that if they fall they roll. Tootles is not the least brave though the most unfortunate of this gallant band. He has been in fewer   55
adventures than any of them because the big things constantly happen while he has stepped round the corner; he will go off, for instance, in some quiet hour to gather firewood, and then when he returns the others will be sweeping up the blood. Instead of souring his nature this has sweetened it and he is the humblest of the band. Nibs is more   60
gay and debonair, Slightly more conceited. Slightly thinks he remembers the days before he was lost, with their manners and customs. Curly is a pickle, and so often has he had to deliver up his person when Peter said sternly, 'Stand forth the one who did this thing,' that now he stands forth whether he has done it or not. The other two are   65
First Twin and Second Twin, who cannot be described because we should probably be describing the wrong one. Hunkering on the ground or peeping out of their holes, the six are not unlike village gossips gathered round the pump.

TOOTLES Has Peter come back yet, Slightly?   70
SLIGHTLY (*with a solemnity that he thinks suits the occasion*) No, Tootles, no.
          (*They are like dogs waiting for the master to tell them that the day has begun*)
CURLY (*as if Peter might be listening*) I do wish he would come back.

TOOTLES I am always afraid of the pirates when Peter is not here to protect us.   75

SLIGHTLY I am not afraid of pirates. Nothing frightens me. But I do wish Peter would come back and tell us whether he has heard anything more about Cinderella.

SECOND TWIN (*with diffidence*) Slightly, I dreamt last night that the prince found Cinderella.   80

FIRST TWIN (*who is intellectually the superior of the two*) Twin, I think you should not have dreamt that, for I didn't, and Peter may say we oughtn't to dream differently, being twins, you know.

TOOTLES I am awfully anxious about Cinderella. You see, not knowing anything about my own mother I am fond of thinking   85
that she was rather like Cinderella.

(*This is received with derision*)

NIBS All I remember about my mother is that she often said to father, 'Oh, how I wish I had a cheque book of my own.'° I don't know what a cheque book is, but I should just love to give my mother one.   90

SLIGHTLY (*as usual*) My mother was fonder of me than your mothers were of you. (*Uproar*) Oh yes, she was. Peter had to make up names for you, but my mother had wrote my name on the pinafore I was lost in. 'Slightly Soiled'; that's my name.

(*They fall upon him pugnaciously; not that they are really worrying about their mothers, who are now as important to them as a piece of string,° but because any excuse is good enough for a shindy. Not for long is he belaboured, for a sound is heard that sends them scurrying down their holes; in a second of time the scene is bereft of human life. What they have heard from near-by is a verse of the dreadful song with which on the Never Land the pirates stealthily trumpet their approach—*)

Yo ho, yo ho, the pirate life,   95
The flag of skull and bones,
A merry hour, a hempen rope,
And hey for Davy Jones!

The pirates appear upon the frozen river dragging a raft, on which reclines among cushions that dark and fearful man, Captain Jas Hook. A more villainous-looking brotherhood of men never hung in a row on Execution Dock.° Here, his great arms bare, pieces of eight° in his ears as ornaments, is the handsome Cecco,° who cut his name on the back of the governor of the prison at Gao.° Heavier in the pull is the gigantic black

*who has had many names since the first one terrified dusky
children on the banks of the Guidjo-mo.° Bill Jukes comes next,
every inch of him tattooed, the same Jukes who got six dozen on
the Walrus from Flint.° Following these are Cookson, said to be
Black Murphy's brother (but this was never proved); and
Gentleman Starkey, once an usher in a school; and Skylights
(Morgan's Skylights);° and Noodler, whose hands are fixed on
backwards; and the spectacled boatswain, Smee,° the only
Nonconformist in Hook's crew; and other ruffians long known
and feared on the Spanish main.*

*Cruellest jewel in that dark setting is Hook himself, cadaverous
and blackavised,° his hair dressed in long curls which look like
black candles about to melt, his eyes blue as the forget-me-not
and of a profound insensibility, save when he claws, at which
time a red spot appears in them. He has an iron hook instead of
a right hand, and it is with this he claws. He is never more
sinister than when he is most polite, and the elegance of his
diction, the distinction of his demeanour, show him one of a
different class from his crew, a solitary among uncultured
companions. This courtliness impresses even his victims on the
high seas, who note that he always says 'Sorry' when prodding
them along the plank.° A man of indomitable courage, the only
thing at which he flinches is the sight of his own blood, which is
thick and of an unusual colour. At his public school° they said
of him that he 'bled yellow.' In dress he apes the dandiacal
associated with Charles II, having heard it said in an earlier
period of his career that he bore a strange resemblance to the
ill-fated Stuarts. A holder of his own contrivance is in his mouth
enabling him to smoke two cigars at once. Those, however, who
have seen him in the flesh, which is an inadequate term for his
earthly tenement, agree that the grimmest part of him is his iron
claw.*

They continue their distasteful singing as they disembark—
> Avast, belay,° yo ho, heave to,
> A-pirating we go,
> And if we're parted by a shot   100
> We're sure to meet below!

*Nibs, the only one of the boys who has not sought safety in his
tree, is seen for a moment near the lagoon, and Starkey's pistol
is at once upraised. The captain twists his hook in him.)*

STARKEY (*abject*) Captain, let go!

HOOK Put back that pistol, first.

STARKEY 'Twas one of those boys you hate; I could have shot him 105
dead.

HOOK Ay, and the sound would have brought Tiger Lily's redskins
on us. Do you want to lose your scalp?

SMEE (*wriggling his cutlass pleasantly*) That is true. Shall I after him,
Captain, and tickle him with Johnny Corkscrew? Johnny is a silent 110
fellow.

HOOK Not now. He is only one, and I want to mischief all the seven.
Scatter and look for them. (*The boatswain whistles his instructions,
and the men disperse on their frightful errand. With none to hear save
Smee, Hook becomes confidential*) Most of all I want their captain, 115
Peter Pan. 'Twas he cut off my arm. I have waited long to shake
his hand with this. (*Luxuriating*) Oh, I'll tear him!

SMEE (*always ready for a chat*) Yet I have oft heard you say your hook
was worth a score of hands, for combing the hair and other homely
uses. 120

HOOK If I was a mother I would pray to have my children born with
this instead of that. (*His left arm creeps nervously behind him. He has
a galling remembrance*) Smee, Pan flung my arm to a crocodile that
happened to be passing by.

SMEE I have often noticed your strange dread of crocodiles. 125

HOOK (*pettishly*) Not of crocodiles but of that one crocodile. (*He lays
bare a lacerated heart*) The brute liked my arm so much, Smee, that
he has followed me ever since, from sea to sea, and from land to
land, licking his lips for the rest of me.

SMEE (*looking for the bright side*) In a way it is a sort of compliment. 130

HOOK (*with dignity*) I want no such compliments; I want Peter Pan,
who first gave the brute his taste for me. Smee, that crocodile
would have had me before now, but by a lucky chance he
swallowed a clock, and it goes tick, tick, tick, tick inside him; and
so before he can reach me I hear the tick and bolt. (*He emits a* 135
hollow rumble) Once I heard it strike six within him.

SMEE (*sombrely*) Some day the clock will run down, and then he'll get
you.

HOOK (*a broken man*) Ay, that is the fear that haunts me. (*He rises*)
Smee, this seat is hot; odds, bobs, hammer and tongs,° I am 140
burning.

(*He has been sitting, he thinks, on one of the island mushrooms,
which are of enormous size. But this is a hand-painted one
placed here in times of danger to conceal a chimney. They*

       remove it, and tell-tale smoke issues; also, alas, the sound of
       children's voices)

SMEE A chimney!

HOOK (*avidly*) Listen! Smee, 'tis plain they live here, beneath the
ground. (*He replaces the mushroom. His brain works tortuously*)

SMEE (*hopefully*) Unrip your plan, Captain.   145

HOOK To return to the boat and cook a large rich cake of jolly
thickness with sugar on it, green sugar. There can be but one room
below, for there is but one chimney. The silly moles had not the
sense to see that they did not need a door apiece. We must leave
the cake on the shore of the mermaids' lagoon. These boys are   150
always swimming about there, trying to catch the mermaids. They
will find the cake and gobble it up, because, having no mother,
they don't know how dangerous 'tis to eat rich damp cake. They
will die!

SMEE (*fascinated*) It is the wickedest, prettiest policy ever I heard of.   155

HOOK (*meaning well*) Shake hands on't.

SMEE No, Captain, no.

       (*He has to link with the hook, but he does not join in the song*)

HOOK   Yo ho, yo ho, when I say 'paw,'
          By fear they're overtook,
          Naught's left upon your bones when you   160
          Have shaken hands with Hook!

       (*Frightened by a tug at his hand, Smee is joining in the chorus*
when another sound stills them both. It is a tick, tick as of a
clock, whose significance Hook is, naturally, the first to recog-
nise. 'The crocodile!' he cries, and totters from the scene. Smee
follows. A huge crocodile, of one thought compact,° passes across,
ticking, and oozes after them. The wood is now so silent that you
may be sure it is full of redskins. Tiger Lily comes first. She is
the belle of the Piccaninny° tribe, whose braves would all have
her to wife, but she wards them off with a hatchet. She puts her
ear to the ground and listens, then beckons, and Great Big Little
Panther° and the tribe are around her, carpeting the ground. Far
away some one treads on a dry leaf)

TIGER LILY Pirates! (*They do not draw their knives; the knives slip into*
their hands) Have um scalps? What you say?

PANTHER Scalp um, oho, velly quick.

THE BRAVES (*in corroboration*) Ugh, ugh, wah.   165

       (*A fire is lit and they dance round and over it till they seem part*
of the leaping flames. Tiger Lily invokes Manitou;° the pipe of

*peace is broken; and they crawl off like a long snake that has
not fed for many moons. Tootles peers after the tail and summons
the other boys, who issue from their holes)*

TOOTLES They are gone.

SLIGHTLY (*almost losing confidence in himself*) I do wish Peter was
here.

FIRST TWIN H'sh! What is that? (*He is gazing at the lagoon and
shrinks back.*) It is wolves, and they are chasing Nibs!   170

    (*The baying wolves are upon them quicker than any boy can
scuttle down his tree*)

NIBS (*falling among his comrades*) Save me, save me!

TOOTLES What should we do?

SECOND TWIN What would Peter do?

SLIGHTLY Peter would look at them through his legs;° let us do what
Peter would do.   175

    (*The boys advance backwards, looking between their legs at the
snarling red-eyed enemy, who trot away foiled*)

FIRST TWIN (*swaggering*) We have saved you, Nibs. Did you see the
pirates?

NIBS (*sitting up, and agreeably aware that the centre of interest is now to
pass to him*) No, but I saw a wonderfuller thing, Twin. (*All mouths
open for the information to be dropped into them*) High over the   180
lagoon I saw the loveliest great white bird. It is flying this way.
(*They search the firmament*)

TOOTLES What kind of a bird, do you think?

NIBS (*awed*) I don't know; but it looked so weary, and as it flies it
moans 'Poor Wendy.'   185

SLIGHTLY (*instantly*) I remember now there are birds called Wen-
dies.

FIRST TWIN (*who has flown to a high branch*) See, it comes, the
Wendy! (*They all see it now*) How white it is! (*A dot of light is
pursuing the bird malignantly*)   190

TOOTLES That is Tinker Bell. Tink is trying to hurt the Wendy. (*He
makes a cup of his hands and calls*) Hullo, Tink! (*A response comes
down in the fairy language*) She says Peter wants us to shoot the
Wendy.

NIBS Let us do what Peter wishes.   195

SLIGHTLY Ay, shoot it; quick, bows and arrows.

TOOTLES (*first with his bow*) Out of the way, Tink; I'll shoot it. (*His
bolt goes home, and Wendy, who has been fluttering among the tree-tops
in her white nightgown, falls straight to earth. No one could be more*

proud than Tootles) I have shot the Wendy; Peter will be so pleased.   200
(*From some tree on which Tink is roosting comes the tinkle we can
now translate, 'You silly ass.' Tootles falters*) Why do you say that?
(*The others feel that he may have blundered, and draw away from
Tootles*)

SLIGHTLY (*examining the fallen one more minutely*) This is no bird; I   205
think it must be a lady.

NIBS (*who would have preferred it to be a bird*) And Tootles has killed
her.

CURLY Now I see, Peter was bringing her to us. (*They wonder for
what object*)   210

SECOND TWIN To take care of us? (*Undoubtedly for some diverting
purpose*)

OMNES° (*though every one of them had wanted to have a shot at her*)
Oh, Tootles!

TOOTLES (*gulping*) I did it. When ladies used to come to me in   215
dreams I said 'Pretty mother,' but when she really came I shot her!
(*He perceives the necessity of a solitary life for him*) Friends,
good-bye.

SEVERAL (*not very enthusiastic*) Don't go.

TOOTLES I must; I am so afraid of Peter.   220
        (*He has gone but a step toward oblivion when he is stopped by
        a crowing as of some victorious cock*)

OMNES Peter!
        (*They make a paling of themselves in front of Wendy as Peter
        skims round the tree-tops and reaches earth*)

PETER Greeting, boys! (*Their silence chafes him*) I am back; why do
you not cheer? Great news, boys, I have brought at last a mother
for us all.

SLIGHTLY (*vaguely*) Ay, ay.   225

PETER She flew this way; have you not seen her?

SECOND TWIN (*as Peter evidently thinks her important*) Oh mournful
day!

TOOTLES (*making a break in the paling*) Peter, I will show her to you.

THE OTHERS (*closing the gap*) No, no.   230

TOOTLES (*majestically*) Stand back all, and let Peter see.
        (*The paling dissolves, and Peter sees Wendy prone on the
        ground*)

PETER Wendy, with an arrow in her heart! (*He plucks it out*) Wendy
is dead.° (*He is not so much pained as puzzled*)

CURLY I thought it was only flowers that die.

PETER Perhaps she is frightened at being dead? (*None of them can say*   235
  as to that) Whose arrow? (*Not one of them looks at Tootles*)
TOOTLES Mine, Peter.
PETER (*raising it as a dagger*) Oh dastard hand!°
TOOTLES (*kneeling and baring his breast*) Strike, Peter; strike true.
PETER (*undergoing a singular experience*) I cannot strike; there is   240
  something stays my hand.
      (*In fact Wendy's arm has risen*)
NIBS 'Tis she, the Wendy lady. See, her arm. (*To help a friend*) I
  think she said 'Poor Tootles.'
PETER (*investigating*) She lives!
SLIGHTLY (*authoritatively*) The Wendy lady lives.   245
      (*The delightful feeling that they have been cleverer than they
      thought comes over them and they applaud themselves*)
PETER (*holding up a button that is attached to her chain*) See, the arrow
  struck against this. It is a kiss I gave her; it has saved her life.
SLIGHTLY I remember kisses; let me see it. (*He takes it in his hand*)
  Ay, that is a kiss.
PETER Wendy, get better quickly and I'll take you to see the   250
  mermaids. She is awfully anxious to see a mermaid.
      (*Tinker Bell, who may have been off visiting her relations,
      returns to the wood and, under the impression that Wendy has
      been got rid of, is whistling as gaily as a canary. She is not
      wholly heartless, but is so small that she has only room for one
      feeling at a time*)
CURLY Listen to Tink rejoicing because she thinks the Wendy is
  dead! (*Regardless of spoiling another's pleasure*) Tink, the Wendy
  lives.
      (*Tink gives expression to fury*)
SECOND TWIN (*tell-tale*) It was she who said that you wanted us to   255
  shoot the Wendy.
PETER She said that? Then listen, Tink, I am your friend no more.
  (*There is a note of acerbity in Tink's reply; it may mean 'Who wants
  you?'*) Begone from me for ever. (*Now it is a very wet tinkle*)
CURLY She is crying.   260
TOOTLES She says she is your fairy.
PETER (*who knows they are not worth worrying about*) Oh well, not for
  ever, but for a whole week.
      (*Tink goes off sulking, no doubt with the intention of giving all
      her friends an entirely false impression of Wendy's appearance*)
  Now what shall we do with Wendy?

CURLY Let us carry her down into the house.   265

SLIGHTLY Ay, that is what one does with ladies.

PETER No, you must not touch her; it wouldn't be sufficiently respectful.

SLIGHTLY That is what I was thinking.

TOOTLES But if she lies there she will die.   270

SLIGHTLY Ay, she will die. It is a pity, but there is no way out.

PETER Yes, there is. Let us build a house around her!° (*Cheers again, meaning that no difficulty baffles Peter*) Leave all to me. Bring the best of what we have. Gut our house. Be sharp. (*They race down their trees*)   275

> (*While Peter is engrossed in measuring Wendy so that the house may fit her, John and Michael, who have probably landed on the island with a bump, wander forward, so draggled and tired that if you were to ask Michael whether he is awake or asleep he would probably answer 'I haven't tried yet.'*)

MICHAEL (*bewildered*) John, John, wake up. Where is Nana, John?

JOHN (*with the help of one eye but not always the same eye*) It is true, we did fly! (*Thankfully*) And here is Peter. Peter, is this the place?

> (*Peter, alas, has already forgotten them, as soon maybe he will forget Wendy. The first thing she should do now that she is here is to sew a handkerchief for him, and knot it as a jog to his memory*)

PETER (*curtly*) Yes.

MICHAEL Where is Wendy? (*Peter points*)   280

JOHN (*who still wears his hat*) She is asleep.

MICHAEL John, let us wake her and get her to make supper for us.

> (*Some of the boys emerge, and he pinches one*)

John, look at them!

PETER (*still house-building*) Curly, see that these boys help in the building of the house.   285

JOHN Build a house?

CURLY For the Wendy.

JOHN (*feeling that there must be some mistake here*) For Wendy? Why, she is only a girl.

CURLY That is why we are her servants.   290

JOHN (*dazed*) Are you Wendy's servants?

PETER Yes, and you also. Away with them. (*In another moment they are woodsmen hacking at trees, with Curly as overseer*) Slightly, fetch a doctor.° (*Slightly reels and goes. He returns professionally in John's hat*) Please, sir, are you a doctor?   295

SLIGHTLY (*trembling in his desire to give satisfaction*) Yes, my little man.

PETER Please, sir, a lady lies very ill.

SLIGHTLY (*taking care not to fall over her*) Tut, tut, where does she lie?   300

PETER In yonder glade. (*It is a variation of a game they play*)

SLIGHTLY I will put a glass thing in her mouth. (*He inserts an imaginary thermometer in Wendy's mouth and gives it a moment to record its verdict. He shakes it and then consults it*)

PETER (*anxiously*) How is she?   305

SLIGHTLY Tut, tut, this has cured her.

PETER (*leaping joyously*) I am glad.

SLIGHTLY I will call again in the evening. Give her beef tea° out of a cup with a spout to it, tut, tut.

> (*The boys are running up with odd articles of furniture*)

PETER (*with an already fading recollection of the Darling nursery*)   310
These are not good enough for Wendy. How I wish I knew the kind of house she would prefer!

FIRST TWIN Peter, she is moving in her sleep.

TOOTLES (*opening Wendy's mouth and gazing down into the depths*) Lovely!   315

PETER Oh, Wendy, if you could sing the kind of house you would like to have.

> (*It is as if she had heard him*)

WENDY (*without opening her eyes*)

> I wish I had a woodland house,
> The littlest ever seen,
> With funny little red walls   320
> And roof of mossy green.

> (*In the time she sings this and two other verses,° such is the urgency of Peter's silent orders that they have knocked down trees, laid a foundation and put up the walls and roof, so that she is now hidden from view. 'Windows,' cries Peter, and Curly rushes them in, 'Roses,' and Tootles arrives breathless with a festoon for the door. Thus springs into existence the most delicious little house for beginners*)

FIRST TWIN I think it is finished.

PETER There is no knocker on the door. (*Tootles hangs up the sole of his shoe*) There is no chimney; we must have a chimney. (*They   325 await his deliberations anxiously*)

JOHN (*unwisely critical*) It certainly does need a chimney.

(He is again wearing his hat, which Peter seizes, knocks the top off it and places on the roof. In the friendliest way smoke begins to come out of the hat)

PETER (*with his hand on the knocker*) All look your best; the first impression is awfully important. (*He knocks, and after a dreadful moment of suspense, in which they cannot help wondering if any one is* 330 *inside, the door opens and who should come out but Wendy! She has evidently been tidying a little. She is quite surprised to find that she has nine children*)

WENDY (*genteelly*) Where am I?

SLIGHTLY Wendy lady, for you we built this house.   335

NIBS and TOOTLES Oh, say you are pleased.

WENDY (*stroking the pretty thing*) Lovely, darling house.

FIRST TWIN And we are your children.

WENDY (*affecting surprise*) Oh?

OMNES (*kneeling, with outstretched arms*) Wendy lady, be our   340 mother!° (*Now that they know it is pretend they acclaim her greedily*)

WENDY (*not to make herself too cheap*) Ought I? Of course it is frightfully fascinating; but you see I am only a little girl; I have no real experience.

OMNES That doesn't matter. What we need is just a nice motherly   345 person.

WENDY Oh dear, I feel that is just exactly what I am.

OMNES It is, it is, we saw it at once.

WENDY Very well then, I will do my best. (*In their glee they go dancing obstreperously round the little house, and she sees she must be* 350 *firm with them as well as kind*) Come inside at once, you naughty children, I am sure your feet are damp. And before I put you to bed I have just time to finish the story of Cinderella.

(They all troop into the enchanting house, whose not least remarkable feature is that it holds them. A vision of Liza passes, not perhaps because she has any right to be there; but she has so few pleasures and is so young that we just let her have a peep at the little house. By and by Peter comes out and marches up and down with drawn sword, for the pirates can be heard carousing far away on the lagoon, and the wolves are on the prowl. The little house, its walls so red and its roof so mossy, looks very cosy and safe, with a bright light showing through the blind, the chimney smoking beautifully, and Peter on guard. On our last sight of him it is so dark that we just guess he is the little figure who has fallen asleep by the door. Dots of light come and go.

They are inquisitive fairies having a look at the house. Any other child in their way they would mischief, but they just tweak Peter's nose and pass on. Fairies, you see, can touch him)

Act 3

THE MERMAIDS' LAGOON°

It is the end of a long playful day on the lagoon. The sun's rays have persuaded him to give them another five minutes, for one more race over the waters before he gathers them up and lets in the moon. There are many mermaids here, going plop-plop, and one might attempt to count the tails did they not flash and disappear so quickly. At times a lovely girl leaps in the air seeking to get rid of her excess of scales, which fall in a silver shower as she shakes them off. From the coral grottoes beneath the lagoon, where are the mermaids' bed-chambers, comes fitful music.

One of the most bewitching of these blue-eyed creatures is lying lazily on Marooners' Rock, combing her long tresses and noting effects in a transparent shell. Peter and his band are in the water unseen behind the rock, whither they have tracked her as if she were a trout, and at a signal ten pairs of arms come whack upon the mermaid to enclose her. Alas, this is only what was meant to happen, for she hears the signal (which is the crow of a cock) and slips through their arms into the water. It has been such a near thing that there are scales on some of their hands. They climb on to the rock crestfallen.

WENDY (*preserving her scales as carefully as if they were rare postage stamps*) I did so want to catch a mermaid.

PETER (*getting rid of his*) It is awfully difficult to catch a mermaid.
> (*The mermaids at times find it just as difficult to catch him, though he sometimes joins them in their one game, which consists in lazily blowing their bubbles into the air and seeing who can catch them. The number of bubbles Peter has flown away with! When the weather grows cold mermaids migrate to the other side of the world, and he once went with a great shoal of them half the way*)

They are such cruel creatures, Wendy, that they try to pull boys and girls like you into the water and drown them.

WENDY (*too guarded by this time to ask what he means precisely by 'like you,' though she is very desirous of knowing*) How hateful!
> (*She is slightly different in appearance now, rather rounder, while John and Michael are not quite so round. The reason is*

*that when new lost children arrive at his underground home
Peter finds new trees for them to go up and down by, and instead
of fitting the tree to them he makes them fit the tree. Sometimes
it can be done by adding or removing garments, but if you are
bumpy, or the tree is an odd shape, he has things done to you
with a roller, and after that you fit.*

*The other boys are now playing King of the Castle, throwing
each other into the water, taking headers and so on; but these
two continue to talk*)

PETER Wendy, this is a fearfully important rock. It is called
Marooners' Rock. Sailors are marooned, you know, when their
captain leaves them on a rock and sails away.

WENDY Leaves them on this little rock to drown?

PETER (*lightly*) Oh, they don't live long. Their hands are tied, so that   30
they can't swim. When the tide is full this rock is covered with
water, and then the sailor drowns.

(*Wendy is uneasy as she surveys the rock, which is the only one
in the lagoon and no larger than a table. Since she last looked
around a threatening change has come over the scene. The sun
has gone, but the moon has not come. What has come is a cold
shiver across the waters which has sent all the wiser mermaids to
their coral recesses. They know that evil is creeping over the
lagoon. Of the boys Peter is of course the first to scent it, and he
has leapt to his feet before the words strike the rock—*

'And if we're parted by a shot
We're sure to meet below.'°

*The games on the rock and around it end so abruptly that several
divers are checked in the air. There they hang waiting for the
word of command from Peter. When they get it they strike the
water simultaneously, and the rock is at once as bare as if
suddenly they had been blown off it. Thus the pirates find it
deserted when their dinghy strikes the rock and is nearly stove in
by the concussion*)

SMEE Luff, you spalpeen,° luff! (*They are Smee and Starkey, with Tiger*   35
Lily, their captive, bound hand and foot) What we have got to do is to
hoist the redskin on to the rock and leave her there to drown.

(*To one of her race this is an end darker than death by fire or
torture, for it is written in the laws of the Piccaninnies that there
is no path through water to the happy hunting ground. Yet her
face is impassive; she is the daughter of a chief and must die as
a chief's daughter; it is enough*)°

STARKEY (*chagrined because she does not mewl*) No mewling. This is your reward for prowling round the ship with a knife in your mouth.   40

TIGER LILY (*stoically*) Enough said.

SMEE (*who would have preferred a farewell palaver*) So that's it! On to the rock with her, mate.

STARKEY (*experiencing for perhaps the last time the stirrings of a man*) Not so rough, Smee; roughish, but not so rough.   45

SMEE (*dragging her on to the rock*) It is the captain's orders.

> (*A stave has in some past time been driven into the rock, probably to mark the burial place of hidden treasure, and to this they moor the dinghy*)

WENDY (*in the water*) Poor Tiger Lily!

STARKEY What was that? (*The children bob.*)

PETER (*who can imitate the captain's voice so perfectly that even the author has a dizzy feeling that at times he was really Hook°*) Ahoy   50
there, you lubbers!

STARKEY It is the captain; he must be swimming out to us.

SMEE (*calling*) We have put the redskin on the rock, Captain.

PETER Set her free.

SMEE But, Captain——   55

PETER Cut her bonds, or I'll plunge my hook in you.

SMEE This is queer!

STARKEY (*unmanned*) Let us follow the captain's orders.

> (*They undo the thongs and Tiger Lily slides between their legs into the lagoon, forgetting in her haste to utter her war-cry, but Peter utters it for her, so naturally that even the lost boys are deceived. It is at this moment that the voice of the true Hook is heard*)

HOOK Boat ahoy!

SMEE (*relieved*) It is the captain.   60

> (*Hook is swimming, and they help him to scale the rock. He is in gloomy mood*)

STARKEY Captain, is all well?

SMEE He sighs.

STARKEY He sighs again.

SMEE (*counting*) And yet a third time he sighs. (*With foreboding*) What's up, Captain?   65

HOOK (*who has perhaps found the large rich damp cake untouched*) The game is up. Those boys have found a mother!

STARKEY Oh evil day!

SMEE What is a mother?°

WENDY (*horrified*) He doesn't know!   70

HOOK (*sharply*) What was that?
     (*Peter makes the splash of a mermaid's tail*)

STARKEY One of them mermaids.

HOOK Dost not know, Smee? A mother is—— (*He finds it more difficult to explain than he had expected, and looks about him for an illustration. He finds one in a great bird which drifts past in a nest as* 75 *large as the roomiest basin*) There is a lesson in mothers for you! The nest must have fallen into the water, but would the bird desert her eggs? (*Peter, who is now more or less off his head, makes the sound of a bird answering in the negative. The nest is borne out of sight*) 80

STARKEY Maybe she is hanging about here to protect Peter?
     (*Hook's face clouds still further and Peter just manages not to call out that he needs no protection*)

SMEE (*not usually a man of ideas*) Captain, could we not kidnap these boys' mother and make her our mother?

HOOK Obesity and bunions, 'tis a princely scheme. We will seize the children, make them walk the plank, and Wendy shall be our 85 mother!

WENDY Never! (*Another splash from Peter*)

HOOK What say you, bullies?°

SMEE There is my hand on't.

STARKEY And mine.   90

HOOK And there is my hook. Swear. (*All swear*). But I had forgot; where is the redskin?

SMEE (*shaken*) That is all right, Captain; we let her go.

HOOK (*terrible*) Let her go?

SMEE 'Twas your own orders, Captain.   95

STARKEY (*whimpering*) You called over the water to us to let her go.

HOOK Brimstone and gall, what cozening is here? (*Disturbed by their faithful faces*) Lads, I gave no such order.

SMEE 'Tis passing queer.

HOOK (*addressing the immensities*) Spirit that haunts this dark lagoon 100 to-night, dost hear me?

PETER (*in the same voice*) Odds, bobs, hammer and tongs, I hear you.

HOOK (*gripping the stave for support*) Who are you, stranger, speak.

PETER (*who is only too ready to speak*) I am Jas Hook, Captain of the *Jolly Roger*.   105

HOOK (*now white to the gills*) No, no, you are not.

PETER Brimstone and gall, say that again and I'll cast anchor in you.

HOOK If you are Hook, come tell me, who am I?

PETER A codfish, only a codfish.

HOOK (*aghast*) A codfish?   110

SMEE (*drawing back from him*) Have we been captained all this time by a codfish?

STARKEY It's lowering to our pride.

HOOK (*feeling that his ego is slipping from him*) Don't desert me, bullies.   115

PETER (*top-heavy*) Paw, fish, paw!

    (*There is a touch of the feminine in Hook, as in all the greatest pirates, and it prompts him to try the guessing game*)

HOOK Have you another name?

PETER (*falling to the lure*) Ay, ay.

HOOK (*thirstily*) Vegetable?

PETER No.   120

HOOK Mineral?

PETER No.

HOOK Animal?

PETER (*after a hurried consultation with Tootles*) Yes.

HOOK Man?   125

PETER (*with scorn*) No.

HOOK Boy?

PETER Yes.

HOOK Ordinary boy?

PETER No!   130

HOOK Wonderful boy?

PETER (*to Wendy's distress*) Yes!

HOOK Are you in England?

PETER No.

HOOK Are you here?   135

PETER Yes.

HOOK (*beaten, though he feels he has very nearly got it*) Smee, you ask him some questions.

SMEE (*rummaging his brains*) I can't think of a thing.

PETER Can't guess, can't guess! (*Foundering in his cockiness*) Do you 140 give it up?

HOOK (*eagerly*) Yes.

PETER All of you?

SMEE and STARKEY Yes.

PETER (*crowing*) Well, then, I am Peter Pan!   145

(*Now they have him*)

HOOK Pan! Into the water, Smee. Starkey, mind the boat. Take him dead or alive!

PETER (*who still has all his baby teeth*) Boys, lam into the pirates!

(*For a moment the only two we can see are in the dinghy, where John throws himself on Starkey. Starkey wriggles into the lagoon and John leaps so quickly after him that he reaches it first. The impression left on Starkey is that he is being attacked by the Twins. The water becomes stained. The dinghy drifts away. Here and there a head shows in the water, and once it is the head of the crocodile. In the growing gloom some strike at their friends, Slightly getting Tootles in the fourth rib while he himself is pinked° by Curly. It looks as if the boys were getting the worse of it, which is perhaps just as well at this point, because Peter, who will be the determining factor in the end, has a perplexing way of changing sides if he is winning too easily. Hook's iron claw makes a circle of black water round him from which opponents flee like fishes. There is only one prepared to enter that dreadful circle. His name is Pan. Strangely, it is not in the water that they meet. Hook has risen to the rock to breathe, and at the same moment Peter scales it on the opposite side. The rock is now wet and as slippery as a ball, and they have to crawl rather than climb. Suddenly they are face to face. Peter gnashes his pretty teeth with joy, and is gathering himself for the spring when he sees he is higher up the rock than his foe. Courteously he waits; Hook sees his intention, and taking advantage of it claws twice. Peter is untouched, but unfairness is what he never can get used to,° and in his bewilderment he rolls off the rock. The crocodile, whose tick has been drowned in the strife, rears its jaws, and Hook, who has almost stepped into them, is pursued by it to land. All is quiet on the lagoon now, not a sound save little waves nibbling at the rock, which is smaller than when we last looked at it. Two boys appear with the dinghy, and the others despite their wounds climb into it. They send the cry 'Peter—Wendy' across the waters, but no answer comes*)

NIBS They must be swimming home.

JOHN Or flying.   150

FIRST TWIN Yes, that is it. Let us be off and call to them as we go.

(*The dinghy disappears with its load, whose hearts would sink it if they knew of the peril of Wendy and her captain. From near*

*and far away come the cries 'Peter—Wendy' till we no longer
hear them.*

*Two small figures are now on the rock, but they have fainted.
A mermaid who has dared to come back in the stillness stretches
up her arms and is slowly pulling Wendy into the water to drown
her. Wendy starts up just in time)*

WENDY Peter!

(He rouses himself and looks around him)

Where are we, Peter?

PETER We are on the rock, but it is getting smaller. Soon the water
will be over it. Listen!   155

(They can hear the wash of the relentless little waves)

WENDY We must go.

PETER Yes.

WENDY Shall we swim or fly?

PETER Wendy, do you think you could swim or fly to the island
without me?   160

WENDY You know I couldn't, Peter; I am just a beginner.

PETER Hook wounded me twice. *(He believes it; he is so good at
pretend that he feels the pain, his arms hang limp)* I can neither swim
nor fly.   165

WENDY Do you mean we shall both be drowned?

PETER Look how the water is rising!

*(They cover their faces with their hands. Something touches
Wendy as lightly as a kiss)*

PETER *(with little interest)* It must be the tail of the kite we made for
Michael; you remember it tore itself out of his hands and floated
away. *(He looks up and sees the kite sailing overhead)* The kite! Why   170
shouldn't it carry you? *(He grips the tail and pulls, and the kite
responds)*

WENDY Both of us!

PETER It can't lift two. Michael and Curly tried.

*(She knows very well that if it can lift her it can lift him also,
for she has been told by the boys as a deadly secret that one of
the queer things about him is that he is no weight at all. But it
is a forbidden subject)*

WENDY I won't go without you. Let us draw lots which is to stay
behind.   175

PETER And you a lady, never! *(The tail is in her hands, and the kite is
tugging hard. She holds out her mouth to Peter, but he knows they
cannot do that)* Ready, Wendy!

(*The kite draws her out of sight across the lagoon.*

The waters are lapping over the rock now, and Peter knows that it will soon be submerged. Pale rays of light mingle with the moving clouds, and from the coral grottoes is to be heard a sound, at once the most musical and the most melancholy in the Never Land, the mermaids calling to the moon to rise. Peter is afraid at last, and a tremor runs through him, like a shudder passing over the lagoon; but on the lagoon one shudder follows another till there are hundreds of them, and he feels just the one)

PETER (*with a drum beating in his breast as if he were a real boy at last*)
To die will be an awfully big adventure.°   180

(*The blind rises again, and the lagoon is now suffused with moonlight. He is on the rock still, but the water is over his feet. The nest is borne nearer, and the bird, after cooing a message to him, leaves it and wings her way upwards.° Peter, who knows the bird language, slips into the nest, first removing the two eggs and placing them in Starkey's hat, which has been left on the stave. The hat drifts away from the rock, but he uses the stave as a mast. The wind is driving him toward the open sea. He takes off his shirt, which he had forgotten to remove while bathing, and unfurls it as a sail. His vessel tacks, and he passes from sight, naked and victorious. The bird returns and sits on the hat*)

Act 4

THE HOME UNDER THE GROUND

We see simultaneously the home under the ground with the children in it and the wood above ground with the redskins on it. Below, the children are gobbling their evening meal; above, the redskins are squatting in their blankets near the little house guarding the children from the pirates. The only way of communicating between these two parties is by means of the hollow trees.

The home has an earthen floor, which is handy for digging in if you want to go fishing; and owing to there being so many entrances there is not much wall space. The table at which the lost ones are sitting is a board on top of a live tree trunk, which has been cut flat but has such growing pains that the board rises as they eat, and they have sometimes to pause in their meals to cut a bit more off the trunk. Their seats are pumpkins or the large gay mushrooms of which we have seen an imitation one concealing the chimney. There is an enormous fireplace which is in almost any part of the room where you care to light it, and across this Wendy has stretched strings, made of fibre, from which she hangs her washing. There are also various tomfool things in the room of no use whatever.

Michael's basket bed is nailed high up on the wall as if to protect him from the cat, but there is no indication at present of where the others sleep. At the back between two of the tree trunks is a grindstone, and near it is a lovely hole, the size of a band-box, with a gay curtain drawn across so that you cannot see what is inside. This is Tink's withdrawing-room and bedchamber, and it is just as well that you cannot see inside, for it is so exquisite in its decoration and in the personal apparel spread out on the bed that you could scarcely resist making off with something. Tink is within at present, as one can guess from a glow showing through the chinks. It is her own glow, for though she has a chandelier for the look of the thing, of course she lights her residence herself. She is probably wasting valuable time just now wondering whether to put on the smoky blue or the apple-blossom.

All the boys except Peter are here, and Wendy has the head of the table, smiling complacently at their captivating ways, but doing her best at the same time to see that they keep the rules about hands-off-

the-table, no-two-to-speak-at-once, and so on. She is wearing romantic woodland garments, sewn by herself, with red berries in her hair
which go charmingly with her complexion, as she knows; indeed she
searched for red berries the morning after she reached the island. The
boys are in picturesque attire of her contrivance, and if these don't   40
always fit well the fault is not hers but the wearers', for they
constantly put on each other's things when they put on anything at
all. Michael is in his cradle on the wall. First Twin is apart on a high
stool and wears a dunce's cap, another invention of Wendy's, but not
wholly successful because everybody wants to be dunce.   45

It is a pretend meal this evening, with nothing whatever on the
table, not a mug, nor a crust, nor a spoon. They often have these
suppers and like them on occasions as well as the other kind, which
consist chiefly of bread-fruit, tappa rolls, yams, mammee apples and
banana splash, washed down with calabashes of poe-poe.° The   50
pretend meals are not Wendy's idea; indeed she was rather startled to
find, on arriving, that Peter knew of no other kind, and she is not
absolutely certain even now that he does eat the other kind, though
no one appears to do it more heartily. He insists that the pretend
meals should be partaken of with gusto,° and we see his band doing   55
their best to obey orders.

WENDY (*her fingers to her ears, for their chatter and clatter are deafening*)
    Si-lence! Is your mug empty, Slightly?
SLIGHTLY (*who would not say this if he had a mug*) Not quite empty,
    thank you.   60
NIBS Mummy, he has not even begun to drink his poe-poe.
SLIGHTLY (*seizing his chance, for this is tale-bearing*) I complain of Nibs!
        (*John holds up his hand*)
WENDY Well, John?
JOHN May I sit in Peter's chair as he is not here?
WENDY In your father's chair? Certainly not.   65
JOHN He is not really our father. He did not even know how to be
    a father till I showed him.
        (*This is insubordination*)
SECOND TWIN I complain of John!
        (*The gentle Tootles raises his hand*)
TOOTLES (*who has the poorest opinion of himself*) I don't suppose
    Michael would let me be baby?   70
MICHAEL No, I won't.
TOOTLES May I be dunce?

FIRST TWIN (*from his perch*) No. It's awfully difficult to be dunce.

TOOTLES As I can't be anything important would any of you like to see me do a trick?   75

OMNES No.

TOOTLES (*subsiding*) I hadn't really any hope.

> (*The tale-telling breaks out again*)

NIBS Slightly is coughing on the table.

CURLY The twins began with tappa rolls.

SLIGHTLY I complain of Nibs!   80

NIBS I complain of Slightly!

WENDY Oh dear, I am sure I sometimes think that spinsters are to be envied.

MICHAEL Wendy, I am too big for a cradle.

WENDY You are the littlest, and a cradle is such a nice homely thing   85
to have about a house. You others can clear away now. (*She sits down on a pumpkin near the fire to her usual evening occupation, darning*) Every heel with a hole in it!

> (*The boys clear away with dispatch, washing dishes they don't have in a non-existent sink and stowing them in a cupboard that isn't there. Instead of sawing the table-leg to-night they crush it into the ground like a concertina, and are now ready for play, in which they indulge hilariously.*
>
> *A movement of the Indians draws our attention to the scene above. Hitherto, with the exception of Panther, who sits on guard on top of the little house, they have been hunkering in their blankets, mute but picturesque; now all rise and prostrate themselves before the majestic figure of Peter, who approaches through the forest carrying a gun and game bag. It is not exactly a gun. He often wanders away alone with this weapon, and when he comes back you are never absolutely certain whether he has had an adventure or not. He may have forgotten it so completely that he says nothing about it; and then when you go out you find the body. On the other hand he may say a great deal about it, and yet you never find the body. Sometimes he comes home with his face scratched, and tells Wendy, as a thing of no importance, that he got these marks from the little people for cheeking them at a fairy wedding, and she listens politely, but she is never quite sure, you know; indeed the only one who is sure about anything on the island is Peter*)

PETER The Great White Father is glad to see the Piccaninny braves protecting his wigwam from the pirates.   90

TIGER LILY The Great White Father save me from pirates. Me his velly nice friend now; no let pirates hurt him.

BRAVES Ugh, ugh, wah!

TIGER LILY Tiger Lily has spoken.

PANTHER Loola, loola! Great Big Little Panther has spoken. 95

PETER It is well. The Great White Father has spoken.

> (*This has a note of finality about it, with the implied 'And now shut up,' which is never far from the courteous receptions of well-meaning inferiors by born leaders of men. He descends his tree, not unheard by Wendy*)

WENDY Children, I hear your father's step. He likes you to meet him at the door. (*Peter scatters pretend nuts among them and watches sharply to see that they crunch with relish*) Peter, you just spoil them, you know!

JOHN (*who would be incredulous if he dare*) Any sport, Peter? 100

PETER Two tigers and a pirate.

JOHN (*boldly*) Where are their heads?

PETER (*contracting his little brows*) In the bag.

JOHN (*No, he doesn't say it. He backs away*)

WENDY (*peeping into the bag*) They are beauties! (*She has learned her 105 lesson*)

FIRST TWIN Mummy, we all want to dance.

WENDY The mother of such an armful dance!

SLIGHTLY As it is Saturday night?

> (*They have long lost count of the days, but always if they want to do anything special they say this is Saturday night, and then they do it*)

WENDY Of course it is Saturday night, Peter? (*He shrugs an indiffer- 110 ent assent*) On with your nighties first.

> (*They disappear into various recesses, and Peter and Wendy with her darning are left by the fire to dodder parentally. She emphasises it by humming a verse of 'John Anderson my Jo,'° which has not the desired effect on Peter. She is too loving to be ignorant that he is not loving enough, and she hesitates like one who knows the answer to her question*)

What is wrong, Peter?

PETER (*scared*) It is only pretend, isn't it, that I am their father?°

WENDY (*drooping*) Oh yes.

> (*His sigh of relief is without consideration for her feelings*)

But they are ours, Peter, yours and mine. 115

PETER (*determined to get at facts, the only things that puzzle him*) But not really?

WENDY Not if you don't wish it.

PETER I don't.

WENDY (*knowing she ought not to probe but driven to it by something* 120
within) What are your exact feelings for me, Peter?

PETER (*in the class-room*) Those of a devoted son, Wendy.

WENDY (*turning away*) I thought so.

PETER You are so puzzling. Tiger Lily is just the same; there is
something or other she wants to be to me, but she says it is not 125
my mother.

WENDY (*with spirit*) No, indeed it isn't.

PETER Then what is it?

WENDY It isn't for a lady to tell.

> (*The curtain of the fairy chamber opens slightly, and Tink, who
> has doubtless been eavesdropping, tinkles a laugh of scorn*)

PETER (*badgered*) I suppose she means that she wants to be my 130
mother.

> (*Tink's comment is 'You silly ass.'*)

WENDY (*who has picked up some of the fairy words*) I almost agree with
her!

> (*The arrival of the boys in their nightgowns turns Wendy's mind
> to practical matters, for the children have to be arranged in line
> and passed or not passed for cleanliness. Slightly is the worst. At
> last we see how they sleep, for in a babel the great bed which
> stands on end by day against the wall is unloosed from custody
> and lowered to the floor. Though large, it is a tight fit for so
> many boys, and Wendy has made a rule that there is to be no
> turning round until one gives the signal, when all turn at once.*
>
> *First Twin is the best dancer and performs mightily on the bed
> and in it and out of it and over it to an accompaniment of pillow
> fights by the less agile; and then there is a rush at Wendy*)

NIBS Now the story you promised to tell us as soon as we were in
bed! 135

WENDY (*severely*) As far as I can see you are not in bed yet.

> (*They scramble into the bed, and the effect is as of a boxful of
> sardines*)

WENDY (*drawing up her stool*) Well, there was once a gentleman——

CURLY I wish he had been a lady.

NIBS I wish he had been a white rat.

WENDY Quiet! There was a lady also. The gentleman's name was Mr 140
Darling and the lady's name was Mrs Darling——

JOHN I knew them!

MICHAEL (*who has been allowed to join the circle*) I think I knew them.

WENDY They were married, you know; and what do you think they had?   145

NIBS White rats?

WENDY No, they had three descendants. White rats are descendants also. Almost everything is a descendant. Now these three children had a faithful nurse called Nana.

MICHAEL (*alas*) What a funny name!   150

WENDY But Mr Darling—(*faltering*) or was it Mrs Darling?—was angry with her and chained her up in the yard; so all the children flew away. They flew away to the Never Land, where the lost boys are.

CURLY I just thought they did; I don't know how it is, but I just   155
thought they did.

TOOTLES Oh, Wendy, was one of the lost boys called Tootles?

WENDY Yes, he was.

TOOTLES (*dazzled*) Am I in a story? Nibs, I am in a story!

PETER (*who is by the fire making Pan's pipes with his knife, and is*   160
determined that Wendy shall have fair play, however beastly a story
he may think it) A little less noise there.

WENDY (*melting over the beauty of her present performance, but without*
any real qualms) Now I want you to consider the feelings of the
unhappy parents with all their children flown away. Think, oh   165
think, of the empty beds. (*The heartless ones° think of them with*
glee)

FIRST TWIN (*cheerfully*) It's awfully sad.

WENDY But our heroine knew that her mother would always leave
the window open for her progeny to fly back by; so they stayed   170
away for years and had a lovely time.

(*Peter is interested at last*)

FIRST TWIN Did they ever go back?

WENDY (*comfortably*) Let us now take a peep into the future. Years
have rolled by, and who is this elegant lady of uncertain age
alighting at London station?   175

(*The tension is unbearable*)

NIBS Oh, Wendy, who is she?

WENDY (*swelling*) Can it be—yes—no—yes, it is the fair Wendy!

TOOTLES I am glad.

WENDY Who are the two noble portly figures accompanying her?
Can they be John and Michael? They are. (*Pride of Michael*) 'See,   180
dear brothers,' says Wendy, pointing upward, 'there is the window

standing open.' So up they flew to their loving parents, and pen cannot inscribe the happy scene over which we draw a veil. (*Her triumph is spoilt by a groan from Peter and she hurries to him*) Peter, what is it? (*Thinking he is ill, and looking lower than his chest*) Where is it? 185

PETER It isn't that kind of pain. Wendy, you are wrong about mothers. I thought like you about the window, so I stayed away for moons and moons, and then I flew back,° but the window was barred, for my mother had forgotten all about me and there was another little boy sleeping in my bed. 190

　　(*This is a general damper*)

JOHN Wendy, let us go back!

WENDY Are you sure mothers are like that?

PETER Yes.

WENDY John, Michael! (*She clasps them to her*) 195

FIRST TWIN (*alarmed*) You are not to leave us, Wendy?

WENDY I must.

NIBS Not to-night?

WENDY At once. Perhaps mother is in half-mourning° by this time! Peter, will you make the necessary arrangements? 200

　　(*She asks it in the steely tones women adopt when they are prepared secretly for opposition*)

PETER (*coolly*) If you wish it.

　　(*He ascends his tree to give the redskins their instructions. The lost boys gather threateningly round Wendy*)

CURLY We won't let you go!

WENDY (*with one of those inspirations women have, in an emergency, to make use of some male who need otherwise have no hope*) Tootles, I appeal to you. 205

TOOTLES (*leaping to his death if necessary*) I am just Tootles and nobody minds me, but the first who does not behave to Wendy I will blood him severely. (*Peter returns*)

PETER (*with awful serenity*) Wendy, I told the braves to guide you through the wood as flying tires you so. Then Tinker Bell will take you across the sea. (*A shrill tinkle from the boudoir probably means 'and drop her into it.'*) 210

NIBS (*fingering the curtain which he is not allowed to open*) Tink, you are to get up and take Wendy on a journey. (*Star-eyed*) She says she won't! 215

PETER (*taking a step toward that chamber*) If you don't get up, Tink, and dress at once—— She is getting up!

WENDY (*quivering now that the time to depart has come*) Dear ones, if
you will all come with me I feel almost sure I can get my father
and mother to adopt you.   220

(*There is joy at this, not that they want parents, but novelty is
their religion*)

NIBS But won't they think us rather a handful?

WENDY (*a swift reckoner*) Oh no, it will only mean having a few beds
in the drawing-room; they can be hidden behind screens on first
Thursdays.°

(*Everything depends on Peter*)

OMNES Peter, may we go?   225

PETER (*carelessly through the pipes to which he is giving a finishing touch*)
All right.

(*They scurry off to dress for the adventure*)

WENDY (*insinuatingly*) Get your clothes, Peter.

PETER (*skipping about and playing fairy music on his pipes, the only
music he knows*) I am not going with you, Wendy.   230

WENDY Yes, Peter!

PETER No.

(*The lost ones run back gaily, each carrying a stick with a bundle
on the end of it*)

WENDY Peter isn't coming!

(*All the faces go blank*)

JOHN (*even John*) Peter not coming!

TOOTLES (*overthrown*) Why, Peter?   235

PETER (*his pipes more riotous than ever*) I just want always to be a little
boy and to have fun.

(*There is a general fear that they are perhaps making the
mistake of their lives*)

Now then, no fuss, no blubbering. (*With dreadful cynicism*) I hope
you will like your mothers!° Are you ready, Tink! Then lead the
way.

(*Tink darts up any tree, but she is the only one. The air above is
suddenly rent with shrieks and the clash of steel. Though they cannot
see, the boys know that Hook and his crew are upon the Indians.
Mouths open and remain open, all in mute appeal° to Peter. He is
the only boy on his feet now, a sword in his hand, the same he slew
Barbicue° with; and in his eye is the lust of battle.*

*We can watch the carnage that is invisible to the children.
Hook has basely broken the two laws of Indian warfare, which
are that the redskins should attack first, and that it should be at*

dawn. They have known the pirate whereabouts since, early in the night, one of Smee's fingers crackled. The brushwood has closed behind their scouts as silently as the sand on the mole; for hours they have imitated the lonely call of the coyote; no stratagem has been overlooked, but alas, they have trusted to the pale-face's honour to await an attack at dawn, when his courage is known to be at the lowest ebb. Hook falls upon them pell-mell, and one cannot withhold a reluctant admiration for the wit that conceived so subtle a scheme and the fell genius with which it is carried out. If the braves would rise quickly they might still have time to scalp, but this they are forbidden to do by the traditions of their race, for it is written that they must never express surprise in the presence of the pale-face. For a brief space they remain recumbent, not a muscle moving, as if the foe were here by invitation. Thus perish the flower of the Piccaninnies, though not unavenged, for with Lean Wolf fall Alf Mason and Canary Robb, while other pirates to bite dust are Black Gilmour and Alan Herb, that same Herb who is still remembered at Manaos for playing skittles with the mate of the Switch *for each other's heads. Chay Turley,° who laughed with the wrong side of his mouth (having no other), is tomahawked by Panther, who eventually cuts a way through the shambles with Tiger Lily and a remnant of the tribe.*

This onslaught passes and is gone like a fierce wind. The victors wipe their cutlasses, and squint, ferret-eyed, at their leader. He remains, as ever, aloof in spirit and in substance. He signs to them to descend the trees, for he is convinced that Pan is down there, and though he has smoked the bees it is the honey he wants. There is something in Peter that at all times goads this extraordinary man to frenzy; it is the boy's cockiness, which disturbs Hook like an insect. If you have seen a lion in a cage futilely pursuing a sparrow you will know what is meant. The pirates try to do their captain's bidding, but the apertures prove to be not wide enough for them; he cannot even ram them down with a pole. He steals to the mouth of a tree and listens)   240

PETER (*prematurely*) All is over!

WENDY But who has won?

PETER Hst! If the Indians have won they will beat the tom-tom; it is always their signal of victory.

(*Hook licks his lips at this and signs to Smee, who is sitting on
it, to hold up the tom-tom. He beats upon it with his claw, and*   245
listens for results)

TOOTLES The tom-tom!

PETER (*sheathing his sword*) An Indian victory!

    (*The cheers from below are music to the black hearts above*)

You are quite safe now, Wendy. Boys, good-bye. (*He resumes his
pipes*)   250

WENDY Peter, you will remember about changing your flannels,°
won't you?

PETER Oh, all right!

WENDY And this is your medicine.

    (*She puts something into a shell and leaves it on a ledge between
two of the trees. It is only water, but she measures it out in drops*)

PETER I won't forget.   255

WENDY Peter, what are you to me?

PETER (*through the pipes*) Your son, Wendy.

WENDY Oh, good-bye!

    (*The travellers start upon their journey, little witting that Hook
has issued his silent orders: a man to the mouth of each tree, and
a row of men between the trees and the little house. As the
children squeeze up they are plucked from their trees, trussed,
thrown like bales of cotton from one pirate to another, and so
piled up in the little house. The only one treated differently is
Wendy, whom Hook escorts to the house on his arm with hateful
politeness. He signs to his dogs to be gone, and they depart
through the wood, carrying the little house with its strange
merchandise and singing their ribald song. The chimney of the
little house emits a jet of smoke fitfully, as if not sure what it
ought to do just now.*

    *Hook and Peter are now, as it were, alone on the island.
Below, Peter is on the bed, asleep, no weapon near him; above,
Hook, armed to the teeth, is searching noiselessly for some tree
down which the nastiness of him can descend. Don't be too much
alarmed by this; it is precisely the situation Peter would have
chosen; indeed if the whole thing were pretend—. One of his
arms droops over the edge of the bed, a leg is arched, and the
mouth is not so tightly closed that we cannot see the little pearls.
He is dreaming, and in his dreams he is always in pursuit of a
boy who was never here, nor anywhere: the only boy who could
beat him.*

Hook finds the tree. It is the one set apart for Slightly who being addicted when hot to the drinking of water has swelled in consequence and surreptitiously scooped his tree for easier descent and egress. Down this the pirate wriggles a passage. In the aperture below his face emerges and goes green as he glares at the sleeping child. Does no feeling of compassion disturb his sombre breast? The man is not wholly evil: he has a Thesaurus in his cabin, and is no mean performer on the flute. What really warps him is a presentiment that he is about to fail. This is not unconnected with a beatific smile on the face of the sleeper, whom he cannot reach owing to being stuck at the foot of the tree. He, however, sees the medicine shell within easy reach, and to Wendy's draught he adds from a bottle five drops of poison distilled when he was weeping from the red in his eye. The expression on Peter's face merely implies that something heavenly is going on. Hook worms his way upwards, and winding his cloak around him, as if to conceal his person from the night of which he is the blackest part, he stalks moodily toward the lagoon.

A dot of light flashes past him and darts down the nearest tree, looking for Peter, only for Peter, quite indifferent about the others when she finds him safe)

PETER (*stirring*) Who is that? (*Tink has to tell her tale, in one long ungrammatical sentence*) The redskins were defeated? Wendy and   260
the boys captured by the pirates! I'll rescue her, I'll rescue her! (*He leaps first at his dagger, and then at his grindstone, to sharpen it. Tink alights near the shell, and rings out a warning cry*) Oh, that is just my medicine. Poisoned? Who could have poisoned it? I promised Wendy to take it, and I will as soon as I have sharpened my dagger.   265
(*Tink, who sees its red colour and remembers the red in the pirate's eye, nobly swallows the draught as Peter's hand is reaching for it*) Why, Tink, you have drunk my medicine! (*She flutters strangely about the room, answering him now in a very thin tinkle*) It was poisoned and you drank it to save my life! Tink, dear Tink, are you dying? (*He   270
has never called her dear Tink before, and for a moment she is gay; she alights on his shoulder, gives his chin a loving bite, whispers 'You silly ass,' and falls on her tiny bed. The boudoir, which is lit by her, flickers ominously. He is on his knees by the opening*)

Her light is growing faint, and if it goes out, that means she is   275
dead! Her voice is so low I can scarcely tell what she is saying. She says—she says she thinks she could get well again if children believed in fairies! (*He rises and throws out his arms he knows not to*

whom, perhaps to the boys and girls of whom he is not one) Do you
believe in fairies? Say quick that you believe! If you believe, clap   280
your hands!° (*Many clap, some don't, a few hiss. Then perhaps there
is a rush of Nanas to the nurseries to see what on earth is happening.
But Tink is saved*) Oh, thank you, thank you, thank you! And now
to rescue Wendy!

> (*Tink is already as merry and impudent as a grig,° with not a
> thought for those who have saved her. Peter ascends his tree as
> if he were shot up it. What he is feeling is 'Hook or me this time!'
> He is frightfully happy. He soon hits the trail, for the smoke
> from the little house has lingered here and there to guide him.
> He takes wing*)

Act 5

Scene 1

THE PIRATE SHIP

THE stage directions for the opening of this scene are as follows:—1
Circuit Amber checked to 80. Battens, all Amber checked, 3 ship's
lanterns alight, Arcs: prompt perch 1. Open dark Amber flooding
back, O.P. perch open dark Amber flooding upper deck. Arc on tall
steps at back of cabin to flood back cloth. Open dark Amber. Warning   5
for slide. Plank ready. Call Hook.°

In the strange light thus described we see what is happening on the
deck of the *Jolly Roger*, which is flying the skull and crossbones and
lies low in the water. There is no need to call Hook, for he is here
already, and indeed there is not a pirate aboard who would dare to   10
call him. Most of them are at present carousing in the bowels of the
vessel, but on the poop Mullins° is visible, in the only great-coat on
the ship, raking with his glass the monstrous rocks within which the
lagoon is cooped. Such a look-out is supererogatory, for the pirate
craft floats immune in the horror of her name.   15

From Hook's cabin at the back Starkey appears and leans over the
bulwark, silently surveying the sullen waters. He is bare-headed and is
perhaps thinking with bitterness of his hat, which he sometimes sees
still drifting past him with the Never bird sitting on it. The black
pirate is asleep on deck, yet even in his dreams rolling mechanically   20
out of the way when Hook draws near. The only sound to be heard is
made by Smee at his sewing-machine, which lends a touch of
domesticity to the night.

Hook is now leaning against the mast, now prowling the deck, the
double cigar in his mouth. With Peter surely at last removed from his   25
path we, who know how vain a tabernacle is man, would not be
surprised to find him bellied out by the winds of his success, but it
is not so; he is still uneasy, looking long and meaninglessly at familiar
objects, such as the ship's bell or the Long Tom,° like one who may
shortly be a stranger to them. It is as if Pan's terrible oath 'Hook or   30
me this time!' had already boarded the ship.

HOOK (*communing with his ego*) How still the night is;° nothing
sounds alive. Now is the hour when children in their homes are

a-bed; their lips bright-browned with the good-night chocolate, and their tongues drowsily searching for belated crumbs housed insecurely on their shining cheeks. Compare with them the children on this boat about to walk the plank. Split my infinitives, but 'tis my hour of triumph! (*Clinging to this fair prospect he dances a few jubilant steps, but they fall below his usual form*) And yet some disky° spirit compels me now to make my dying speech, lest when dying there may be no time for it. All mortals envy me, yet better perhaps for Hook to have had less ambition! O fame, fame, thou glittering bauble, what if the very——(*Smee, engrossed in his labours at the sewing-machine, tears a piece of calico with a rending sound which makes the Solitary think for a moment that the untoward has happened to his garments*) No little children love me.° I am told they play at Peter Pan, and that the strongest always chooses to be Peter. They would rather be a Twin than Hook; they force the baby to be Hook. The baby! that is where the canker gnaws. (*He contemplàtes his industrious boatswain*) 'Tis said they find Smee lovable. But an hour agone I found him letting the youngest of them try on his spectacles. Pathetic Smee, the Nonconformist pirate, a happy smile upon his face because he thinks they fear him! How can I break it to him that they think him lovable? No, bi-carbonate of Soda, no, not even——(*Another rending of the calico disturbs him, and he has a private consultation with Starkey, who turns him round and evidently assures him that all is well. The peroration of his speech is nevertheless for ever lost, as eight bells strikes and his crew pour forth in bacchanalian orgy. From the poop he watches their dance till it frets him beyond bearing*) Quiet, you dogs, or I'll cast anchor in you! (*He descends to a barrel on which there are playing-cards, and his crew stand waiting, as ever, like whipped curs*) Are all the prisoners chained, so that they can't fly away?

JUKES Ay, ay, Captain.

HOOK Then hoist them up.

STARKEY (*raising the door of the hold*) Tumble up, you ungentlemanly lubbers.

> (*The terrified boys are prodded up and tossed about the deck. Hook seems to have forgotten them; he is sitting by the barrel with his cards*)

HOOK (*suddenly*) So! Now then, you bullies, six of you walk the plank to-night, but I have room for two cabin-boys. Which of you is it to be? (*He returns to his cards*)

TOOTLES (*hoping to soothe him by putting the blame on the only person, vaguely remembered, who is always willing to act as a buffer*) You

see, sir, I don't think my mother would like me to be a pirate.
Would your mother like you to be a pirate, Slightly?

SLIGHTLY (*implying that otherwise it would be a pleasure to him to*   75
oblige) I don't think so. Twin, would your mother like——

HOOK Stow this gab.° (*To John*) You boy, you look as if you had a
little pluck in you. Didst never want to be a pirate, my hearty?

JOHN (*dazzled by being singled out*) When I was at school I—what do
you think, Michael?   80

MICHAEL (*stepping into prominence*) What would you call me if I
joined?

HOOK Blackbeard Joe.

MICHAEL John, what do you think?

JOHN Stop, should we still be respectful subjects of King George?°   85

HOOK You would have to swear 'Down with King George.'

JOHN (*grandly*) Then I refuse!

MICHAEL And I refuse.

HOOK That seals your doom. Bring up their mother.

> (*Wendy is driven up from the hold and thrown to him. She
> sees at the first glance that the deck has not been scrubbed for
> years*)

So, my beauty, you are to see your children walk the plank.   90

WENDY (*with noble calmness*) Are they to die?

HOOK They are. Silence all, for a mother's last words to her children.

WENDY These are my last words. Dear boys, I feel that I have a
message to you from your real mothers, and it is this, 'We hope
our sons will die like English gentlemen.'   95

> (*The boys go on fire*)

TOOTLES I am going to do what my mother hopes. What are you to
do, Twin?

FIRST TWIN What my mother hopes. John, what are——

HOOK Tie her up! Get the plank ready.

> (*Wendy is róped to the mast; but no one regards her, for all eyes
> are fixed upon the plank now protruding from the poop over the
> ship's side. A great change, however, occurs in the time Hook
> takes to raise his claw and point to this deadly engine. No one
> is now looking at the plank: for the tick, tick of the crocodile is
> heard. Yet it is not to bear on the crocodile that all eyes slew
> round, it is that they may bear on Hook. Otherwise prisoners and
> captors are equally inert, like actors in some play who have
> found themselves 'on' in a scene in which they are not personally
> concerned. Even the iron claw hangs inactive, as if aware that*

the crocodile is not coming for it. Affection for their captain, now cowering from view, is not what has given Hook his dominance over the crew, but as the menacing sound draws nearer they close their eyes respectfully.

There is no crocodile. It is Peter, who has been circling the pirate ship, ticking as he flies far more superbly than any clock. He drops into the water and climbs aboard, warning the captives with upraised finger (but still ticking) not for the moment to give audible expression to their natural admiration. Only one pirate sees him, Whibbles of the eye patch,° who comes up from below. John claps a hand on Whibbles's mouth to stifle the groan; four boys hold him to prevent the thud; Peter delivers the blow, and the carrion is thrown overboard. 'One!' says Slightly, beginning to count.

Starkey is the first pirate to open his eyes. The ship seems to him to be precisely as when he closed them. He cannot interpret the sparkle that has come into the faces of the captives, who are cleverly pretending to be as afraid as ever. He little knows that the door of the dark cabin has just closed on one more boy. Indeed it is for Hook alone he looks, and he is a little surprised to see him)

STARKEY (*hoarsely*) It is gone, Captain! There is not a sound.   100
(*The tenement that is Hook heaves tumultuously and he is himself again*)

HOOK (*now convinced that some fair spirit watches over him*) Then here is to Johnny Plank——
   Avast, belay, the English brig
   We took and quickly sank,
   And for a warning to the crew   105
   We made them walk the plank!
(*As he sings he capers detestably along an imaginary plank and his copy-cats do likewise, joining in the chorus*)
   Yo ho, yo ho, the frisky plank,
   You walks along it so,
   Till it goes down and you goes down
   To tooral looral lo!   110
(*The brave children try to stem this monstrous torrent by breaking into the National Anthem*)

STARKEY (*paling*) I don't like it, messmates!

HOOK Stow that, Starkey. Do you boys want a touch of the cat° before you walk the plank? (*He is more pitiless than ever now that*

he believes he has a charmed life) Fetch the cat, Jukes; it is in the   115
cabin.

JUKES Ay, ay, sir. (*It is one of his commonest remarks, and it is only
recorded now because he never makes another. The stage direction 'Exit
Jukes' has in this case a special significance. But only the children know
that some one is awaiting this unfortunate in the cabin, and Hook
tramples them down as he resumes his ditty:*)   120

> Yo ho, yo ho, the scratching cat
> Its tails are nine you know,
> And when they're writ upon your back,
> You're fit to——

(*The last words will ever remain a matter of conjecture, for from
the dark cabin comes a curdling screech which wails through the
ship and dies away. It is followed by a sound, almost more eerie
in the circumstances, that can only be likened to the crowing of
a cock*)

HOOK What was that?   125
SLIGHTLY (*solemnly*) Two!
> (*Cecco swings into the cabin, and in a moment returns, livid°*)
HOOK (*with an effort*) What is the matter with Bill Jukes, you dog?
CECCO The matter with him is he is dead—stabbed.
PIRATES Bill Jukes dead!
CECCO The cabin is as black as a pit, but there is something terrible   130
in there: the thing you heard a-crowing.
HOOK (*slowly*) Cecco, go back and fetch me out that doodle-doo.
CECCO (*unstrung*) No, Captain, no. (*He supplicates on his knees, but his
master advances on him implacably*)
HOOK (*in his most syrupy voice*) Did you say you would go, Cecco?   135
> (*Cecco goes. All listen. There is one screech, one crow*)
SLIGHTLY (*as if he were a bell tolling*) Three!
HOOK 'Sdeath° and oddsfish, who is to bring me out that doodle-
doo?
> (*No one steps forward*)
STARKEY (*injudiciously*) Wait till Cecco comes out.
> (*The black looks of some others encourage him*)
HOOK I think I heard you volunteer, Starkey.   140
STARKEY (*emphatically*) No, by thunder!
HOOK (*in that syrupy voice which might be more engaging when
accompanied by his flute*) My hook thinks you did. I wonder if it
would not be advisable, Starkey, to humour the hook?
STARKEY I'll swing° before I go in there.   145

HOOK (*gleaming*) Is it mutiny? Starkey is ringleader. Shake hands, Starkey.

> (*Starkey recoils from the claw. It follows him till he leaps overboard*)

Did any other gentleman say mutiny?

> (*They indicate that they did not even know the late Starkey*)

SLIGHTLY Four!

HOOK I will bring out that doodle-doo myself.   150

> (*He raises a blunderbuss but casts it from him with a menacing gesture which means that he has more faith in the claw. With a lighted lantern in his hand he enters the cabin. Not a sound is to be heard now on the ship, unless it be Slightly wetting his lips to say 'Five.' Hook staggers out*)

HOOK (*unsteadily*) Something blew out the light.

MULLINS (*with dark meaning*) Some—thing?

NOODLER What of Cecco?

HOOK He is as dead as Jukes.

> (*They are superstitious like all sailors, and Mullins has planted a dire conception in their minds*)

COOKSON They do say as the surest sign a ship's accurst is when   155
there is one aboard° more than can be accounted for.

NOODLER I've heard he allus boards the pirate craft at last. (*With dreadful significance*) Has he a tail, Captain?

MULLINS They say that when he comes it is in the likeness of the wickedest man aboard.   160

COOKSON (*clinching it*) Has he a hook, Captain?

> (*Knives and pistols come to hand, and there is a general cry 'The ship is doomed!' But it is not his dogs that can frighten Jas Hook. Hearing something like a cheer from the boys he wheels round, and his face brings them to their knees*)

HOOK So you like it, do you! By Caius and Balbus, bullies, here is a notion: open the cabin door and drive them in. Let them fight the doodle-doo for their lives. If they kill him we are so much the better; if he kills them we are none the worse.   165

> (*This masterly stroke restores their confidence; and the boys, affecting fear, are driven into the cabin. Desperadoes though the pirates are, some of them have been boys themselves, and all turn their backs to the cabin and listen, with arms outstretched° to it as if to ward off the horrors that are being enacted there.
>
> Relieved by Peter of their manacles, and armed with such weapons as they can lay their hands on, the boys steal out softly*)

*as snowflakes, and under their captain's hushed order find
hiding-places on the poop. He releases Wendy; and now it would
be easy for them all to fly away, but it is to be Hook or him this
time. He signs to her to join the others, and with awful grimness
folding her cloak around him, the hood over his head, he takes
her place by the mast, and crows)*

MULLINS The doodle-doo has killed them all!

SEVERAL The ship's bewitched.
        (They are snapping at Hook again)

HOOK I've thought it out, lads; there is a Jonah° aboard.

SEVERAL *(advancing upon him)* Ay, a man with a hook.
        *(If he were to withdraw one step their knives would be in him,
        but he does not flinch)*

HOOK *(temporising)* No, lads, no, it is the girl. Never was luck on a   170
pirate ship wi' a woman aboard. We'll right the ship when she has
gone.

MULLINS *(lowering his cutlass)* It's worth trying.

HOOK Throw the girl overboard.

MULLINS *(jeering)* There is none can save you now, missy.   175

PETER There is one.

MULLINS Who is that?

PETER *(casting off the cloak)* Peter Pan, the avenger!
        (He continues standing there to let the effect sink in)

HOOK *(throwing out a suggestion)* Cleave him to the brisket.
        (But he has a sinking that this boy has no brisket)

NOODLER The ship's accurst!   180

PETER Down, boys, and at them!
        *(The boys leap from their concealment and the clash of arms
        resounds through the vessel. Man to man the pirates are the
        stronger, but they are unnerved by the suddenness of the
        onslaught and they scatter, thus enabling their opponents to hunt
        in couples and choose their quarry. Some are hurled into the
        lagoon; others are dragged from dark recesses. There is no boy
        whose weapon is not reeking save Slightly, who runs about with
        a lantern, counting, ever counting)*

WENDY *(meeting Michael in a moment's lull)* Oh, Michael, stay with
me, protect me!

MICHAEL *(reeling)* Wendy, I've killed a pirate!

WENDY It's awful, awful.   185

MICHAEL No, it isn't, I like it, I like it.

(*He casts himself into the group of boys who are encircling Hook.
Again and again they close upon him and again and again he
hews a clear space*)

HOOK Back, back, you mice. It's Hook; do you like him? (*He lifts up
Michael with his claw and uses him as a buckler.° A terrible voice
breaks in*)

PETER Put up your swords, boys. This man is mine.   190

(*Hook shakes Michael off his claw as if he were a drop of water,
and these two antagonists face each other for their final bout.
They measure swords at arms' length, make a sweeping motion
with them, and bringing the points to the deck rest their hands
upon the hilts°*)

HOOK (*with curling lip*) So, Pan, this is all your doing!

PETER Ay, Jas Hook, it is all my doing.

HOOK Proud and insolent youth, prepare to meet thy doom.

PETER Dark and sinister man, have at thee.

(*Some say that he had to ask Tootles whether the word was
sinister or canister.*

*Hook or Peter this time! They fall to without another word.
Peter is a rare swordsman, and parries with dazzling rapidity,
sometimes before the other can make his stroke. Hook, if not
quite so nimble in wrist play, has the advantage of a yard or two
in reach, but though they close he cannot give the quietus° with
his claw, which seems to find nothing to tear at. He does not,
especially in the most heated moments, quite see Peter, who to
his eyes, now blurred or opened clearly for the first time, is less
like a boy than a mote of dust dancing in the sun. By some
impalpable stroke Hook's sword is whipped from his grasp, and
when he stoops to raise it a little foot is on its blade. There is no
deep gash on Hook, but he is suffering torment as from
innumerable jags*)

BOYS (*exulting*) Now, Peter, now!   195

(*Peter raises the sword by its blade, and with an inclination of
the head that is perhaps slightly overdone, presents the hilt to his
enemy*)

HOOK 'Tis some fiend fighting me! Pan, who and what art thou?

(*The children listen eagerly for the answer, none quite so eagerly
as Wendy*)

PETER (*at a venture*) I'm youth, I'm joy, I'm a little bird that has
broken out of the egg.

HOOK To't again!

> (*He has now a damp feeling that this boy is the weapon which is to strike him from the lists of man; but the grandeur of his mind still holds and, true to the traditions of his flag, he fights on like a human flail. Peter flutters round and through and over these gyrations as if the wind of them blew him out of the danger zone, and again and again he darts in and jags*)

HOOK (*stung to madness*) I'll fire the powder magazine. (*He disappears they know not where*) 200

CHILDREN Peter, save us!

> (*Peter, alas, goes the wrong way and Hook returns*)

HOOK (*sitting on the hold with gloomy satisfaction*) In two minutes the ship will be blown to pieces.

> (*They cast themselves before him in entreaty*)

CHILDREN Mercy, mercy! 205

HOOK Back, you pewling° spawn. I'll show you now the road to dusty death.° A holocaust of children, there is something grand in the idea!

> (*Peter appears with a smoking bomb° in his hand and tosses it overboard. Hook has not really had much hope, and he rushes at his other persecutors with his head down like some exasperated bull in the ring; but with bantering cries they easily elude him by flying among the rigging.*
>
> *Where is Peter? The incredible boy has apparently forgotten the recent doings, and is sitting on a barrel playing upon his pipes. This may surprise others but does not surprise Hook. Lifting a blunderbuss he strikes forlornly not at the boy but at the barrel, which is hurled across the deck. Peter remains sitting in the air still playing upon his pipes. At this sight the great heart of Hook breaks. That not wholly unheroic figure climbs the bulwarks murmuring 'Floreat Etona,'° and prostrates himself into the water, where the crocodile is waiting for him open-mouthed. Hook knows the purpose of this yawning cavity, but after what he has gone through he enters it like one greeting a friend.*
>
> *The curtain rises° to show Peter a very Napoleon on his ship.° It must not rise again lest we see him on the poop in Hook's hat and cigars, and with a small iron claw*)

Scene 2°

THE NURSERY AND THE TREE-TOPS

The old nursery appears again with everything just as it was at the beginning of the play, except that the kennel has gone and that the window is standing open. So Peter was wrong about mothers; indeed there is no subject on which he is so likely to be wrong.

Mrs Darling is asleep on a chair near the window, her eyes tired with searching the heavens. Nana is stretched out listless on the floor. She is the cynical one, and though custom has made her hang the children's night things on the fire-guard for an airing, she surveys them not hopefully but with some self-contempt.

MRS DARLING (*starting up as if we had whispered to her that her brats are coming back*) Wendy, John, Michael! (*Nana lifts a sympathetic paw to the poor soul's lap*) I see you have put their night things out again, Nana! It touches my heart to watch you do that night after night. But they will never come back.

> (*In trouble the difference of station can be completely ignored, and it is not strange to see these two using the same handkerchief. Enter Liza, who in the gentleness with which the house has been run of late is perhaps a little more masterful than of yore*)

LIZA (*feeling herself degraded by the announcement*) Nana's dinner is served.

> (*Nana, who quite understands what are Liza's feelings, departs for the dining-room with an exasperating leisureliness, instead of running, as we would all do if we followed our instincts*)

LIZA To think I have a master as have changed places with his dog!

MRS DARLING (*gently*) Out of remorse, Liza.

LIZA (*surely exaggerating*) I am a married woman myself. I don't think it's respectable to go to his office in a kennel, with the street boys running alongside cheering. (*Even this does not rouse her mistress, which may have been the honourable intention*) There, that is the cab fetching him back! (*Amid interested cheers from the street the kennel is conveyed to its old place by a cabby and friend, and Mr Darling scrambles out of it in his office clothes*)

MR DARLING (*giving her his hat loftily*) If you will be so good, Liza. (*The cheering is resumed*) It is very gratifying!

LIZA (*contemptuous*) Lot of little boys.

MR DARLING (*with the new sweetness of one who has sworn never to lose his temper again*) There were several adults to–day.   30

> (*She goes off scornfully with the hat and the two men, but he has not a word of reproach for her. It ought to melt us when we see how humbly grateful he is for a kiss from his wife, so much more than he feels he deserves. One may think he is wrong to exchange into the kennel, but sorrow has taught him that he is the kind of man who whatever he does contritely he must do to excess; otherwise he soon abandons doing it*)

MRS DARLING (*who has known this for quite a long time*) What sort of a day have you had, George?

> (*He is sitting on the floor by the kennel*)

MR DARLING There were never less than a hundred running round the cab cheering, and when we passed the Stock Exchange the members came out and waved.   35

> (*He is exultant but uncertain of himself, and with a word she could dispirit him utterly*)

MRS DARLING (*bravely*) I am so proud, George.

MR DARLING (*commendation from the dearest quarter ever going to his head*) I have been put on a picture postcard, dear.

MRS DARLING (*nobly*) Never!

MR DARLING (*thoughtlessly*) Ah, Mary, we should not be such celebrities if the children hadn't flown away.   40

MRS DARLING (*startled*) George, you are sure you are not enjoying it?

MR DARLING (*anxiously*) Enjoying it! See my punishment: living in a kennel.   45

MRS DARLING Forgive me, dear one.

MR DARLING It is I who need forgiveness, always I, never you. And now I feel drowsy. (*He retires into the kennel*) Won't you play me to sleep on the nursery piano? And shut that window, Mary dearest; I feel a draught.   50

MRS DARLING Oh, George, never ask me to do that. The window must always be left open for them, always, always.

> (*She goes into the day nursery, from which we presently hear her playing the sad song of Margaret.° She little knows that her last remark has been overheard by a boy crouching at the window. He steals into the room accompanied by a ball of light*)

PETER Tink, where are you? Quick, close the window. (*It closes*) Bar it. (*The bar slams down*) Now when Wendy comes she will think her mother has barred her out, and she will have to come back to   55 me! (*Tinker Bell sulks*) Now, Tink, you and I must go out by the door. (*Doors, however, are confusing things to those who are used to windows, and he is puzzled when he finds that this one does not open on to the firmament. He tries the other, and sees the piano player*) It is Wendy's mother! (*Tink pops on to his shoulder and they peep together*) She is a pretty lady, but not so pretty as my mother. (*This is a pure guess*) She is making the box say 'Come home, Wendy.' You will never see Wendy again, lady, for the window is barred! (*He flutters about the room joyously like a bird, but has to return to that door*) She has laid her head down on the box. There are two wet things sitting on her eyes. As soon as they go away another two come and sit on her eyes. (*She is heard moaning 'Wendy, Wendy, Wendy'.*) She wants me to unbar the window. I won't! She is awfully fond of Wendy. I am fond of her too. We can't both have her, lady! (*A funny feeling comes over him*) Come on, Tink; we don't want any silly mothers.

    (*He opens the window and they fly out.*

      It is thus that the truants find entrance easy when they alight on the sill, John to his credit having the tired Michael on his shoulders. They have nothing else to their credit; no compunction for what they have done, not the tiniest fear that any just person may be awaiting them with a stick. The youngest is in a daze, but the two others are shining virtuously like holy people who are about to give two other people a treat)

MICHAEL (*looking about him*) I think I have been here before.

JOHN It's your home, you stupid.

WENDY There is your old bed, Michael.

MICHAEL I had nearly forgotten.

JOHN I say, the kennel!

WENDY Perhaps Nana is in it.

JOHN (*peering*) There is a man asleep in it.

WENDY (*remembering him by the bald patch*) It's father!

JOHN So it is!

MICHAEL Let me see father. (*Disappointed*) He is not as big as the pirate I killed.

JOHN (*perplexed*) Wendy, surely father didn't use to sleep in the kennel?

WENDY (*with misgivings*) Perhaps we don't remember the old life as well as we thought we did.

JOHN (*chilled*) It is very careless of mother not to be here when we come back.

(*The piano is heard again*)

WENDY H'sh! (*She goes to the door and peeps*) That is her playing! (*They all have a peep*)   90

MICHAEL Who is that lady?

JOHN H'sh! It's mother.

MICHAEL Then are you not really our mother, Wendy?

WENDY (*with conviction*) Oh dear, it is quite time to be back!

JOHN Let us creep in and put our hands over her eyes.   95

WENDY (*more considerate*) No, let us break it to her gently.

> (*She slips between the sheets of her bed; and the others, seeing the idea at once, get into their beds. Then when the music stops they cover their heads. There are now three distinct bumps in the beds. Mrs Darling sees the bumps as soon as she comes in, but she does not believe she sees them*)

MRS DARLING I see them in their beds so often in my dreams that I seem still to see them when I am awake! I'll not look again. (*She sits down and turns away her face from the bumps, though of course they are still reflected in her mind*) So often their silver voices call   100 me, my little children whom I'll see no more.

> (*Silver voices is a good one, especially about John; but the heads pop up*)

WENDY (*perhaps rather silvery*) Mother!

MRS DARLING (*without moving*) That is Wendy.

JOHN (*quite gruff*) Mother!

MRS DARLING Now it is John.   105

MICHAEL (*no better than a squeak*) Mother!

MRS DARLING Now Michael. And when they call I stretch out my arms to them, but they never come, they never come!°

> (*This time, however, they come, and there is joy once more in the Darling household. The little boy who is crouching at the window sees the joke of the bumps in the beds, but cannot understand what all the rest of the fuss is about.*)
>
> *The scene changes*° *from the inside of the house to the outside, and we see Mr Darling romping in at the door, with the lost boys hanging gaily to his coat-tails. So we may conclude that Wendy has told them to wait outside until she explains the situation to her mother, who has then sent Mr Darling down to tell them that they are adopted. Of course they could have flown in by the window like a covey of birds, but they think it better fun to enter by a door. There is a moment's trouble*

about Slightly, who somehow gets shut out. Fortunately Liza finds him)

LIZA What is the matter, boy?

SLIGHTLY They have all got a mother except me.   110

LIZA *(starting back)* Is your name Slightly?

SLIGHTLY Yes'm.

LIZA Then I am your mother.

SLIGHTLY How do you know?

LIZA *(the good-natured creature)* I feel it in my bones.   115

> *(They go into the house and there is none happier now than Slightly, unless it be Nana as she passes with the importance of a nurse who will never have another day off. Wendy looks out at the nursery window and sees a friend below, who is hovering in the air knocking off tall hats with his feet. The wearers don't see him. They are too old. You can't see Peter if you are old. They think he is a draught at the corner)*

WENDY Peter!

PETER *(looking up casually)* Hullo, Wendy.

> *(She flies down to him, to the horror of her mother, who rushes to the window)*

WENDY *(making a last attempt)* You don't feel you would like to say anything to my parents, Peter, about a very sweet subject?

PETER No, Wendy.   120

WENDY About me, Peter?

PETER No. *(He gets out his pipes, which she knows is a very bad sign. She appeals with her arms to Mrs Darling, who is probably thinking that these children will all need to be tied to their beds at night)*

MRS DARLING *(from the window)* Peter, where are you? Let me adopt   125
you too.

> *(She is the loveliest age for a woman, but too old to see Peter clearly)*

PETER Would you send me to school?

MRS DARLING *(obligingly)* Yes.

PETER And then to an office?

MRS DARLING I suppose so.   130

PETER Soon I should be a man?

MRS DARLING Very soon.

PETER *(passionately)* I don't want to go to school and learn solemn things. No one is going to catch me, lady, and make me a man. I want always to be a little boy and to have fun.   135

> *(So perhaps he thinks, but it is only his greatest pretend)°*

MRS DARLING (*shivering every time Wendy pursues him in the air*)
    Where are you to live, Peter?
PETER In the house we built for Wendy. The fairies are to put it high
    up among the tree-tops where they sleep at night.
WENDY (*rapturously*) To think of it!   140
MRS DARLING I thought all the fairies were dead.
WENDY (*almost reprovingly*) No indeed! Their mothers drop the
    babies into the Never birds' nests, all mixed up with the eggs, and
    the mauve fairies are boys and the white ones are girls, and there
    are some colours who don't know what they are. The row the   145
    children and the birds make at bath time is positively deafening.
PETER I throw things at them.
WENDY You will be rather lonely in the evenings, Peter.
PETER I shall have Tink.
WENDY (*flying up to the window*) Mother, may I go?   150
MRS DARLING (*gripping her for ever*)° Certainly not. I have got you
    home again, and I mean to keep you.
WENDY But he does so need a mother.
MRS DARLING So do you, my love.
PETER Oh, all right.   155
MRS DARLING (*magnanimously*) But, Peter, I shall let her go to you
    once a year for a week to do your Spring Cleaning.
        (*Wendy revels in this, but Peter, who has no notion what a
        Spring Cleaning is, waves a rather careless thanks*)
MRS DARLING Say good-night, Wendy.
WENDY I couldn't go down just for a minute?
MRS DARLING No.   160
WENDY Good-night, Peter!
PETER Good-night, Wendy!
WENDY Peter, you won't forget me, will you, before Spring-Cleaning
    time comes?
        (*There is no answer, for he is already soaring high. For a
        moment after he is gone we still hear the pipes. Mrs Darling
        closes and bars the window*°)

We are dreaming now of the Never Land a year later. It is bed-time   165
on the island, and the blind goes up to the whispers of the lovely
Never music. The blue haze that makes the wood below magical by
day comes up to the tree-tops to sleep, and through it we see
numberless nests all lit up, fairies and birds quarrelling for possession,
others flying around just for the fun of the thing and perhaps making   170

bets about where the little house will appear to-night. It always comes and snuggles on some tree-top, but you can never be sure which; here it is again, you see John's hat first as up comes the house so softly that it knocks some gossips off their perch. When it has settled comfortably it lights up, and out come Peter and Wendy. 175

Wendy looks a little older, but Peter is just the same. She is cloaked for a journey, and a sad confession must be made about her; she flies so badly now that she has to use a broomstick.

WENDY (*who knows better this time than to be demonstrative at partings*)
Well, good-bye, Peter; and remember not to bite your nails. 180
PETER Good-bye, Wendy.
WENDY I'll tell mother all about the Spring Cleaning and the house.
PETER (*who sometimes forgets that she has been here before*) You do like the house?
WENDY Of course it is small. But most people of our size wouldn't 185
have a house at all. (*She should not have mentioned size, for he has already expressed displeasure at her growth. Another thing, one he has scarcely noticed, though it disturbs her, is that she does not see him quite so clearly now as she used to do*) When you come for me next year, Peter—you will come, won't you? 190
PETER Yes. (*Gloating*) To hear stories about me!
WENDY It is so queer that the stories you like best should be the ones about yourself.
PETER (*touchy*) Well, then?
WENDY Fancy your forgetting the lost boys, and even Captain Hook! 195
PETER Well, then?
WENDY I haven't seen Tink this time.
PETER Who?
WENDY Oh dear! I suppose it is because you have so many adven-
tures. 200
PETER (*relieved*) 'Course it is.
WENDY If another little girl—if one younger than I am——(*She can't go on*) Oh, Peter, how I wish I could take you up and squdge you! (*He draws back*) Yes, I know. (*She gets astride her broomstick*) Home! (*It carries her from him over the tree-tops.* 205

> In a sort of way he understands what she means by 'Yes, I know,' but in most sorts of ways he doesn't. It has something to do with the riddle of his being. If he could get the hang of the thing his cry might become 'To live would be an awfully big adventure!' but he can never quite get the hang of it, and so no

one is as gay as he. With rapturous face he produces his pipes, and the Never birds and the fairies gather closer, till the roof of the little house is so thick with his admirers that some of them fall down the chimney. He plays on and on till we wake up)

WHEN WENDY
GREW UP:
An Afterthought

CHARACTERS

Peter Pan
Wendy
Jane (her Daughter)
Nana

An Afterthought

The Scene is the same nursery, with this slight change—Michael's bed is now where Wendy's was and vice versa, and in front of John's bed, hiding the upper part of it from the audience, is a clothes horse on which depend (covering it), a little girl's garments to air at the fire. Time early evening. Lights in.°

Wendy emerges from bathroom. She is now a grown-up woman, wearing a pretty dress with train, and she sails forward to fire in an excessively matronly manner. She comes straight to audience, points out to them° with pride her long skirt and that her hair is up. Then takes a child's nightgown off fireguard and after pointing it out with rapture to audience exit into bathroom. She comes out with her little daughter Jane, who is in the nightgown. Wendy is drying Jane's hair.

JANE (*naughty*) Won't go to bed, Mummy, won't go to bed!

WENDY (*excessively prim*) Jane! When *I* was a little girl I went to bed the *moment* I was told. Come at once! (*Jane dodges her and after pursuit is caught.*) Naughtikins! (*sits by fire with Jane on her knee warming toes*) to run your poor old Mother out of breath! When   5
she's not so young as she used to be!

JANE How young used you to be, Mummy?

WENDY Quite young. How time flies!

JANE Does it fly the way you flew when you were a little girl?

WENDY The way I flew. Do you know Darling it is all so long ago.   10
I sometimes wonder whether I ever did really fly.

JANE Yes you did.

WENDY Those dear old days.

JANE Why can't you fly now, Mother?

WENDY Because I'm grown up sweetheart; when people grow up   15
they forget the way.

JANE Why do they forget the way?

WENDY Because they are no longer young and innocent. It is only the young and innocent that can fly.

JANE What is young and innocent? I do wish I were young and   20
innocent! (*Wendy suddenly hugs her*)

WENDY Come to bed, dearest. (*Takes her to bed right, down stage*)

JANE Tell me a story. Tell me about Peter Pan.

WENDY (*standing at foot of bed*) I've told it you so often that I believe
you could tell it to me now better than *I* could tell it to you.   25

JANE (*putting bed clothes round them to suggest a tent*) Go on Mother.
This is the Little House. What do you see?

WENDY I see—just this nursery.

JANE But what do you see long ago in it?

WENDY I see—little Wendy in her bed.   30

JANE Yes, and Uncle Michael here and Uncle John over there.

WENDY Heigh ho! and to think that John has a beard now, and that
Michael is an engine driver. Lie down, Petty.

JANE But do tell me. Tell me that bit—about how you grew up and
Peter didn't. Begin where he promised to come for you every year,   35
and take you to the Tree Tops to do his Spring Cleaning. Lucky
you!

WENDY Well then! (*now on bed behind Jane*) On the conclusion of the
adventures described in our last chapter which left our heroine,
Wendy, in her Mummy's arms, she was very quickly packed off to   40
school again—a day school.

JANE And so were all the boys.

WENDY Yes—Mummy adopted them. They were fearfully anxious
because John had said to them that, if they didn't fit in, they would
all have to be sent to the Dogs' Home. However they all fitted in,   45
and they went to school in a bus every day, but sometimes they
were very naughty, for when the conductor clambered up to collect
the fares they flew off, so as not to have to pay their pennies. You
should have seen Nana taking them to church. It was like a Collie
herding sheep.   50

JANE Did they ever wish they were back in the Never Never Land?

WENDY (*hesitating*) I—I don't know.

JANE (*with conviction*) *I* know.

WENDY Of course they missed the fun. Even Wendy sometimes
couldn't help flying, the littlest thing lifted her up in the air. The 55
sight of a hat blown off a gentleman's head for instance. If it flew
off, so did she! So a year passed, and the first Spring Cleaning time
came round, when Peter was to come and take her to the Tree
Tops.

JANE OO! OO!   60

WENDY *How* she prepared for him! *How* she sat at that window in
her going-away frock—and he came—and away they flew to his
Spring Cleaning—and he was exactly the same, and he never
noticed that she was any different.

JANE How was she different?   65

WENDY She had to let the frock down two inches! She was so
   terrified that he might notice it, for she had promised him never
   to have growing pains. However, he never noticed, he was so full
   of lovely talk about himself.

JANE (*gleefully*) He was always awful cocky.   70

WENDY I think ladies rather love cocky gentlemen.

JANE So do I love them.

WENDY There was one sad thing I noticed. He had forgotten a lot.
   He had even forgotten Tinker Bell. I think she was no more.

JANE Oh dear!   75

WENDY You see Darling, a fairy only lives as long a time as a feather
   is blown about the air on a windy day. But fairies are so little
   that a short time seems a good while to them. As the feather
   flutters they have quite an enjoyable life, with time to be born
   respectably and have a look round, and to dance once and to cry   80
   once and to bring up their children—just as one can go a long way
   quickly in a motor car. And so motor cars help us to understand
   fairies.

JANE Everybody grows up and dies except Peter, doesn't they?

WENDY Yes, you see he had no sense of time. He thought all the past   85
   was just yesterday. He spoke as if it was just yesterday that he and
   I had parted and it was a whole year.

JANE Oh dearie Dear!

WENDY We had a lovely time, but soon I had to go back home, and
   another year passed, and Spring Cleaning time came again. And   90
   oh the terror of me sitting waiting for him—for I was another two
   inches round the waist! But he never came. How I cried! Another
   year passed, and still I got into my little frock somehow, and that
   year he came—and the strangest thing was that he never knew that
   he had missed a year. I didn't tell him. I meant to, but I said to   95
   him 'What am I to you Peter?' and he said 'You are my
   mother'—so of course after that I couldn't tell him. But that was
   the last. Many Spring Cleaning times came round, but never Peter
   any more. 'Just always be waiting for me' he said, 'and then some
   time you will hear me crow', but I never heard him crow again.   100
   It's just as well Sweetie, for you see he would think all the past
   was yesterday, and he would expect to find me a little girl
   still—and that would be too tragic. And now you must sleep.
   (*Rises*)

JANE I am fearfully awake. Tell me about Nana.   105

WENDY (*at foot of bed*) Of course I see now that Nana wasn't a *perfect* nurse. She was rather old-fashioned in her ideas—she had too much faith in your stocking round your throat, and so on—and two or three times she became just an ordinary dog, and stayed out so late at night with bad companions that father had to get up at two in the morning in his pyjamas to let her in. But she was so fond of children that her favourite way of spending her afternoons off was to go to Kensington Gardens, and follow careless nurses to their homes and report them to their mistresses. As she's old now I have to coddle her a good deal and that's why we give her John's bed to sleep in. (*Looking left*) Dear Nana! (*Flings kiss to the hidden bed*)

JANE Now tell me about being married in white with a pink sash.

WENDY Most of the boys married their favourite heroines in fiction and Slightly married a lady of title and so he became a lord.°

JANE And one of them married Wendy and so he became my Papa!

WENDY Yes and we bought this house at 3 per cents from Grand-Papa because he felt the stairs. And Papa is very clever, and knows all about Stocks and Shares. Of course he doesn't really know about them, nobody really knows, but in the mornings when he wakes up fresh he says 'Stocks are up and Shares are down' in a way that makes Mummy very, very proud of him.

JANE Now tell me about *me*.

WENDY At last there came to our heroine a little daughter. I don't know how it is but I just always thought that some day Wendy would have a little daughter.

JANE So did *I*, mother,° so did *I*! Tell me what she's like.

WENDY Pen cannot describe her, she would have to be written with a golden splash! (*Hugs her*) That's the end. You *must* sleep.

JANE I am not a bit sleepy.

WENDY (*leaving her*) Hsh!

JANE Mother, I think—(*pause*)

WENDY Well dear, what do you think? (*Pause again—Wendy goes and looks and sees that Jane has suddenly fallen asleep*) Asleep! (*Tucks her in bed, removes the clothes on screen, leisurely, folds and puts them away and then Nana is revealed lying asleep in John's bed beneath the coverlet. She puts down light and sits by fire to sew. Pause—then the night-light over Jane's bed quivers and goes out. Then Peter's crow is heard—Wendy starts up breathless—then the window opens and Peter flies into the room. He is not a day altered. He is gay. Wendy gasps, sinks back in chair. He sees Nana in bed and is startled. Nana moans,*

*he comes forward avoiding Nana's bed, sees Wendy's dress, thinks she's
playing a trick on him*)

PETER (*gaily jumping in front of her*) Hulloh Wendy! (*She turns
lamplight away from her*) Thimbles! (*He leaps on to her knee and   150
kisses her*)

WENDY (*not knowing what to do*) Peter! Peter, do you know how long
it is since you were here before?

PETER It was yesterday.

WENDY Oh! (*He feels her cheek*)   155

PETER Why is there wet on your face? (*She can't answer*) I know! It's
'cos you are so glad I've come for you. (*Suddenly remembers
Nana—jumps up*) Why is Nana in John's bed?

WENDY (*quivering*) John—doesn't sleep here now.

PETER Oh the cheek! (*Looking carelessly at Jane's bed*) Is Michael   160
asleep?

WENDY (*after hesitating*) Yes. (*Horrified at herself*) That isn't Michael! (*Peter peeps curiously*)

PETER (*going*) Hullo, it's a new one!

WENDY Yes.   165

PETER Boy or girl?

WENDY Girl.

PETER Do you like her?

WENDY Yes! (*Desperate*) Peter, don't you see whose child she is?

PETER Of course I do. She's your mother's child. I say, I like her too! 170

WENDY (*crying*) Why?

PETER 'Cos now your mother can let you stay longer with me for
Spring Cleaning. (*Agony of Wendy*)

WENDY Peter. I—I have something to tell you.

PETER (*running to her gaily*) Is it a secret?   175

WENDY Oh! Peter, when Captain Hook carried us away—

PETER Who's Captain Hook? Is it a story? Tell it me.

WENDY (*aghast*) Do you mean to say you've even forgotten Captain
Hook, and how you killed him and saved all our lives?

PETER (*fidgeting*) I forget them after I kill them.   180

WENDY Oh, Peter, you forget everything!

PETER Everything except mother Wendy. (*Hugs her*)

WENDY Oh!

PETER Come on Wendy.

WENDY (*miserably*) Where to?   185

PETER To the Little House. (*A little strong*) Have you forgotten it is
Spring Cleaning time—it's you that forgets.

WENDY Peter, Peter! By this time the little house must have rotted
all away.

PETER So it has, but there are new ones, even littler.   190

WENDY Did you build them yourself?

PETER Oh no, I just found them. You see the little house was a
Mother and it has young ones.

WENDY You sweet.

PETER So come on. (*Pulling her*) I'm Captain.   195

WENDY I can't come, Peter—I have forgotten how to fly.

PETER I'll soon teach you again. (*Blows fairy dust on her*)

WENDY Peter, Peter, you are wasting the fairy dust.

PETER (*at last alarmed*) What is it, Wendy? Is something wrong?
Don't cheat me mother Wendy,—I'm only a little boy.   200

WENDY I can't come with you, Peter—because I'm no longer young
and innocent.

PETER (*with a cry*) Yes you are.

WENDY I'm going to turn up the light, and then you will see for
yourself.   205

PETER (*frightened—hastily*) Wendy, don't turn up the light.

WENDY Yes. But first I want to say to you for the last time something
I said often and often in the dear Never Never Land. Peter, what
are your exact feelings for me?

PETER Those of a devoted son, Wendy. (*Silently she lets her hand play*   210
with his hair°—she caresses his face, smiling through her tears—
then she turns lamp up near the fire and faces him—a bewildered
understanding comes to him—she puts out her arms—but he shrinks
back)
What is it? What is it?   215

WENDY Peter, I'm grown up—I couldn't help it! (*He backs again*)
I'm a married woman Peter—and that little girl is my baby.

PETER (*after pause—fiercely*) What does she call you?

WENDY (*softly, after pause*) Mother.

PETER Mother! (*He takes step towards child with a little dagger in his* 220
hand upraised, then is about to fly away, then flings self on floor and
sobs)

WENDY Peter, Peter! Oh! (*Knows not what to do, rushes in agony from*
the room—long pause in which nothing is heard but Peter's sobs. Nana
is restless. Peter is on the same spot as when crying about Shadow in   225
Act 1. Presently his sobbing wakes Jane. She sits up)

JANE Boy, why are you crying?

        (*Peter rises—they bow as in Act 1*)

JANE What's your name?

PETER Peter Pan.

JANE I just thought it would be you.   230

PETER I came for my mother to take her to the Never Never Land to do my Spring Cleaning.

JANE Yes I know, I've been waiting for you.

PETER Will *you* be my mother?

JANE Oh, yes. (*Simply*)   235
> (*She gets out of bed and stands beside him, arms round him in a child's conception of a mother—Peter very happy. The lamp flickers° and goes out as night-light did*)

PETER I hear Wendy coming—Hide!
> (*They hide. Then Peter is seen teaching Jane to fly. They are very gay. Wendy enters and stands right, taking in situation and much more. They don't see her*)

PETER Hooray! Hooray!

JANE (*flying*) Oh! Lucky me!

PETER And you'll come with me?

JANE If Mummy says I may.   240

WENDY Oh!

JANE May I, Mummy?

WENDY May I come too?

PETER You can't fly.

JANE It's just for a week.   245

PETER And I do so need a mother.

WENDY (*nobly yielding*) Yes my love, you may go. (*Kisses and squeals of rapture, Wendy puts slippers and cloak on Jane and suddenly Peter and Jane fly out hand in hand right into the night, Wendy waving to them—Nana wakens, rises, is weak on legs, barks feebly—Wendy 250 comes and gets on her knees beside Nana*)

WENDY Don't be anxious Nana. This is how I planned it if he ever came back. Every Spring Cleaning, except when he forgets, I'll let Jane fly away with him to the darling Never Never Land, and when she grows up I will hope *she* will have a little daughter, who 255 will fly away with him in turn—and in this way may I go on for ever and ever, dear Nana, so long as children are young and innocent.°
> (*Gradual darkness—then two little lights seen moving slowly through heavens*)

CURTAIN

WHAT EVERY
WOMAN KNOWS

CHARACTERS
(in order of appearance)

James Wylie	Comtesse De La Brière
Alick Wylie	Lady Sybil Tenterden
David Wylie	Maid
Maggie Wylie	Charles Venables
John Shand	Footman

Act 1

James Wylie is about to make a move on the dambrod,° and in the
little Scotch room there is an awful silence befitting the occasion.
James with his hand poised—for if he touches a piece he has to play
it, Alick will see to that—raises his red head suddenly to read Alick's
face. His father, who is Alick, is pretending to be in a panic lest James   5
should make this move. James grins heartlessly, and his fingers are
about to close on the 'man' when some instinct of self-preservation
makes him peep once more. This time Alick is caught: the unholy
ecstasy on his face tells as plain as porridge that he has been luring
James to destruction. James glares; and, too late, his opponent is a   10
simple old father again. James mops his head, sprawls in the manner
most conducive to thought in the Wylie family, and, protruding his
underlip, settles down to a reconsideration of the board. Alick blows
out his cheeks, and a drop of water settles on the point of his nose.

You will find them thus any Saturday night (after family worship,   15
which sends the servant to bed); and sometimes the pauses are so long
that in the end they forget whose move it is.

It is not the room you would be shown into if you were calling
socially on Miss Wylie. The drawing-room for you, and Miss Wylie
in a coloured merino° to receive you; very likely she would exclaim,   20
'This is a pleasant surprise!' though she has seen you coming up the
avenue and has just had time to whip the dustcloths° off the chairs,
and to warn Alick, David and James, that they had better not dare
come in to see you before they have put on a dickey.° Nor is this the
room in which you would dine in solemn grandeur if invited to drop   25
in and take pot-luck, which is how the Wylies invite, it being a family
weakness to pretend that they sit down in the dining-room daily. It
is the real living-room of the house, where Alick, who will never get
used to fashionable ways, can take off his collar and sit happily in his
stocking-soles, and James at times would do so also; but catch Maggie   30
letting him.

There is one very fine chair, but, heavens, not for sitting on; just
to give the room a social standing in an emergency. It sneers at the
other chairs with an air of insolent superiority, like a haughty bride
who has married into the house for money. Otherwise the furniture   35
is homely; most of it has come from that smaller house where the
Wylies began. There is the large and shiny chair which can be turned

into a bed if you look the other way for a moment. James cannot sit on this chair without gradually sliding down it till he is lying luxuriously on the small of his back, his legs indicating, like the hands of a clock, that it is ten past twelve; a position in which Maggie shudders to see him receiving company.

The other chairs are horse-hair, than which nothing is more comfortable if there be a good slit down the seat. The seats are heavily dented, because all the Wylie family sit down with a dump.° The draught-board is on the edge of a large centre table, which also displays four books placed at equal distances from each other, one of them a Bible, and another the family album. If these were the only books they would not justify Maggie in calling this chamber the library, her dogged name for it; while David and James call it the west-room and Alick calls it 'the room,' which is to him the natural name for any apartment without a bed in it. There is a bookcase of pitch pine, which contains six hundred books, with glass doors to prevent your getting at them.

No one does try to get at the books, for the Wylies are not a reading family. They like you to gasp when you see so much literature gathered together in one prison-house, but they gasp themselves at the thought that there are persons, chiefly clergymen, who, having finished one book, coolly begin another. Nevertheless it was not all vainglory that made David buy this library: it was rather a mighty respect for education, as something that he has missed. This same feeling makes him take in the *Contemporary Review*° and stand up to it like a man. Alick, who also has a respect for education, tries to read the *Contemporary*, but becomes dispirited, and may be heard muttering over its pages, 'No, no use, no use, no,' and sometimes even 'Oh hell.' James has no respect for education; and Maggie is at present of an open mind.

They are Wylie and Sons of the local granite quarry, in which Alick was throughout his working days a mason. It is David who has raised them to this position; he climbed up himself step by step (and hewed the steps), and drew the others up after him. 'Wylie Brothers,' Alick would have had the firm called, but David said No, and James said No, and Maggie said No; first honour must be to their father; and Alick now likes it on the whole, though he often sighs at having to shave every day; and on some snell mornings° he still creeps from his couch at four and even at two (thinking that his mallet and chisel are calling him), and begins to pull on his trousers, until the grandeur of them reminds him that he can go to bed again. Sometimes he cries a

little, because there is no more work for him to do for ever and ever;
and then Maggie gives him a spade (without telling David) or David   80
gives him the logs to saw (without telling Maggie).

We have given James a longer time to make his move than our kind
friends in front° will give him, but in the meantime something has
been happening. David has come in, wearing a black coat and his
Sabbath boots, for he has been to a public meeting. David is nigh   85
forty years of age, whiskered like his father and brother (Alick's
whiskers being worn as a sort of cravat round the neck), and he has
the too brisk manner of one who must arrive anywhere a little before
any one else. The painter who did the three of them for fifteen
pounds (you may observe the canvases on the walls) has caught this   90
characteristic, perhaps accidentally, for David is almost stepping out
of his frame, as if to hurry off somewhere; while Alick and James look
as if they were pinned to the wall for life. All the six of them, men
and pictures, however, have a family resemblance, like granite blocks
from their own quarry. They are as Scotch as peat for instance, and   95
they might exchange eyes without any neighbour noticing the
difference, inquisitive little blue eyes that seem to be always totting
up the price of things.

The dambrod players pay no attention to David, nor does he regard
them. Dumping down on the sofa he removes his 'lastic sides,° as his   100
Sabbath boots are called, by pushing one foot against the other, gets
into a pair of hand-sewn slippers, deposits the boots as according to
rule in the ottoman, and crosses to the fire. There must be something
on David's mind to-night, for he pays no attention to the game,
neither gives advice (than which nothing is more maddening) nor   105
exchanges a wink with Alick over the parlous condition of James's
crown. You can hear the wag-at-the-wall clock° in the lobby ticking.
Then David lets himself go; it runs out of him like a hymn:

DAVID   Oh, let the solid ground
                    Not fail beneath my feet,   110
                    Before my life has found
                    What some have found so sweet.°
            (*This is not a soliloquy, but is offered as a definite statement. The
            players emerge from their game with difficulty*)
ALICK (*with James's crown in his hand*) What's that you're saying,
    David?
DAVID (*like a public speaker explaining the situation in a few well-chosen*   115
    words) The thing I'm speaking about is Love.

JAMES (*keeping control of himself*) Do you stand there and say you're in love, David Wylie?

DAVID Me; what would I do with the thing?

JAMES (*who is by no means without pluck*) I see no necessity for calling   120
it a thing.

> (*They are two bachelors who all their lives have been afraid of nothing but Woman. David in his sportive days—which continue—has done roguish things with his arm when conducting a lady home under an umbrella from a soirée,° and has both chuckled and been scared on thinking of it afterwards. James, a commoner fellow altogether, has discussed the sex over a glass, but is too canny° to be in the company of less than two young women at a time*)

DAVID (*derisively*) Oho, has she got you, James?

JAMES (*feeling the sting of it*) Nobody has got me.

DAVID They'll catch you yet, lad.

JAMES They'll never catch me. You've been nearer catched yourself.   125

ALICK Yes, Kitty Menzies, David.

DAVID (*feeling himself under the umbrella*) It was a kind of a shave° that.

ALICK (*who knows all that is to be known about women and can speak of them without a tremor*) It's a curious thing, but a man cannot   130
help winking when he hears that one of his friends has been catched.

DAVID That's so.

JAMES (*clinging to his manhood*) And fear of that wink is what has kept the two of us single men. And yet what's the glory of being   135
single?

DAVID There's no particular glory in it, but it's safe.

JAMES (*putting away his aspirations*) Yes, it's lonely, but it's safe. But who did you mean the poetry for, then?

DAVID For Maggie, of course.   140

> (*You don't know David and James till you know how they love their sister Maggie*)

ALICK I thought that.

DAVID (*coming to the second point of his statement about Love*) I saw her reading poetry and saying those words over to herself.

JAMES She has such a poetical mind.

DAVID Love. There's no doubt as that's what Maggie has set her   145
heart on. And not merely love, but one of those grand noble loves; for though Maggie is undersized she has a passion for romance.

JAMES (*wandering miserably about the room*) It's terrible not to be able to give Maggie what her heart is set on.

> (*The others never pay much attention to James, though he is quite a smart figure in less important houses*)

ALICK (*violently*) Those idiots of men.   150

DAVID Father, did you tell her who had got the minister of Galashiels?°

ALICK (*wagging his head sadly*) I had to tell her. And then I—I—bought her a sealskin muff, and I just slipped it into her hands and came away.   155

JAMES (*illustrating the sense of justice in the Wylie family*) Of course, to be fair to the man, he never pretended he wanted her.

DAVID None of them wants her; that's what depresses her. I was thinking, father, I would buy her that gold watch and chain in Snibby's window. She hankers after it.   160

JAMES (*slapping his pocket*) You're too late, David; I've got them for her.

DAVID It's ill done of the minister. Many a pound of steak has that man had in this house.

ALICK You mind the slippers she worked° for him?   165

JAMES I mind them fine; she began them for William Cathro. She's getting on in years, too, though she looks so young.

ALICK I never can make up my mind, David, whether her curls make her look younger or older.

DAVID (*determinedly*) Younger. Whisht!° I hear her winding the   170
clock. Mind, not a word about the minister to her, James. Don't even mention religion this day.

JAMES Would it be like me to do such a thing?

DAVID It would be very like you. And there's that other matter: say not a syllable about our having a reason for sitting up late to-night.   175
When she says it's bed-time, just all pretend we're not sleepy.

ALICK Exactly, and when——

> (*Here Maggie enters, and all three are suddenly engrossed in the dambrod. We could describe Maggie at great length. But what is the use? What you really want to know is whether she was good-looking. No, she was not. Enter Maggie, who is not good-looking. When this is said, all is said. Enter Maggie, as it were, with her throat cut from ear to ear. She has a soft Scotch voice and a more resolute manner than is perhaps fitting to her plainness; and she stops short at sight of James sprawling unconsciously in the company chair*)

MAGGIE James, I wouldn't sit on the fine chair.

JAMES I forgot again.

(*But he wishes she had spoken more sharply. Even profanation of the fine chair has not roused her. She takes up her knitting, and they all suspect that she knows what they have been talking about*)

MAGGIE You're late, David, it's nearly bed-time.   180

DAVID (*finding the subject a safe one*) I was kept late at the public meeting.

ALICK (*glad to get so far away from Galashiels*) Was it a good meeting?

DAVID Fairish. (*With some heat*) That young John Shand *would* make a speech.°   185

MAGGIE John Shand? Is that the student Shand?

DAVID The same. It's true he's a student at Glasgow University in the winter months, but in summer he's just the railway porter here; and I think it's very presumptuous of a young lad like that to make a speech when he hasn't a penny to bless himself with.   190

ALICK The Shands were always an impudent family, and jealous. I suppose that's the reason they haven't been on speaking terms with us this six years. Was it a good speech?

DAVID (*illustrating the family's generosity*) It was very fine; but he needn't have made fun of *me*.   195

MAGGIE (*losing a stitch*) He dared?

DAVID (*depressed*) You see I can *not* get started on a speech without saying things like 'In rising *for* to make a few remarks.'

JAMES What's wrong with it?

DAVID He mimicked me, and said, 'Will our worthy chairman come   200
for to go for to answer my questions?' and so on; and they roared.

JAMES (*slapping his money pocket*) The sacket.°

DAVID I did feel bitterly, father, the want of education.° (*Without knowing it, he has a beautiful way of pronouncing this noble word*)

MAGGIE (*holding out a kind hand to him*) David.   205

ALICK I've missed it sore, David. Even now I feel the want of it in the very marrow of me. I'm shamed to think I never gave you your chance. But when you were young I was so desperate poor, how could I do it, Maggie?

MAGGIE It wasn't possible, father.   210

ALICK (*gazing at the book-shelves*) To be able to understand these books! To up with them one at a time and scrape them as clean as though they were a bowl of brose.° Lads, it's not to riches, it's to scholarship that I make my humble bow.

JAMES (*who is good at bathos*) There's ten yards of them. And they 215
    were selected by the minister of Galashiels. He said——

DAVID (*quickly*) James.

JAMES I mean—I mean——

MAGGIE (*calmly*) I suppose you mean what you say, James. I hear,
    David, that the minister of Galashiels is to be married on that Miss 220
    Turnbull.

DAVID (*on guard*) So they were saying.

ALICK All I can say is she has made a poor bargain.

MAGGIE (*the damned*) I wonder at you, father. He's a very nice
    gentleman. I'm sure I hope he has chosen wisely. 225

JAMES Not him.

MAGGIE (*getting near her tragedy*) How can you say that when you
    don't know her? I expect she is full of charm.°

ALICK Charm? It's the very word he used.

DAVID Havering° idiot. 230

ALICK What *is* charm, exactly, Maggie?

MAGGIE Oh, it's—it's a sort of bloom on a woman. If you have it,
    you don't need to have anything else; and if you don't have it, it
    doesn't much matter what else you have. Some women, the few,
    have charm for all; and most have charm for one. But some have 235
    charm for none.

    (*Somehow she has stopped knitting. Her men-folk are very
    depressed. James brings his fist down on the table with a crash*)

JAMES (*shouting*) I have a sister that has charm.

MAGGIE No, James, you haven't.

JAMES (*rushing at her with the watch and chain*) Ha'e,° Maggie.
    (*She lets them lie in her lap*)

DAVID Maggie, would you like a silk? 240

MAGGIE What could I do with a silk? (*With a gust of passion*) You
    might as well dress up a little brown hen.
    (*They wriggle miserably*)

JAMES (*stamping*) Bring him here to me.

MAGGIE Bring whom, James?

JAMES David, I would be obliged if you wouldn't kick me beneath 245
    the table.

MAGGIE (*rising*) Let's be practical; let's go to our beds.
    (*This reminds them that they have a job on hand in which she
    is not to share*)

DAVID (*slily*) I don't feel very sleepy yet.

ALICK Nor me either.

JAMES You've just taken the very words out of my mouth. 250

DAVID (*with unusual politeness*) Good-night to you, Maggie.

MAGGIE (*fixing the three of them*) *All* of you unsleepy,° when, as is well known, ten o'clock is your regular bed-time?

JAMES Yes, it's common knowledge that we go to our beds at ten. (*Chuckling*) That's what we're counting on. 255

MAGGIE Counting on?

DAVID You stupid whelp.

JAMES What have *I* done?

MAGGIE (*folding her arms*) There's something up. You've got to tell me, David. 260

DAVID (*who knows when he is beaten*) Go out and watch, James.

MAGGIE Watch?

(*James takes himself off, armed, as Maggie notices, with a stick*)

DAVID (*in his alert business way*) Maggie, there are burglars about.

MAGGIE Burglars? (*She sits rigid, but she is not the kind to scream*)

DAVID We hadn't meant for to tell you till we nabbed them; but 265
they've been in this room twice of late. We sat up last night waiting for them, and we're to sit up again to-night.

MAGGIE The silver plate.

DAVID It's all safe as yet. That makes us think that they were either frightened away these other times, or that they are coming back 270
for to make a clean sweep.

MAGGIE How did you get to know about this?

DAVID It was on Tuesday that the polissman called at the quarry with a very queer story. He had seen a man climbing out at this window at ten past two. 275

MAGGIE Did he chase him?

DAVID It was so dark he lost sight of him at once.

ALICK Tell her about the window.

DAVID We've found out that the catch of the window has been pushed back by slipping the blade of a knife between the wood- 280
work.

MAGGIE David.

ALICK The polissman said he was carrying a little carpet bag.°

MAGGIE The silver plate *is* gone.

DAVID No, no. We were thinking that very likely he has bunches of 285
keys in the bag.

MAGGIE Or weapons.

DAVID As for that, we have some pretty stout weapons ourselves in the umbrella stand. So, if you'll go to your bed, Maggie——

MAGGIE Me? and my brothers in danger.   290

ALICK There's just one of them.

MAGGIE The polissman just saw one.

DAVID (*licking his palms*) I would be very pleased if there were three
of them.

MAGGIE I watch° with you. I would be very pleased if there were   295
four of them.

DAVID And they say she has no charm!

> (*James returns on tiptoe as if the burglars were beneath the
> table. He signs to every one to breathe no more, and then
> whispers his news*)

JAMES He's there. I had no sooner gone out than I saw him sliding
down the garden wall, close to the rhubarbs.

ALICK What's he like?   .   300

JAMES He's an ugly customer. That's all I could see. There was a
little carpet bag in his hand.

DAVID That's him.

JAMES He slunk into the rhodydendrons, and he's there now,
watching the window.   305

DAVID We have him. Out with the light.

> (*The room is beautified by a chandelier fitted for three gas jets,
> but with the advance of progress one of these has been removed
> and the incandescent light° put in its place. This alone is lit.
> Alick climbs a chair, pulls a little chain, and the room is now
> but vaguely lit by the fire. It plays fitfully on four sparkling
> faces*)

MAGGIE Do you think he saw you, James?

JAMES I couldn't say, but in any case I was too clever for him. I
looked up at the stars, and yawned loud at them as if I was
tremendous sleepy.   310

> (*There is a long pause during which they are lurking in the
> shadows. At last they hear some movement, and they steal like
> ghosts from the room. We see David turning out the lobby light;
> then the door closes and an empty room awaits the intruder with
> a shudder of expectancy. The window opens and shuts as softly
> as if this were a mother peering in to see whether her baby is
> asleep. Then the head of a man shows between the curtains. The
> remainder of him follows. He is carrying a little carpet bag. He
> stands irresolute; what puzzles him evidently is that the Wylies
> should have retired to rest without lifting that piece of coal off
> the fire.° He opens the door and peeps into the lobby, listening*)

to the wag-at-the-wall clock. All seems serene, and he turns on the light. We see him clearly now. He is John Shand, age twenty-one, boots muddy, as an indignant carpet can testify. He wears a shabby topcoat and a cockerty bonnet;° otherwise he is in the well-worn corduroys of a railway porter. His movements, at first stealthy, become almost homely as he feels that he is secure. He opens the bag and takes out a bunch of keys, a small paper parcel, and a black implement that may be a burglar's jemmy. This cool customer examines the fire and piles on more coals. With the keys he opens the door of the bookcase, selects two large volumes, and brings them to the table. He takes off his topcoat and opens his parcel, which we now see contains sheets of foolscap paper. His next action shows that the 'jemmy' is really a ruler. He knows where the pen and ink are kept. He pulls the fine chair nearer to the table, sits on it, and proceeds to write, occasionally dotting the carpet with ink as he stabs the air with his pen. He is so occupied that he does not see the door opening, and the Wylie family staring at him.° They are armed with sticks)

ALICK (*at last*) When you're ready, John Shand.
    (*John hints back,° and then he has the grace to rise, dogged and expressionless*)

JAMES (*like a railway porter*) Ticket, please.

DAVID You can't think of anything clever for to go for to say now, John.

MAGGIE I hope you find that chair comfortable,° young man.   315

JOHN I have no complaint to make against the chair.

ALICK (*who is really distressed*) A native of the town. The disgrace to your family! I feel pity for the Shands this night.

JOHN (*glowering*) I'll thank you, Mr Wylie, not to pity my family.

JAMES Canny, canny.°   320

MAGGIE (*that sense of justice again*) I think you should let the young man explain. It mayn't be so bad as we thought.

DAVID Explain away, my billie.°

JOHN Only the uneducated would need an explanation. I'm a student, (*with a little passion*) and I'm desperate for want of books.   325
You have all I want here; no use to you but for display; well, I came here to study. I come twice weekly. (*Amazement of his hosts*)

DAVID (*who is the first to recover*) By the window.

JOHN Do you think a Shand would so far lower himself as to enter your door? Well, is it a case for the police?   330

JAMES It is.

MAGGIE (*not so much out of the goodness of her heart as to patronise the Shands*) It seems to me it's a case for us all to go to our beds and leave the young man to study; but not on that chair. (*And she wheels the chair away from him*) 335

JOHN Thank you, Miss Maggie, but I couldn't be beholden to you.

JAMES My opinion is that he's nobody, so out with him.

JOHN Yes, out with me. And you'll be cheered to hear I'm likely to be a nobody for a long time to come.

DAVID (*who had been beginning to respect him*) Are you a poor scholar? 340

JOHN On the contrary, I'm a brilliant scholar.

DAVID It's siller,° then?

JOHN (*glorified by experiences he has shared with many a gallant soul*) My first year at college I lived on a barrel of potatoes, and we had just a sofa-bed between two of us; when the one lay down the other 345 had to get up. Do you think it was hardship? It was sublime. But this year I can't afford it. I'll have to stay on here, collecting the tickets of the illiterate, such as you, when I might be with Romulus and Remus° among the stars.

JAMES (*summing up*) Havers.° 350

DAVID (*in whose head some design is vaguely taking shape*) Whisht, James. I must say, young lad, I like your spirit. Now tell me, what's your professors' opinion of your future.

JOHN They think me a young man of extraordinary promise.

DAVID You have a name here for high moral character. 355

JOHN And justly.

DAVID Are you serious-minded?

JOHN I never laughed in my life.

DAVID Who do you sit under° in Glasgow?

JOHN Mr Flemister of the Sauchiehall High. 360

DAVID Are you a Sabbath-school teacher?

JOHN I am.

DAVID One more question. Are you promised?

JOHN To a lady?

DAVID Yes. 365

JOHN I've never given one of them a single word of encouragement. I'm too much occupied thinking about my career.

DAVID So. (*He reflects, and finally indicates by a jerk of the head that he wishes to talk with his father behind the door*)

JAMES (*longingly*) Do you want me too? 370
        (*But they go out without even answering him*)

MAGGIE I don't know what maggot they have in their heads,° but sit down, young man, till they come back.

JOHN My name's Mr Shand, and till I'm called that I decline to sit down again in this house.

MAGGIE Then I'm thinking, young sir, you'll have a weary wait.   375
          (*While he waits you can see how pinched his face is. He is little more than a boy, and he seldom has enough to eat. David and Alick return presently, looking as sly as if they had been discussing some move on the dambrod, as indeed they have*)

DAVID (*suddenly become genial*) Sit down, Mr Shand, and pull in your chair. You'll have a thimbleful of something to keep the cold out? (*Briskly*) Glasses, Maggie.
          (*She wonders, but gets glasses and decanter from the sideboard, which James calls the chiffy.° David and Alick, in the most friendly manner, also draw up to the table*)
    You're not a totaller,° I hope?

JOHN (*guardedly*) I'm practically a totaller.   380

DAVID So are we. How do you take it? Is there any hot water, Maggie?

JOHN If I take it at all, and I haven't made up my mind yet, I'll take it cold.

DAVID You'll take it hot, James?   385

JAMES (*also sitting at the table but completely befogged*) No, I——

DAVID (*decisively*) I think you'll take it hot, James.

JAMES (*sulking*) I'll take it hot.

DAVID The kettle, Maggie.
          (*James has evidently to take it hot so that they can get at the business now on hand while Maggie goes kitchenward for the kettle*)

ALICK Now, David, quick, before she comes back.   390

DAVID Mr Shand, we have an offer to make you.

JOHN (*warningly*) No patronage.

ALICK It's strictly a business affair.

DAVID Leave it to me, father. It's this——(*But to his annoyance the suspicious Maggie has already returned with the kettle*) Maggie, don't   395
    you see that you're not wanted?

MAGGIE (*sitting down by the fire and resuming her knitting*) I do, David.

DAVID I have a proposition to put before Mr Shand, and women are out of place in business transactions.
          (*The needles continue to click*)

ALICK (*sighing*) We'll have to let her bide, David.   400

DAVID (*sternly*) Woman. (*But even this does not budge her*) Very well then, sit there, but don't interfere, mind. Mr Shand, we're willing, the three of us, to lay out £300 on your education if——

JOHN Take care.

DAVID (*slowly, which is not his wont*) On condition that five years from now, Maggie Wylie, if still unmarried, can claim to marry you, should such be her wish; the thing to be perfectly open on her side, but you to be strictly tied down.

JAMES (*enlightened*) So, so.

DAVID (*resuming his smart manner*) Now, what have you to say? Decide.

JOHN (*after a pause*) I regret to say——

MAGGIE It doesn't matter what he regrets to say, because I decide against it. And I think it was very ill-done of you to make any such proposal.

DAVID (*without looking at her*) Quiet, Maggie.

JOHN (*looking at her*) I must say, Miss Maggie, I don't see what reasons *you* can have for being so set against it.

MAGGIE If you would grow a beard,° Mr Shand, the reasons wouldn't be quite so obvious.

JOHN I'll never grow a beard.

MAGGIE Then you're done for at the start.

ALICK Come, come.

MAGGIE Seeing I have refused the young man——

JOHN Refused!

DAVID That's no reason why we shouldn't have his friendly opinion. Your objections, Mr Shand?

JOHN Simply, it's a one-sided bargain. I admit I'm no catch at present; but what could a man of my abilities not soar to with three hundred pounds? Something far above what she could aspire to.

MAGGIE Oh, indeed!

DAVID The position is that without the three hundred you can't soar.

JOHN You have me there.

MAGGIE Yes, but——

ALICK You see *you're* safeguarded, Maggie; you don't need to take him unless you like, but he has to take you.

JOHN That's an unfair arrangement also.

MAGGIE I wouldn't dream of it without that condition.

JOHN Then you *are* thinking of it?

MAGGIE Poof!

DAVID It's a good arrangement for you, Mr Shand. The chances are you'll never have to go on with it, for in all probability she'll marry soon.

JAMES She's tremendous run after.   445

JOHN Even if that's true, it's just keeping me in reserve in case she misses doing better.

DAVID (*relieved*) That's the situation in a nutshell.°

JOHN Another thing. Supposing I was to get fond of her?

ALICK (*wistfully*) It's very likely.   450

JOHN Yes, and then suppose she was to give me the go-by?

DAVID You have to risk that.

JOHN Or take it the other way. Supposing as I got to know her I *could not* endure her?

DAVID (*suavely*) You have to take both risks.   455

JAMES (*less suavely*) What you need, John Shand, is a clout on the head.

JOHN Three hundred pounds is no great sum.

DAVID You can take it or leave it.

ALICK No great sum for a student studying for the ministry!   460

JOHN Do you think that with that amount of money I would stop short at being a minister?

DAVID That's how I like to hear you speak. A young Scotsman of your ability let loose upon the world with £300, what could he not do? It's almost appalling to think of; especially if he went among 465 the English.°

JOHN What do you think, Miss Maggie?

MAGGIE (*who is knitting*) I have no thoughts on the subject either way.

JOHN (*after looking her over*) What's her age? She looks young, but 470 they say it's the curls that does it.

DAVID (*rather happily*) She's one of those women who are eternally young.

JOHN I can't take that for an answer.

DAVID She's twenty-five.   475

JOHN I'm just twenty-one.

JAMES I read in a book that about four years' difference in the ages is the ideal thing. (*As usual he is disregarded*)

DAVID Well, Mr Shand?

JOHN (*where is his mother?*) I'm willing if she's willing.   480

DAVID Maggie?

MAGGIE There can be no 'if' about it. It must be an offer.

JOHN A Shand give a Wylie such a chance to humiliate him? Never.

MAGGIE Then all is off.

DAVID Come, come, Mr Shand, it's just a form.   485

JOHN (*reluctantly*) Miss Maggie, will you?

MAGGIE (*doggedly*) Is it an offer?

JOHN (*dourly*) Yes.

MAGGIE (*rising*) Before I answer I want first to give you a chance of
drawing back.   490

DAVID Maggie.

MAGGIE (*bravely*) When they said that I have been run after they
were misleading you. I'm without charm; nobody has ever been
after me.

JOHN Oho!   495

ALICK They will be yet.

JOHN (*the innocent*) It shows at least that you haven't been after
them.

    (*His hosts exchange a self-conscious glance*)

MAGGIE One thing more; David said I'm twenty-five, I'm twenty-
six.   500

JOHN Aha!

MAGGIE Now be practical. Do you withdraw from the bargain, or do
you not?

JOHN (*on reflection*) It's a bargain.

MAGGIE Then so be it.   505

DAVID (*hurriedly*) And that's settled. Did you say you would take it
hot, Mr Shand?

JOHN I think I'll take it neat.

    (*The others decide to take it hot, and there is some careful
business here with the toddy° ladles*)

ALICK Here's to you, and your career.

JOHN Thank you. To you, Miss Maggie. Had we not better draw up   510
a legal document? Lawyer Crosbie could do it on the quiet.

DAVID Should we do that, or should we just trust to one another's
honour?

ALICK (*gallantly*) Let Maggie decide.

MAGGIE I think we would better have a legal document.°   515

DAVID We'll have it drawn up to-morrow. I was thinking the best
way would be for to pay the money in five yearly instalments.

JOHN I was thinking, better bank the whole sum in my name at once.

ALICK I think David's plan's the best.

JOHN I think not. Of course if it's not convenient to you°——   520

DAVID (*touched to the quick*) It's perfectly convenient. What do you say, Maggie?

MAGGIE I agree with John.

DAVID (*with an odd feeling that Maggie is now on the other side*) Very well.   525

JOHN Then as that's settled I think I'll be stepping.° (*He is putting his papers back in the bag*)

ALICK (*politely*) If you would like to sit on at your books——

JOHN As I can come at any orra time° now I think I'll be stepping. (*Maggie helps him into his topcoat*)   530

MAGGIE Have you a muffler, John?

JOHN I have. (*He gets it from his pocket.*)

MAGGIE You had better put it twice round.° (*She does this for him*)

DAVID Well, good-night to you, Mr Shand.

ALICK And good luck.   535

JOHN Thank you. The same to you. And I'll cry in° at your office in the morning before the 6.20 is due.

DAVID I'll have the document ready for you. (*There is the awkward pause that sometimes follows great events*) I think, Maggie, you might see Mr Shand to the door.   540

MAGGIE Certainly. (*John is going by the window*) This way, John.
    (*She takes him off by the more usual exit*)

DAVID He's a fine frank fellow; and you saw how cleverly he got the better of me about banking the money. (*As the heads of the conspirators come gleefully together*) I tell you, father, he has a grand business head.   545

ALICK Lads, he's canny. He's cannier than any of us.

JAMES Except maybe Maggie. He has no idea what a remarkable woman Maggie is.

ALICK Best he shouldn't know. Men are nervous of remarkable women.   550

JAMES She's a long time in coming back.

DAVID (*not quite comfortable*) It's a good sign. H'sh. [*Re-enter Maggie*] What sort of a night is it, Maggie?

MAGGIE It's a little blowy.
    (*She gets a large dust-cloth which is lying folded on a shelf, and proceeds to spread it over the fine chair. The men exchange self-conscious glances*)

DAVID (*stretching himself*) Yes—well, well, oh yes. It's getting late.   555
What is it with you, father?

ALICK I'm ten forty-two.°

JAMES I'm ten-forty.

DAVID Ten forty-two.

    (*They wind up their watches*)

MAGGIE It's high time we were bedded. (*She puts her hands on their*   560
*shoulders lovingly, which is the very thing they have been trying to
avoid*) You're very kind to me.

DAVID Havers.

ALICK Havers.

JAMES (*but this does not matter*) Havers.   565

MAGGIE (*a little dolefully*) I'm a sort of sorry for the young man,
David.

DAVID Not at all. You'll be the making of him. (*She lifts the two
volumes*) Are you taking the books to your bed, Maggie?

MAGGIE Yes. I don't want him to know things I don't know myself.   570
    (*She departs with the books; and Alick and David, the villains,
now want to get away from each other*)

ALICK Yes—yes. Oh yes—ay, man—it is so—umpha. You'll lift the
big coals off, David.

    (*He wanders away to his spring mattress. David removes the
coals*)

JAMES (*who would like to sit down and have an argy-bargy*) It's a most
romantical affair. (*But he gets no answer*) I wonder how it'll turn
out? (*No answer*) She's queer, Maggie. I wonder how some clever   575
writer has never noticed how queer women are. It's my belief you
could write a whole book about them.° (*David remains obdurate*) It
was very noble of her to tell him she's twenty-six. (*Muttering as he
too wanders away*) But I thought she was twenty-seven.

    (*David turns out the light*)

Act 2

Six years have elapsed and John Shand's great hour has come. Perhaps his great hour really lies ahead of him, perhaps he had it six years ago; it often passes us by in the night with such a faint call that we don't even turn in our beds. But according to the trumpets this is John's great hour; it is the hour for which he has long been working 5 with his coat off; and now the coat is on again (broadcloth but ill-fitting),° for there is no more to do but await results. He is standing for Parliament, and this is election night.

As the scene discloses itself you get, so to speak, one of John Shand's posters in the face. Vote for Shand. Shand, Shand, Shand. 10 Civil and Religious Liberty, Faith, Hope, Freedom. They are all fly-blown names for Shand. Have a placard about Shand, have a hundred placards about him, it is snowing Shand to-night in Glasgow; take the paste out of your eye, and you will see that we are in one of Shand's committee rooms. It has been a hairdresser's empor- 15 ium, but Shand, Shand, Shand has swept through it like a wind, leaving nothing but the fixtures; why shave, why have your head doused in those basins when you can be brushed and scraped and washed up for ever by simply voting for Shand?

There are a few hard chairs for yelling Shand from, and then 20 rushing away. There is an iron spiral staircase that once led to the ladies' hairdressing apartments, but now leads to more Shand, Shand, Shand. A glass door at the back opens on to the shop proper, screaming Civil and Religious Liberty, Shand, as it opens, and beyond is the street crammed with still more Shand pro and con. Men in 25 every sort of garb rush in and out, up and down the stair, shouting the magic word. Then there is a lull, and down the stair comes Maggie Wylie, decidedly overdressed in blue velvet and (let us get this over) less good-looking than ever. She raises her hands to heaven, she spins round like a little teetotum.° To her from the street, 30 suffering from a determination° of the word Shand to the mouth, rush Alick and David. Alick is thinner (being older), David is stouter (being older), and they are both in tweeds and silk hats.

MAGGIE David—have they—is he? quick, quick!
DAVID There's no news yet, no news. It's terrible. 35
(*The teetotum revolves more quickly*)

ALICK For God's sake, Maggie, sit down.

MAGGIE I can't, I can't!

DAVID Hold her down.

> (*They press her into a chair; James darts in, stouter also. His necktie has gone; he will never again be able to attend a funeral in that hat*)

JAMES (*wildly*) John Shand's the man for you. John Shand's the man for you. John Shand's the man for you.   40

DAVID (*clutching him*) Have you heard anything?

JAMES Not a word.

ALICK Look at her.

DAVID Maggie. (*He goes on his knees beside her, pressing her to him in affectionate anxiety*) It was mad of him to dare.   45

MAGGIE It was grand of him.

ALICK (*moving about distraught*) Insane ambition.

MAGGIE Glorious ambition.

DAVID Maggie, Maggie, my lamb, best be prepared for the worst.

MAGGIE (*husky*) I am prepared.   50

ALICK Six weary years has she waited for this night.

MAGGIE Six brave years has John toiled for this night.

JAMES And you could have had him, Maggie, at the end of five. The document says five.

MAGGIE Do you think I grudge not being married to him yet? Was   55
I to hamper him till the fight was won?

DAVID (*with wrinkled brows*) But if it's lost?

> (*She can't answer.*)

ALICK (*starting*) What's that?

> (*The three listen at the door; the shouting dies down*)

DAVID They're terrible still; what can make them so still?

> (*James spirits himself away. Alick and David blanch to hear Maggie speaking softly as if to John*)

MAGGIE Did you say you had lost, John?° Of course you would lose the   60
first time, dear John. Six years. Very well, we'll begin another six
to–night. You'll win yet. (*Fiercely*) Never give in, John, never give in!

> (*The roar of the multitude breaks out again and comes rolling nearer*)

DAVID I think he's coming.

> (*James is fired into the room like a squeezed onion*)

JAMES He's coming!

> (*They may go on speaking, but through the clang outside none could hear. The populace seem to be trying to take the committee*)

room by assault. Out of the scrimmage° a man emerges dish-
evelled and bursts into the room, closing the door behind him. It
is John Shand in a five guinea suit,° including the hat. There
are other changes in him also, for he has been delving his way
through loamy ground all those years. His right shoulder, which
he used to raise to pound a path through the crowd, now remains
permanently in that position. His mouth tends to close like a box.
His eyes are tired, they need some one to pull the lids over them
and send him to sleep for a week. But they are honest eyes still,
and faithful, and could even light up his face at times with a
smile, if the mouth would give a little help)

JOHN (*clinging to a chair that he may not fly straight to heaven*) I'm in;   65
I'm elected. Majority two hundred and forty-four; I'm John
Shand, *MP*.

    (*The crowd have the news by this time and their roar breaks the*
door open. James is off at once to tell them that he is to be
Shand's brother-in-law. A teardrop clings to Alick's nose; David
hits out playfully at John, and John in an ecstasy returns the
blow)

DAVID Fling yourself at the door, father, and bar them out. Maggie,
what keeps you so quiet now?

MAGGIE (*weak in her limbs*) You're sure you're in, John?   70

JOHN Majority 244. I've beaten the baronet. I've done it, Maggie,
and not a soul to help me; I've done it alone. (*His voice breaks; you*
could almost pick up the pieces) I'm as hoarse as a crow, and I have
to address the Cowcaddens Club yet; David, pump some oxygen
into me.°   75

DAVID Certainly, Mr Shand. (*While he does it, Maggie is seeing visions*)

ALICK What are you doing, Maggie?

MAGGIE This is the House of Commons, and I'm John, catching the
Speaker's eye for the first time. Do you see a queer little old wifie
sitting away up there in the Ladies' Gallery? That's me. Mr   80
Speaker, sir, I rise to make my historic maiden speech. I am no
orator, sir; voice from Ladies' Gallery, 'Are you not, John? you'll
soon let them see that'; cries of 'Silence, woman,' and general
indignation. Mr Speaker, sir, I stand here diffidently with my eyes
on the Treasury Bench; voice from the Ladies' Gallery, 'And   85
you'll soon have your coat-tails on it, John'; loud cries of 'Remove
that little old wifie,' in which she is forcibly ejected, and the
honourable gentleman resumes his seat in a torrent of admiring
applause.°

(*Alick and David waggle their proud heads*)

JOHN (*tolerantly*) Maggie, Maggie. 90

MAGGIE You're not angry with me, John?

JOHN No, no.

MAGGIE But you glowered.

JOHN I was thinking of Sir Peregrine. Just because I beat him at the poll he took a shabby revenge; he congratulated me in French, a 95 language I haven't taken the trouble to master.

MAGGIE (*becoming a little taller*) Would it help you, John, if you were to marry a woman that could speak French?

DAVID (*quickly*) Not at all.

MAGGIE (*gloriously*) *Mon cher Jean, laissez-moi parler le français,* 100 *voulez-vous un interprète?*°

JOHN Hullo!

MAGGIE *Je suis la sœur française de mes deux frères écossais.*°

DAVID (*worshipping her*) She's been learning French.

JOHN (*lightly*) Well done. 105

MAGGIE (*grandly*) They're arriving.

ALICK Who?

MAGGIE Our guests. This is London, and Mrs John Shand° is giving her first reception. (*Airily*) Have I told you, darling, who are coming to-night? There's that dear Sir Peregrine. (*To Alick*) Sir 110 Peregrine, this *is* a pleasure. *Avez-vous* . . . So sorry we beat you at the poll.

JOHN I'm doubting the baronet would sit on you,° Maggie.

MAGGIE I've invited a lord to sit on the baronet. *Voilà!*

DAVID (*delighted*) You thing! You'll find the lords expensive. 115

MAGGIE Just a little cheap lord. (*James enters importantly*) My dear Lord Cheap, this is kind of you.

(*James hopes that Maggie's reason is not unbalanced*)

DAVID (*who really ought to have had education*) How de doo, Cheap?

JAMES (*bewildered*) Maggie—— 120

MAGGIE Yes, do call me Maggie.

ALICK (*grinning*) She's practising her first party, James. The swells° are at the door.

JAMES (*heavily*) That's what I came to say. They *are* at the door.

JOHN Who? 125

JAMES The swells; in their motor. (*He gives John three cards*)

JOHN 'Mr Tenterden.'

DAVID Him that was speaking for you?

JOHN The same. He's a whip and an Honourable.° 'Lady Sybil
    Tenterden.' (*Frowns*) Her! She's his sister.   130

MAGGIE A married woman?

JOHN No. 'The Comtesse de la Brière.'

MAGGIE (*the scholar*) She must be French.

JOHN Yes; I think she's some relation. She's a widow.

JAMES But what am I to say to them? ('*Mr Shand's compliments, and*   135
    he will be proud to receive them' is the very least that the Wylies
    expect)

JOHN (*who was evidently made for great ends*) Say I'm very busy, but
    if they care to wait I hope presently to give them a few minutes.

JAMES (*thunderstruck*) Good God, Mr Shand!   140
        (*But it makes him John's more humble servant than ever, and*
        he departs with the message)

JOHN (*not unaware of the sensation he has created*) I'll go up and let
    the crowd see me from the window.

MAGGIE But—but—what are we to do with these ladies?

JOHN (*as he tramps upwards*) It's your reception, Maggie; this will
    prove you.°   145

MAGGIE (*growing smaller*) Tell me what you know about this Lady
    Sybil?

JOHN The only thing I know about her is that she thinks me vulgar.

MAGGIE You?

JOHN She has attended some of my meetings, and I'm told she said   150
    that.

MAGGIE What could the woman mean?

JOHN I wonder. When I come down I'll ask her.
    (*With his departure Maggie's nervousness increases*)

ALICK (*encouragingly*) In at them, Maggie, with your French.

MAGGIE It's all slipping from me, father.   155

DAVID (*gloomily*) I'm sure to say 'for to come for to go.'
    (*The newcomers glorify the room, and Maggie feels that they
    have lifted her up with the tongs and deposited her in one of the
    basins. They are far from intending to be rude; it is not their
    fault that thus do swans scatter the ducks. They do not know
    that they are guests of the family, they think merely that they
    are waiting with other strangers in a public room; they undulate°
    inquiringly, and if Maggie could undulate in return she would
    have no cause for offence. But she suddenly realises that this is
    an art as yet denied her, and that though David might buy her
    evening-gowns as fine as theirs (and is at this moment probably*

deciding to do so), she would look better carrying them in her arms than on her person. She also feels that to emerge from wraps as they are doing is more difficult than to plank your money on the counter for them. The Comtesse she could forgive, for she is old; but Lady Sybil is young and beautiful and comes lazily to rest like a stately ship of Tarsus°)

COMTESSE (*smiling divinely, and speaking with such a pretty accent*) I hope one is not in the way. We were told we might wait.

MAGGIE (*bravely climbing out of the basin*) Certainly—I am sure—if you will be so—it is——   160
    (*She knows that David and her father are very sorry for her*)
    (*A high voice is heard orating outside*)

SYBIL (*screwing her nose deliciously*) He is at it again, auntie.

COMTESSE *Mon Dieu!* (*Like one begging pardon of the universe*) It is Mr Tenterden, you understand, making one more of his delightful speeches to the crowd. *Would* you be so charming as to shut the door?   165
    (*This to David in such appeal that she is evidently making the petition of her life. David saves her*)

MAGGIE (*determined not to go under*) *J'espère que vous—trouvez—cette —réunion— intéressante?*

COMTESSE *Vous parlez français? Mais c'est charmant! Voyons, causons un peu. Racontez moi tout de ce grand homme, toutes les choses merveilleuses qu'il a faites.*   170

MAGGIE *I—I—Je connais——*° (*Alas!*)

COMTESSE (*naughtily*) Forgive me, mademoiselle, I thought you spoke French.

SYBIL (*who knows that David admires her shoulders*) How wicked of you, auntie. (*To Maggie*) I assure you none of us can understand   175 her when she gallops at that pace.

MAGGIE (*crushed*) It doesn't matter. I will tell Mr Shand that you are here.

SYBIL (*drawling*) Please don't trouble him. We are really only waiting till my brother recovers and can take us back to our hotel.   180

MAGGIE I'll tell him.
    (*She is glad to disappear up the stair*)

COMTESSE The lady seems distressed. Is she a relation of Mr Shand?

DAVID Not for to say a relation. She's my sister. Our name is Wylie.
    (*But granite quarries are nothing to them*)

COMTESSE How do you do? You are the committee man of Mr Shand?   185

DAVID No, just friends.

COMTESSE (*gaily to the basins*) Aha! I know you. Next, please! Sybil, do you weigh yourself, or are you asleep?

>   (*Lady Sybil has sunk indolently into a weighing-chair°*)

SYBIL Not quite, auntie.

COMTESSE (*the mirror of la politesse*) Tell me all about Mr Shand. 190
Was it here that he—picked up the pin?°

DAVID The pin?

COMTESSE As *I* have read, a self-made man always begins by picking up a pin. After that, as the memoirs say, his rise was rapid.

>   (*David, however, is once more master of himself, and indeed has begun to tot up the cost of their garments*)

DAVID It wasn't a pin he picked up, my lady; it was £300.   195

ALICK (*who feels that John's greatness has been outside the conversation quite long enough*) And his rise wasn't so rapid, just at first, David!

DAVID He had his fight. His original intention was to become a minister; he's university-educated, you know; he's not a working-man member.   200

ALICK (*with reverence*) He's an MA. But while he was a student he got a place in an iron-cementer's business.

COMTESSE (*now far out of her depths*) Iron-cementer?

DAVID They scrape boilers.

COMTESSE I see. The fun men have, Sybil!   205

DAVID (*with some solemnity*) There have been millions made in scraping boilers. They say, father, he went into business so as to be able to pay off the £300.

ALICK (*slily*) So I've heard.

COMTESSE Aha—it was a loan?   210

>   (*David and Alick are astride their great subject now*)

DAVID No, a gift—of a sort—from some well-wishers. But they wouldn't hear of his paying it off, father!

ALICK Not them!

COMTESSE (*restraining an impulse to think of other things*) That was kind, charming.   215

ALICK (*with a look at David*) Yes. Well, my lady, he developed a perfect genius for the iron-cementing.

DAVID But his ambition wasn't satisfied. Soon he had public life in his eye. As a heckler he was something fearsome; they had to seat him on the platform for to keep him quiet. Next they had to let   220
him into the Chair. After that he did all the speaking; he cleared all roads before him like a fire-engine; and when this vacancy

occurred, you could hardly say it did occur, so quickly did he step
into it. My lady, there are few more impressive sights in the world
than a Scotsman on the make.°   225
COMTESSE I can well believe it. And now he has said farewell to
boilers?
DAVID (*impressively*) Not at all; the firm promised if he was elected
for to make him their London manager at £800 a year.
COMTESSE There is a strong man for you, Sybil; but I believe you   230
are asleep.
SYBIL (*stirring herself*) Honestly I'm not. (*Sweetly to the others*) But
would you mind finding out whether my brother is drawing to a
close?

> (*David goes out, leaving poor Alick marooned. The Comtesse is
> kind to him*)

COMTESSE Thank you very much. (*Which helps Alick out*) Don't you   235
love a strong man, sleepy head?
SYBIL (*preening herself*) I never met one.
COMTESSE Neither have I. But if you *did* meet one, would he wake
you up?
SYBIL I dare say he would find there were two of us.   240
COMTESSE (*considering her*) Yes, I think he would. Ever been in love,
you cold thing?
SYBIL (*yawning*) I have never shot up in flame, auntie.
COMTESSE Think you could manage it?
SYBIL If Mr Right came along.   245
COMTESSE As a girl of to-day it would be your duty to tame him.
SYBIL As a girl of to-day I would try to do my duty.
COMTESSE And if it turned out that *he* tamed you instead?
SYBIL He would have to do that if he were *my* Mr Right.
COMTESSE And then?   250
SYBIL Then, of course, I should adore him. Auntie, I think if I ever
really love it will be like Mary Queen of Scots, who said of her
Bothwell° that she could follow him round the world in her nighty.
COMTESSE My petite!
SYBIL I believe I mean it.   255
COMTESSE Oh, it is quite my conception of your character. Do you
know, I am rather sorry for this Mr John Shand.
SYBIL (*opening her fine eyes*) Why? He is quite a boor, is he not?
COMTESSE For that very reason. Because his great hour is already
nearly sped. That wild bull manner that moves the multitude—   260
they will laugh at it in your House of Commons.

SYBIL (*indifferent*) I suppose so.

COMTESSE Yet if he had education—

SYBIL Have we not been hearing how superbly he is educated?

COMTESSE It is such as you or me that he needs to educate him now.   265
 You could do it almost too well.

SYBIL (*with that pretty stretch of neck*) I am not sufficiently interested.
 I retire in your favour. How would you begin?

COMTESSE By asking him to drop in, about five, of course. By the
 way, I wonder is there a Mrs Shand?   270

SYBIL I have no idea. But they marry young.°

COMTESSE If there is not, there is probably a lady waiting for him,
 somewhere in a boiler.

SYBIL I dare say.
      (*Maggie descends*)

MAGGIE Mr Shand will be down directly.   275

COMTESSE Thank you. Your brother has been giving us such an
 interesting account of his career. I forget, Sybil, whether he said
 that he was married.

MAGGIE No, he's not married; but he will be soon.

COMTESSE Ah! (*She is merely making conversation*) A friend of   280
 yours?

MAGGIE (*now a scorner of herself*) I don't think much of her.°

COMTESSE In that case, tell me all about her.

MAGGIE There's not much to tell. She's common, and stupid. One
 of those who go in for self-culture; and then when the test comes   285
 they break down. (*With sinister enjoyment*) She'll be the ruin of
 him.

COMTESSE But is not that sad! Figure to yourself how many men
 with greatness before them have been shipwrecked by marrying in
 the rank from which they sprang.   290

MAGGIE I've told her that.

COMTESSE But she will not give him up?

MAGGIE No.

SYBIL Why should she if he cares for her? What is her name?

MAGGIE It's—Maggie.   295

COMTESSE (*still uninterested*) Well, I am afraid that Maggie is to do
 for John. (*John comes down*) Ah, our hero!

JOHN Sorry I have kept you waiting. The Comtesse?

COMTESSE And my niece Lady Sybil Tenterden. (*Sybil's head inclines
 on its stem*) She is not really all my niece; I mean I am only half   300
 of her aunt. What a triumph, Mr Shand!

JOHN Oh, pretty fair, pretty fair. Your brother has just finished addressing the crowd, Lady Sybil.

SYBIL Then we must not detain Mr Shand, auntie.

COMTESSE (*who unless her heart is touched thinks insincerity charming*) 305 Only one word. I heard you speak last night. Sublime! Just the sort of impassioned eloquence that your House of Commons loves.

JOHN It's very good of you to say so.

COMTESSE But we must run. *Bon soir.*
(*Sybil bows as to some one far away*)

JOHN Good-night, Lady Sybil. I hear you think I'm vulgar. 310
(*Eyebrows are raised*)

COMTESSE My dear Mr Shand, what absurd——

JOHN I was told she said that after hearing me speak.

COMTESSE Quite a mistake, I——

JOHN (*doggedly*) Is it not true?

SYBIL ('*waking up*') You seem to know, Mr Shand; and as you press 315 me so unnecessarily—well, yes, that is how you struck me.

COMTESSE My child!

SYBIL (*who is a little agitated*) He would have it.

JOHN (*perplexed*) What's the matter? I just wanted to know, because if it's true I must alter it. 320

COMTESSE There, Sybil, see how he values your good opinion.

SYBIL (*her svelte figure giving like a fishing-rod*) It is very nice of you to put it in that way, Mr Shand. Forgive me.

JOHN But I don't quite understand yet. Of course, it can't matter to me, Lady Sybil, what you think of me; what I mean is, that I 325 mustn't be vulgar if it would be injurious to my career.
(*The fishing-rod regains its rigidity*)

SYBIL I see. No, of course, I could not affect your career, Mr Shand.

JOHN (*who quite understands that he is being challenged*) That's so, Lady Sybil, meaning no offence. 330

SYBIL (*who has a naughty little impediment in her voice when she is most alluring*) Of course not. And we are friends again?

JOHN Certainly.

SYBIL Then I hope you will come to see me in London as I present no terrors. 335

JOHN (*he is a man, is John*) I'll be very pleased.

SYBIL Any afternoon about five.

JOHN Much obliged. And you can teach me the things I don't know yet, if you'll be so kind.

SYBIL (*the impediment becoming more assertive*) If you wish it, I shall   340
do my best.

JOHN Thank you, Lady Sybil. And who knows there may be one or
two things I can teach you.

SYBIL (*it has now become an angel's hiccough*) Yes, we can help one
another. Good-bye till then.   345

JOHN Good-bye. Maggie, the ladies are going.°
(*During this skirmish Maggie has stood apart. At the mention of
her name they glance at one another. John escorts Sybil, but the
Comtesse turns back*)

COMTESSE Are you, then, *the* Maggie?° (*Maggie nods rather defiantly
and the Comtesse is distressed*) But if I had known I would not have
said those things. Please forgive an old woman.

MAGGIE It doesn't matter.   350

COMTESSE I—I dare say it will be all right. Mademoiselle, if I were
you I would not encourage those *tête-à-têtes* with Lady Sybil. I am
the rude one, but she is the dangerous one; and I am afraid his
impudence has attracted her. *Bon voyage*, Miss Maggie.

MAGGIE Good-bye—but I *can* speak French. *Je parle français.* Isn't   355
that right?

COMTESSE But yes, it is excellent. (*Making things easy for her*) *C'est
très bien.*

MAGGIE *Je me suis embrouillée—la dernière fois.*

COMTESSE Good! Shall I speak more slowly?   360

MAGGIE No, no. *Non, non,* faster, faster.

COMTESSE *J'admire votre courage!*

MAGGIE *Je comprends chaque mot.*

COMTESSE *Parfait!* Bravo!

MAGGIE *Voilà!*   365

COMTESSE *Superbe!*
(*She goes, applauding; and Maggie has a moment of elation,
which however has passed before John returns for his hat*)

MAGGIE Have you more speaking to do, John?
(*He is somehow in high good-humour*)

JOHN I must run across and address the Cowcaddens Club. (*He sprays
his throat with a hand-spray*) I wonder if I *am* vulgar, Maggie?

MAGGIE You are not, but *I* am.   370

JOHN Not that *I* can see.

MAGGIE Look how overdressed I am, John! I knew it was too showy
when I ordered it, and yet I could not resist the thing. But I will
tone down, I will. What did you think of Lady Sybil?

JOHN That young woman had better be careful. She's a bit of a 375
besom,° Maggie.

MAGGIE She's beautiful, John.

JOHN She has a neat way of stretching herself. For playing with she
would do as well as another.
(*She looks at him wistfully*)

MAGGIE You couldn't stay and have a talk for a few minutes? 380

JOHN If you want me, Maggie. The longer you keep them waiting,
the more they think of you.

MAGGIE When are you to announce that we're to be married, John?

JOHN I won't be long. You've waited a year more than you need have
done, so I think it's your due I should hurry things now. 385

MAGGIE I think it's noble of you.

JOHN Not at all, Maggie; the nobleness has been yours in waiting so
patiently. And your brothers would insist on it at any rate. They're
watching me like cats with a mouse.

MAGGIE It's so little I've done to help. 390

JOHN Three hundred pounds.

MAGGIE I'm getting a thousand per cent for it.

JOHN And very pleased I am you should think so, Maggie.

MAGGIE Is it terrible hard to you, John?

JOHN It's not hard at all. I can say truthfully, Maggie, that all, or 395
nearly all, I've seen of you in these six years has gone to increase
my respect for you.

MAGGIE Respect!

JOHN And a bargain's a bargain.

MAGGIE If it wasn't that you're so glorious to me, John, I would let 400
you off.°
(*There is a gleam in his eye, but he puts it out*)

JOHN In my opinion, Maggie, we'll be a very happy pair.
(*She accepts this eagerly*)

MAGGIE We know each other so well, John, don't we?

JOHN I'm an extraordinary queer character, and I suppose nobody
knows me well except myself; but I know you, Maggie, to the very 405
roots of you.
(*She magnanimously lets this remark alone*)

MAGGIE And it's not as if there was any other woman you—fancied
more, John.

JOHN There's none whatever.

MAGGIE If there ever should be—oh, if there ever should be! Some 410
woman with charm.

JOHN Maggie, you forget yourself. There couldn't be another woman once I was a married man.

MAGGIE One has heard of such things.

JOHN Not in Scotsmen,° Maggie; not in Scotsmen.   415

MAGGIE I've sometimes thought, John, that the difference between us and the English is that the Scotch are hard in all other respects but soft with women, and the English are hard with women but soft in all other respects.

JOHN You've forgotten the grandest moral attribute of a Scotsman,   420
Maggie, that he'll do nothing which might damage his career.

MAGGIE Ah, but John, whatever you do, you do it so tremendously; and if you were to love, what a passion it would be.

JOHN There's something in that, I suppose.

MAGGIE And then, what could I do? For the desire of my life now,   425
John, is to help you to get everything you want, except just that I want you to have me, too.

JOHN We'll get on fine, Maggie.

MAGGIE You're just making the best of it. They say that love is sympathy, and if that's so, mine must be a great love for you, for   430
I see all you are feeling this night and bravely hiding; I feel for you as if I was John Shand myself. (*He sighs*)

JOHN I had best go to the meeting, Maggie.

MAGGIE Not yet. Can you look me in the face, John, and deny that there is surging within you a mighty desire to be free, to begin the   435
new life untrammelled?

JOHN Leave such maggots alone, Maggie.

MAGGIE It's a shame of me not to give you up.

JOHN I would consider you a very foolish woman if you did.

MAGGIE If I were John Shand I would no more want to take Maggie   440
Wylie with me through the beautiful door that has opened wide for you than I would want to take an old pair of shoon.° Why don't you bang the door in my face, John? (*A tremor runs through John*)

JOHN A bargain's a bargain, Maggie.

(*Maggie moves about, an eerie figure, breaking into little cries. She flutters round him, threateningly*)

MAGGIE Say one word about wanting to get out of it, and I'll put the   445
lawyers on you.

JOHN Have I hinted at such a thing?

MAGGIE The document holds you hard and fast.

JOHN It does.

(*She gloats miserably*)

MAGGIE The woman never rises with the man. I'll drag you down,   450
John. I'll drag you down.

JOHN Have no fear of that, I won't let you. I'm too strong.

MAGGIE You'll miss the prettiest thing in the world, and all owing
to me.

JOHN What's that?   455

MAGGIE Romance.

JOHN Poof!

MAGGIE All's cold and grey without it, John. They that have had it
have slipped in and out of heaven.

JOHN You're exaggerating, Maggie.   460

MAGGIE You've worked so hard, you've had none of the fun that
comes to most men long before they're your age.

JOHN I never was one for fun. I cannot call to mind, Maggie, ever
having laughed in my life.

MAGGIE You have no sense of humour.   465

JOHN Not a spark.

MAGGIE I've sometimes thought that if you had, it might make you
fonder of me. I think one needs a sense of humour to be fond of
me.

JOHN I remember reading of some one that said it needed a surgical   470
operation to get a joke into a Scotsman's head.

MAGGIE Yes, that's been said.

JOHN What beats me, Maggie, is how you could insert a joke with
an operation.°

     (*He considers this and gives it up*)

MAGGIE That's not the kind of fun I was thinking of. I mean fun   475
with the lasses, John—gay, jolly, harmless fun. They could be
impudent fashionable beauties now, stretching themselves to attract you, like that hiccoughing little devil, and running away from
you, and crooking their fingers to you to run after them.

     (*He draws a big breath*)

JOHN No, I never had that.   480

MAGGIE It's every man's birthright, and you would have it now but
for me.

JOHN I can do without, Maggie.

MAGGIE It's like missing out all the Saturdays.

JOHN You feel sure, I suppose, that an older man wouldn't suit you   485
better, Maggie?

MAGGIE I couldn't feel surer of anything. You're just my ideal.

JOHN Yes, yes. Well, that's as it should be.

(*She threatens him again*)

MAGGIE David has the document. It's carefully locked away.

JOHN He would naturally take good care of it.   490

(*The pride of the Wylies deserts her*)

MAGGIE John, I make you a solemn promise that, in consideration of
the circumstances of our marriage, if you should ever fall in love
I'll act differently from other wives.

JOHN There will be no occasion, Maggie.

(*Her voice becomes tremulous*)

MAGGIE John, David doesn't have the document. He thinks he has, 495
but I have it here.

(*Somewhat heavily John surveys the fatal paper*)

JOHN Well do I mind the look of it, Maggie. Yes, yes, that's it.
Umpha!

MAGGIE You don't ask why I've brought it.

JOHN Why did you?   500

MAGGIE Because I thought I might perhaps have the courage and the
womanliness° to give it back to you. (*John has a brief dream*) Will
you never hold it up against me in the future that I couldn't do
that?

JOHN I promise you, Maggie, I never will.   505

MAGGIE To go back to the Pans° and take up my old life there, when
all these six years my eyes have been centred on this night! I've
been waiting for this night as long as you have been; and now to
go back there, and wizen and dry up, when I might be married to
John Shand!   510

JOHN And you will be, Maggie. You have my word.

MAGGIE Never—never—never. (*She tears up the document. He
remains seated immovable, but the gleam returns to his eye. She rages
first at herself and then at him*) I'm a fool, a fool, to let you go. I
tell you, you'll rue this day, for you need me, you'll come to   515
grief without me. There's nobody can help you as I could have
helped you. I'm essential to your career, and you're blind not to
see it.

JOHN What's that, Maggie? In no circumstances would I allow any
meddling with my career.   520

MAGGIE You would never have known I was meddling with it. But
that's over. Don't be in too great a hurry to marry, John. Have
your fling with the beautiful dolls first. Get the whiphand of the
haughty ones, John. Give them their licks.° Every time they
hiccough let them have an extra slap in memory of me. And be   525

sure to remember this, my man, that the one who marries you will find you out.

JOHN Find me out?

MAGGIE However careful a man is, his wife always finds out his failings. 530

JOHN I don't know, Maggie, to what failings you refer.

> (*The Cowcaddens Club has burst its walls, and is pouring this way to raise the new Member on its crest. The first wave hurls itself against the barber's shop with cries of 'Shand, Shand, Shand!' For a moment John stems the torrent by planting his back against the door*)

You are acting under an impulse, Maggie, and I can't take advantage of it. Think the matter over, and we'll speak about it in the morning.

MAGGIE No, I can't go through it again. It ends to-night and now. 535 Good luck, John.

> (*She is immediately submerged in the sea that surges through the door, bringing much wreckage with it. In a moment the place is so full that another cupful could not find standing room. Some slippery ones are squeezed upwards and remain aloft as warnings. John has jumped on to the stair, and harangues the flood vainly like another Canute.° It is something about freedom and noble minds, and, though unheard, goes to all heads, including the speaker's. By the time he is audible sentiment has him for her own*)

JOHN But, gentlemen, one may have too much even of freedom. (*No, no*) Yes, Mr Adamson. One may want to be tied. (*Never, never*) I say yes, Willie Cameron; and I have found a young lady who I am proud to say is willing to be tied to me. I'm to be married! (*Uproar*) 540 Her name's Miss Wylie. (*Transport*) Quiet; she's here now. (*Frenzy*) She was here! Where are you, Maggie? (*A small voice—* 'I'm here.' *A hundred great voices—*'Where—where—where?' *The small voice—*'I'm so little none of you can see me.')

> (*Three men, name of Wylie, buffet their way forward*)

DAVID James, father, have you grip of her? 545

ALICK We've got her.

DAVID Then hoist her up.

> (*The queer little elated figure is raised aloft. With her fingers she can just touch the stars. Not unconscious of the nobility of his behaviour, the hero of the evening points an impressive finger at her*)

JOHN Gentlemen, the future Mrs John Shand! (*Cries of 'Speech, speech!'*) No, no, being a lady she can't make a speech, but——

(*The heroine of the evening surprises him*)

MAGGIE I can make a speech, and I will make a speech, and it's in   550
two words, and they're these—(*holding out her arms to enfold all the
members of the Cowcaddens Club*)—My Constituents!° (*Dementia*)

Act 3

[Scene 1]

A few minutes ago the Comtesse de la Brière, who has not recently been in England, was shown into the London home of the Shands. Though not sufficiently interested to express her surprise in words, she raised her eyebrows on finding herself in a charming room; she had presumed that the Shand scheme of decoration would be as impossible as themselves.

It is the little room behind the dining-room for which English architects have long been famous; 'Make something of this, and you will indeed be a clever one,' they seem to say to you as they unveil it. The Comtesse finds that John has undoubtedly made something of it. It is his 'study' (mon Dieu, the words these English use!) and there is nothing in it that offends; there is so much not in it too that might so easily have been there. It is not in the least ornate; there are no colours quarrelling with each other (unseen, unheard by the blissful occupant of the revolving chair); the Comtesse has not even the gentle satisfaction of noting a 'suite' in stained oak. Nature might have taken a share in the decorations, so restful are they to the eyes; it is the working room of a man of culture, probably lately down from Oxford; at a first meeting there is nothing in it that pretends to be what it is not. Our visitor is a little disappointed, but being fair-minded blows her absent host a kiss for disappointing her.

He has even, she observes with a twinkle, made something of the most difficult of his possessions, the little wife. For Maggie, who is here receiving her, has been quite creditably toned down. He has put her into a little grey frock that not only deals gently with her personal defects, but is in harmony with the room. Evidently, however, she has not 'risen' with him, for she is as stupid as ever; the Comtesse, who remembers having liked her the better of the two, could shake her for being so stupid. For instance, why is she not asserting herself in that other apartment?

The other apartment is really a correctly solemn dining-room, of which we have a glimpse through partly open folding-doors. At this moment it is harbouring Mr Shand's ladies' committee, who sit with pens and foolscap round the large table, awaiting the advent of their leader. There are nobly wise ones and some foolish ones among them,

for we are back in the strange days when it was considered 'un-
womanly' for women to have minds.° The Comtesse peeps at them
with curiosity, as they arrange their papers or are ushered into the
dining-room through a door which we cannot see. To her frivolous
ladyship they are a species of wild fowl, and she is specially amused   40
to find her niece among them. She demands an explanation as soon
as the communicating doors close.

COMTESSE Tell me, since when has my dear Sybil become one of
    these ladies? It is not like her.
        (*Maggie is obviously not clever enough to understand the woman
        question.° Her eye rests longingly on a half-finished stocking as
        she innocently but densely replies*)
MAGGIE I think it was about the time that my husband took up their   45
    cause.
        (*The Comtesse has been hearing tales of Lady Sybil and the
        barbarian; and after having the grace to hesitate, she speaks with
        the directness for which she is famed in Mayfair*)
COMTESSE Mrs Shand, excuse me for saying that if half of what I
    hear be true, your husband is seeing that lady a great deal too
    often. (*Maggie is expressionless; she reaches for her stocking, whereat
    her guest loses patience*) Oh, *mon Dieu*, put that down; you can buy   50
    them at two francs the pair. Mrs Shand, why do not you compel
    yourself to take an intelligent interest in your husband's work?
MAGGIE I typewrite his speeches.
COMTESSE But do you know what they are about?
MAGGIE They are about various subjects.   55
COMTESSE Oh!
        (*Did Maggie give her an unseen quizzical glance before demure-
        ly resuming the knitting? One is not certain, as John has come
        in, and this obliterates her. 'A Scotsman on the make,' of whom
        David has spoken reverently, is still to be read—in a somewhat
        better bound volume—in John Shand's person; but it is as
        doggedly honest a face as ever; and he champions women, not
        for personal ends, but because his blessed days of poverty gave
        him a light upon their needs. His self-satisfaction, however, has
        increased, and he has pleasantly forgotten some things. For
        instance, he can now call out 'Porter' at railway stations without
        dropping his hands for the barrow. Maggie introduces the
        Comtesse, and he is still undaunted*)
JOHN I remember you well—at Glasgow.

COMTESSE It must be quite two years ago, Mr Shand.

    (*John has no objection to showing that he has had a classical education*)

JOHN *Tempus fugit,*° Comtesse.

COMTESSE I have not been much in this country since then, and I   60
return to find you a coming man.

    (*Fortunately his learning is tempered with modesty*)

JOHN Oh, I don't know, I don't know.

COMTESSE The Ladies' Champion.

    (*His modesty is tempered with a respect for truth*)

JOHN Well, well.

COMTESSE And you are about, as I understand, to introduce a bill to   65
give women an equal right with men to grow beards° (*which is all she knows about it. He takes the remark literally*).

JOHN There's nothing about beards in it, Comtesse. (*She gives him time to cogitate, and is pleased to note that there is no result*) Have you typed my speech, Maggie?   70

MAGGIE Yes; twenty-six pages. (*She produces it from a drawer*)

    (*Perhaps John wishes to impress the visitor*)

JOHN I'm to give the ladies' committee a general idea of it. Just see, Maggie, if I know the peroration. 'In conclusion, Mr Speaker, these are the reasonable demands of every intelligent English-woman'—I had better say British woman—'and I am proud to nail   75
them to my flag'—

    (*The visitor is properly impressed*)

COMTESSE Oho! defies his leaders!

JOHN —'so long as I can do so without embarrassing the Government.'

COMTESSE Ah, ah, Mr Shand!   80

JOHN 'I call upon the Front Bench, sir, loyally but firmly'—

COMTESSE Firm again!

JOHN —'either to accept my Bill, or to promise *without delay* to bring in one of their own; and if they decline to do so I solemnly warn them that though I will not press the matter to a division° just   85
now'—

COMTESSE Ahem!

JOHN —'I will bring it forward again in the near future.' And now, Comtesse, *you* know that I'm not going to divide—and not another soul knows it.   90

COMTESSE I am indeed flattered by your confidence.

JOHN I've only told you because I don't care who knows now.

COMTESSE Oh!
       (*Somehow Maggie seems to be dissatisfied*)
MAGGIE But why is that, John?
JOHN I daren't keep the Government in doubt any longer about what   95
    I mean to do. I'll show the whips the speech privately to-night.
MAGGIE (*who still wants to know*) But not to go to a division is
    hedging, isn't it? Is that strong?
JOHN To make the speech at all, Maggie, is stronger than most
    would dare. They would *do* for me if I went to a division.   100
MAGGIE Bark but not bite?
JOHN Now, now, Maggie, you're out of your depth.
MAGGIE I suppose that's it.
       (*The Comtesse remains in the shallows*)
COMTESSE But what will the ladies say, Mr Shand?
JOHN They won't like it, Comtesse, but they've got to lump it.   105
       (*Here the maid appears with a card for Maggie, who considers
       it quietly*)
JOHN Any one of importance?
MAGGIE No.
JOHN Then I'm ready, Maggie.
       (*This is evidently an intimation that she is to open the folding-
       doors, and he makes an effective entrance into the dining-room,
       his thumb in his waistcoat. There is a delicious clapping of hands
       from the committee, and the door closes. Not till then does
       Maggie, who has grown thoughtful, tell her maid to admit the
       visitor*)°
COMTESSE Another lady, Mrs Shand?
MAGGIE The card says 'Mr Charles Venables.'   110
       (*The Comtesse is really interested at last*)
COMTESSE Charles Venables! Do *you* know him?
MAGGIE I think I call to mind meeting one of that name at the
    Foreign Office party.
COMTESSE One of that name! He who is a Minister of your Cabinet.
    But as you know him so little why should he call on you?   115
MAGGIE I wonder.
       (*Maggie's glance wanders to the drawer in which she has
       replaced John's speech*)
COMTESSE Well, well, I shall take care of you, petite.
MAGGIE Do *you* know him?
COMTESSE Do I know him! The last time I saw him he asked me
    to—to—hem!—*ma chérie*, it was thirty years ago.   120

MAGGIE Thirty years!

COMTESSE I was a pretty woman then. I dare say I shall detest him
now; but if I find I do not—let us have a little plot—I shall drop
this book; and then perhaps you will be so charming as—as not to
be here for a little while?   125

> (*Mr Venables, who enters, is such a courtly seigneur that he
> seems to bring the eighteenth century with him; you feel that his
> sedan chair° is at the door. He stoops over Maggie's plebeian
> hand*)

VENABLES I hope you will pardon my calling, Mrs Shand; we had
such a pleasant talk the other evening.

> (*Maggie, of course, is at once deceived by his gracious manner*)

MAGGIE I think it's kind of you. Do you know each other? The
Comtesse de la Brière.

> (*He repeats the name with some emotion, and the Comtesse, half
> mischievously, half sadly, holds a hand before her face*)

VENABLES Comtesse.   130

COMTESSE Thirty years, Mr Venables.

> (*He gallantly removes the hand that screens her face*)

VENABLES It does not seem so much.

> (*She gives him a similar scrutiny*)

COMTESSE *Mon Dieu*, it seems all that!

> (*They smile rather ruefully. Maggie like a kind hostess relieves
> the tension*)

MAGGIE The Comtesse has taken a cottage in Surrey for the summer.

VENABLES I am overjoyed.   135

COMTESSE No, Charles, you are not. You no longer care. Fickle one!
And it is only thirty years.

> (*He sinks into a chair beside her*)

VENABLES Those heavenly evenings, Comtesse, on the Bosphorus.°

COMTESSE I refuse to talk of them. I hate you.

> (*But she drops the book, and Maggie fades from the room. It is
> not a very clever departure, and the old diplomatist smiles. Then
> he sighs a beautiful sigh, for he does all things beautifully*)

VENABLES It is moonlight, Comtesse, on the Golden Horn.°   140

COMTESSE Who are those two young things in a caïque?°

VENABLES Is he the brave Leander, Comtesse, and is she Hero of the
Lamp?°

COMTESSE No, she is the foolish wife of the French Ambassador, and
he is a good-for-nothing British attaché trying to get her husband's   145
secrets out of her.

VENABLES Is it possible! They part at a certain garden gate.

COMTESSE Oh, Charles, Charles!

VENABLES But you promised to come back; I waited there till dawn. Blanche, if you *had* come back——   150

COMTESSE How is Mrs Venables?

VENABLES She is rather poorly. *I* think it's gout.

COMTESSE And you?

VENABLES I creak a little in the mornings.

COMTESSE So do I. There is such a good man at Wiesbaden.   155

VENABLES The Homburg°   fellow is better. The way he patched me up last summer—Oh, Lord, Lord!

COMTESSE Yes, Charles, the game is up; we are two old fogies. (*They groan in unison; then she raps him sharply on the knuckles*) Tell me, sir, what are you doing here?   160

VENABLES Merely a friendly call.

COMTESSE I do not believe it.

VENABLES The same woman; the old delightful candour.

COMTESSE The same man; the old fibs. (*She sees that the door is asking a question*) Yes, come, Mrs Shand, I have had quite enough   165 of him; I warn you he is here for some crafty purpose.°

MAGGIE (*drawing back timidly*) Surely not?

VENABLES Really, Comtesse, you make conversation difficult. To show that my intentions are innocent, Mrs Shand, I propose that you choose the subject.   170

MAGGIE (*relieved*) There, Comtesse.

VENABLES I hope your husband is well?

MAGGIE Yes, thank you. (*With a happy thought*) I decide that we talk about him.

VENABLES If you wish it.   175

COMTESSE Be careful; *he* has chosen the subject.

MAGGIE *I* chose it, didn't I?

VENABLES You know you did.

MAGGIE (*appealingly*) You admire John?

VENABLES Very much. But he puzzles me a little. You Scots, Mrs   180 Shand, are such a mixture of the practical and the emotional that you escape out of an Englishman's hand like a trout.

MAGGIE (*open-eyed*) Do we?

VENABLES Well, not you, but your husband. I have known few men make a worse beginning in the House. He had the most atrocious   185 bow-wow public-park manner——

COMTESSE I remember that manner!

MAGGIE No, he hadn't.

VENABLES (*soothingly*) At first. But by his second session° he had shed all that, and he is now a pleasure to listen to. By the way, Comtesse, have you found any dark intention in that?   190

COMTESSE You wanted to know whether he talks over these matters with his wife; and she has told you that he does not.

MAGGIE (*indignantly*) I haven't said a word about it, have I?

VENABLES Not a word. Then, again, I admire him for his impromptu speeches.   195

MAGGIE What is impromptu?

VENABLES Unprepared. They have contained some grave blunders, not so much of judgment as of taste——

MAGGIE (*hotly*) *I* don't think so.   200

VENABLES Pardon me. But he has righted himself subsequently in the neatest way. I have always found that the man whose second thoughts are good is worth watching. Well, Comtesse, I see you have something to say.

COMTESSE You are wondering whether she can tell you who gives him his second thoughts.   205

MAGGIE Gives them to John? I would like to see anybody try to give thoughts to John.

VENABLES Quite so.

COMTESSE Is there anything more that has roused your admiration, Charles?   210

VENABLES (*purring*) Let me see. Yes, we are all much edified by his humour.

COMTESSE (*surprised indeed*) His humour? That man!

MAGGIE (*with hauteur*) Why not?   215

VENABLES I assure you, Comtesse, some of the neat things in his speeches convulse the House. A word has even been coined for them—Shandisms.

COMTESSE (*slowly recovering from a blow*) Humour!

VENABLES In conversation, I admit, he strikes one as being—ah—somewhat lacking in humour.   220

COMTESSE (*pouncing*) You are wondering who supplies his speeches with the humour.

MAGGIE Supplies John?

VENABLES Now that you mention it, some of his Shandisms do have a curiously feminine quality.   225

COMTESSE You have thought it might be a woman.

VENABLES Really, Comtesse——

COMTESSE I see it all. Charles, you thought it might be the wife!

VENABLES (*flinging up his hands*) I own up.   230

MAGGIE (*bewildered*) Me?

VENABLES Forgive me, I see I was wrong.

MAGGIE (*alarmed*) Have I been doing John any harm?

VENABLES On the contrary, I am relieved to know that there are no hairpins in his speeches. If he is at home, Mrs Shand, may I see   235
him? I am going to be rather charming to him.

MAGGIE (*drawn in two directions*) Yes, he is—oh yes—but——

VENABLES That is to say, Comtesse, if he proves himself the man I believe him to be.

> (*This arrests Maggie almost as she has reached the dining-room door*)

MAGGIE (*hesitating*) He is very busy just now.   240

VENABLES (*smiling*) I think he will see me.

MAGGIE Is it something about his speech?

VENABLES (*the smile hardening*) Well, yes, it is.

MAGGIE Then I dare say I could tell you what you want to know without troubling him, as I've been typing it.   245

VENABLES (*with a sigh*) I don't acquire information in that way.

COMTESSE I trust not.

MAGGIE There's no secret about it. He is to show it to the whips to-night.

VENABLES (*sharply*) You are sure of that?   250

COMTESSE It is quite true, Charles. I heard him say so; and indeed he repeated what he called the 'peroration' before me.

MAGGIE I know it by heart. (*She plays a bold game*) 'These are the demands of all intelligent British women, and I am proud to nail them to my flag'—   255

COMTESSE The very words, Mrs Shand.

MAGGIE (*looking at her imploringly*) 'And I don't care how they may embarrass the Government.'° (*The Comtesse is bereft of speech, so suddenly has she been introduced to the real Maggie Shand*) 'If the right honourable gentleman will give us his pledge to introduce a similar   260
Bill this session I will willingly withdraw mine; but otherwise I solemnly warn him that I will press the matter now to a division.'

> (*She turns her face from the great man; she has gone white*)

VENABLES (*after a pause*) Capital.

> (*The blood returns to Maggie's heart*)

COMTESSE (*who is beginning to enjoy herself very much*) Then you are pleased to know that he means to, as you say, go to a division?   265

VENABLES Delighted. The courage of it will be the making of him.

COMTESSE I see.

VENABLES Had he been to hedge° we should have known that he was a pasteboard knight and have disregarded him.

COMTESSE I see.   270

     (*She desires to catch the eye of Maggie, but it is carefully turned from her*)

VENABLES Mrs Shand, let us have him in at once.

COMTESSE Yes, yes, indeed.

     (*Maggie's anxiety returns, but she has to call John in*)

JOHN (*impressed*) Mr Venables! This is an honour.

VENABLES How are you, Shand?

JOHN Sit down, sit down. (*Becoming himself again*) I can guess what   275
you have come about.

VENABLES Ah, you Scotsmen.

JOHN Of course I know I'm harassing the Government a good deal——

VENABLES (*blandly*) Not at all, Shand. The Government are very   280
pleased.

JOHN You don't expect me to believe that?

VENABLES I called here to give you the proof of it. You may know that we are to have a big meeting at Leeds on the 24th, when two Ministers are to speak. There is room for a third speaker, and I   285
am authorised to offer that place to you.

JOHN To me!

VENABLES Yes.

JOHN (*swelling*) It would be—the Government taking me up.

VENABLES Don't make too much of it; it would be an acknow-   290
ledgment that they look upon you as one of their likely young men.

MAGGIE John!

JOHN (*not found wanting in a trying hour*) It's a bribe. You are offering me this on condition that I don't make my speech. How can you think so meanly of me as to believe that I would play the women's   295
cause false for the sake of my own advancement. I refuse your bribe.

VENABLES (*liking him for the first time*) Good. But you are wrong. There are no conditions, and we want you to make your speech. Now do you accept?   300

JOHN (*still suspicious*) If you make me the same offer after you have read it. I insist on your reading it first.

VENABLES (*sighing*) By all means.

(*Maggie is in an agony as she sees John hand the speech to his
leader. On the other hand, the Comtesse thrills*)

But I assure you we look on the speech as a small matter. The
important thing is your intention of going to a division; and we   305
agree to that also.

JOHN (*losing his head*) What's that?

VENABLES Yes, we agree.

JOHN But—but—why, you have been threatening to excommunic-
ate° me if I dared.   310

VENABLES All done to test you, Shand.

JOHN To test me?

VENABLES We know that a division on your Bill can have no serious
significance; we shall see to that. And so the test was to be whether
you had the pluck to divide the House. Had you been intending   315
to talk big in this speech, and then hedge, through fear of the
Government, they would have had no further use for you.

JOHN (*heavily*) I understand. (*But there is one thing he cannot
understand, which is, why Venables should be so sure that he is not to
hedge*)   320

VENABLES (*turning over the pages carelessly*) Any of your good things
in this, Shand?

JOHN (*whose one desire is to get the pages back*) No, I—no—it isn't
necessary you should read it now.

VENABLES (*from politeness only*) Merely for my own pleasure. I shall   325
look through it this evening. (*He rolls up the speech to put it in his
pocket. John turns despairingly to Maggie, though well aware that no
help can come from her*)

MAGGIE That's the only copy there is, John. (*To Venables*) Let me
make a fresh one, and send it to you in an hour or two.   330

VENABLES (*good-naturedly*) I could not put you to that trouble, Mrs
Shand. I will take good care of it.

MAGGIE If anything were to happen to you on the way home,
wouldn't whatever is in your pocket be considered to be the
property of your heirs?   335

VENABLES (*laughing*) Now there is forethought! Shand, I think that
after that——! (*He returns the speech to John, whose hand swallows
it greedily*) She is Scotch° too, Comtesse.

COMTESSE (*delighted*) Yes, she is Scotch too.

VENABLES Though the only persons likely to do for me in the street,   340
Shand, are your ladies' committee. Ever since they took the horse
out of my brougham,° I can scent them a mile away.

COMTESSE A mile? Charles, peep in there.

> (*He softly turns the handle of the dining-room door, and realises that his scent is not so good as he had thought it. He bids his hostess and the Comtesse good-bye in a burlesque whisper and tiptoes off to safer places. John having gone out with him, Maggie can no longer avoid the Comtesse's reproachful eye. That much injured lady advances upon her with accusing finger*)

COMTESSE So, madam!

> (*Maggie is prepared for her*)

MAGGIE I don't know what you mean.   345

COMTESSE Yes, you do. I mean that there *is* some one who 'helps' our Mr Shand.

MAGGIE There's not.

COMTESSE And it *is* a woman, and it's you.

MAGGIE I help in the little things.   350

COMTESSE The little things! You are the Pin he picked up and that is to make his fortune. And now what I want to know is whether your John is aware that you help at all.

> (*John returns, and at once provides the answer*)

JOHN Maggie, Comtesse, I've done it again!

MAGGIE I'm so glad, John.   355

> (*The Comtesse is in an ecstasy*)

COMTESSE And all because you were not to hedge, Mr Shand.

> (*His appeal to her with the wistfulness of a schoolboy makes him rather attractive*)

JOHN You won't tell on me, Comtesse! (*He thinks it out*) They had just guessed I would be firm because they know I'm a strong man. You little saw, Maggie, what a good turn you were doing me when you said you wanted to make another copy of the speech.   360

> (*She is dense*)

MAGGIE How, John?

JOHN Because now I can alter the end.

> (*She is enlightened*)

MAGGIE So you can!

JOHN Here's another lucky thing, Maggie: I hadn't told the ladies' committee that I was to hedge, and so they need never know.   365 Comtesse, I tell you there's a little cherub who sits up aloft and looks after the career of John Shand.

> (*The Comtesse looks not aloft but toward the chair at present occupied by Maggie*)

COMTESSE Where does she sit, Mr Shand?

(*He knows that women are not well read*)

JOHN It's just a figure of speech.

(*He returns airily to his committee room; and now again you may hear the click of Maggie's needles. They no longer annoy the Comtesse; she is setting them to music*)

COMTESSE It is not down here she sits, Mrs Shand, knitting a   370
stocking.

MAGGIE No, it isn't.

COMTESSE And when I came in I gave him credit for everything; even for the prettiness of the room!

MAGGIE He has beautiful taste.   375

COMTESSE Good-bye, Scotchy.

MAGGIE Good-bye, Comtesse, and thank you for coming.

COMTESSE Good-bye—Miss Pin.

(*Maggie rings genteelly*)

MAGGIE Good-bye.

(*The Comtesse is now lost in admiration of her*)

COMTESSE You divine little wife. He can't be worthy of it, no man   380
could be worthy of it. Why do you do it?

(*Maggie shivers a little*)

MAGGIE He loves to think he does it all himself; that's the way of men. I'm six years older than he is. I'm plain, and I have no charm. I shouldn't have let him marry me. I'm trying to make up for it.

(*The Comtesse kisses her and goes away. Maggie, somewhat foolishly, resumes her knitting*)

[Scene 2 *The same*]

(*Some days later this same room is listening—with the same inattention—to the outpouring of John Shand's love for the lady of the hiccoughs. We arrive—by arrangement—rather late; and thus we miss some of the most delightful of the pangs.*

One can see that these two are playing no game, or, if they are, that they little know it. The wonders of the world (so strange are the instruments chosen by Love) have been revealed to John in hiccoughs; he shakes in Sybil's presence; never were more swimming eyes; he who has been of a wooden face till now, with ways to match, has gone on flame like a piece of paper; emotion is in flood in him. We may be almost fond of John for being so worshipful of love. Much has come to him that we had almost despaired of his acquiring, including nearly all the divine attributes except that sense of humour. The beautiful Sybil has always possessed but little of it also, and what she had has been struck from her by Cupid's flail.° Naked of the saving grace, they face each other in awful rapture)

JOHN In a room, Sybil, I go to you as a cold man to a fire. You fill me like a peal of bells in an empty house.

(She is being brutally treated by the dear impediment, for which hiccough is such an inadequate name that even to spell it is an abomination though a sign of ability. How to describe a sound that is noiseless? Let us put it thus, that when Sybil wants to say something very much there are little obstacles in her way; she falters, falls perhaps once, and then is over, the while her appealing orbs beg you not to be angry with her. We may express those sweet pauses in precious dots, which some clever person can afterwards string together and make a pearl necklace of them)

SYBIL I should not . . . let you say it, . . . but . . . you . . . say it so beautifully.

JOHN You must have guessed. 5

SYBIL I dreamed . . . I feared . . . but you were . . . Scotch, and I didn't know what to think.

JOHN Do you know what first attracted me to you, Sybil? It was your insolence. I thought, 'I'll break her insolence for her.'

SYBIL And I thought . . . 'I'll break his str . . . ength!' 10

JOHN And now your cooing voice plays round me; the softness of you, Sybil, in your pretty clothes makes me think of young birds. *(The impediment is now insurmountable; she has to swim for it, she swims toward him)* It is you who inspire my work.

(He thrills to find that she can be touched without breaking)

SYBIL I am so glad . . . so proud . . . 15

JOHN And others know it, Sybil, as well as I. Only yesterday the Comtesse said to me, 'No man could get on so fast unaided. *Cherchez la femme*, Mr Shand.'

SYBIL Auntie said that?

JOHN I said 'Find her yourself, Comtesse.'° 20

SYBIL And she?

JOHN She said 'I have found her,' and I said in my blunt way, 'You mean Lady Sybil,' and she went away laughing.

SYBIL Laughing?

JOHN I seem to amuse the woman. 25

(*Sybil grows sad*)

SYBIL If Mrs Shand—— It is so cruel to her. Whom did you say she had gone to the station to meet?

JOHN Her father and brothers.

SYBIL It is so cruel to them. We must think no more of this. It is mad . . . ness.   30

JOHN It's fate. Sybil, let us declare our love openly.

SYBIL You can't ask that, now in the first moment that you tell me of it.

JOHN The one thing I won't do even for you is to live a life of underhand.   35

SYBIL The . . . blow to her.

JOHN Yes. But at least she has always known that I never loved her.

SYBIL It is asking me to give . . . up everything, every one, for you.

JOHN It's too much.

       (*John is humble at last*)

SYBIL To a woman who truly loves, even that is not too much. Oh!   40
it is not I who matter—it is you.

JOHN My dear, my dear.

SYBIL So gladly would I do it to save you; but, oh, if it were to bring you down!

JOHN Nothing can keep me down if I have you to help me.   45

SYBIL I am dazed, John, I . . .

JOHN My love, my love.

SYBIL I . . . oh . . . here . . .

JOHN Be brave, Sybil, be brave.

SYBIL   50

       (*In this bewilderment of pearls she melts into his arms. Maggie
       happens to open the door just then; but neither fond heart hears
       her*)

JOHN I can't walk along the streets, Sybil, without looking in all the
shop windows for what I think would become you best. (*As
awkwardly as though his heart still beat against corduroy,*° *he takes
from his pocket a pendant and its chain. He is shy, and she drops pearls
over the beauty of the ruby which is its only stone*) It is a drop of my   55
blood, Sybil.

       (*Her lovely neck is outstretched, and he puts the chain round it.
       Maggie withdraws as silently as she had come; but perhaps the
       door whispered 'd—n' as it closed, for Sybil wakes out of
       Paradise*)

SYBIL I thought——Did the door shut?

JOHN It was shut already.

(*Perhaps it is only that Sybil is bewildered to find herself once again in a world that has doors*)

SYBIL It seemed to me——

JOHN There was nothing. But I think I hear voices; they may have arrived. 60

(*Some pretty instinct makes Sybil go farther from him. Maggie kindly gives her time for this by speaking before opening the door*)

MAGGIE That will do perfectly, David. The maid knows where to put them. (*She comes in*) They've come, John; they *would* help with the luggage. (*John goes out. Maggie is agreeably surprised to find a visitor*) How do you do, Lady Sybil? This is nice of you. 65

SYBIL I was so sorry not to find you in, Mrs Shand.

(*The impediment has run away. It is only for those who love it*)

MAGGIE Thank you. You'll sit down?

SYBIL I think not; your relatives——

MAGGIE They will be so proud to see that you are my friend.

(*If Maggie were less simple her guest would feel more comfortable. She tries to make conversation*)

SYBIL It is their first visit to London? 70

(*Instead of relieving her anxiety on this point, Maggie has a long look at the gorgeous armful*)

MAGGIE I'm glad you are so beautiful, Lady Sybil.

(*The beautiful one is somehow not flattered. She pursues her investigations with growing uneasiness*)

SYBIL One of them is married now, isn't he? (*Still there is no answer; Maggie continues looking at her, and shivers slightly*) Have they travelled from Scotland to-day? Mrs Shand, why do you look at me so? The door did open! (*Maggie nods*) What are you to do? 75

MAGGIE That would be telling. Sit down, my pretty.

(*As Sybil subsides into what the Wylies with one glance would call the best chair, Maggie's men-folk are brought in by John, all carrying silk hats and looking very active after their long rest in the train. They are gazing about them. They would like this lady, they would like John, they would even like Maggie to go away for a little and leave them to examine the room. Is that linen on the walls, for instance, or just paper? Is the carpet as thick as it feels, or is there brown paper beneath it? Had Maggie got anything off that bookcase on account of the worm-holes? David even discovers that we were simpletons when we said there*) *was nothing in the room that pretended to be what it was not. He taps the marble mantelpiece, and is favourably impressed by the tinny sound)*

DAVID Very fine imitation. It's a capital house, Maggie.

MAGGIE I'm so glad you like it. Do you know one another? This is my father and my brothers, Lady Sybil.

(The lovely form inclines towards them. Alick and John remain firm on their legs, but James totters)

JAMES A ladyship! Well done, Maggie. 80

ALICK *(sharply)* James! I remember you, my lady.

MAGGIE Sit down, father. This is the study.

(James wanders round it inquisitively until called to order)

SYBIL You must be tired after your long journey.

DAVID *(drawing the portraits of himself and partners in one lightning sketch)* Tired, your ladyship? We sat on cushioned seats the whole way. 85

JAMES *(looking about him for the chair you sit on)* Every seat in this room is cushioned.

MAGGIE You may say all my life is cushioned now, James, by this dear man of mine.

(She gives John's shoulder a loving pressure, which Sybil feels is a telegraphic communication to herself in a cypher that she cannot read. Alick and the brothers bask in the evidence of Maggie's happiness)

JOHN *(uncomfortably)* And is Elizabeth hearty, James? 90

JAMES *(looking down his nose in the manner proper to young husbands when addressed about their wives)* She's very well, I thank you kindly.

MAGGIE James is a married man now, Lady Sybil.

(Sybil murmurs her congratulations)

JAMES I thank you kindly. *(Courageously)* Yes, I'm married. *(He looks at David and Alick to see if they are smiling; and they are)* It wasn't 95 a case of being catched; it was entirely of my own free will. *(He looks again; and the mean fellows are smiling still)* Is your ladyship married?

SYBIL Alas! no.

DAVID James! *(Politely)* You will be yet, my lady. 100

(Sybil indicates that he is kind indeed)

JOHN Perhaps they would like you to show them their rooms, Maggie?

DAVID Fine would we like to see all the house as well as the sleeping accommodation. But first——*(He gives his father the look with which chairmen call on the next speaker)* 105

ALICK I take you,° David. (*He produces a paper parcel from a roomy pocket*) It wasn't likely, Mr Shand, that we should forget the day.

JOHN The day?

DAVID The second anniversary of your marriage. We came purposely for the day.   110

JAMES (*his fingers itching to take the parcel from his father*) It's a lace shawl, Maggie, from the three of us, a pure Tobermory;° you would never dare wear it if you knew the cost.

> (*The shawl in its beauty is revealed, and Maggie hails it with little cries of joy. She rushes at the donors and kisses each of them just as if she were a pretty woman. They are much pleased and give expression to their pleasure in a not very dissimilar manner*)

ALICK Havers.

DAVID Havers.   115

JAMES Havers.

JOHN It's a very fine shawl.

> (*He should not have spoken, for he has set James's volatile mind working*)

JAMES You may say so. What did you give her, Mr Shand?

JOHN (*suddenly deserted by God and man*) Me?

ALICK Yes, yes, let's see it.   120

JOHN Oh—I——

> (*He is not deserted by Maggie, but she can think of no way out*)

SYBIL (*prompted by the impediment, which is in hiding, quite close*) Did he . . . forget?

> (*There is more than a touch of malice in the question. It is a challenge, and the Wylies as a family are almost too quick to accept a challenge*)

MAGGIE (*lifting the gage° of battle*) John forget? Never! It's a pendant, father.   125

> (*The impediment bolts. John rises*)

ALICK A pendant? One of those things on a chain?

> (*He grins, remembering how once, about sixty years ago, he and a lady and a pendant—but we have no time for this*)

MAGGIE Yes.

DAVID (*who has felt the note of antagonism and is troubled*) You were slow in speaking of it, Mr Shand.

MAGGIE (*This is her fight*) He was shy, because he thought you might 130
blame him for extravagance.

DAVID (*relieved*) Oh, that's it.

JAMES (*licking his lips*) Let's see it.

MAGGIE (*a daughter of the devil*) Where did you put it, John?
(*John's mouth opens but has nothing to contribute*)

SYBIL (*the impediment has stolen back again*) Perhaps it has been . . .   135
mislaid.
(*The brothers echo the word incredulously*)

MAGGIE Not it. I can't think where we laid it down, John. It's not
on that table, is it, James? (*The Wylies turn to look and Maggie's
hand goes out to Lady Sybil: John Shand, witness. It is a very
determined hand, and presently a pendant is placed in it*) Here it is!   140
(*Alick and the brothers cluster round it, weigh it and appraise it*)

ALICK Preserve me. Is that stone real, Mr Shand?

JOHN (*who has begun to look his grimmest*) Yes.

MAGGIE (*who is now ready, if he wishes it, to take him on too*) John says
it's a drop of his blood.   145

JOHN (*wishing it*) And so it is.

DAVID Well said, Mr Shand.

MAGGIE (*scared*) And now, if you'll all come with me, I think John
has something he wants to talk over with Lady Sybil. (*Recovering
and taking him on*) Or would you prefer, John, to say it before us   150
all?

SYBIL (*gasping*) No!

JOHN (*flinging back his head*) Yes, I prefer to say it before you all.

MAGGIE (*flinging back hers*) Then sit down again.
(*The Wylies wonderingly obey*)

SYBIL Mr Shand, Mr Shand!——   155

JOHN Maggie knows, and it was only for her I was troubled. Do you
think I'm afraid of *them*? (*With mighty relief*) Now we can be open.

DAVID (*lowering*)° What is it? What's wrong, John Shand?

JOHN (*facing him squarely*) It was to Lady Sybil I gave the pendant,
and all my love with it. (*Perhaps James utters a cry, but the silence*   160
of Alick and David is more terrible)

SYBIL (*whose voice is smaller than we had thought*) What are you to
do?
(*It is to Maggie she is speaking*)

DAVID She'll leave it for us to do.

JOHN That's what I want.   165
(*The lords of creation look at the ladies*)

MAGGIE (*interpreting*) You and I are expected to retire, Lady Sybil,
while the men decide our fate. (*Sybil is ready to obey the law, but
Maggie remains seated*) Man's the oak, woman's the ivy. Which of
us is it that's to cling to you, John?

(*With three stalwarts glaring at him, John rather grandly takes Sybil's hand. They are two against the world*)

SYBIL (*a heroine*) I hesitated, but I am afraid no longer; whatever he 170 asks of me I will do.

(*Evidently the first thing he asks of her is to await him in the dining-room*)

It will mean surrendering everything for him. I am glad it means all that. (*She passes into the dining-room looking as pretty as a kiss*)

MAGGIE So that settles it.

ALICK I'm thinking that doesn't settle it. 175

DAVID No, by God! (*But his love for Maggie steadies him. There is even a note of entreaty in his voice*) Have you nothing to say to her, man?

JOHN I have things to say to her, but not before you.

DAVID (*sternly*) Go away, Maggie. Leave him to us.

JAMES (*who thinks it is about time that he said something*) Yes, leave 180 him to us.

MAGGIE No, David, I want to hear what is to become of me; I promise not to take any side.

(*And sitting by the fire she resumes her knitting. The four regard her as on an evening at The Pans a good many years ago*)

DAVID (*barking*) How long has this been going on?

JOHN If you mean how long has that lady been the apple of my eye, 185 I'm not sure; but I never told her of it until to-day.

MAGGIE (*thoughtfully and without dropping a stitch*) I think it wasn't till about six months ago, John, that she began to be very dear to you. At first you liked to bring in her name when talking to me, so that I could tell you of any little things I might have heard she 190 was doing. But afterwards, as she became more and more to you, you avoided mentioning her name.

JOHN (*surprised*) Did you notice that?

MAGGIE (*in her old-fashioned way*) Yes.

JOHN I tried to be done with it for your sake. I've often had a sore 195 heart for you, Maggie.

JAMES You're proving it!

MAGGIE Yes, James, he had. I've often seen him looking at me very sorrowfully of late because of what was in his mind; and many a kindly little thing he has done for me that he didn't use to do. 200

JOHN You noticed that too!

MAGGIE Yes.

DAVID (*controlling himself*) Well, we won't go into that; the thing to be thankful for is that it's ended.

ALICK (*who is looking very old*) Yes, yes, that's the great thing.   205

JOHN All useless, sir, it's not ended; it's to go on.

DAVID There's a devil in you, John Shand.

JOHN (*who is an unhappy man just now*) I dare say there is. But do you think he had a walk over, Mr David?

JAMES Man, I could knock you down!   210

MAGGIE There's not one of you could knock John down.°

DAVID (*exasperated*) Quiet, Maggie. One would think you were taking his part.

MAGGIE Do you expect me to desert him at the very moment that he needs me most?   215

DAVID It's him that's deserting you.

JOHN Yes, Maggie, that's what it is.

ALICK Where's your marriage vow? And your church attendances?

JAMES (*with terrible irony*) And your prize for moral philosophy?

JOHN (*recklessly*) All gone whistling down the wind.   220

DAVID I suppose you understand that you'll have to resign your seat?

JOHN (*his underlip much in evidence*) There are hundreds of seats, but there's only one John Shand.

MAGGIE (*but we don't hear her*)° That's how I like to hear him speak.

DAVID (*the ablest person in the room*) Think, man, I'm old by you, and   225 for long I've had a pride in you. It will be beginning the world again with more against you than there was eight years ago.

JOHN I have a better head to begin it with than I had eight years ago.

ALICK (*hoping this will bite*) She'll have her own money, David!   230

JOHN She's as poor as a mouse.

JAMES (*thinking possibly of his Elizabeth's mother*) We'll go to her friends, and tell them all. They'll stop it.

JOHN She's of age.

JAMES They'll take her far away.   235

JOHN I'll follow, and tear her from them.

ALICK Your career——

JOHN (*to his credit*) To hell with my career. Do you think I don't know I'm on the rocks? What can you, or you, or you, understand of the passions of a man! I've fought, and I've given in. When a   240 ship founders, as I suppose I'm foundering, it's not a thing to yelp at. Peace, all of you. (*He strides into the dining-room, where we see him at times pacing the floor*)

DAVID (*to James, who gives signs of a desire to take off his coat*) Let him be. We can't budge him. (*With bitter wisdom*) It's true what he says,   245 true at any rate about me. What do I know of the passions of a man! I'm up against something I don't understand.

ALICK It's something wicked.

DAVID I dare say it is, but it's something big.

JAMES It's that damned charm.   250

MAGGIE (*still by the fire*) That's it. What was it that made you fancy Elizabeth, James?

JAMES (*sheepishly*) I can scarcely say.

MAGGIE It was her charm.

DAVID *Her* charm!   255

JAMES (*pugnaciously*) Yes, *her* charm.

MAGGIE She had charm for James.
　　　(*This somehow breaks them up. Maggie goes from one to another with an odd little smile flickering on her face*)

DAVID Put on your things, Maggie, and we'll leave his house.

MAGGIE (*patting his kind head*) Not me, David.
　　　(*This is a Maggie they have known but forgotten; all three brighten*)

DAVID You haven't given in!   260
　　　(*The smile flickers and expires*)

MAGGIE I want you all to go upstairs, and let me have my try now.

JAMES Your try?

ALICK Maggie, you put new life into me.

JAMES And into me.
　　　(*David says nothing; the way he grips her shoulder says it for him*)

MAGGIE I'll save him, David, if I can.   265

DAVID Does he deserve to be saved after the way he has treated you?

MAGGIE You stupid David. What has that to do with it?
　　　(*When they have gone, John comes to the door of the dining-room. There is welling up in him a great pity for Maggie, but it has to subside a little when he sees that the knitting is still in her hand. No man likes to be so soon supplanted. Sybil follows, and the two of them gaze at the active needles*)

MAGGIE (*perceiving that she has visitors*) Come in, John. Sit down, Lady Sybil, and make yourself comfortable. I'm afraid we've put you about.   270
　　　(*She is, after all, only a few years older than they and scarcely looks her age; yet it must have been in some such way as this that the little old woman who lived in a shoe° addressed her numerous progeny*)

JOHN I'm mortal sorry, Maggie.

SYBIL (*who would be more courageous if she could hold his hand*) And I also.

MAGGIE (*soothingly*) I'm sure you are. But as it can't be helped I see no reason why we three shouldn't talk the matter over in a practical   275
way.

　　　(*Sybil looks doubtful, but John hangs on desperately to the word practical*)

JOHN If you could understand, Maggie, what an inspiration she is to me and my work.

SYBIL Indeed, Mrs Shand, I think of nothing else.

MAGGIE That's fine. That's as it should be.   280

SYBIL (*talking too much*) Mrs Shand, I think you are very kind to take it so reasonably.

MAGGIE That's the Scotch way. When were you thinking of leaving me, John?

　　　(*Perhaps this is the Scotch way also; but Sybil is English, and from the manner in which she starts you would say that something has fallen on her toes*)

JOHN (*who has heard nothing fall*) I think, now that it has come to a   285
breach, the sooner the better. (*His tone becomes that of James when asked after the health of his wife*) When it is convenient to you, Maggie.

MAGGIE (*making a rapid calculation*) It couldn't well be before Wednesday. That's the day the laundry comes home.   290

　　　(*Sybil has to draw in her toes again*)

JOHN And it's the day the House rises.° (*Stifling a groan*) It may be my last appearance in the House.

SYBIL (*her arms yearning for him*) No, no, please don't say that.

MAGGIE (*surveying them sympathetically*) You love the House, don't you, John, next to her? It's a pity you can't wait till after your   295
speech at Leeds. Mr Venables won't let you speak at Leeds, I fear, if you leave me.

JOHN What a chance it would have been. But let it go.

MAGGIE The meeting is in less than a month. Could you not make it such a speech that they would be very loth to lose you?   300

JOHN (*swelling*) That's what was in my mind.

SYBIL (*with noble confidence*) And he could have done it.

MAGGIE Then we've come to something practical.

JOHN (*exercising his imagination with powerful effect*) No, it wouldn't be fair to you if I was to stay on now.   305

222

MAGGIE Do you think I'll let myself be considered when your career is at stake? A month will soon pass for me; I'll have a lot of packing to do.

JOHN It's noble of you, but I don't deserve it, and I can't take it from you.   310

MAGGIE Now's the time, Lady Sybil, for you to have one of your inspiring ideas.

SYBIL (*ever ready*) Yes, yes—but what?
          (*It is odd that they should both turn to Maggie at this moment*)

MAGGIE (*who has already been saying it to herself*) What do you think of this: I can stay on here with my father and brothers; and you,   315
John, can go away somewhere and devote yourself to your speech?

SYBIL Yes.

JOHN That might be. (*Considerately*) Away from both of you? Where could I go?

SYBIL (*ever ready*) Where?   320

MAGGIE I know.
          (*She has called up a number on the telephone before they have time to check her*)

JOHN (*on his dignity*) Don't be in such a hurry, Maggie.

MAGGIE Is this Lamb's Hotel? Put me on to the Comtesse de la Brière, please.

SYBIL (*with a sinking*) What do you want with auntie?   325

MAGGIE Her cottage in the country would be the very place. She invited John and me.

JOHN Yes, but——

MAGGIE (*arguing*) And Mr Venables is to be there. Think of the impression you could make on *him*, seeing him daily for three   330
weeks.

JOHN There's something in that.

MAGGIE Is it you, Comtesse? I'm Maggie Shand.

SYBIL You are not to tell her that——?

MAGGIE No. (*To the Comtesse*) Oh, I'm very well, never was better.   335
Yes, yes; you see I can't, because my folk have never been in London before, and I must take them about and show them the sights. But John could come to you alone; why not?

JOHN (*with proper pride*) If she's not keen to have me, I won't go.

MAGGIE She's very keen. Comtesse, I could come for a day by and   340
by to see how you are getting on. Yes—yes—certainly. (*To John*) She says she'll be delighted.

JOHN (*thoughtfully*) You're not doing this, Maggie, thinking that my being absent from Sybil for a few weeks can make any difference? Of course it's natural you should want us to keep apart, but—— 345

MAGGIE (*grimly*) I'm founding no hope on keeping you apart, John.

JOHN It's what other wives would do.

MAGGIE I promised to be different.

JOHN (*his position as a strong man assured*) Then tell her I accept. (*He wanders back into the dining-room*) 350

SYBIL I think—(*she is not sure what she thinks*)—I think you are very wonderful.

MAGGIE Was that John calling to you?

SYBIL Was it? (*She is glad to join him in the dining-room*)

MAGGIE Comtesse, hold the line a minute. (*She is alone, and she has 355 nearly reached the end of her self-control. She shakes emotionally and utters painful little cries; there is something she wants to do, and she is loth to do it. But she does it*) Are you there, Comtesse? There's one other thing, dear Comtesse; I want you to invite Lady Sybil also; yes, for the whole time that John is there. No, I'm not mad; as a 360 great favour to me; yes, I have a very particular reason, but I won't tell you what it is; oh, call me Scotchy as much as you like, but consent; do, do, do. Thank you, thank you, good-bye.

> (*She has control of herself now, and is determined not to let it slip from her again. When they reappear the stubborn one is writing a letter*)

JOHN I thought I heard the telephone again.

MAGGIE (*looking up from her labours*) It was the Comtesse; she says 365 she's to invite Lady Sybil to the cottage at the same time.

SYBIL Me!

JOHN To invite Sybil? Then of course I won't go, Maggie.

MAGGIE (*wondering seemingly at these niceties*) What does it matter? Is anything to be considered except the speech? (*It has been admitted 370 that she was a little devil*) And, with Sybil on the spot, John, *to help you and inspire you*, what a speech it will be!

JOHN (*carried away*) Maggie, you really are a very generous woman.°

SYBIL (*convinced at last*) She is indeed.

JOHN And you're queer too. How many women in the circumstances 375 would sit down to write a letter!

MAGGIE It's a letter to you, John.

JOHN To me?

MAGGIE I'll give it to you when it's finished, but I ask you not to open it till your visit to the Comtesse ends. 380

JOHN What is it about?

MAGGIE It's practical.

SYBIL (*rather faintly*) Practical? (*She has heard the word so frequently to-day that it is beginning to have a Scotch sound. She feels she ought to like Maggie, but that she would like her better if they were farther apart. She indicates that the doctors are troubled about her heart, and murmuring her adieux she goes. John, who is accompanying her, pauses at the door*)

JOHN (*with a queer sort of admiration for his wife*) Maggie, I wish I was fond of you.

MAGGIE (*heartily*) I wish you were, John.

> (*He goes, and she resumes her letter. The stocking is lying at hand, and she pushes it to the floor. She is done for a time with knitting*)

Act 4

Man's most pleasant invention is the lawn-mower. All the birds know this, and that is why, when it is at rest, there is always at least one of them sitting on the handle with his head cocked, wondering how the delicious whirring sound is made. When they find out, they will change their note. As it is, you must sometimes have thought that you heard the mower very early in the morning, and perhaps you peeped in *négligé*° from your lattice window to see who was up so early. It was really the birds trying to get the note.°

On this broiling morning, however, we are at noon, and whoever looks will see that the whirring is done by Mr Venables. He is in a linen suit with the coat discarded (the bird is sitting on it), and he comes and goes across the Comtesse's lawns, pleasantly mopping his face. We see him through a crooked bowed window generously open, roses intruding into it as if to prevent its ever being closed at night; there are other roses in such armfuls on the tables that one could not easily say where the room ends and the garden begins.

In the Comtesse's pretty comic drawing-room (for she likes the comic touch when she is in England) sits John Shand with his hostess, on chairs at a great distance from each other. No linen garments for John, nor flannels, nor even knickerbockers;° he envies the English way of dressing for trees and lawns, but is too Scotch to be able to imitate it; he wears tweeds, just as he would do in his native country where they would be in kilts. Like many another Scot, the first time he ever saw a kilt was on a Sassenach;° indeed kilts were perhaps invented, like golf, to draw the English north. John is doing nothing, which again is not a Scotch accomplishment, and he looks rather miserable and dour. The Comtesse is already at her Patience cards, and occasionally she smiles on him as if not displeased with his long silence. At last she speaks:

COMTESSE I feel it rather a shame to detain you here on such a lovely day, Mr Shand, entertaining an old woman.

JOHN I don't pretend to think I'm entertaining you, Comtesse.

COMTESSE But you *are*, you know.

JOHN I would be pleased to be told how?

> (*She shrugs her impertinent shoulders, and presently there is another heavy sigh from John*)

226

COMTESSE Again! Why do not you go out on the river?

JOHN Yes, I can do that. (*He rises*)

COMTESSE And take Sybil with you. (*He sits again*) No?

JOHN I have been on the river with her twenty times.

COMTESSE Then take her for a long walk through the Fairloe woods.

JOHN We were there twice last week.

COMTESSE There is a romantically damp little arbour at the end of what the villagers call the Lovers' Lane.

JOHN One can't go there every day. I see nothing to laugh at.

COMTESSE Did I laugh? I must have been translating the situation into French.

> (*Perhaps the music of the lawn-mower is not to John's mood, for he betakes himself to another room. Mr Venables pauses in his labours to greet a lady who has appeared on the lawn, and who is Maggie. She is as neat as if she were one of the army of typists (who are quite the nicest kind of women), and carries a little bag. She comes in through the window, and puts her hands over the Comtesse's eyes*)

COMTESSE They are a strong pair of hands, at any rate.

MAGGIE And not very white, and biggish for my size. Now guess.

> (*The Comtesse guesses, and takes both the hands in hers as if she valued them. She pulls off Maggie's hat as if to prevent her flying away*)

COMTESSE Dear abominable one, not to let me know you were coming.

MAGGIE It is just a surprise visit, Comtesse. I walked up from the station. (*For a moment Maggie seems to have borrowed Sybil's impediment*) How is—everybody?

COMTESSE He is quite well. But, my child, he seems to me to be a most unhappy man.

> (*This sad news does not seem to make a most unhappy woman of the child. The Comtesse is puzzled, as she knows nothing of the situation save what she has discovered for herself*)

Why should that please you, O heartless one?

MAGGIE I won't tell you.

COMTESSE I could take you and shake you, Maggie. Here have I put my house at your disposal for so many days for some sly Scotch purpose, and you will not tell me what it is.

MAGGIE No.

COMTESSE Very well, then, but I have what you call a nasty one for you. (*The Comtesse lures Mr Venables into the room by holding up what might be a foaming glass of lemon squash*) Alas, Charles, it is

but a flower vase. I want you to tell Mrs Shand what you think of
her husband's speech.

(*Mr Venables gives his hostess a reproachful look*)

VENABLES Eh—ah—Shand will prefer to do that himself. I promised   65
the gardener—I must not disappoint him—excuse me——

COMTESSE You must tell her, Charles.

MAGGIE Please, Mr Venables, I should like to know.

(*He sits down with a sigh and obeys*)

VENABLES Your husband has been writing the speech here, and by
his own wish he read it to me three days ago. The occasion is to   70
be an important one; and, well, there are a dozen young men in
the party at present, all capable of filling a certain small ministerial
post. (*He looks longingly at the mower, but it sends no message to his
aid*) And as he is one of them I was anxious that he should show
in this speech of what he is capable.   75

MAGGIE And hasn't he?

(*Not for the first time Mr Venables wishes that he was not in
politics*)

VENABLES I am afraid he has.

COMTESSE What is wrong with the speech, Charles?

VENABLES Nothing—and he can still deliver it. It is a powerful,
well-thought-out piece of work, such as only a very able man could   80
produce. But it has no *special quality* of its own—none of the little
touches that used to make an old stager like myself want to pat
Shand on the shoulder. (*The Comtesse's mouth twitches, but Maggie
declines to notice it*) He pounds on manfully enough, but, if I may
say so, with a wooden leg. It is as good, I dare say, as the rest of   85
them could have done; but they start with such inherited advant-
ages, Mrs Shand, that he had to do better.

MAGGIE Yes, I can understand that.

VENABLES I am sorry, Mrs Shand, for he interested me. His career
has set me wondering whether if *I* had begun as a railway porter   90
I might not still be calling out, 'By your leave.'°

(*Maggie thinks it probable but not important*)

MAGGIE Mr Venables, now that I think of it, surely John wrote to
me that you were dissatisfied with his first speech, and that he was
writing another.

(*The Comtesse's eyes open very wide indeed*)

VENABLES I have heard nothing of that, Mrs Shand. (*He shakes his   95
wise head*) And in any case, I am afraid——(*He still hears the
wooden leg*)

MAGGIE But you said yourself that his second thoughts were sometimes such an improvement on the first.
(*The Comtesse comes to the help of the baggage*)

COMTESSE I remember your saying that, Charles. 100

VENABLES Yes, that has struck me. (*Politely*) Well, if he has anything
to show me——In the meantime——
(*He regains the lawn, like one glad to escape attendance at
John's obsequies. The Comtesse is brought back to speech by the
sound of the mower—nothing wooden in it*)

COMTESSE What are you up to now, Miss Pin? You know as well as
I do that there is no such speech.
(*Maggie's mouth tightens*)

MAGGIE I do not. 105

COMTESSE It is a duel, is it, my friend?
(*The Comtesse rings the bell and Maggie's guilty mind is
agitated*)

MAGGIE What are you ringing for?

COMTESSE As the challenged one, Miss Pin, I have the choice of
weapons. I am going to send for your husband to ask him if he has
written such a speech. After which, I suppose, *you* will ask me to 110
leave you while you and he write it together.
(*Maggie wrings her hands*)

MAGGIE You are wrong, Comtesse; but please don't do that.

COMTESSE You but make me more curious, and my doctor says that
I must be told everything. (*The Comtesse assumes the pose of her sex
in melodrama*) Put your cards on the table, Maggie Shand, or—— 115
(*She indicates that she always pinks° her man. Maggie dolefully
produces a roll of paper from her bag*) What precisely is that?
(*The reply is little more than a squeak*)

MAGGIE John's speech.

COMTESSE You have written it yourself!
(*Maggie is naturally indignant*)

MAGGIE It's typed. 120

COMTESSE You guessed that the speech he wrote unaided would not
satisfy, and you prepared this to take its place!

MAGGIE Not at all, Comtesse. It is the draft of his speech that he left
at home. That's all.

COMTESSE With a few trivial alterations by yourself, I swear. Can 125
you deny it?
(*No wonder that Maggie is outraged. She replaces John's speech
in the bag with becoming hauteur*)

MAGGIE Comtesse, these insinuations are unworthy of you. May I ask where is my husband?

(*The Comtesse drops her a curtsey*)

COMTESSE I believe your Haughtiness may find him in the Dutch garden. Oh, I see through you. You are not to show him   130
your speech. But you are to get him to write another one, and somehow all your additions will be in it. Think not, creature, that you can deceive one so old in iniquity as the Comtesse de la Brière.

(*There can be but one reply from a good wife to such a charge, and at once the Comtesse is left alone with her shame. Anon a footman appears. You know how they come and go*)

FOOTMAN You rang, my lady?   135

COMTESSE Did I? Ah, yes, but why? (*He is but lately from the ploughshare° and cannot help her. In this quandary her eyes alight upon the bag. She is unfortunately too abandoned to feel her shame; she still thinks that she has the choice of weapons. She takes the speech from the bag and bestows it on her servitor*) Take this to Mr   140
Venables, please, and say it is from Mr Shand. (*Thomas—but in the end we shall probably call him John—departs with the dangerous papers; and when Maggie returns she finds that the Comtesse is once more engaged on her interrupted game of Patience*) You did not find him?   145

(*All the bravery has dropped from Maggie's face*)

MAGGIE I didn't see him, but I heard him. *She* is with him. I think they are coming here.

(*The Comtesse is suddenly kind again*)

COMTESSE Sybil? Shall I get rid of her?

MAGGIE No, I want her to be here, too. Now I shall know.

(*The Comtesse twists the little thing round*)

COMTESSE Know what?   150

MAGGIE As soon as I look into his face I shall know.

(*A delicious scent ushers in the fair Sybil, who is as sweet as a milking stool. She greets Mrs Shand with some alarm*)

How do you do, Lady Sybil? How pretty you look in that frock. (*Sybil rustles uncomfortably*) You are a feast to the eye.

SYBIL Please, I wish you would not.

(*Shall we describe Sybil's frock, in which she looks like a great strawberry that knows it ought to be plucked; or would it be easier to watch the coming of John? Let us watch John*)

JOHN You, Maggie! You never wrote that you were coming.   155

(*No, let us watch Maggie.*° *As soon as she looked into his face she was to know something of importance*)

MAGGIE (*not dissatisfied with what she sees*) No, John, it's a surprise visit. I just ran down to say good-bye.

(*At this his face falls, which does not seem to pain her*)

SYBIL (*foreseeing another horrible Scotch scene*) To say good-bye?

COMTESSE (*thrilling with expectation*) To whom, Maggie?

SYBIL (*deserted by the impediment, which is probably playing with rough boys in the Lovers' Lane*) Auntie, do leave us, won't you? 160

COMTESSE Not I. It is becoming far too interesting.

MAGGIE I suppose there's no reason the Comtesse shouldn't be told, as she will know so soon at any rate?

JOHN That's so. (*Sybil sees with discomfort that he is to be practical also*) 165

MAGGIE It's so simple. You see, Comtesse, John and Lady Sybil have fallen in love with one another, and they are to go off as soon as the meeting at Leeds has taken place.

(*The Comtesse's breast is too suddenly introduced to Caledonia*° *and its varied charms*)

COMTESSE *Mon Dieu!* 170

MAGGIE I think that's putting it correctly, John.

JOHN In a sense. But I'm not to attend the meeting at Leeds. My speech doesn't find favour. (*With a strange humility*) There's something wrong with it.

COMTESSE I never expected to hear you say that, Mr Shand. 175

JOHN (*wondering also*) I never expected it myself. I meant to make it the speech of my career. But somehow my hand seems to have lost its cunning.°

COMTESSE And you don't know how?

JOHN It's inexplicable. My brain was never clearer. 180

COMTESSE You might have helped him, Sybil.

SYBIL (*quite sulkily*) I did.

COMTESSE But I thought she was such an inspiration to you, Mr Shand.

JOHN (*going bravely to Sybil's side*) She slaved at it with me. 185

COMTESSE Strange. (*Wickedly becoming practical also*) So now there is nothing to detain you. Shall I send for a fly,° Sybil?

SYBIL (*with a cry of the heart*) Auntie, do leave us.

COMTESSE I can understand your impatience to be gone, Mr Shand.

JOHN (*heavily*) I promised Maggie to wait till the 24th, and I'm a man of my word. 190

MAGGIE But I give you back your word, John. You can go now.
(*John looks at Sybil, and Sybil looks at John, and the
impediment arrives in time to take a peep at both of them*)

SYBIL (*groping for the practical, to which we must all come in the end*)
He must make satisfactory arrangements about you first. I insist
on that.   195

MAGGIE (*with no more imagination than a hen*) Thank you, Lady
Sybil, but I have made all my arrangements.

JOHN (*stung*) Maggie, that was my part.

MAGGIE You see, my brothers feel they can't be away from their
business any longer; and so, if it would be convenient to you, John,   200
I could travel north with them by the night train on Wednesday.

SYBIL I—I——The way you put things——!

JOHN This is just the 21st.

MAGGIE My things are all packed. I think you'll find the house in
good order, Lady Sybil. I have had the vacuum cleaners in. I'll   205
give you the keys of the linen and the silver plate; I have them in
that bag. The carpet on the upper landing is a good deal frayed,
but——

SYBIL Please, I don't want to hear any more.

MAGGIE The ceiling of the dining-room would be the better of a new   210
lick of paint——

SYBIL (*stamping her foot, small fours*) Can't you stop her?

JOHN (*soothingly*) She's meaning well. Maggie, I know it's natural to
you to value those things, because your outlook on life is bounded
by them; but all this jars on me.   215

MAGGIE Does it?

JOHN Why should you be so ready to go?

MAGGIE I promised not to stand in your way.

JOHN (*stoutly*) You needn't be in such a hurry. There are three days
to run yet. (*The French are so different from us that we shall probably*   220
never be able to understand why the Comtesse laughed aloud here) It's
just a joke to the Comtesse.

COMTESSE It seems to be no joke to you, Mr Shand. Sybil, my pet,
are you to let him off?

SYBIL (*flashing*) Let him off? If he wishes it. Do you?   225

JOHN (*manfully*) I want it to go on. (*Something seems to have caught
in his throat: perhaps it is the impediment trying a temporary home*)
It's the one wish of my heart. If you come with me, Sybil, I'll do
all in a man's power to make you never regret it.
(*Triumph of the Vere de Veres*)

MAGGIE (*bringing them back to earth with a dump*) And I can make my   230
    arrangements for Wednesday?

SYBIL (*seeking the Comtesse's protection*) No, you can't. Auntie, I am
    not going on with this. I'm very sorry for you, John, but I see
    now—I couldn't face it——

        (*She can't face anything at this moment except the sofa pillows*)

COMTESSE (*noticing John's big sigh of relief*) So *that* is all right, Mr   235
    Shand!

MAGGIE Don't you love her any more, John? Be practical.

SYBIL (*to the pillows*) At any rate I have tired of him. Oh, best to tell
    the horrid truth. I am ashamed of myself. I have been crying my
    eyes out over it—I thought I was such a different kind of woman.   240
    But I am weary of him. I think him—oh, so dull.

JOHN (*his face lighting up*) Are you sure that is how you have come
    to think of me?

SYBIL I'm sorry; (*with all her soul*) but yes—yes—yes.

JOHN By God, it's more than I deserve.   245

COMTESSE Congratulations to you both.

        (*Sybil runs away; and in the fullness of time she married
        successfully in cloth of silver,° which was afterwards turned into
        a bed-spread*)

MAGGIE You haven't read my letter yet, John, have you?

JOHN No.

COMTESSE (*imploringly*) May I know to what darling letter you refer?

MAGGIE It's a letter I wrote to him before he left London. I gave it   250
    to him closed, not to be opened until his time here was ended.

JOHN (*as his hand strays to his pocket*) Am I to read it now?

MAGGIE Not before her. Please go away, Comtesse.

COMTESSE Every word you say makes me more determined to remain.

MAGGIE It will hurt you, John. (*Distressed*) Don't read it; tear it up.   255

JOHN You make me very curious, Maggie. And yet I don't see what
    can be in it.

COMTESSE But you feel a little nervous? Give *me* the dagger.°

MAGGIE (*quickly*) No. (*But the Comtesse has already got it*)

COMTESSE May I? (*She must have thought they said Yes, for she opens*   260
    the letter. She shares its contents with them) 'Dearest John, It is at
    my request that the Comtesse is having Lady Sybil at the cottage
    at the same time as yourself.'

JOHN What?

COMTESSE Yes, she begged me to invite you together.   265

JOHN But why?

MAGGIE I promised you not to behave as other wives would do.

JOHN It's not understandable.

COMTESSE 'You may ask why I do this, John, and my reason is, I think that after a few weeks of Lady Sybil, every day, and all day, 270 you will become sick to death of her. I am also giving her the chance to help you and inspire you with your work, so that you may both learn what her help and her inspiration amount to. Of course, if your love is the great strong passion you think it, then those weeks will make you love her more than ever and I can only 275 say good-bye. But if, as I suspect, you don't even now know what true love is, then by the next time we meet, dear John, you will have had enough of her.—Your affectionate wife, Maggie.' Oh, why was not Sybil present at the reading of the will!° And now, if you two will kindly excuse me, I think I must go and get that poor 280 sufferer the eau de Cologne.

JOHN It's almost enough to make a man lose faith in himself.

COMTESSE Oh, don't say that, Mr Shand.

MAGGIE (*defending him*) You mustn't hurt him. If you haven't loved deep and true, that's just because you have never met a woman 285 yet, John, capable of inspiring it.

COMTESSE (*putting her hand on Maggie's shoulder*) Have you not, Mr Shand?

JOHN I see what you mean. But Maggie wouldn't think better of me for any false pretences. She knows my feelings for her now are 290 neither more nor less than what they have always been.

MAGGIE (*who sees that he is looking at her as solemnly as a volume of sermons printed by request*) I think no one could be fond of me that can't laugh a little at me.

JOHN How could that help? 295

COMTESSE (*exasperated*) Mr Shand, I give you up.

MAGGIE I admire his honesty.

COMTESSE Oh, I give you up also. Arcades ambo.° Scotchies both.

JOHN (*when she has gone*) But this letter, it's not like you. By Gosh, Maggie, you're no fool. 300

(*She beams at this, as any wife would*)

But how could I have made such a mistake? It's not like a strong man. (*Evidently he has an inspiration*)

MAGGIE What is it?

JOHN (*the inspiration*) *Am* I a strong man?

MAGGIE You? Of course you are. And self-made. Has anybody ever 305 helped you in the smallest way?

JOHN (*thinking it out again*) No, nobody.

MAGGIE Not even Lady Sybil?

JOHN I'm beginning to doubt it. It's very curious, though, Maggie, that this speech should be disappointing.   310

MAGGIE It's just that Mr Venables hasn't the brains to see how good it is.

JOHN That must be it. (*But he is too good a man to rest satisfied with this*) No, Maggie, it's not. Somehow I seem to have lost my neat way of saying things.   315

MAGGIE (*almost cooing*) It will come back to you.

JOHN (*forlorn*) If you knew how I've tried.

MAGGIE (*cautiously*) Maybe if you were to try again; and I'll just come and sit beside you, and knit. I think the click of the needles sometimes put you in the mood.   320

JOHN Hardly that; and yet many a Shandism have I knocked off while you were sitting beside me knitting. I suppose it was the quietness.

MAGGIE Very likely.

JOHN (*with another inspiration*) Maggie!   325

MAGGIE (*again*) What is it, John?

JOHN What if it was you that put those queer ideas into my head!

MAGGIE Me?

JOHN Without your knowing it, I mean.

MAGGIE But how?   330

JOHN We used to talk bits over; and it may be that you dropped the seed, so to speak.

MAGGIE John, could it be this, that I sometimes had the idea in a rough womanish° sort of way and then you polished it up till it came out a Shandism?   335

JOHN (*slowly slapping his knee*) I believe you've hit it, Maggie: to think that you may have been helping me all the time—and neither of us knew it!

> (*He has so nearly reached a smile that no one can say what might have happened within the next moment if the Comtesse had not reappeared*)

COMTESSE Mr Venables wishes to see you, Mr Shand.

JOHN (*lost, stolen, or strayed° a smile in the making*) Hum!   340

COMTESSE He is coming now.

JOHN (*grumpy*) Indeed!

COMTESSE (*sweetly*) It is about your speech.

JOHN He has said all he need say on that subject, and more.

COMTESSE (*quaking a little*) I think it is about the second speech.   345
JOHN What second speech?
    (*Maggie runs to her bag and opens it*)
MAGGIE (*horrified*) Comtesse, you have given it to him!
COMTESSE (*impudently*) Wasn't I meant to?
JOHN What is it? What second speech?
MAGGIE Cruel, cruel. (*Willing to go on her knees*) You had left the   350
    first draft of your speech at home, John, and I brought it here
    with—with a few little things I've added myself.
JOHN (*a seven-footer*) What's that?
MAGGIE (*four foot ten at most*) Just trifles—things I was to suggest to
    you—while I was knitting—and then, if you liked any of them you   355
    could have polished them—and turned them into something good.
    John, John—and now she has shown it to Mr Venables.
JOHN (*thundering*) As my work, Comtesse?
    (*But the Comtesse is not of the women who are afraid of thunder*)
MAGGIE It is your work—nine-tenths of it.
JOHN (*in the black cap*)° You presumed, Maggie Shand! Very well,   360
    then, here he comes, and now we'll see to what extent you've
    helped me.
VENABLES My dear fellow. My dear Shand, I congratulate you. Give
    me your hand.
JOHN The speech?   365
VENABLES You have improved it out of knowledge. It is the same
    speech, but those new touches make all the difference. (*John sits
    down heavily*) Mrs Shand, be proud of him.
MAGGIE I am. I am, John.
COMTESSE You always said that his second thoughts were best,   370
    Charles.
VENABLES (*pleased to be reminded of it*) Didn't I, didn't I? Those
    delicious little touches! How good that is, Shand, about the flowing
    tide.
COMTESSE The flowing tide?   375
VENABLES In the first speech it was something like this—
    'Gentlemen, the Opposition are calling to you to vote for them and
    the flowing tide, but I solemnly warn you to beware lest the
    flowing tide does not engulf you.' The second way is much better.
COMTESSE What is the second way, Mr Shand?   380
    (*John does not tell her*)
VENABLES This is how he puts it now. (*John cannot help raising his
    head to listen*) 'Gentlemen, the Opposition are calling to you to vote

for them and the flowing tide, but I ask you cheerfully to vote for us and *dam* the flowing tide.'

> (*Venables and his old friend the Comtesse laugh heartily, but for different reasons*)

COMTESSE It *is* better, Mr Shand.   385

MAGGIE *I* don't think so.

VENABLES Yes, yes, it's so virile. Excuse me, Comtesse, I'm off to read the whole thing again. (*For the first time he notices that John is strangely quiet*) I think this has rather bowled you over, Shand.

> (*John's head sinks lower*)

Well, well, good news doesn't kill.   390

MAGGIE (*counsel for the defence*) Surely the important thing about the speech is its strength and knowledge and eloquence, the things that were in the first speech as well as in the second.

VENABLES That of course is largely true. The wit would not be enough without them, just as they were not enough without the   395 wit. It is the combination that is irresistible. (*John's head rises a little*) Shand, you are our man, remember that, it is emphatically the best thing you have ever done. How this will go down at Leeds!

> (*He returns gaily to his hammock; but lower sinks John's head, and even the Comtesse has the grace to take herself off. Maggie's arms flutter near her husband, not daring to alight*)

MAGGIE You heard what he said, John. It's the combination. Is it so   400 terrible to you to find that my love for you had made me able to help you in the little things?

JOHN The little things! It seems strange to me to hear you call me by my name, Maggie. It's as if I looked on you for the first time.

MAGGIE Look at me, John, for the first time. What do you see?   405

JOHN I see a woman who has brought her husband low.

MAGGIE Only that?

JOHN I see the tragedy of a man who has found himself out.° Eh, I can't live with you again, Maggie.

> (*He shivers*)

MAGGIE Why did you shiver, John?   410

JOHN It was at myself for saying that I couldn't live with you again, when I should have been wondering how for so long you have lived with me. And I suppose you have forgiven me all the time. (*She nods*) And forgive me still? (*She nods again*) Dear God!

MAGGIE John, am I to go? or are you to keep me on? (*She is now a*   415 *little bundle near his feet*) I'm willing to stay because I'm useful to you, if it can't be for a better reason. (*His hand feels for her, and the bundle wriggles nearer*) It's nothing unusual I've done, John. Every man who is high up loves to think that he has done it all himself; and the wife smiles, and lets it go at that. It's our only joke. Every woman knows that. (*He stares at her in hopeless perplexity*) Oh, John, if only you could laugh at me.   420

JOHN   I can't laugh, Maggie.

(*But as he continues to stare at her a strange disorder appears in his face. Maggie feels that it is to be now or never*)

MAGGIE   Laugh, John, laugh. Watch me; see how easy it is.

(*A terrible struggle is taking place within him. He creaks. Something that may be mirth forces a passage, at first painfully, no more joy in it than in the discoloured water from a spring that has long been dry. Soon, however, he laughs loud and long. The spring water is becoming clear. Maggie claps her hands. He is saved*)

MARY ROSE

CHARACTERS
(in order of appearance)

Mrs Otery
Harry Morland Blake
Mr Morland
Mrs Morland

Mr Amy
Mary Rose
Simon Blake
Mr Cameron

Act 1

The scene is a room in a small Sussex manor house that has long been for sale. It is such a silent room that whoever speaks first here is a bold one, unless indeed he merely mutters to himself, which they perhaps allow. All of this room's past which can be taken away has gone. Such light as there is comes from the only window, which is at the back and is incompletely shrouded in sacking. For a moment this is a mellow light, and if a photograph could be taken quickly we might find a disturbing smile on the room's face, perhaps like the Monna Lisa's,° which came, surely, of her knowing what only the dead should know. There are two doors, one leading downstairs; the other is at the back, very insignificant, though it is the centre of this disturbing history. The wallpaper, heavy in the adherence of other papers of a still older date, has peeled and leans forward here and there in a grotesque bow, as men have hung in chains; one might predict that the next sound heard here will be in the distant future when another piece of paper loosens. Save for two packing-cases, the only furniture is a worn easy-chair doddering by the unlit fire, like some foolish old man. We might play with the disquieting fancy that this room, once warm with love, is still alive but is shrinking from observation, and that with our departure they cunningly set to again at the apparently never-ending search which goes on in some empty old houses.

Some one is heard clumping up the stair, and the caretaker enters. It is not she, however, who clumps; she has been here for several years, and has become sufficiently a part of the house to move noiselessly in it. The first thing we know about her is that she does not like to be in this room. She is an elderly woman of gaunt frame and with a singular control over herself. There may be some one, somewhere, who can make her laugh still, one never knows, but the effort would hurt her face. Even the war, lately ended, meant very little to her. She has shown a number of possible purchasers over the house, just as she is showing one over it now, with the true caretaker's indifference whether you buy or not. The few duties imposed on her here she performs conscientiously, but her greatest capacity is for sitting still in the dark. Her work over, her mind a blank, she sits thus rather than pay for a candle. One knows a little more about life when he knows the Mrs Oterys, but she herself is unaware that she is

peculiar, and probably thinks that in some such way do people in general pass the hour before bedtime. Nevertheless, though saving of her candle in other empty houses, she always lights it on the approach   40
of evening in this one.

The man who has clumped up the stairs in her wake is a young Australian soldier, a private, such as in those days you met by the dozen in any London street, slouching along it forlornly if alone, with sudden stoppages to pass the time (in which you ran against him), or   45
in affable converse with a young lady. In his voice is the Australian tang that became such a friendly sound to us.° He is a rough fellow, sinewy, with the clear eye of the man with the axe whose chief life-struggle till the war came was to fell trees and see to it that they did not crash down on him. Mrs Otery is showing him the house,   50
which he has evidently known in other days, but though interested he is unsentimental and looks about him with a tolerant grin.

MRS OTERY This was the drawing-room.

HARRY Not it, no, no, never. This wasn't the drawing-room, my
cabbage;° at least not in my time.   55

MRS OTERY (*indifferently*) I only came here about three years ago and
I never saw the house furnished, but I was told to say this was the
drawing-room. (*With a flicker of spirit*) And I would thank you not
to call me your cabbage.

HARRY (*whom this kind of retort helps to put at his ease*) No offence. It's   60
a French expression, and many a happy moment have I given to the
mademoiselles by calling them cabbages. But the drawing-room! I
was a little shaver when I was here last, but I mind we called the
drawing-room the Big Room; it wasn't a little box like this.

MRS OTERY This is the biggest room in the house. (*She quotes   65
drearily from some advertisement which is probably hanging in rags on
the gate*) Specially charming is the drawing-room with its superb
view of the Downs. This room is upstairs and is approached
by——

HARRY By a stair, containing some romantic rat-holes. Snakes,   70
whether it's the room or not, it strikes cold; there is something
shiversome about it.

(*For the first time she gives him a sharp glance*)

I've shivered in many a shanty in Australy, and thought of the big
room at home and the warmth of it. The warmth! And now this
is the best it can do for the prodigal when he returns to it expecting   75
to see that calf done to a turn.° We live and learn, missis.

MRS OTERY We live, at any rate.

HARRY Well said, my cabbage.

MRS OTERY Thank you, my rhododendron.

HARRY (*cheered*) I like your spirit. You and me would get on great if   80
I had time to devote to your amusement. But, see here, I can make
sure whether this was the drawing-room. If it was, there is an
apple-tree outside there, with one of its branches scraping on the
window. I ought to know, for it was out at the window down that
apple-tree to the ground that I slided one dark night when I   85
was a twelve-year-old, ran away from home, the naughty blue-
eyed angel that I was, and set off to make my fortune on the
blasted ocean. The fortune, my—my lady friend—has still got the
start of me, but the apple-tree should be there to welcome her
darling boy.   90

> (*He pulls down the sacking, which lets a little more light into the
> room. We see that the window, which reaches to the floor, opens
> outwards. There were probably long ago steps from it down into
> the garden, but they are gone now, and gone too is the apple-tree*)

I've won! No tree: no drawing-room.

MRS OTERY I have heard tell there was once a tree there; and you
can see the root if you look down.

HARRY Yes, yes, I see it in the long grass, and a bit of the seat that
used to be round it. This is the drawing-room right enough,   95
Harry, my boy. There were blue curtains to that window, and I
used to hide behind them and pounce out upon Robinson Crusoe.
There was a sofa at this end, and I had my first lessons in
swimming on it. You are a fortunate woman, my petite, to be here
drinking in these moving memories. There used to be a peacock,   100
too. Now, what the hell could a peacock be doing in this noble
apartment?

MRS OTERY I have been told a cloth used to hang on the wall here,
tapestries they're called, and that it had pictures of peacocks on it.
I dare say that was your peacock.   105

HARRY Gone, even my peacock! And I could have sworn I used to
pull the feathers out of its tail. The clock was in this corner, and
it had a wheezy little figure of a smith that used to come out and
strike the hour on an anvil. My old man used to wind that clock
up every night, and I mind his rage when he found out it was an   110
eight-day clock.° The padre had to reprove him for swearing.
Padre? What's the English for padre? Damme, I'm forgetting my
own language. Oh yes, parson. Is *he* in the land of the living still?

I can see him clear, a long thin man with a hard sharp face. He
was always quarrelling about pictures he collected.   115
MRS OTERY The parson here is a very old man, but he is not tall and
thin, he is little and roundish with a soft face and white whiskers.
HARRY Whiskers? I can't think he had whiskers. (*Ruminating*) *Had*
he whiskers? Stop a bit, I believe it is his wife I'm thinking about.
I doubt I don't give satisfaction as a sentimental character. Is there 120
any objection, your ladyship, to smoking in the drawing-room?
MRS OTERY (*ungraciously*) Smoke if you want.
        (*He hacks into a cake of tobacco with a large clasp knife*)
That's a fearsome-looking knife.
HARRY Useful in trench warfare. It's not a knife, it's a visiting-card.
You leave it on favoured parties° like this.   125
        (*He casts it at one of the packing-cases, and it sticks quivering
        in the wood*)
MRS OTERY Were you an officer?
HARRY For a few minutes now and again.
MRS OTERY You're playing with me.
HARRY You're so *ir*resistible.
MRS OTERY Do you want to see the other rooms?   130
HARRY I was fondly hoping you would ask me that.
MRS OTERY Come along, then. (*She wants to lead him downstairs, but
the little door at the back has caught his eye*)
HARRY What does that door open on?
MRS OTERY (*avoiding looking at it*) Nothing, it's just a cupboard door. 135
HARRY (*considering her*) Who is playing with me now?
MRS OTERY I don't know what you mean. Come this way.
HARRY (*not budging*) I'll explain what I mean. That door—it's
coming back to me—it leads into a little dark passage.
MRS OTERY That's all.   140
HARRY That can't be all. Who ever heard of a passage wandering
about by itself in a respectable house! It leads—yes—to a single
room, and the door of the room faces this way.
        (*He opens the door, and a door beyond is disclosed*)
There's a memory for you! But what the hell made you want to
deceive me?   145
MRS OTERY It's of no consequence.
HARRY I think—yes—the room in there has two stone windows—
and wooden rafters.
MRS OTERY It's the oldest part of the house.
HARRY It comes back to me that I used to sleep there.   150

MRS OTERY That may be. If you'll come down with me——

HARRY I'm curious to see that room first.

     (She bars the way)

MRS OTERY *(thin-lipped and determined)* You can't go in there.

HARRY Your reasons?

MRS OTERY It's—locked. I tell you it's just an empty room.   155

HARRY There must be a key.

MRS OTERY It's—lost.

HARRY Queer your anxiety to stop me, when you knew I would find the door locked.

MRS OTERY Sometimes it's locked; sometimes not.   160

HARRY Is it not you that locks it?

MRS OTERY *(reluctantly)* It's never locked, it's held.

HARRY Who holds it?

MRS OTERY *(in a little outburst)* Quiet, man.

HARRY You're all shivering.   165

MRS OTERY I'm not.

HARRY *(cunningly)* I suppose you are just shivering because the room is so chilly.

MRS OTERY *(falling into the trap)* That's it.

HARRY So you *are* shivering!   170

     (She makes no answer, and he reflects with the help of his pipe)

May I put a light to these bits of sticks?

MRS OTERY If you like. My orders are to have fires once a week.

     (He lights the twigs in the fireplace, and they burn up easily, but will be ashes in a few minutes)

You can't have the money to buy a house like this.

HARRY Not me. It was just my manly curiosity to see the old home that brought me. I'm for Australy again. *(Suddenly turning on her)*   175
What is wrong with this house?

MRS OTERY *(on her guard)* There is nothing wrong with it.

HARRY Then how is it going so cheap?

MRS OTERY It's—in bad repair.

HARRY Why has it stood empty so long?   180

MRS OTERY It's—far from a town.

HARRY What made the last tenant leave in such a hurry?

MRS OTERY *(wetting her lips)* You have heard that, have you? Gossiping in the village, I suppose?

HARRY I have heard some other things as well. I have heard they had   185
to get a caretaker from a distance, because no woman hereabout would live alone in this house.

MRS OTERY A pack o' cowards.

HARRY I have heard that that caretaker was bold and buxom° when
    she came, and that now she is a scared woman.   190

MRS OTERY I'm not.

HARRY I have heard she's been known to run out into the fields and
    stay there trembling half the night.

       (*She does not answer, and he resorts to cunning again*)

    Of course, I see they couldn't have meant you. Just foolish stories
    that gather about an old house.   195

MRS OTERY (*relieved*) That's all.

HARRY (*quickly, as he looks at the little door*) What's that?

       (*Mrs Otery screams*)

    I got you that time! What was it you expected to see?

       (*No answer*)

    Is it a ghost? They say it's a ghost. What is it gives this house an
    ill name?   200

MRS OTERY Use as brave words as you like when you have gone, but
    I advise you, my lad, to keep a civil tongue while you are here. (*In
    her everyday voice*) There is no use showing you the rest of the
    house. If you want to be stepping,° I have my work to do.

HARRY We have got on so nicely, I wonder if you would give me a   205
    mug of tea. Not a cup, we drink it by the mugful where I hail
    from.

MRS OTERY (*ungraciously*) I have no objection.

HARRY Since you are so pressing, I accept.

MRS OTERY Come down, then, to the kitchen.   210

HARRY No, no, I'm sure the Prodigal got his tea in the drawing-
    room, though what made them make such a fuss about that man
    beats me.

MRS OTERY (*sullenly*) You are meaning to go into that room. I
    wouldn't if I was you.   215

HARRY If you were me you would.

MRS OTERY (*closing the little door*) Until I have your promise——

HARRY (*liking the tenacity of her*) Very well, I promise—unless, of
    course, she comes peeping out at the handsome gentleman. Your
    ghost has naught to do wi' me. It's a woman, isn't it?   220

       (*Her silence is perhaps an assent*)

    See here, I'll sit in this chair till you come back, saying my prayers.
    (*Feeling the chair*) You're clammy cold, old dear. It's not the
    ghost's chair by any chance, is it?

       (*No answer*)

You needn't look so scared, woman; she doesn't walk till midnight,
does she?   225
MRS OTERY (*looking at his knife in the wood*) I wouldn't leave that
  knife lying about.
HARRY Oh, come, give the old girl a chance.
MRS OTERY I'll not be more than ten minutes.
HARRY She can't do much in ten minutes.   230
    (*At which remark Mrs Otery fixes him with her eyes and
    departs*)

Harry is now sitting sunk in the chair, staring at the fire. It goes out,
but he remains there motionless, and in the increasing dusk he ceases
to be an intruder. He is now part of the room, the part long waited
for, come back at last. The house is shaken to its foundation by his
presence, we may conceive a thousand whispers. Then the crafty work   235
begins.° The little door at the back opens slowly to the extent of a
foot. Thus might a breath of wind blow it if there were any wind.
Presently Harry starts to his feet, convinced that there is some one in
the room, very near his knife. He is so sure of the exact spot where
she is that for a moment he looks nowhere else.   240
    In that moment the door slowly closes. He has not seen it close,
but he opens it and calls out, 'Who is that? Is any one there?' With
some distaste he enters the passage and tries the inner door, but
whether it be locked or held it will not open. He is about to pocket
his knife, then with a shrug of bravado sends it quivering back into   245
the wood—for her if she can get it. He returns to the chair, but not
to close his eyes: to watch and to be watched. The room is in a
tremble of desire to get started upon that nightly travail which can
never be completed till this man is here to provide the end.
    The figure of Harry becomes indistinct and fades from sight. When   250
the haze lifts we are looking at the room as it was some thirty years
earlier on the serene afternoon that began its troubled story. There
are rooms that are always smiling, so that you may see them at it if
you peep through the keyhole, and Mrs Morland's little drawing-
room is one of them. Perhaps these are smiles that she has left lying   255
about. She leaves many things lying about; for instance, one could
deduce the shape of her from studying that corner of the sofa which
is her favourite seat, and all her garments grow so like her that her
wardrobes are full of herself hanging on nails or folded away in
drawers. The pictures on her walls in time take on a resemblance to   260
her or hers though they may be meant to represent a waterfall, every

present given to her assumes some characteristic of the donor, and no doubt the necktie she is at present knitting will soon be able to pass as the person for whom it is being knit. It is only delightful ladies at the most agreeable age who have this personal way with their belongings. Among Mrs Morland's friends in the room are several of whom we have already heard, such as the blue curtains from which Harry pounced upon the castaway, the sofa on which he had his first swimming lessons, the peacock on the wall, the clock with the smart smith ready to step out and strike his anvil, and the apple-tree is in full blossom at the open window, one of its branches has even stepped into the room.

Mr Morland and the local clergyman are chatting importantly about some matter of no importance, while Mrs Morland is on her sofa at the other side of the room, coming into the conversation occasionally with a cough or a click of her needles, which is her clandestine way of telling her husband not to be so assertive to his guest. They are all middle-aged people who have found life to be on the whole an easy and happy adventure, and have done their tranquil best to make it so for their neighbours. The squire is lean, the clergyman of full habit,° but could you enter into them you would have difficulty in deciding which was clergyman and which was squire; both can be peppery, the same pepper. They are benignant creatures, but could exchange benignancies without altering. Mrs Morland knows everything about her husband except that she does nearly all his work for him. She really does not know this. His work, though he rises early to be at it, is not much larger than a lady's handkerchief, and consists of magisterial duties,° with now and then an impressive scene about a tenant's cowshed. She then makes up his mind for him, and is still unaware that she is doing it. He has so often heard her say (believing it, too)° that he is difficult to move when once he puts his foot down that he accepts himself modestly as a man of this character, and never tries to remember when it was that he last put down his foot. In the odd talks which the happily married sometimes hold about the future he always hopes he will be taken first, being the managing one, and she says little beyond pressing his hand, but privately she has decided that there must be another arrangement. Probably life at the vicarage is on not dissimilar lines, but we cannot tell, as we never meet Mr Amy's wife. Mr Amy is even more sociable than Mr Morland; he is reputed to know every one in the county, and has several times fallen off his horse because he will salute all passers-by. On his visits to London he usually returns

depressed because there are so many people in the streets to whom
he may not give a friendly bow. He likes to read a book if he knows
the residence or a relative of the author, and at the play it is far more   305
to him to learn that the actress has three children, one of them down
with measles, than to follow her histrionic genius. He and his host
have the pleasant habit of print-collecting, and a very common scene
between them is that which now follows. They are bent over the
squire's latest purchase.   310

MR AMY Very interesting. A nice little lot. I must say, James, you
have the collector's flair.

MR MORLAND Oh, well, I'm keen, you know, and when I run up to
London I can't resist going a bust° in my small way. I picked these
up quite cheap.   315

MR AMY The flair. That is what you have.

MR MORLAND Oh, I don't know.

MR AMY Yes, you have, James. You got them at Peterkin's in
Dean Street, didn't you? Yes, I know you did. I saw them there.
I wanted them too, but they told me you had already got the   320
refusal.

MR MORLAND Sorry to have been too quick for you, George, but it
is my way to nip in. You have some nice prints yourself.

MR AMY I haven't got your flair, James.

MR MORLAND I admit I don't miss much.   325
        (*So far it has been a competition in saintliness*)

MR AMY No. (*The saint leaves him*) You missed something yesterday
at Peterkin's, though.

MR MORLAND How do you mean?

MR AMY You didn't examine the little lot lying beneath this lot.

MR MORLAND I turned them over; just a few odds and ends of no   330
account.

MR AMY (*with horrible complacency*) All except one, James.

MR MORLAND (*twitching*) Something good?

MR AMY (*at his meekest*) Just a little trifle of a Gainsborough.°

MR MORLAND (*faintly*) What! You've got it?   335

MR AMY I've got it. I am a poor man, but I thought ten pounds
wasn't too much for a Gainsborough.
        (*The devil now has them both*)

MR MORLAND Ten pounds! Is it signed?

MR AMY No, it isn't signed.

MR MORLAND (*almost his friend again*) Ah!   340

MR AMY What do you precisely mean by that 'Ah,' James? If it had been signed, could I have got it for ten pounds? You are always speaking about your flair; I suppose I can have a little flair sometimes too.

MR MORLAND I am not always speaking about my flair, and I don't believe it is a Gainsborough.   345

MR AMY (*with dignity*) Please don't get hot, James. If I had thought you would grudge me my little find—which *you* missed—I wouldn't have brought it to show you.

> (*With shocking exultation he produces a roll of paper*)

MR MORLAND (*backing from it*) So that's it.   350

MR AMY This is it. (*The squire has to examine it like a Christian*) There! I have the luck this time. I hope you will have it next. (*The exultation passes from the one face into the other*)

MR MORLAND Interesting, George—quite. But definitely not a Gainsborough.   355

MR AMY I say definitely a Gainsborough.

MR MORLAND Definitely not a Gainsborough.

> (*By this time the needles have entered into the controversy, but they are disregarded*)

I should say the work of a clever amateur.

MR AMY Look at the drawing of the cart and the figure beside it.

MR MORLAND Weak and laboured. Look at that horse.   360

MR AMY Gainsborough did some very funny horses.

MR MORLAND Granted, but he never placed them badly. That horse destroys the whole balance of the composition.

MR AMY James, I had no idea you had such a small nature.

MR MORLAND I don't like that remark; for your sake I don't like   365
it. No one would have been more pleased than myself if you had picked up a Gainsborough. But this! Besides, look at the paper.

MR AMY What is wrong with the paper, Mr Morland?

MR MORLAND It is machine-made.° Gainsborough was in his grave   370
years before that paper was made.

> (*After further inspection Mr Amy is convinced against his will, and the find is returned to his pocket less carefully than it had been produced*)

Don't get into a tantrum about it, George.

MR AMY (*grandly*) I am not in a tantrum, and I should be obliged if you wouldn't George me. Smile on, Mr Morland, I congratulate you on your triumph; you have hurt an old friend to the quick.   375

Bravo, bravo. Thank you, Mrs Morland, for a very pleasant visit.
Good-day.

MRS MORLAND (*prepared*) I shall see you into your coat, George.

MR AMY I thank you, Mrs Morland, but I need no one to see me
into my coat. Good-day.   380

    (*He goes, and she blandly follows him. She returns with the culprit*)

MRS MORLAND Now which of you is to say it first?

MR AMY James, I am heartily ashamed of myself.

MR MORLAND George, I apologise.

MR AMY I quite see that it isn't a Gainsborough.

MR MORLAND After all, it's certainly in the Gainsborough school.   385

    (*They clasp hands sheepishly, but the peacemaker helps the
    situation by showing a roguish face, and Mr Amy departs
    shaking a humorous fist at her*)

MRS MORLAND I coughed so often, James; and you must have heard
me clicking.

MR MORLAND I heard all right. Good old George! It's a pity he has
no flair. He might as well order his prints by wireless.°

MRS MORLAND What is that?   390

MR MORLAND Wireless it's to be called. There is an article about it
in that paper. The fellow says that before many years have passed
we shall be able to talk to ships on the ocean.

MRS MORLAND (*who has resumed her knitting*) Nonsense, James.

MR MORLAND Of course it's nonsense. And yet there is no denying,   395
as he says, that there are more things in heaven and earth than are
dreamt of in our philosophy.°

MRS MORLAND (*becoming grave*) You and I know that to be true, James.

    (*For a moment he does not know to what she is referring*)

MR MORLAND (*edging away from trouble*) Oh, that. My dear, that is
all dead and done with long ago.   400

MRS MORLAND (*thankfully*) Yes. But sometimes when I look at
Mary Rose—so happy——

MR MORLAND She will never know anything about it.

MRS MORLAND No, indeed. But some day she will fall in love——

MR MORLAND (*wriggling*) That infant! Fanny, is it wise to seek   405
trouble before it comes?

MRS MORLAND She can't marry, James, without your first telling the
man. We agreed.

MR MORLAND Yes, I suppose I must—though I'm not certain I
ought to. Sleeping dogs——Still, I'll keep my word, I'll tell him   410
everything.

MRS MORLAND Poor Mary Rose.

MR MORLAND (*manfully*) Now then, none of that. Where is she now?

MRS MORLAND Down at the boat-house with Simon, I think.

MR MORLAND That is all right. Let her play about with Simon and   415
the like. It may make a tomboy of her, but it will keep young men
out of her head.

(*She wonders at his obtuseness*)

MRS MORLAND You still think of Simon as a boy?

MR MORLAND Bless the woman, he is only a midshipman.°

MRS MORLAND A sub-lieutenant now.   420

MR MORLAND Same thing. Why, Fanny, I still tip him.° At least I
did a year ago. And he liked it: 'Thanks no end, you are a trump,'
he said, and then slipped behind the screen to see how much it
was.

MRS MORLAND He is a very delightful creature; but he isn't a boy   425
any more.

MR MORLAND It's not nice of you to put such ideas into my head.
I'll go down to the boat-house at once. If this new invention was
in working order, Fanny, I could send him packing without rising
from my seat. I should simply say from this sofa, 'Is my little Mary   430
Rose there?'

(*To their surprise there is an answer from Mary Rose unseen*)

MARY ROSE (*in a voice more quaking than is its wont*) I'm here,
Daddy.

MR MORLAND (*rising*) Where are you, Mary Rose?

MARY ROSE I am in the apple-tree.   435

(*Mrs Morland smiles and is going to the window, but her
husband checks her with a further exhibition of the marvel of the
future*)

MR MORLAND What are you doing in the apple-tree, hoyden?

MARY ROSE I'm hiding.

MR MORLAND From Simon?

MARY ROSE No; I'm not sure whom I'm hiding from. From myself,
I think. Daddy, I'm frightened.   440

MR MORLAND What has frightened you? Simon?

MARY ROSE Yes—partly.

MR MORLAND Who else?

MARY ROSE I am most afraid of my daddy.

MR MORLAND (*rather flattered*) Of me?   445

(*If there is anything strange about this girl of eighteen who steps
from the tree into the room, it is an elusiveness of which she is*

*unaware. It has remained hidden from her girl friends, though
in the after years, in the brief space before they forget her, they
will probably say, because of what happened, that there was
always something a little odd about Mary Rose. This oddness
might be expressed thus, that the happiness and glee of which she
is almost overfull know of another attribute of her that never
plays with them.*

*There is nothing splendid about Mary Rose, never can she
become one of those secret women so much less innocent than she,
yet perhaps so much sweeter in the kernel, who are the bane or
glory, or the bane and glory, of greater lovers than she could ever
understand. She is just a rare and lovely flower, far less fitted
than those others for the tragic role.°*

*She butts her head into Mrs Morland with a childish
impulsiveness that might overthrow a less accustomed bosom)*

MARY ROSE (*telling everything*) Mother!

MR MORLAND You don't mean that anything has really frightened
you, Mary Rose?

MARY ROSE I am not sure. Hold me tight, Mother.

MRS MORLAND Darling, has Simon been disturbing you?   450

MARY ROSE (*liking this way of putting it*) Yes, he has. It is all Simon's
fault.

MR MORLAND But you said you were afraid even of me.

MARY ROSE You are the only one.

MR MORLAND Is this some game? Where is Simon?   455

MARY ROSE (*in little mouthfuls*) He is at the foot of the tree. He is
not coming up by the tree. He wants to come in by the door. That
shows how important it is.

MR MORLAND What is?

MARY ROSE You see, his leave is up to-morrow, and he—wants to   460
see you, Daddy, before he goes.

MR MORLAND I am sure he does. And I know why. I told you,
Fanny. Mary Rose, do you see my purse lying about?

MARY ROSE Your purse, Dad?

MR MORLAND Yes, you gosling. There is a fiver in it, and *that* is   465
what Master Simon wants to see me about. .

(*Mary Rose again seeks her mother's breast*)

MRS MORLAND Oh, James! Dearest, tell me what Simon has been
saying to you; whisper it, my love.

(*Mary Rose whispers*)

Yes, I thought it was that.

MARY ROSE I am frightened to tell Daddy.   470

MRS MORLAND James, you may as well be told bluntly; it isn't your
   fiver that Simon wants, it is your daughter.
      (*Mr Morland is aghast, and Mary Rose rushes into his arms to
      help him in this terrible hour*)

MARY ROSE (*as the injured party*) You will scold him, won't you,
   Dad?

MR MORLAND (*vainly trying to push her from him*) By—by—by   475
   the—by all that is horrible I'll do more than scold him. The
   puppy, I'll—I'll——

MARY ROSE (*entreating*) Not more than scold him, Daddy—not
   more. Mary Rose couldn't bear it if it was more.

MR MORLAND (*blankly*) You are not in love with Simon, are you?   480

MARY ROSE Oh-h-h-h!
      (*She makes little runnings from the one parent to the other,
      carrying kisses for the wounds*)
   Daddy, I am so awfully sorry that this has occurred. Mummy,
   what can we do? (*She cries*)

MRS MORLAND (*soothing her*) My own, my pet. But he is only a boy,
   Mary Rose, just a very nice boy.   485

MARY ROSE (*awed*) Mother, that is the wonderful, wonderful thing.
   He was just a boy—I quite understand that—he was a mere boy
   till to-day; and then, Daddy, he suddenly changed; all at once he
   became a man. It was while he was—telling me. You will scarcely
   know him now, Mother.   490

MRS MORLAND Darling, he breakfasted with us; I think I shall know
   him still.

MARY ROSE He is quite different from breakfast-time. He doesn't
   laugh any more, he would never think of capsizing the punt
   intentionally now, he has grown so grave, so manly, so—so   495
   protective, he thinks of everything now, of freeholds and leaseholds,
   and gravel soil, and hot and cold, and the hire system.°
      (*She cries again, but her eyes are sparkling through the rain*)

MR MORLAND (*with spirit*) He has got as far as that, has he! Does he
   propose that this marriage should take place to-morrow?

MARY ROSE (*eager to soften the blow*) Oh no, not for quite a long time. 500
   At earliest, not till his next leave.

MRS MORLAND Mary Rose!

MARY ROSE He is waiting down there, Mummy. May I bring him
   in?

MRS MORLAND Of course, dearest.   505

254

MR MORLAND Don't come with him, though.

MARY ROSE Oh! (*She wonders what this means*) You know how shy
Simon is.

MR MORLAND I do not.

MRS MORLAND Your father and I must have a talk with him alone,   510
you see.

MARY ROSE I—I suppose so. He so wants to do the right thing,
Mother.

MRS MORLAND I am sure he does.

MARY ROSE Do you mind my going upstairs into the apple-room   515
and sometimes knocking on the floor? I think it would be a help
to him to know I am so near by.

MRS MORLAND It would be a help to all of us, my sweet.

MARY ROSE (*plaintively*) You—you won't try to put him against me,
Daddy?   520

MR MORLAND I would try my hardest if I thought I had any chance.
(*When she has gone they are a somewhat forlorn pair*)
Poor old mother!

MRS MORLAND Poor old father! There couldn't be a nicer boy, though.

MR MORLAND No, but——(*He has a distressing thought*)

MRS MORLAND (*quietly*) Yes, there's that.   525

MR MORLAND It got me on the quick when she said, 'You won't try
to put him against me, Daddy'—because that is just what I
suppose I have got to do.

MRS MORLAND He must be told.

MR MORLAND (*weakly*) Fanny, let us keep it to ourselves.   530

MRS MORLAND It would not be fair to him.

MR MORLAND No, it wouldn't. (*Testily*) He will be an ass if it
bothers him.

MRS MORLAND (*timidly*) Yes.

> (*Simon comes in, a manly youth of twenty-three in naval
> uniform. Whether he has changed much since breakfast-time we
> have no means of determining, but he is sufficiently attractive to
> make one hope that there will be no further change in the
> immediate future. He seems younger even than his years, because
> he is trying to look as if a decade or so had passed since the
> incident of the boat-house and he were now a married man of
> approved standing. He has come with honeyed words upon his
> lips, but suddenly finds that he is in the dock. His judges survey
> him silently, and he can only reply with an idiotic but perhaps
> ingratiating laugh*)

SIMON Ha, ha, ha, ha, ha, ha, ha, ha! (*He ceases uncomfortably, like*   535
one *who has made his statement*)

MR MORLAND You will need to say more than that, you know,
Simon, to justify your conduct.

MRS MORLAND Oh, Simon, how could you!

SIMON (*with a sinking*) It seems almost like stealing.   540

MR MORLAND It is stealing.

SIMON (*prudently*) Ha, ha, ha, ha, ha, ha!
(*From the ceiling there comes a gentle tapping, as from a senior
officer who is indicating that England expects her lieutenant this
day to do his duty. Simon inflates*)
It is beastly hard on you, of course; but if you knew what Mary
Rose is!

MRS MORLAND (*pardonably*) We feel that even we know to some   545
extent what Mary Rose is.

SIMON (*tacking*)° Yes, rather; and so you can see how it has come
about. (*This effort cheers him*) I would let myself be cut into little
chips for her; I should almost like it. (*With a brief glance at his
misspent youth*) Perhaps you have thought that I was a rather larky°   550
sort in the past?

MR MORLAND (*sarcastically*) We see an extraordinary change in you,
Simon.

SIMON (*eagerly*) Have you noticed that? Mary Rose has noticed it
too. That is my inner man coming out. (*Carefully*) To some young   555
people marriage is a thing to be entered on lightly, but that is not
my style. What I want is to give up larks, and all that, and insure
my life, and read the political articles.
(*Further knocking from above reminds him of something else*)
Yes, and I promise you it won't be like losing a daughter but like
gaining a son.   560

MRS MORLAND Did Mary Rose tell you to say that?

SIMON (*guiltily*) Well——(*Tap, tap*) Oh, another thing, I should
consider it well worth being married to Mary Rose just to have
you, Mrs Morland, for a mother-in-law.

MR MORLAND (*pleased*) Well said, Simon; I like you the better for that.   565

MRS MORLAND (*a demon*) Did she tell you to say that also?

SIMON Well——At any rate, never shall I forget the respect and
affection I owe to the parents of my beloved wife.

MR MORLAND She is not your wife yet, you know.

SIMON (*handsomely*) No, she isn't. But can she be? Mrs Morland, can   570
she be?

MRS MORLAND That is as may be, Simon. It is only a possible engagement that we are discussing at present.

SIMON Yes, yes, of course. (*Becoming more difficult to resist as his reason goes*) I used to be careless about money, but I have thought 575 of a trick of writing the word Economy in the inside of my watch, so that I'll see it every time I wind up. My people°——

MR MORLAND We like them, Simon.
        (*The tapping is resumed*)

SIMON I don't know whether you have noticed a sound from up above? 580

MR MORLAND I did think I heard something.

SIMON That is Mary Rose in the apple-room.

MRS MORLAND No!

SIMON Yes; she is doing that to help me. I promised to knock back as soon as I thought things were going well. What do you 585 say? May I?
        (*He gives them an imploring look, and mounts a chair, part of a fishing-rod in his hand*)

MR MORLAND (*an easy road in sight*) I think, Fanny, he might?

MRS MORLAND (*braver*) No. (*Tremulously*) There is a little thing, Simon, that Mary Rose's father and I feel we ought to tell you about her before—before you knock, my dear. It is not very 590 important, I think, but it is something she doesn't know of herself, and it makes her a little different from other girls.

SIMON (*alighting—sharply*) I won't believe anything against Mary Rose.

MRS MORLAND We have nothing to tell you against her. 595

MR MORLAND It is just something that happened, Simon. She couldn't help it. It hasn't troubled us in the least for years, but we always agreed that she mustn't be engaged before we told the man. We must have your promise, before we tell you, that you will keep it to yourself. 600

SIMON (*frowning*) I promise.

MRS MORLAND You must never speak of it even to her.

SIMON Not to Mary Rose? I wish you would say quickly what it is.
        (*They are now sitting round the little table*)

MR MORLAND It can't be told quite in a word. It happened seven years ago, when Mary Rose was eleven. We were in a remote part 605 of Scotland—in the Outer Hebrides.

SIMON I once went on shore there from the *Gadfly*, very bleak and barren, rocks and rough grass, I never saw a tree.

MR MORLAND It is mostly like that. There is a whaling-station. We
went because I was fond of fishing. I haven't had the heart to fish   610
since. Quite close to the inn where we put up there is—a little
island.

(*He sees that little island so clearly that he forgets to go on*)

MRS MORLAND It is quite a small island, Simon, uninhabited, no
sheep even. I suppose there are only about six acres of it. There
are trees there, quite a number of them, Scotch firs and a few   615
rowan-trees,—they have red berries, you know. There seemed to
us to be nothing very particular about the island, unless, perhaps,
that it is curiously complete in itself. There is a tiny pool in it that
might be called a lake, out of which a stream flows. It has hillocks
and a glade, a sort of miniature land. That was all we noticed,   620
though it became the most dreaded place in the world to us.

MR MORLAND (*considerately*) I can tell him without your being here,
Fanny.

MRS MORLAND I prefer to stay, James.

MR MORLAND I fished a great deal in the loch between that island   625
and the larger one. The sea-trout were wonderful. I often rowed
Mary Rose across to the island and left her there to sketch. She
was fond of sketching in those days, we thought them pretty
things. I could see her from the boat most of the time, and we used
to wave to each other. Then I would go back for her when I   630
stopped fishing.

MRS MORLAND I didn't often go with them. We didn't know at the
time that the natives had a superstition against landing on the
island, and that it was supposed to resent this. It had a Gaelic name
which means 'The Island that Likes to be Visited.' Mary Rose   635
knew nothing of this, and she was very fond of her island. She
used to talk to it, call it her darling, things like that.

SIMON (*restless*) Tell me what happened.

MR MORLAND It was on what was to be our last day. I had landed
her on this island as usual, and in the early evening I pulled across   640
to take her off. From the boat I saw her, sitting on a stump of a
tree that was her favourite seat, and she waved gaily to me and I
to her. Then I rowed over, with, of course, my back to her. I had
less than a hundred yards to go, but, Simon, when I got across she
wasn't there.   645

SIMON You seem so serious about it. She was hiding from you?

MRS MORLAND She wasn't on the island, Simon.

SIMON But—but—oh, but——

MR MORLAND Don't you think I searched and searched?

MRS MORLAND All of us. No one in the village went to bed that   650
night. It was then we learned how they feared the island.

MR MORLAND The little pool was dragged. There was nothing we
didn't try; but she was gone.

SIMON (*distressed*) I can't—there couldn't—but never mind that. Tell
me how you found her.   655

MRS MORLAND It was the twentieth day after she disappeared.
Twenty days!

SIMON Some boat——?

MR MORLAND There was no boat but mine.

SIMON Tell me.   660

MRS MORLAND The search had long been given up, but we couldn't
come away.

MR MORLAND I was wandering one day along the shore of the loch,
you can imagine in what state of mind. I stopped and stood looking
across the water at the island, and, Simon, I saw her sitting on the   665
tree-trunk sketching.

MRS MORLAND Mary Rose!

MR MORLAND She waved to me and went on sketching. I—I waved
back to her. I got into the boat and rowed across just in the old
way, except that I sat facing her, so that I could see her all the   670
time. When I landed, the first thing she said to me was, 'Why did
you row in that funny way, Dad?' Then I saw at once that she
didn't know anything had happened.

SIMON Mr Morland! How could——? Where did she say she had been?

MRS MORLAND She didn't know she had been anywhere, Simon.   675

MR MORLAND She thought I had just come for her at the usual time.

SIMON Twenty days. You mean she had been on the island all that
time?

MR MORLAND We don't know.

MRS MORLAND James brought her back to me just the same merry   680
unselfconscious girl, with no idea that she had been away from me
for more than an hour or two.

SIMON But when you told her——

MRS MORLAND We never told her; she doesn't know now.

SIMON Surely you——   685

MRS MORLAND We had her back again, Simon; that was the great
thing. At first we thought to tell her after we got her home; and
then, it was all so inexplicable, we were afraid to alarm her, to take
the bloom off her. In the end we decided never to tell her.

SIMON You told no one?   690

MR MORLAND Several doctors.

SIMON How did they explain it?

MR MORLAND They had no explanation for it except that it never took place. You can think that, too, if you like.

SIMON I don't know what to think. It has had no effect on her, at   695
any rate.

MR MORLAND None whatever—and you can guess how we used to watch.

MRS MORLAND Simon, I am very anxious to be honest with you. I have sometimes thought that our girl is curiously young for her   700
age—as if—you know how just a touch of frost may stop the growth of a plant and yet leave it blooming°—it has sometimes seemed to me as if a cold finger had once touched my Mary Rose.

SIMON Mrs Morland!

MRS MORLAND There is nothing in it.   705

SIMON What you are worrying about is just her innocence—which seems a holy thing to me.

MRS MORLAND And indeed it is.

SIMON If that is all——   ·

MR MORLAND We have sometimes thought that she had momentary   710
glimpses back into that time, but before we could question her in a cautious way about them the gates had closed and she remembered nothing. You never saw her talking to—to some person who wasn't there?

SIMON No.   715

MRS MORLAND Nor listening, as it were, for some sound that never came?

SIMON A sound? Do you mean a sound from the island?

MRS MORLAND Yes, we think so. But at any rate she has long outgrown those fancies.   720

(*She fetches a sketch-book from a drawer*)

Here are the sketches she made. You can take the book away with you and look at them at your leisure.

SIMON It is a little curious that she has never spoken to me of that holiday. She tells me everything.

MRS MORLAND No, that isn't curious, it is just that the island has   725
faded from her memory. I should be troubled if she began to recall it. Well, Simon, we felt we had to tell you. That is all we know, I am sure it is all we shall ever know. What are you going to do?

SIMON What do you think!

(*He mounts the chair again, and knocks triumphantly. A happy tapping replies*)

You heard? That means it's all right. You'll see how she'll come   730
tearing down to us!

MRS MORLAND (*kissing him*) You dear boy, you will see how I shall
go tearing up to her. (*She goes off*)

SIMON I do love Mary Rose, sir.

MR MORLAND So do we, Simon. I suppose that made us love her a   735
little more than other daughters are loved. Well, it is dead and
done with, and it doesn't disturb me now at all. I hope you won't
let it disturb you.

SIMON (*undisturbed*) Rather not. (*Disturbed*) I say, I wonder whether
I *have* noticed her listening for a sound?   740

MR MORLAND Not you. We did wisely, didn't we, in not questioning
her?

SIMON Oh lord, yes. 'The Island that Likes to be Visited.' It is a
queer name. (*Boyishly*) I say, let's forget all about it. (*He looks at
the ceiling*) I almost wish her mother hadn't gone up to her. It will   745
make Mary Rose longer in coming down.

MR MORLAND (*humorous*) Fanny will think of nicer things to say to
her than you could think of, Simon.

SIMON Yes, I know. Ah, now you are chaffing° me. (*Apologetically*)
You see, sir, my leave is up to-morrow.   750

(*Mary Rose comes rushing in*)

Mary Rose!

(*She darts past him into her father's arms*)

MARY ROSE It isn't you I am thinking of; it is father, it is poor father.
Oh, Simon, how could you? Isn't it hateful of him, Daddy!

MR MORLAND I should just say it is. Is your mother crying too?

MARY ROSE (*squeaking*) Yes.   755

MR MORLAND I see I am going to have an abominable day. If you
two don't mind very much being left alone, I think I'll go up and
sit in the apple-room and cry with your mother. It is close and
dark and musty up there, and when we feel we can't stick it any
longer I'll knock on the floor, Simon, as a sign that we are coming   760
down.

(*He departs on this light note. We see how the minds of these two
children° match*)

SIMON Mary Rose!

MARY ROSE Oh, Simon—you and me.

SIMON You and me, that's it. We are *us*, now. Do you like it?

MARY ROSE It is so fearfully solemn.   765
SIMON You are not frightened, are you?
     (*She nods*)
  Not at me?
     (*She shakes her head*)
  What at?
MARY ROSE At *it*——Being——married. Simon, after we are married
  you will sometimes let me play, won't you?   770
SIMON Games?
     (*She nods.*)
  Rather. Why, I'll go on playing rugger myself. Lots of married
  people play games.
MARY ROSE (*relieved*) I'm glad; Simon, do you love me?
SIMON Dearest—precious—my life—my sweetheart. Which name do   775
  you like best?
MARY ROSE I'm not sure. They are all very nice. (*She is conscious of
  the ceiling*) Oughtn't we to knock to those beloveds to come down?
SIMON Please don't. I know a lot about old people, darling. I assure
  you they don't mind very much sitting in dull places.   780
MARY ROSE We mustn't be selfish.
SIMON Honest Injun,° it isn't selfishness. You see, I have a ton of
  things to tell you. About how I put it to them, and how I
  remembered what you told me to say, and the way I got the soft
  side of them. They have heard it all already, so it would really be   785
  selfish to bring them down.
MARY ROSE I'm not so sure.
SIMON I'll tell you what we'll do. Let's go back to the boat-house,
  and then they can come down and be cosy here.
MARY ROSE (*gleeful*) Let's! We can stay there till tea-time. (*She*   790
  wants to whirl him away at once.)
SIMON It is fresh down there; put on a jacket, my star.
MARY ROSE Oh, bother!
SIMON (*firmly*) My child, you are in my care now; I am responsible
  for you, and I order you to put on a jacket.   795
MARY ROSE Order! Simon, you do say the loveliest things. I'll put it
  on at once.
     (*She is going towards the little door at the back, but turns to say*
     something important)
  Simon, I'll tell you a funny thing about me. I may be wrong, but
  I think I'll sometimes love you to kiss me, and sometimes it will
  be better not.   800

SIMON All right. Tell me, what were you thinking as you sat up there in the apple-room, waiting?

MARY ROSE Holy things.

SIMON About love?

    (*She nods*)

MARY ROSE We'll try to be good, won't we, Simon, please?   805

SIMON Rather. Honest Injun, we'll be nailers.° Did you think of—our wedding-day?

MARY ROSE A little.

SIMON Only a little?

MARY ROSE But frightfully clearly. (*Suddenly*) Simon, I had such a 810 delicious idea about our honeymoon. There is a place in Scotland—in the Hebrides—I should love to go there.

SIMON (*taken aback*) The Hebrides?

MARY ROSE We once went to it when I was little. Isn't it funny, I had almost forgotten about that island, and then suddenly I saw it 815 quite clearly as I was sitting up there. (*Senselessly*) Of course it was the little old woman° who pointed it out to me.

    (*Simon is disturbed*)

SIMON (*gently*) Mary Rose, there are only yourselves and the three maids in the house, aren't there?

MARY ROSE (*surprised*) You know there are. Whatever makes you 820 ask?

SIMON (*cautiously*) I thought—I thought I had a glimpse of a little old woman on the stair to-day.

MARY ROSE (*interested*) Who on earth could that be?

SIMON It doesn't matter, I had made a mistake. Tell me, what was 825 there particular about that place in the Hebrides?

MARY ROSE Oh, the fishing for father. But there was an island where I often——My little island!

SIMON (*perhaps quite unnecessarily*) What are you listening for, Mary Rose?   830

MARY ROSE Was I? I don't hear anything. Oh, my dear, my dear, I should love to show you the tree-trunk and the rowan-tree where I used to sketch while father was in the boat. I expect he used to land me on the island because it was such a safe place.

SIMON (*troubled*) That had been the idea. I am not going to spend 835 my honeymoon by the sea, though. And yet I should like to go to the Hebrides—some day—to see that island.

MARY ROSE Yes, let's.

    (*She darts off through the little door for her jacket*)

Act 2

An island in the Outer Hebrides. A hundred yards away, across the loch
at the back, may be seen the greater island of which this might be but a
stone cast into the sea by some giant hand: perhaps an evil stone which
the big island had to spew forth but could not sink. It is fair to look upon
to-day, all its menace hidden under mosses of various hues that are a bath   5
to the eye; an island placid as a cow grazing or a sulky lady asleep. The
sun which has left the bleak hills beyond is playing hide and seek on it;
one suddenly has the curious fancy to ask, with whom? A blessed spot it
might be thought, rather than sinister, were there not those two trees, a
fir and a rowan, their arms outstretched for ever southward, as if they   10
had been struck while in full flight and could no longer pray to their gods
to carry them away from this island. A young Highlander, a Cameron,
passes in a boat at the back. Mary Rose and Simon come into view on
the island. We have already heard them swishing a way through
whins° and bracken that are unseen. They are dressed as English people   15
dress in Scotland. They have been married for four years and are still
the gay young creatures of their engagement day. Their talk is the happy
nonsense that leaves no ripple unless the unexpected happens.

MARY ROSE (*thrilled*) I think, I think, I don't think at all, I am quite
    sure. This is the place. Simon, kiss me, kiss me quick. You   20
    promised to kiss me quick when we found the place.
SIMON (*obeying*) I am not the man to break my word. At the same
    time, Mary Rose, I would point out to you that this is the third
    spot you have picked out as being the place, and three times have
    I kissed you quick on that understanding. This can't go on, you   25
    know. As for your wonderful island, it turns out to be about the
    size of the Round Pond.°
MARY ROSE I always said it was little like myself.
SIMON It was obviously made to fit you, or you to fit it; one of you
    was measured for the other. At any rate, we have now been all   30
    round it, and all through it, as my bleeding limbs testify. (*The
    whins have been tearing at him, and he rubs his legs*)
MARY ROSE They didn't hurt me at all.
SIMON Perhaps they like you better than me. Well, we have made a
    good search for the place where you used to sit and sketch, and   35
    you must now take your choice.

MARY ROSE It was here. I told you of the fir and the rowan-tree.

SIMON There were a fir and a rowan at each of the other places.

MARY ROSE Not this fir, not this rowan.

SIMON You have me there.

MARY ROSE Simon, I know I'm not clever, but I'm always right. The rowan-berries! I used to put them in my hair. (*She puts them in her hair again*) Darling rowan-tree, are you glad to see me back? You don't look a bit older, how do you think *I* am wearing? I shall tell you a secret. You too, firry. Come closer, both of you. Put your arms around me, and listen: I am married!
        (*The branch of which she has been making a scarf disengages itself*) It didn't like that, Simon, it is jealous. After all, it knew me first. Dearest trees, if I had known that you felt for me in that way—but it is too late now. I have been married for nearly four years, and this is the man. His name is Lieutenant Simon Sobersides. (*She darts about making discoveries*)

SIMON (*tranquilly smoking*) What is it now?

MARY ROSE That moss! I feel sure there is a tree-trunk beneath it, the very root on which I used to sit and sketch.
        (*He clears away some of the moss*)

SIMON It is a tree-trunk right enough.

MARY ROSE I believe—I believe I cut my name on it with a knife.

SIMON This looks like it. 'M—A—R—' and there it stops. That is always where the blade of the knife breaks.

MARY ROSE My ownest seat, how I have missed you.

SIMON Don't you believe it, old tree-trunk. She had forgotten all about you, and you just came vaguely back to her mind because we happened to be in the neighbourhood.

MARY ROSE Yes, I suppose that is true. You were the one who wanted to come, Simon. I wonder why?

SIMON (*with his answer ready*) No particular reason. I wanted to see a place you had visited as a child; that was all. But what a trumpery° island it proves to be.

MARY ROSE (*who perhaps agrees with him*) How can you? Even if it is true, you needn't say it before them all, hurting their feelings. Dear seat, here is one for each year I have been away. (*She kisses the trunk a number of times*)

SIMON (*counting*) Eleven. Go on, give it all the news. Tell it we don't have a house of our own yet.

MARY ROSE You see, dear seat, we live with my daddy and mother, because Simon is so often away at sea. You know, the loveliest thing in the world is the navy, and the loveliest thing in the navy is HMS *Valiant*, and the loveliest thing on HMS *Valiant* is Lieutenant Simon Sobersides, and the loveliest thing on Lieutenant Simon Sobersides is the little tuft of hair which will keep standing up at the back of his head.   80

> (*Simon, who is lolling on the moss, is so used to her prattle that his eyes close*)

But, listen, you trees, I have a much more wonderful secret than that. You can have three guesses. It is this . . . I—have—got—a baby! A girl? No thank you. He is two years and nine months, and he says such beautiful things to me about loving me. Oh, rowan, do you think he means them?   85

SIMON I distinctly heard it say yes.

> (*He opens his eyes, to see her gazing entranced across the water*)

You needn't pretend that you can see him.

MARY ROSE I do. Can't you? He is waving his bib to us.

SIMON That is nurse's cap.

MARY ROSE Then he is waving it. How clever of him. (*She waves*   90
her handkerchief*) Now they are gone. Isn't it funny to think that from this very spot I used to wave to father? That was a happy time.

SIMON I should be happier here if I wasn't so hungry. I wonder where Cameron is. I told him after he landed us to tie up the boat   95
at any good place and make a fire. I suppose I had better try to make it myself.

MARY ROSE How you can think of food at such a time!

SIMON (*who is collecting sticks*) All very well, but you will presently be eating more than your share.   100

MARY ROSE Do you know, Simon, I don't think daddy and mother like this island.

SIMON (*on his guard*) Help me with the fire, you chatterbox.

> (*He has long ceased to credit the story he heard four years ago, but he is ever watchful for Mary Rose*)

MARY ROSE They never seem to want to speak of it.

SIMON Forgotten it, I suppose.   105

MARY ROSE I shall write to them from the inn this evening. How surprised they will be to know I am there again.

SIMON (*casually*) I wouldn't write from there. Wait till we cross to the mainland.

MARY ROSE Why not from there?   110

266

SIMON Oh, no reason. But if they have a distaste for the place, perhaps they wouldn't like our coming. I say, praise me, I have got this fire alight.

MARY ROSE (*who is occasionally pertinacious*) Simon, why did you want to come to my island without me?

SIMON Did I? Oh, I merely suggested your remaining at the inn because I thought you seemed tired. I wonder where Cameron can have got to?

MARY ROSE Here he comes. (*Solicitously*) Do be polite to him, dear; you know how touchy they are.

SIMON I am learning!

    (*The boat, with Cameron, draws in. He is a gawky youth of twenty, in the poor but honourable garb of the gillie,° and is not specially impressive until you question him about the universe*)

CAMERON (*in the soft voice of the Highlander*) Iss it the wish of Mr Blake that I should land?°

SIMON Yes, yes, Cameron, with the luncheon.

    (*Cameron steps ashore with a fishing basket*)

CAMERON Iss it the wish of Mr Blake that I open the basket?

SIMON We shall tumble out the luncheon if you bring a trout or two. I want you to show my wife, Cameron, how one cooks fish by the water's edge.

CAMERON I will do it with pleasure. (*He pauses*) There iss one little matter;° it iss of small importance. You may haf noticed that I always address you as Mr Blake. I notice that you always address me as Cameron; I take no offence.

MARY ROSE Oh dear, I am sure I always address you as Mr Cameron.

CAMERON That iss so, ma'am. You may haf noticed that I always address you as 'ma'am.' It iss my way of indicating that I consider you a ferry genteel young matron,° and of all such I am the humble servant. (*He pauses*) In saying I am your humble servant I do not imply that I am not as good as you are. With this brief explanation, ma'am, I will now fetch the trouts.

SIMON (*taking advantage of his departure*) That is one in the eye for me. But I'm hanged if I mister him.

MARY ROSE Simon, do be careful. If you want to say anything to me that is dangerous, say it in French.

    (*Cameron returns with two small sea-trout*)

CAMERON The trouts, ma'am, having been cleaned in a thorough and yet easy manner by pulling them up and down in the water, the next procedure iss as follows.

*(He wraps up the trout in a piece of newspaper and soaks them
in the water)*

I now place the soaking little parcels on the fire, and when the
paper begins to burn it will be a sure sign that the trouts iss now
ready, like myself, ma'am, to be your humble servants.° *(He is
returning to the boat)* 150

MARY ROSE *(who has been preparing the feast)* Don't go away.

CAMERON If it iss agreeable to Mistress Blake I would wish to go
back to the boat.

MARY ROSE Why?

(Cameron is not comfortable)

It would be more agreeable to me if you would stay. 155

CAMERON *(shuffling)* I will stay.

SIMON Good man—and look after the trout. It is the most heavenly
way of cooking fish, Mary Rose.

CAMERON It iss a tasty way, Mr Blake, but I would not use the word
heavenly in this connection. 160

SIMON I stand corrected. *(Tartly)* I must say——

MARY ROSE *Prenez garde, mon brave!*

SIMON *Mon Dieu! Qu'il est un drôle!*

MARY ROSE *Mais moi, je l'aime; il est tellement*°——What is the
French for an original? 165

SIMON That stumps me.

CAMERON Colloquially *coquin*° might be used, though the classic
writers would probably say simply *un original.*

SIMON *(with a groan)* Phew, this is serious. What was that book you
were reading, Cameron, while I was fishing? 170

CAMERON It iss a small Euripides° I carry in the pocket, Mr Blake.

SIMON Latin, Mary Rose!

CAMERON It may be Latin, but in these parts we know no better than
to call it Greek.

SIMON Crushed again! But I dare say it is good for me. Sit down and 175
have pot-luck with us.

CAMERON I thank you, Mr Blake, but it would not be good manners
for a paid man to sit with his employers.

MARY ROSE When I ask you, Mr Cameron?

CAMERON It iss kindly meant, but I haf not been introduced to 180
you.

MARY ROSE Oh, but—oh, do let me. My husband Mr Blake—Mr
Cameron.

CAMERON I hope you are ferry well, sir.

SIMON The same to you, Mr Cameron. How do you do? Lovely day,   185
 isn't it?

CAMERON It iss a fairly fine day. (*He is not yet appeased*)

MARY ROSE (*to the rescue*) Simon!

SIMON Ah! Do you know my wife? Mr Cameron—Mrs Blake.

CAMERON I am ferry pleased to make Mistress Blake's acquaintance.   190
 Iss Mistress Blake making a long stay° in these parts?

MARY ROSE No, alas, we go across° to-morrow.

CAMERON I hope the weather will be favourable.

MARY ROSE Thank you (*passing him the sandwiches*). And now, you
 know, you are our guest.   195

CAMERON I am much obliged. (*He examines the sandwiches with
 curiosity*) Butcher-meat! This iss ferry excellent.
  (*He bursts into a surprising fit of laughter, and suddenly cuts it
  off*)
 Please to excuse my behaviour. You haf been laughing at me all
 this time, but you did not know I haf been laughing at myself also,
 though keeping a remarkable control over my features. I will now   200
 haf my laugh out, and then I will explain. (*He finishes his laugh*) I
 will now explain. I am not the solemn prig I haf pretended to you
 to be, I am really a fairly attractive young man, but I am shy and
 I haf been guarding against your taking liberties with me, not
 because of myself, who am nothing, but because of the noble   205
 profession it iss my ambition to enter. (*They discover that they like
 him*)

MARY ROSE Do tell us what that is.

CAMERON It iss the ministry. I am a student of Aberdeen University,
 and in the vacation I am a boatman, or a gillie, or anything you   210
 please, to help to pay my fees.

SIMON Well done!

CAMERON I am obliged to Mr Blake. And I may say, now that we
 know one another socially, that there iss much in Mr Blake which
 I am trying to copy.   215

SIMON Something in me worth copying!

CAMERON It iss not Mr Blake's learning; he has not much learning,
 but I haf always understood that the English manage without it.
 What I admire in you iss your ferry nice manners and your general
 deportment,° in all which I haf a great deal to learn yet, and I   220
 watch these things in Mr Blake and take memoranda of them in a
 little note-book.
  (*Simon expands*)

MARY ROSE Mr Cameron, do tell me that I also am in the little
note-book?

CAMERON You are not, ma'am, it would not be seemly in me. But it   225
iss written in my heart, and also I haf said it to my father, that I
will remain a bachelor unless I can marry some lady who iss ferry
like Mistress Blake.

MARY ROSE Simon, you never said anything to me as pretty as that.
Is your father a crofter° in the village?   230

CAMERON Yes, ma'am, when he iss not at the University of Aberdeen.

SIMON My stars, does he go there too?

CAMERON He does so. We share a ferry small room between us.

SIMON Father and son. Is he going into the ministry also?   235

CAMERON Such iss not his purpose. When he has taken his degree
he will return and be a crofter again.

SIMON In that case I don't see what he is getting out of it.

CAMERON He iss getting the grandest thing in the world out of it;
he iss getting education.   240

> (*Simon feels that he is being gradually rubbed out, and it is a
> relief to him that Cameron has now to attend to the trout. The
> paper they are wrapped in has begun to burn*)

MARY ROSE (*for the first time eating of trout as it should be cooked*)
Delicious! (*She offers a portion to Cameron*)

CAMERON No, I thank you. I haf lived on trouts most of my life.
This butcher-meat iss more of an excellent novelty to me.

> (*He has been standing all this time*)

MARY ROSE Do sit down, Mr Cameron.   245

CAMERON I am doing ferry well here, I thank you.

MARY ROSE But, please.

CAMERON (*with decision*) I will not sit down on this island.

SIMON (*curiously*) Come, come, are you superstitious, you who are
going into the ministry?   250

CAMERON This island has a bad name. I haf never landed on it
before.

MARY ROSE A bad name, Mr Cameron? Oh, but what a shame!
When I was here long ago, I often came to the island.

CAMERON Iss that so? It was not a chancey° thing to do.   255

MARY ROSE But it is a darling island.

CAMERON That iss the proper way to speak of it.

MARY ROSE I am sure I never heard a word against it. Have you,
Simon?

SIMON (*brazenly*) Not I. I have heard that its Gaelic name has an odd 260
    meaning—'The Island that Likes to be Visited,' but there is
    nothing terrifying in that.

MARY ROSE The name is new to me, Mr Cameron. I think it is
    sweet.

CAMERON That iss as it may be, Mistress Blake. 265

SIMON What is there against the island?

CAMERON For one thing, they are saying it has no authority to be
    here. It was not always here, so they are saying. Then one day it
    was here.

SIMON That little incident happened before your time, I should say, 270
    Mr Cameron.

CAMERON It happened before the time of anyone now alive, Mr
    Blake.

SIMON I thought so. And does the island ever go away for a jaunt in
    the same way? 275

CAMERON There are some who say that it does.

SIMON But you have not seen it on the move yourself?

CAMERON I am not always watching it, Mr Blake.

SIMON Anything else against it?

CAMERON There iss the birds. Too many birds come here. The birds 280
    like this island more than iss seemly.

SIMON Birds here! What could bring them here?

CAMERON It iss said they come to listen.

SIMON To listen to the silence? An island that is as still as an empty
    church. 285

CAMERON I do not know; that iss what they say.

MARY ROSE I think it is a lovely story about the birds. I expect the
    kind things come because this island likes to be visited.

CAMERON That iss another thing; for, mark you, Mistress Blake, an
    island that had visitors would not need to want to be visited. And 290
    why has it not visitors? Because they are afraid to visit it.

MARY ROSE Whatever are they afraid of?

CAMERON That iss what I say to them. Whateffer are you afraid of,
    I say.

MARY ROSE But what are *you* afraid of, Mr Cameron? 295

CAMERON The same thing that they are afraid of. There are stories,
    ma'am.

MARY ROSE Do tell us. Simon, wouldn't it be lovely if he would tell
    us some misty, eerie Highland stories?

SIMON I don't know; not unless they are pretty ones. 300

MARY ROSE Please, Mr Cameron! I love to have my blood curdled.

CAMERON There iss many stories. There iss that one of the boy who was brought to this island. He was no older than your baby.

SIMON What happened to him?

CAMERON No one knows, Mr Blake. His father and mother and their   305
friends, they were gathering rowans on the island, and when they looked round he was gone.

SIMON Lost?

CAMERON He could not be found. He was never found.

MARY ROSE Never! He had fallen into the water?   310

CAMERON That iss a good thing to say,° that he had fallen into the water. That iss what I say.

SIMON But you don't believe it?

CAMERON I do not.

MARY ROSE What do the people in the village say?   315

CAMERON Some say he iss on the island still.

SIMON Mr Cameron! Oh, Mr Cameron! What does your father say?

CAMERON He will be saying° that they are not here always, but that they come and go.

SIMON They? Who are they?   320

CAMERON (uncomfortably) I do not know.

SIMON Perhaps he heard what the birds come to listen to!

CAMERON That iss what they say. He had heard the island calling.

SIMON (hesitating) How does the island call?

CAMERON I do not know.   325

SIMON Do you know anyone who has heard the call?

CAMERON I do not. No one can hear it but those for whom it iss meant.

MARY ROSE But if that child heard it, the others must have heard it also, as they were with him.   330

CAMERON They heard nothing. This iss how it will be. I might be standing close to you, Mistress Blake, as it were here, and I might hear it, ferry loud, terrible, or in soft whispers—no one knows—but I would haf to go, and you will not haf heard a sound.

MARY ROSE Simon, isn't it creepy!   335

SIMON But full of holes, I have no doubt. How long ago is this supposed to have happened, credulous one?°

CAMERON It was before I was born.

SIMON I thought so.

MARY ROSE Simon, don't make fun of my island. Do you know any   340
more ducky° stories about it, Mr Cameron?

CAMERON I cannot tell them if Mr Blake will be saying things the
island might not like to hear.

SIMON Not 'chancey,' I suppose.

MARY ROSE Simon, promise to be good.   345

SIMON All right, Cameron.

CAMERON This one iss about a young English miss, and they say she
was about ten years of age.

MARY ROSE Not so much younger than I was when I came here.
How long ago was it?   350

CAMERON I think it iss ten years ago this summer.

MARY ROSE Simon, it must have been the year after I was here!
      (*Simon thinks she has heard enough*)

SIMON Very likely. But, I say, we mustn't stay on gossiping. We
must be getting back. Did you bail out the boat?

CAMERON I did not, but I will do it now if such iss your wish.   355

MARY ROSE The story first; I won't go without the story.

CAMERON Well, then, the father of this miss he will be fond of the
fishing,° and he sometimes landed the little one on the island while
he fished round it from the boat.

MARY ROSE Just as father used to do with me!   360

SIMON I dare say lots of bold tourists come over here.

CAMERON That iss so, if ignorance be boldness, and sometimes——

SIMON Quite so. But I really think we must be starting.

MARY ROSE No, dear. Please go on, Mr Cameron.

CAMERON One day the father pulled over for his little one as usual. He   365
saw her from the boat, and it iss said she kissed her hand to him.
Then in a moment more he reached the island, but she was gone.

MARY ROSE Gone?

CAMERON She had heard the call of the island, though no sound
came to him.   370

MARY ROSE Doesn't it make one shiver!

CAMERON My father was one of the searchers; for many days they
searched.

MARY ROSE But it would not take many minutes to search this
darling little island.   375

CAMERON They searched, ma'am, long after there was no sense in
searching.

MARY ROSE What a curdling° story! Simon dear, it might have been
Mary Rose. Is there any more?

CAMERON There iss more. It was about a month afterwards. Her   380
father was walking on the shore, over there, and he saw something

moving on the island. All in a tremble, ma'am, he came across in the boat, and it was his little miss.

MARY ROSE Alive?

CAMERON Yes, ma'am.   385

MARY ROSE I am glad: but it rather spoils the mystery.

SIMON How, Mary Rose?

MARY ROSE Because she could tell them what happened, stupid. Whatever was it?

CAMERON It iss not so easy as that. She did not know that anything   390
had happened. She thought she had been parted from her father for but an hour.

(*Mary Rose shivers and takes her husband's hand*)

SIMON (*speaking more lightly than he is feeling*) You and your bogies and wraiths, you man of the mists.

MARY ROSE (*smiling*) Don't be alarmed, Simon; I was only pretend- 395
ing.

CAMERON . It iss not good to disbelieve the stories when you are in these parts. I believe them all when I am here, though I turn the cold light of remorseless Reason° on them when I am in Aberdeen.

SIMON Is that 'chancey,' my friend? An island that has such extraord- 400
inary powers could surely send its call to Aberdeen or farther.

CAMERON (*troubled*) I had not thought of that. That may be ferry true.

SIMON Beware, Mr Cameron, lest some day when you are preaching far from here the call plucks you out of the very pulpit and brings   405
you back to the island like a trout on a long cast.°

CAMERON I do not like Mr Blake's way of talking. I will go and bail the boat.

(*He goes back to the boat, which soon drifts out of sight*)

MARY ROSE (*pleasantly thrilled*) Suppose it were true, Simon!

SIMON (*stoutly*) But it isn't.   410

MARY ROSE No, of course not; but if it had been, how awful for the girl when her father told her that she had been away for weeks.

SIMON Perhaps she was never told. He may have thought it wiser not to disturb her.

MARY ROSE Poor girl! Yes, I suppose that would have been best.   415
And yet—it was taking a risk.

SIMON How?

MARY ROSE Well, not knowing what had happened before, she might come back and—and be caught again. (*She draws closer to him*) Little island, I don't think I like you to-day.   420

SIMON If she ever comes back, let us hope it is with an able-bodied husband to protect her.

MARY ROSE (*comfortably*) Nice people, husbands. You won't let them catch me, will you, Simon?

SIMON Let 'em try. (*Gaily*) And now to pack up the remnants of the feast and escape from the scene of the crime. We will never come back again, Mary Rose, I'm too frightened! 425
  (*She helps him to pack*)

MARY ROSE It is a shame to be funny about my island. You poor, lonely isle. I never knew about your liking to be visited, and I dare say I shall never visit you any more. The last time of anything is always sad, don't you think, Simon? 430

SIMON (*briskly*) There must always be a last time, dearest dear.

MARY ROSE Yes—I suppose—for everything. There must be a last time I shall see you, Simon. (*Playing with his hair*) Some day I shall flatten this tuft for the thousandth time, and then never do it again. 435

SIMON Some day I shall look for it and it won't be there. That day I shall say 'Good riddance.'

MARY ROSE I shall cry. (*She is whimsical rather than merry and merry rather than sad*)
  (*Simon touches her hair with his lips*)
Some day, Simon, you will kiss me for the last time. 440

SIMON That wasn't the last time, at any rate. (*To prove it he kisses her again, sportively, little thinking that this may be the last time. She quivers*) What is it?

MARY ROSE I don't know; something seemed to pass over me.

SIMON You and your last times. Let me tell you, Mistress Blake, 445 there will be a last time of seeing your baby. (*Hurriedly*) I mean only that he can't always be infantile; but the day after you have seen him for the last time as a baby you will see him for the first time as a little gentleman. Think of that.

MARY ROSE (*clapping her hands*) The loveliest time of all will be 450 when he is a man and takes me on his knee instead of my putting him on mine. Oh, gorgeous! (*With one of her sudden changes*) Don't you think the sad thing is that we seldom know when the last time has come? We could make so much more of it.

SIMON Don't you believe that. To know would spoil it all. 455
  (*The packing is nearly completed*)
I suppose I ought to stamp out the fire?

MARY ROSE Let Cameron do that. I want you to come and sit beside me, Simon, and make love to me.

SIMON   What a life. Let me see now, how does one begin? Which arm
is it? I believe I have forgotten the way.   460

MARY ROSE   Then I shall make love to you. (*Playing with his hair*)
Have I been a nice wife to you, Simon?° I don't mean always and
always. There was that awful day when I threw the butter-dish at
you. I am so sorry. But have I been a tolerably good wife on the
whole, not a wonderful one, but a wife that would pass in a crowd?   465

SIMON   Look here, if you are going to butt me with your head in that
way, you must take that pin out of your hair.

MARY ROSE   Have I been all right as a mother, Simon? Have I been
the sort of mother a child could both love and respect?

SIMON   That is a very awkward question. You must ask that of Harry   470
Morland Blake.

MARY ROSE   Have I——?

SIMON   Shut up, Mary Rose. I know you: you will be crying in a
moment, and you don't have a handkerchief, for I wrapped it
round the trout whose head came off.   475

MARY ROSE   At any rate, Simon Blake, say you forgive me about the
butter-dish.

SIMON   I am not so sure of that.

MARY ROSE   And there were some other things—almost worse than
the butter-dish.   480

SIMON   I should just say there were.

MARY ROSE   Simon, how can you? There was nothing so bad as that.

SIMON   (*shaking his head*) I can smile at it now, but at the time I was
a miserable man. I wonder I didn't take to drink.

MARY ROSE   Poor old Simon. But how stupid you were, dear, not to   485
understand.

SIMON   How could an ignorant young husband understand that it was
a good sign when his wife threw the butter-dish at him?

MARY ROSE   You should have guessed.

SIMON   No doubt I was a ninny. But I had always understood that   490
when a young wife°—that then she took the husband aside and
went red, or white, and hid her head on his bosom, and whispered
the rest. I admit I was hoping for that; but all I got was the
butter-dish.

MARY ROSE   I suppose different women have different ways.   495

SIMON   I hope so. (*Severely*) And that was a dastard trick you played
me afterwards.

MARY ROSE   Which? Oh, that! I just wanted you to be out of the way
till all was over.

SIMON I don't mean your getting me out of the house, sending me   500
to Plymouth. The dastardliness was in not letting them tell me,
when I got back, that—that he had arrived.

MARY ROSE It was very naughty of me. You remember, Simon,
when you came in to my room you tried to comfort me by saying
it wouldn't be long now—and I let you maunder on, you darling.   505

SIMON Gazing at me with solemn, innocent eyes. You unutterable
brat, Mary Rose!

MARY ROSE You should have been able to read in my face how clever
I had been. Oh, Simon, when I said at last, 'Dearest, what is that
funny thing in the bassinette?'° and you went and looked, never   510
shall I forget your face.

SIMON I thought at first it was some baby you had borrowed.

MARY ROSE I sometimes think so still. I didn't, did I?

SIMON You are a droll one. Always just when I think I know you at
last I have to begin at the beginning again.   515

MARY ROSE (*suddenly*) Simon, if one of us had to—to go—and we
could choose which one——

SIMON (*sighing*) She's off again.

MARY ROSE Well, but if—I wonder which would be best? I mean for
Harry, of course.   520

SIMON Oh, I should have to hop it.

MARY ROSE Dear!

SIMON Oh, I haven't popped off yet. Steady, you nearly knocked
over the pickles. (*He regards her curiously*) If I did go, I know your
first thought would be 'The happiness of Harry must not be   525
interfered with for a moment.' You would blot me out for ever,
Mary Rose, rather than he should lose one of his hundred laughs
a day.

>   (*She hides her face*)

It's true, isn't it?

MARY ROSE It is true, at any rate, that if I was the one to go, that is   530
what I should like you to do.

SIMON Get off the table-cloth.

>   (*Her mouth opens*)

Don't step on the marmalade.

MARY ROSE (*gloriously*) Simon, isn't life lovely! I am so happy,
happy, happy. Aren't you?   535

SIMON Rather.

MARY ROSE But you can tie up marmalade.° Why don't you scream
with happiness? One of us has got to scream.

SIMON Then I know which one it will be. Scream away, it will give
Cameron the jumps.   540
    (*Cameron draws in*)
There you are, Cameron. We are still safe, you see. You can count
us—two.
CAMERON I am ferry glad.
SIMON Here you are (*handing him the luncheon basket*). You needn't
tie the boat up. Stay there and I'll stamp out the fire myself.   545
CAMERON As Mr Blake pleases.
SIMON Ready, Mary Rose?
MARY ROSE I must say good-bye to my island first. Good-bye, old
mossy seat, nice rowan. Good-bye, little island that likes too much
to be visited. Perhaps I shall come back when I am an old lady   550
with wrinkles, and you won't know your Mary Rose.
SIMON I say, dear, do dry up. I can't help listening to you when I
ought to be getting this fire out.
MARY ROSE I won't say another word.
SIMON Just as it seems to be out, sparks come again. Do you think   555
if I were to get some stones——?
    (*He looks up and she signs that she has promised not to talk.
    They laugh to each other. He is then occupied for a little time
    in dumping wet stones from the loch upon the fire. Cameron is
    in the boat with his Euripides. Mary Rose is sitting demure but
    gay, holding her tongue with her fingers like a child.*
        *Something else is happening;° the call has come to Mary Rose.
    It is at first as soft and furtive as whisperings from holes in the
    ground, 'Mary Rose, Mary Rose.' Then in a fury as of storm
    and whistling winds that might be an unholy organ it rushes upon
    the island, raking every bush for her. These sounds increase
    rapidly in volume till the mere loudness of them is horrible. They
    are not without an opponent. Struggling through them, and also
    calling her name, is to be heard music of an unearthly sweetness
    that is seeking perhaps to beat them back and put a girdle of
    safety round her. Once Mary Rose's arms go out to her husband
    for help, but thereafter she is oblivious of his existence. Her face
    is rapt, but there is neither fear nor joy in it. Thus she passes
    from view. The island immediately resumes its stillness. The sun
    has gone down. Simon by the fire and Cameron in the boat have
    heard nothing*)
SIMON (*on his knees*) I think the fire is done for at last, and that we
can go now. How cold and grey it has become. (*Smiling, but without*

looking up) You needn't grip your tongue any longer, you know. (*He rises*) Mary Rose, where have you got to? Please don't hide. 560 Dearest, don't. Cameron, where is my wife?

> (*Cameron rises in the boat, and he is afraid to land. His face alarms Simon, who runs this way and that and is lost to sight calling her by name again and again. He returns livid*)

Cameron, I can't find her. Mary Rose! Mary Rose! Mary Rose!

Act 3

Twenty-five years have passed, and the scene is again that cosy room in the Morlands' house, not much changed since we last saw it. If chintzes have faded, others as smiling have taken their place. The time is a crisp autumn afternoon just before twilight comes. The apple-tree, not so easy to renew as the chintzes, has become smaller, but there are a few gallant apples on it. The fire is burning, and round it sit Mr and Mrs Morland and Mr Amy, the Morlands gone smaller like the apple-tree and Mr Amy bulky, but all three on the whole still bearing their apples. Inwardly they have changed still less; hear them at it as of yore.

MR MORLAND What are you laughing over, Fanny?

MRS MORLAND It is this week's *Punch*, so very amusing.

MR AMY Ah, *Punch*, it isn't what it used to be.°

MR MORLAND No, indeed.

MRS MORLAND I disagree. You two try if you can look at this picture without laughing.

     (*They are unable to stand the test*)

MR MORLAND I think I can say that I enjoy a joke as much as ever.

MRS MORLAND You light-hearted old man!

MR MORLAND (*humorously*) Not so old, Fanny. Please to remember that I am two months younger than you.

MRS MORLAND How can I forget it when you have been casting it up against me all our married life?

MR MORLAND (*not without curiosity*) Fanny and I are seventy-three; you are a bit younger, George, I think?

MR AMY Oh yes, oh dear yes.

MR MORLAND You never say precisely what your age is.

MR AMY I am in the late sixties. I am sure I have told you that before.

MR MORLAND It seems to me you have been in the sixties longer than it is usual to be in them.

MRS MORLAND (*with her needles*) James!

MR MORLAND No offence, George. I was only going to say that at seventy-three I certainly don't feel my age. How do you feel, George, at—at sixty-six? (*More loudly, as if Mr Amy were a little deaf*) Do you feel your sixty-six years?

MR AMY (*testily*) I am more than sixty-six. But I certainly don't feel my age. It was only last winter that I learned to skate.

MR MORLAND I still go out with the hounds. You forgot to come last time, George.

MR AMY If you are implying anything against my memory, James.   40

MR MORLAND (*peering through his glasses*) What do you say?

MR AMY I was saying that I have never used glasses in my life.

MR MORLAND If I wear glasses occasionally it certainly isn't because there is anything defective in my eyesight. But the type used by newspapers nowadays is so vile——   45

MR AMY There I agree with you. Especially Bradshaw.°

MR MORLAND (*not hearing him*) I say the type used by newspapers of to-day is vile. Don't you think so?

MR AMY I have just said so. (*Pleasantly*) You are getting rather dull of hearing, James.   50

MR MORLAND I am? I like that, George! Why, I have constantly to shout to you nowadays.

MR AMY What annoys me is not that you are a little deaf, you can't help that. But from the nature of your replies I often see that you are pretending to have heard what I said when you did not. That   55
is rather vain, James.

MR MORLAND Vain! Now you brought this on yourself, George. I have got something here I might well be vain of, and I meant not to show it to you because it will make you squirm.
(*Mrs Morland taps warningly*)

MR MORLAND I didn't mean that, George. I am sure that you will   60
be delighted. What do you think of this?
(*He produces a water-colour which his friend examines at arm's length*)
Let me hold it out for you, as your arms are so short.
(*The offer is declined*)

MR AMY (*with a sinking*) Very nice. What do you call it?

MR MORLAND Have you any doubt? I haven't the slightest. I am sure that it is an early Turner.°   65

MR AMY (*paling*) Turner!

MR MORLAND What else can it be? Holman suggested a Girtin° or even a Dayes.° Absurd! Why, Dayes was only a glorified drawing-master. I flatter myself I can't make a mistake about a Turner. There is something about a Turner difficult to define, but unmis-   70
takable, an absolute something. It is a charming view, too; Kirkstall Abbey° obviously.

MR AMY Rievaulx,° I am convinced.

MR MORLAND I say Kirkstall.

MRS MORLAND (*with her needles*) James!   75

MR MORLAND Well, you may be right, the place doesn't matter.

MR AMY There is an engraving of Rievaulx in that Copperplate
Magazine° we were looking at. (*He turns up the page*) I have got it,
Rievaulx. (*He brightens*) Why, this is funny. It is an engraving of
that very picture. Hello, hello, hello. (*Examining it through his*   80
private glass°) And it is signed E. Dayes.

> (*Mr Morland holds the sketch so close to him that it brushes his*
> *eyelashes*)

I wouldn't eat it, James. So it is by Dayes, the drawing-master,
after all. I am sorry you have had this disappointment.

> (*Mrs Morland taps warningly, but her husband is now possessed*)

MR MORLAND You sixty-six, Mr. Amy, you sixty-six!

MR AMY James, this is very painful. Your chagrin I can well   85
understand, but surely your sense of manhood—I regret that I
have outstayed my welcome. I bid you good afternoon. Thank you,
Mrs Morland, for your unvarying hospitality.

MRS MORLAND I shall see you into your coat, George.

MR AMY It is very kind of you, but I need no one to see me into my   90
coat.

MR MORLAND You will never see your way into it by yourself.

> (*This unworthy remark is perhaps not heard, for Mrs Morland*
> *succeeds once more in bringing the guest back*)

MR AMY James, I cannot leave this friendly house in wrath.

MR MORLAND I am an irascible old beggar, George. What I should
do without you——   95

MR AMY Or I without you. Or either of us without that little old
dear, to whom we are a never-failing source of mirth.

> (*The little old dear curtseys, looking very frail as she does so*)

Tell Simon when he comes that I shall be in to see him tomorrow.
Good-bye, Fanny; I suppose you think of the pair of us as in our
second childhood?   100

MRS MORLAND Not your second, George. I have never known any
men who have quite passed their first.

> (*He goes smiling*)

MR MORLAND (*ruminating by the fire*) He is a good fellow, George,
but how touchy he is about his age! And he has a way of tottering
off to sleep while one is talking to him.   105

MRS MORLAND He is not the only one of us who does that.

(She is standing by the window)

MR MORLAND What are you thinking about, Fanny?

MRS MORLAND I was thinking about the apple-tree, and that you have given the order for its destruction.

MR MORLAND It must come down. It is becoming a danger, might   110
fall on some one down there any day.

MRS MORLAND I quite see that it has to go. *(She can speak of Mary Rose without a tremor now)* But her tree! How often she made it a ladder from this room to the ground!

(Mr Morland does not ask who, but he very nearly does so)

MR MORLAND Oh yes, of course. Did she use to climb the apple-   115
tree? Yes, I think she did.

(He goes to his wife, as it were for protection)

MRS MORLAND *(not failing him)* Had you forgotten that also, James?

MR MORLAND I am afraid I forget a lot of things.

MRS MORLAND Just as well.

MR MORLAND It is so long since she—how long is it, Fanny?   120

MRS MORLAND Twenty-five years, a third of our lifetime. It will soon be dark; I can see the twilight running across the fields. Draw the curtains, dear.

(He does so and turns on the lights; they are electric lights now) Simon's train must be nearly due, is it not?

MR MORLAND In ten minutes or so. Did you forward his telegram?   125

MRS MORLAND No, I thought he would probably get it sooner if I kept it here.

MR MORLAND I dare say. *(He joins her on the sofa, and she sees that he is troubled)*

MRS MORLAND What is it, dear?   130

MR MORLAND I am afraid I was rather thoughtless about the apple-tree, Fanny. I hurt you.

MRS MORLAND *(brightly)* Such nonsense! Have another pipe, James.

MR MORLAND *(doggedly)* I will not have another pipe. I hereby undertake to give up smoking for a week as a punishment to   135
myself. *(His breast swells a little)*

MRS MORLAND You will regret this, you know.

MR MORLAND *(his breast ceasing to swell)* Why is my heart not broken? If I had been a man of real feeling it would have broken twenty-five years ago, just as yours did.   140

MRS MORLAND Mine didn't, dear.

MR MORLAND In a way it did. As for me, at the time I thought I could never raise my head again, but there is a deal of the old

Adam° in me still. I ride and shoot and laugh and give pompous
decisions on the bench and wrangle with old George as if nothing   145
much had happened to me. I never think of the island now; I dare
say I could go back there and fish. (*He finds that despite his outburst
his hand has strayed towards his tobacco-pouch*) See what I am doing!
(*He casts his pouch aside as if it were the culprit*) I am a man
enamoured of myself. Why, I have actually been considering,   150
Fanny, whether I should have another dress suit.

MRS MORLAND (*picking up the pouch*) And why shouldn't you?

MR MORLAND At my age! Fanny, this should be put on my
tombstone: 'In spite of some adversity he remained a lively old
blade° to the end.'   155

MRS MORLAND Perhaps that would be a rather creditable epitaph for
any man, James, who has gone through as much as you have. What
better encouragement to the young than to be able to tell them that
happiness keeps breaking through? (*She puts the pipe, which she has
been filling, in his mouth*)   160

MR MORLAND If I smoke, Fanny, I shall despise myself more than
ever.

MRS MORLAND To please me.

MR MORLAND (*as she holds the light*) I don't feel easy about it, not at
all easy. (*With a happy thought*) At any rate, I won't get the dress   165
suit.

MRS MORLAND Your dress suit is shining like a mirror.

MR MORLAND Isn't it! I thought of a jacket suit° only. The V-shaped
waistcoat seems to be what they are all wearing now.

MRS MORLAND Would you have braid on the trousers?   170

MR MORLAND I was wondering. You see——Oh, Fanny, you are
just humouring me.

MRS MORLAND Not at all. And as for the old Adam in you, dear
Adam, there is still something of the old Eve in me. Our trip to
Switzerland two years ago, with Simon, I enjoyed every hour of it.   175
The little card parties here, am I not called the noisy one? Think
of the girls I have chaperoned and teased and laughed with, just as
if I had never had a girl myself.

MR MORLAND Your brightness hasn't been all pretence?

MRS MORLAND No, indeed; I have passed through the valley of the   180
shadow,° dear, but I can say thankfully that I have come out again
into the sunlight. (*A little tremulously*) I suppose it is all to the good
that as the years go by the dead should recede farther from us.

MR MORLAND Some say they don't.

MRS MORLAND You and I know better, James.   185

MR MORLAND Up there in the misty Hebrides I dare say they think of her as on the island still. Fanny, how long is it since—since you half thought *that* yourself?

MRS MORLAND Ever so many years. Perhaps not the first year. I did cling for a time——   190

MR MORLAND The neighbours here didn't like it.

MRS MORLAND She wasn't their Mary Rose, you see.

MR MORLAND And yet her first disappearance——

MRS MORLAND It is all unfathomable. It is as if Mary Rose was just something beautiful that you and I and Simon had dreamt   195 together. You have forgotten much, but so have I. Even that room (*she looks towards the little door*) that was hers and her child's during all her short married life—I often go into it now without remembering that it was theirs.

MR MORLAND It is strange. It is rather terrible. You are pretty nigh   200 forgotten, Mary Rose.

MRS MORLAND That isn't true, dear. Mary Rose belongs to the past, and we have to live in the present, for a very little longer. Just a little longer, and then we shall understand all. Even if we could drag her back to tell us now what these things mean, I think it   205 would be a shame.

MR MORLAND Yes, I suppose so. Do you think Simon is a philosopher about it also?

MRS MORLAND Don't be bitter, James, to your old wife. Simon was very fond of her. He was a true lover.   210

MR MORLAND Was, was! Is it all 'was' about Mary Rose?

MRS MORLAND It just has to be. He had all the clever ones of the day advising, suggesting, probing. He went back to the island every year for a long time.

MR MORLAND Yes, and then he missed a year, and that somehow   215 ended it.

MRS MORLAND He never married again. Most men would.

MR MORLAND His work took her place.. What a jolly, hearty fellow he is!

MRS MORLAND If you mean he isn't heart-broken, he isn't. Merci-   220 fully the wound has healed.

MR MORLAND I am not criticising, Fanny. I suppose anyone who came back after twenty-five years—however much they had been loved—it might—we—should we know what to say to them, Fanny?   225

MRS MORLAND Don't, James. (*She rises*) Simon is late, isn't he?

MR MORLAND Very little. I heard the train a short time ago, and he might be here—just—if he had the luck to find a cab. But not if he is walking across the fields.

MRS MORLAND Listen! 230

MR MORLAND Yes, wheels. That is probably Simon. He had got a cab.

MRS MORLAND I do hope he won't laugh at me for having lit a fire in his room.

MR MORLAND (*with masculine humour*) I hope you put him out some bed-socks. 235

MRS MORLAND (*eagerly*) Do you think he would let me? You wretch! (*She hurries out, and returns in Simon's arms.*

> *He is in a greatcoat and mufti. He looks his years, grizzled with grey hair and not very much of it, and the tuft is gone. He is heavier and more commanding, full of vigour, a rollicking sea-dog° for the moment, but it is a face that could be stern to harshness*)

SIMON (*saluting*) Come aboard, sir.

MRS MORLAND Let me down, you great bear. You know how I hate to be rumpled.

MR MORLAND Not she, loves it. Always did. Get off your greatcoat, 240 Simon. Down with it anywhere.

MRS MORLAND (*fussing delightedly*) How cold your hands are. Come nearer to the fire.

MR MORLAND He is looking fit, though.

SIMON We need to be fit—these days. 245

MRS MORLAND So nice to have you again. You do like duck, don't you? The train was late, wasn't it?

SIMON A few minutes only. I made a selfish bolt for the one cab, and got it.

MR MORLAND We thought you might be walking across the fields. 250

SIMON No, I left the fields to the two other people who got out of the train. One of them was a lady; I thought something about her walk was familiar to me, but it was darkish, and I didn't make her out.

MRS MORLAND Bertha Colinton, I expect. She was in London 255 to-day.

SIMON If I had thought it was Mrs Colinton I would have offered her a lift. (*For a moment he gleams boyishly like the young husband of other days*) Mother, I have news; I have got the *Bellerophon*,° honest Injun! 260

MRS MORLAND The very ship you wanted.

SIMON Rather.

MR MORLAND Bravo, Simon.

SIMON It is like realising the ambition of one's life. I'm one of the
lucky folk, I admit.   265

    (*He says this, and neither of them notices it as a strange remark*)

MR MORLAND (*twinkling*) Beastly life, a sailor's.

SIMON (*cordially*) Beastly. I have loathed it ever since I slept in the
old *Britannia*, with my feet out at the port-hole to give them air.
We all slept that way; must have been a pretty sight from the
water. Oh, a beast of a life, but I wouldn't exchange it for any other   270
in the world. (*Lowering*) And if this war does come——

MR MORLAND (*characteristically*) It won't, I'm sure.

SIMON I dare say not. But they say—however.

MRS MORLAND Simon, I had forgotten. There is a telegram for you.

SIMON Avaunt!° I do trust it is not recalling me. I had hoped for at   275
least five clear days.

MRS MORLAND (*giving it to him*) We didn't open it.

SIMON Two to one it is recalling me.

MRS MORLAND It came two days ago. I don't like them, Simon,
never did; they have broken so many hearts.   280

SIMON They have made many a heart glad too. It may be from my
Harry—at last. Mother, do you think I was sometimes a bit harsh
to him?

MRS MORLAND I think you sometimes were, my son.

MR MORLAND Open it, Simon.   285

    (*Simon opens the telegram and many unseen devils steal into the
room*)

MRS MORLAND (*shrinking from his face*) It can't be so bad as that. We
are all here,° Simon.

    (*For a moment he has not been here himself, he has been on an
island. He is a good son to Mrs Morland now, thinking of her
only, placing her on the sofa, going on his knees beside her and
stroking her kind face. Her arms go out to her husband, who has
been reading the telegram*)

MR MORLAND (*dazed*) Can't be, can't be!

SIMON (*like some better father than he perhaps has been*) It is all right,
Mother. Don't you be afraid. It is good news. You are a brave one,   290
you have come through much, you will be brave for another
minute, won't you?

    (*She nods, with a frightened smile*)

Mother dear, it is Mary Rose.

MR MORLAND It can't be true. It is too—too glorious to be true.

MRS MORLAND Glorious? Is my Mary Rose alive?   295

SIMON It is all right, all right. I wouldn't say it, surely, if it wasn't
true. Mary Rose has come back. The telegram is from Cameron.
You remember who he was. He is minister there now. Hold my
hand, and I'll read it. 'Your wife has come back. She was found
to-day on the island. I am bringing her to you. She is quite well,   300
but you will all have to be very careful.'

MRS MORLAND Simon, can it be?

SIMON I believe it absolutely. Cameron would not deceive me.

MR MORLAND He might be deceived himself; he was a mere
acquaintance.   305

SIMON I am sure it is true. He knew her by sight as well as any of
us.

MR MORLAND But after twenty-five years!

SIMON Do you think I wouldn't know her after twenty-five years?

MRS MORLAND My—my—she will be—very changed.   310

SIMON However changed, Mother, wouldn't I know my Mary Rose
at once! Her hair may be as grey as mine—her face—her little
figure—her pretty ways—though they were all gone, don't you
think I would know Mary Rose at once? (*He is suddenly stricken
with a painful thought*) Oh, my God, I saw her, and I didn't know   315
her!

MRS MORLAND Simon!

SIMON It had been Cameron with her. They must have come in my
train. Mother, it was she I saw going across the fields—her little
walk when she was excited, half a run, I recognised it, but I didn't   320
remember it was hers.

(*Those unseen devils chuckle*)

MR MORLAND It was getting dark.

SIMON (*slowly*) Mary Rose is coming across the fields.°

(*He goes out. Morland peers weakly through the window
curtains. Mrs Morland goes on her knees to pray*)

MR MORLAND It is rather dark. I—I shouldn't wonder though there
was a touch of frost to-night. I wish I was more use.   325

(*Cameron enters, a bearded clergyman now*)

MRS MORLAND Mr Cameron? Tell us quickly, Mr Cameron, is it true?

CAMERON It iss true, ma'am. Mr Blake met us at the gate and he iss
with her now. I hurried on to tell you the things necessary. It iss
good for her you should know them at once.

MRS MORLAND Please, quick.   330

CAMERON You must be prepared to find her—different.

MRS MORLAND We are all different. Her age——

CAMERON I mean, Mrs Morland, different from what you expect.
She iss not different as we are different. They will be saying° she
iss just as she was on the day she went away.   335

    (*Mrs Morland shrinks*)

These five-and-twenty years, she will be thinking° they were just
an hour in which Mr Blake and I had left her in some incomprehensible jest.

MRS MORLAND James, just as it was before!

MR MORLAND But when you told her the truth?   340

CAMERON She will not have it.

MRS MORLAND She must have seen how much older you are.

CAMERON She does not know me, ma'am, as the boy who was with
her that day. When she did not recognise me I thought it best—she
was so troubled already—not to tell her.   345

MR MORLAND (*appealing*) But now that she has seen Simon. His
appearance, his grey hair—when she saw him she would know.

CAMERON (*unhappy*) I am not sure; it iss dark out there.

MR MORLAND She must have known that he would never have left
her and come home.   350

CAMERON That secretly troubles her, but she will not speak of it.
There iss some terrible dread lying on her heart.

MR MORLAND A dread?

MRS MORLAND Harry. James, if she should think that Harry is still
a child!   355

CAMERON· I never heard what became of the boy.

MRS MORLAND He ran away to sea when he was twelve years old.
We had a few letters from Australia, very few; we don't know
where he is now.

MR MORLAND How was she found, Mr Cameron?   360

CAMERON Two men fishing from a boat saw her. She was asleep by
the shore at the very spot where Mr Blake made a fire so long ago.
There was a rowan-tree beside it. At first they were afraid to land,
but they did. They said there was such a joy on her face as she
slept that it was a shame to waken her.   365

MR MORLAND Joy?

CAMERON That iss so, sir. I have sometimes thought——

    (*There is a gleeful clattering on the stairs of some one to whom
they must be familiar; and if her father and mother have doubted*

they know now before they see her that Mary Rose has come back. She enters. She is just as we saw her last except that we cannot see her quite so clearly. She is leaping towards her mother in the old impulsive way, and the mother responds in her way, but something steps between them)

MARY ROSE (*puzzled*) What is it?

  (*It is the years*)

MRS MORLAND My love.

MR MORLAND Mary Rose.   370

MARY ROSE Father.

  (*But the obstacle is still there. She turns timidly to Simon, who has come in with her*)

What is it, Simon?

  (*She goes confidently to him till she sees what the years have done with him. She shakes now*)

SIMON My beloved wife.

  (*He takes her in his arms and so does her mother, and she is glad to be there, but it is not of them she is thinking, and soon she softly disengages herself*)

MR MORLAND We are so glad you—had you a comfortable journey, Mary Rose? You would like a cup of tea, wouldn't you? Is there 375
anything *I* can do?

  (*Mary Rose's eyes go from him to the little door at the back*)

MARY ROSE (*coaxingly to her father*) Tell me.

MR MORLAND Tell you what, dear?

MARY ROSE (*appealing to Cameron*) You?

  (*He presses her hand and turns away. She goes to Simon and makes much of him, cajoling him*)

Simon, my Simon. Be nice to me, Simon. Be nice to me, dear 380
Simon, and tell me.

SIMON Dearest love, since I lost you—it was a long time ago——

MARY ROSE (*petulant*) It wasn't—please, it wasn't. (*She goes to her mother*) Tell me, my mother dear.

MR MORLAND I don't know what she wants to be told.   385

MRS MORLAND I know.

MARY ROSE (*an unhappy child*) Where is my baby?

  (*They cannot face her, and she goes to seek an answer from the room that lies beyond the little door. Her mother and husband follow her.*

   Mr Morland and Cameron left alone are very conscious of what may be going on in that inner room)

MR MORLAND Have you been in this part of the country before, Mr Cameron?

CAMERON I haf not, sir. It iss my first visit to England. You cannot 390
hear the sea in this house at all, which iss very strange to me.

MR MORLAND If I might show you our Downs——

CAMERON I thank you, Mr Morland, but—in such circumstances do not trouble about me at all.
>   (*They listen*)

MR MORLAND I do not know if you are interested in prints. I have 395
a pencil sketch by Cozens°—undoubtedly genuine——

CAMERON I regret my ignorance on the subject. This matter, so strange—so inexplicable——

MR MORLAND Please don't talk of it to me, sir. I am—an old man.
I have been so occupied all my life with little things—very 400
pleasant—I cannot cope—cannot cope——
>   (*A hand is placed on his shoulder so sympathetically that he dares to ask a question*)

Do you think she should have come back, Mr Cameron?
>   (*The stage darkens and they are blotted out. Into this darkness Mrs Otery enters with a candle, and we see that the scene has changed to the dismantled room of the first act. Harry is sunk in the chair as we last saw him*)

MRS OTERY (*who in her other hand has a large cup and saucer*) Here is your tea, mister. Are you sitting in the dark? I haven't been more than the ten minutes I promised you. I was—— 405
>   (*She stops short, struck by his appearance. She holds the candle nearer him. He is staring wide-eyed into the fire, motionless*)

What is the matter, mister? Here is the tea, mister.
>   (*He looks at her blankly*)

I have brought you a cup of tea, I have just been the ten minutes.

HARRY (*rising*) Wait a mo.
>   (*He looks about him, like one taking his bearings*)

Gimme the tea. That's better. Thank you, missis.

MRS OTERY Have you seen anything? 410

HARRY See here, as I sat in that chair—I wasn't sleeping, mind you—it's no dream—but things of the far past connected with this old house—things I knew naught of—they came crowding out of their holes and gathered round me till I saw—I saw them all so clear that I don't know what to think, woman. (*He is a grave man* 415
now) Never mind about that. Tell me about this—ghost.

MRS OTERY It's no concern of yours.

HARRY Yes, it is some concern of mine. The folk that used to live here—the Morlands——

MRS OTERY That was the name. I suppose you heard it in the village?   420

HARRY I have heard it all my days. It is one of the names I bear. I am one of the family.

MRS OTERY I suspicioned that.

HARRY I suppose that is what made them come to me as I sat here.   425
Tell me about them.

MRS OTERY It is little I know. They were dead and gone before my time, the old man and his wife.

HARRY It's not them I am asking you about.

MRS OTERY They had a son-in-law, a sailor. The war made a great   430
man of him before it drowned him.

HARRY I know that; he was my father. Hard I used to think him, but I know better now. Go on, there's the other one.

MRS OTERY (*reluctantly*) That was all.

HARRY There is one more.   435

MRS OTERY If you must speak of her, she is dead too. I never saw her in life.

HARRY Where is she buried?

MRS OTERY Down by the church.

HARRY Is there a stone?   440

MRS OTERY Yes.

HARRY Does it say her age?

MRS OTERY No.

HARRY Is that holy spot well taken care of?

MRS OTERY You can see for yourself.   445

HARRY I will see for myself. And so it is her ghost that haunts this house?

  (*She makes no answer. He struggles with himself*)

There is no such thing as ghosts. And yet——Is it true about folk having lived in this house and left in a hurry?

MRS OTERY It's true.   450

HARRY Because of a ghost—a thing that can't be.

MRS OTERY When I came in your eyes were staring; I thought you had seen her.

HARRY Have you ever seen her yourself?

  (*She shivers*)

Where? In this room?   455

  (*She looks at the little door*)

In there? Has she ever been seen out of that room?

MRS OTERY All over the house, in every room and on the stairs. I tell you I've met her on the stairs, and she drew back to let me pass and said 'Good evening' too, timidlike, and at another time she has gone by me like a rush of wind.   460

HARRY What is she like? Is she dressed in white? They are allus° dressed in white, aren't they?

MRS OTERY She looks just like you or me. But for all that she's as light as air. I've seen—things.

HARRY You look like it, too. But she is harmless, it seems?   465

MRS OTERY There's some wouldn't say that; them that left in a hurry. If she thought you were keeping it from her she would do you a mischief.

HARRY Keeping what from her?

MRS OTERY Whatever it is she prowls about this cold house search- 470
ing for, searching, searching. I don't know what it is.

HARRY (grimly) Maybe I could tell you. I dare say I could even put her in the way of finding him.

MRS OTERY Then I wish to God you would, and let her rest.

HARRY My old dear, there are worse things than not finding what 475
you are looking for; there is finding them so different from what you had hoped. (He moves about) A ghost. Oh no—and yet, and yet—— See here, I am going into that room.

MRS OTERY As you like; I care not.

HARRY I'll burst open the door.   480

MRS OTERY No need; it's not locked; I cheated you about that.

HARRY But I tried it and it wouldn't open.

        (Mrs Otery is very unhappy)

You think she is in there?

MRS OTERY She may be.

HARRY (taking a deep breath) Give me air.   485

        (He throws open the window and we see that it is a night of stars)

Leave me here now. I have a call to make.

MRS OTERY (hesitating) I dunno. You think you're in no danger, but——

HARRY That is how it is to be, missis. Just ten minutes you were out of the room, did you say?   490

MRS OTERY That was all.

HARRY God!

        (She leaves him. After a moment's irresolution he sets off upon his quest carrying the candle, which takes with it all the light of

*the room. He is visible on the other side of the darkness, in the
little passage and opening the door beyond. He returns, and now
we see the pale ghost of Mary Rose standing in the middle of the
room, as if made out of the light he has brought back with him)*

MARY ROSE (*bowing to him timidly*) Have you come to buy the house?

HARRY (*more startled by his own voice than by hers*) Not me.

MARY ROSE It is a very nice house. (*Doubtfully*) Isn't it?   495

HARRY It was a nice house once.

MARY ROSE (*pleased*) Wasn't it! (*Suspiciously*) Did you know this
house?

HARRY When I was a young shaver.°

MARY ROSE Young? Was it you who laughed?   500

HARRY When was that?

MARY ROSE (*puzzled*) There was once some one who laughed in this
house. Don't you think laughter is a very pretty sound?

HARRY (*out of his depths*) Is it? I dare say. I never thought about it.

MARY ROSE You are quite old.   505

HARRY I'm getting on.

MARY ROSE (*confidentially*) Would you mind telling me why every
one is so old? I don't know you, do I?

HARRY I wonder. Take a look. You might have seen me in the old
days—playing about—outside in the garden—or even inside.   510

MARY ROSE You—you are not Simon, are you?

HARRY No. (*Venturing*) My name is Harry.

MARY ROSE (*stiffening*) *I* don't think so. I strongly object to your
saying that.

HARRY I'm a queer sort of cove,° and I would like to hear you call   515
me Harry.

MARY ROSE (*firmly*) I decline. I regret, but I absolutely decline.

HARRY No offence.

MARY ROSE I think you are sorry for me.

HARRY I am that.   520

MARY ROSE I am sorry for me, too.

HARRY (*desperately desirous to help her*) If only there was something
I——I know nothing about ghosts—not a thing; can they sit down?
Could you——?
        (*He turns the chair toward her*)

MARY ROSE That is your chair.   525

HARRY What do you mean by that?

MARY ROSE That is where you were sitting.

HARRY Were you in this room when I was sitting there?

MARY ROSE I came in to look at you.
>   (*A sudden thought makes him cross with the candle to where he had left his knife. It is gone*)

HARRY Where is my knife? Were you standing looking at me with   530
my knife in your hand?
>   (*She is sullenly silent*)

Give me my knife.
>   (*She gives it to him*)

What made you take it?

MARY ROSE I thought you were perhaps the one.

HARRY The one?   535

MARY ROSE The one who stole him from me.

HARRY I see. Godsake, in a sort of way I suppose I am.
>   (*He sits in the chair*)

MARY ROSE Give him back to me.

HARRY I wish I could. But I'm doubting he is gone beyond recall.

MARY ROSE (*unexpectedly*) Who is he?°   540

HARRY Do you mean you have forgotten who it is you are searching
for?

MARY ROSE I knew once. It is such a long time ago. I am so tired;
please can I go away and play now?

HARRY Go away? Where? You mean back to that—that place?   545
>   (*She nods*)

What sort of a place is it? Is it good to be there?

MARY ROSE Lovely, lovely, lovely.

HARRY It's not just the island, is it, that's so lovely, lovely?
>   (*She is perplexed*)

Have you forgotten the island too?

MARY ROSE I am sorry.   550

HARRY The island, the place where you heard the call.

MARY ROSE What is that?

HARRY You have even forgotten the call! (*With vision*) As far as I can
make out, it was as if, in a way, there were two kinds of dogs out
hunting you—the good and the bad.   555

MARY ROSE (*who thinks he is chiding her*) Please don't be cross with
me.

HARRY I am far from cross with you. I begin to think it was the good
dogs that got you. Are they ghosts in that place?

MARY ROSE (*with surprising certainty*) No.   560

HARRY You are sure?

MARY ROSE Honest Injun!

HARRY What fairly does me is, if the place is so lovely, what made
you leave it?

MARY ROSE (*frightened*) I don't know.   565

HARRY Do you think you could have fallen out?°

MARY ROSE I don't know. (*She thinks his power is great*) Please, I
don't want to be a ghost any more.

HARRY As far as I can see, if you wasn't a ghost there you made
yourself one by coming back. But it's no use your expecting me to   570
be able to help you. (*She droops at this and he holds out his arms*)
Come to me, ghostie; I wish you would.

MARY ROSE (*prim again*) Certainly not.

HARRY If you come, I'll try to help you.
          (*She goes at once and sits on his knee*)
See here, when I was sitting by the fire alone I seemed to hear you   575
as you once were saying that some day when he was a man you
would like to sit on your Harry's knee.

MARY ROSE (*vaguely quoting she knows not whom*) The loveliest time
of all° will be when he is a man and takes me on his knee instead
of my taking him on mine.   580

HARRY Do you see who I am now?

MARY ROSE Nice man.

HARRY Is that all you know about me?

MARY ROSE Yes.

HARRY There is a name I would like to call you by, but my best   585
course is not to worry you. Poor soul, I wonder if there was ever
a man with a ghost on his knee before.

MARY ROSE I don't know.

HARRY Seems to me you're feared of being a ghost. I dare say, to a
timid thing, being a ghost is worse than seeing them.   590

MARY ROSE Yes.

HARRY Is it lonely being a ghost?

MARY ROSE Yes.

HARRY Do you know any other ghost?

MARY ROSE No.   595

HARRY Would you like to know other ghosts?

MARY ROSE Yes.

HARRY I can understand that. And now you would like to go away
and play?

MARY ROSE Please.   600

HARRY In this cold house, when you should be searching, do you
sometimes play by yourself instead?

MARY ROSE (*whispering*) Don't tell.

HARRY Not me. You're a pretty thing. What beautiful shoes you
    have.   605
        (*She holds out her feet complacently*)

MARY ROSE Nice buckles.

HARRY I like your hair.

MARY ROSE Pretty hair.

HARRY Do you mind° the tuft that used to stand up at the back
    of—of Simon's head?   610

MARY ROSE (*merrily*) Naughty tuft.

HARRY I have one like that.

MARY ROSE (*smoothing it down*) Oh dear, oh dear, what a naughty
    tuft!

HARRY My name is Harry.   615

MARY ROSE (*liking the pretty sound*) Harry, Harry, Harry, Harry.

HARRY But you don't know what Harry I am.

MARY ROSE No.

HARRY And this brings us no nearer what's to be done with you. I
    would willingly stay here though I have my clearing in Australy,   620
    but you're just a ghost. They say there are ways of laying ghosts,
    but I am so ignorant.

MARY ROSE (*imploringly*) Tell me.

HARRY I wish I could; you are even more ignorant than I am.

MARY ROSE Tell me.   625

HARRY All I know about them for certain is that they are unhappy
    because they can't find something, and then once they've got the
    thing they want, they go away happy and never come back.

MARY ROSE Oh, nice!

HARRY The one thing clear to me is that you have got that thing at   630
    last, but you are too dog-tired to know or care. What you need
    now is to get back to the place you say is lovely, lovely.

MARY ROSE Yes, yes.

HARRY It sounds as if it might be Heaven, or near thereby.
        (*She wants him to find out for her*)
    Queer, you that know so much can tell nothing, and them that   635
    know nothing can tell so much. If there was any way of getting
    you to that glory place!

MARY ROSE Tell me.

HARRY (*desperate*) He would surely send for you, if He wanted you.

MARY ROSE (*crushed*) Yes.   640

HARRY It's like as if He had forgotten you.

MARY ROSE Yes.

HARRY It's as if nobody wanted you, either there or here.

MARY ROSE Yes. (*She rises*) Bad man.

HARRY It's easy to call me names, but the thing fair beats me. There   645
is nothing I wouldn't do for you, but a mere man is so helpless.
How should the likes of me know what to do with a ghost that has
lost her way on earth? I wonder if what it means is that you broke
some law, just to come back for the sake of—of that Harry? If it
was that, it's surely time He overlooked it.   650

MARY ROSE Yes.

(*He looks at the open window*)

HARRY What a night of stars! Good old glitterers, I dare say they are
in the know, but I am thinking you are too small a thing to get a
helping hand from them.

MARY ROSE Yes.   655

(*The call is again heard, but there is in it now no unholy sound.
It is a celestial music that is calling for Mary Rose, Mary Rose,
first in whispers and soon so loudly that, for one who can hear,
it is the only sound in the world. Mary Rose, Mary Rose. As it
wraps her round, the weary little ghost knows that her long day
is done. Her face is shining. The smallest star shoots down for
her, and with her arms stretched forth to it trustingly she walks
out through the window into the empyrean. The music passes
with her. Harry hears nothing, but he knows that somehow a
prayer has been answered*)

EXPLANATORY NOTES

The Admirable Crichton

1.1.12 S.D. *spats*: short gaiters reaching a little above the ankle.

13 S.D. *Athenaeum*: i.e. an undergraduate club; a general term for a literary or scientific society tracing its ancestry to the cultural life of classical Greece. The Athenaeum in London was the most prestigious in terms of social standing.

18 S.D. *sup*: take a late supper (after the theatre, for example).

21 S.D. *at Westminster*: i.e. in the Government, the seat of which is the Palace of Westminster.

35 S.D. *to the scandal of all good houses*: in a way that will outrage socially elevated families. In this tone of light and gentle satire the stage directions open the theme which Crichton's dialogue opens in the text, namely a shaking-up of conventional social attitudes. The humorous and teasing nature of the play makes palatable to its original London audience what would otherwise, at the time of first production, have been a radical and provocative social message. Barrie needs to disarm his readers just as productions must disarm the theatre audience, if he is to get away with the social inversions of this play.

37 S.D. *the pantry and the boudoir*: the pantry was the butler's headquarters and the boudoir was a lady's private room. This innocent-seeming but prophetic linking of these two locations is again lightly provocative, linking public opinion on the part of the mistress and servant. The stage direction makes explicit the play's social implications, but does so with the same engaging tone of humorous mischief as the dialogue.

S.D. *We*: Barrie adopts a mocking form of royal plural, as if he were presiding over the unfolding events of his play and distanced from it, rather than its author. In this way he is characteristically present as an 'implied audience' for his own work.

52 S.D. *those who are anybody*: those with claims to social rank.

64 S.D. *losing caste*: forfeiting inherited social class.

77 *servants' hall*: the communal centre of the household's domestic servants, where they took their meals. The first act of the play emphasizes that as strict a social hierarchy operates here as in the high society these people serve, and the dramatic success of the play as a whole depends on performances from the actors playing servants in this opening scene which clearly indicate its ranks and rigidities.

86 *Radical views*: Mackail, *The Story of J.M.B.* (1941), reports this entry in Barrie's notebook for 1899: 'Scene—Servants entertained in drawing-room by mistress and master à la Carlisle family.' He notes: 'Somebody must have told Barrie of this, and the reference is obviously to Rosalind, Countess of Carlisle, who was Lady Airlie's sister, and combined advanced radical principles with a manner which terrified members of every class . . . She, or this story about her, had planted the first germ of *The Admirable Crichton*,' (p. 288).

118 S.D. *crumb-brush*: a small brush and wooden pan for sweeping up table crumbs was standard equipment for dining-rooms.

125 S.D. *club member*: member of a gentlemen's London club (like the Athenaeum).

165 *bowl with your head*: use your intelligence when bowling in a cricket match (but not, Ernest implies, at any other time).

172 *breaks both ways*: can bowl both off-breaks and leg-breaks, and is therefore a spin bowler very difficult to bat against.

173 S.D. *uncut*: having pages which must be slit and separated by the reader after purchase.

S.D. *Let laws and learning, art and commerce die*: Barrie misquotes Lord John Manners, Duke of Rutland (1818–1906): 'Let wealth and commerce, laws and learning die | But leave us still our old nobility!' (*England's Trust*, iii. 227).

S.D. *Piccadilly or Holborn*: fashionable shopping areas for men's clothes.

190 *don't like it*: doesn't like it: an idiosyncrasy of aristocratic grammar put to much comic effect by writers in the first half of the twentieth century, notably by P. G. Wodehouse.

201 *You are the same . . . myself*: a comic reversal of customary egalitarianism, prior to the play's far more subversive displacement of ordinary class assumptions.

206 S.D. *Lowering*: looking threateningly ('ow' as in 'how').

211 *do anything*: perform any party piece.

293 *If it's spared*: if it doesn't die. This act of sexual clairvoyance can only have preceded the birth, so undermining Lord Loam's previous democratic guesswork. The acting of the role here should show Lord Loam as completely unable to doff his aristocracy, despite his best efforts: even his mistake is aristocratically overridden. The greater the failure here, the greater the surprise later.

297 *I'm ashamed to be seen talking to you*: the words invert their normal social implications, but emphasize the omnipresence of accepted natural hierarchy which pervades this scene. See the 'etiquette of the servants' hall' in Crichton's next speech.

306 *Upper House*: House of Lords.

323 *Nature*: under its light surface, the play brilliantly juxtaposes two theories of original nature, that of equality (Lord Loam) and that of adaptive hierarchy (Crichton). (Darwin would have been on Crichton's side.)

336 *looking daggers*: looking angry.

354 *I hear you laughing*: many of the most effective moments in the play depend not on dialogue but on moments of silence, brief intervals of awkwardness and passages of action, as here. These 'freeze-frames', or short episodes of 'silent film' are both retrospectively recorded for the reader *and* signalled to the actor/director by Barrie's full stage directions: a mere indication of entrances, exits, and moves cannot do justice to their choreographic intricacy. The timing of the (very brief) pause, before Lord Loam *does* hear the compulsory laughter he is democratically insisting upon, is essential to the scene's effect.

365 *entirely and utterly out of the question*: Lord Loam is anxious to excite democratic ideas and prudently to stamp on them. Crichton shares his view here, from a totally different philosophical standpoint!

369 *under way*: i.e. aboard ship and moving through the water. (Barrie's text uses the erroneous form 'under weigh', which presumably arose by mistaken association with the term 'weigh anchor'.)

389 *Crichton*: faced with a similar emergency, Lady Macbeth ordered the Scottish nobles to 'Stand not upon the order of your going | But go at once.' Crichton's band of servants go at once, but he does not omit to stand upon the order of their going. The movement required here is thematically very expressive.

416 S.D. *tragic thoughts*: as usual, Barrie's use of the word 'tragic' is intentionally reductive.

447 We *don't do it*: i.e. ladies' maids do not: Fisher refers her behaviour to the standards of a social group which, like any other, has its rigid corporate pride.

449 S.D. *weeps*: the dialogue is again offset by action, and the full stage direction combines authorial judgement with precise instructions for performance and effect.

495 *keeping company*: courting.

521 *lawks!*: expression of astonishment ('Lord have mercy').

526 *character*: testimonial.

538 *Crichton . . . wages*: you will be compensated in your wages for the inconvenience of being separated from Crichton.

549 *The ingrate! The smug! The fop!*: a 'smug' is a self-satisfied person; 'fop' is used in the obsolete sense of 'conceited person'.

559 *the party*: i.e. the potential valet.

568 S.D. *appalled*: mock-usage in the archaic sense 'made pale with terror' (by realizing her temerity in proposing to Crichton such

humiliating forfeiture of rank). A valet was markedly inferior in status to a butler.

582 *a valet's hand*: Crichton reproves Agatha for her unseemly condescension in offering her hand to a hand so much reduced in status as his own. All these hyperbolic plays on social difference protect the *comedy* of the island revolution, when it eventually comes.

595 *Circumstances might alter cases*: the play's provisional title was 'The Case is Altered'.

602 *kept in his place*: in Crichton's description of his social ideal (ll. 587–9) this phrase was wholly innocent, but the rationale he has just given imparts to it a slightly sinister ambiguity.

604 *for the house*: for the family.

621 *time to dress*: i.e. to dress for dinner.

2.1.16 S.D. *perhaps it was ourselves*: again Barrie affects a mock-detachment from his characters, and a pose as author-spectator which enables him to identify conspiratorially with those very features of assumed superiority on the part of the audience which his play is intended gently to subvert.

40 S.D. *that valuable time*: i.e. the three minutes before the boat sank.

45 S.D. *before the mast*: ordinary sailors (who had their quarters in that part of the ship, forward of the mast). The ladies have been playing at being sailors, and Barrie's costumes for them at this point are in contrast to the authentic garb for practical contingencies which they have acquired by Act 3.

136 *You are a man*: a pivotal statement in the shift enacted in this scene between one social order and another: for the first time in the play Lady Mary detaches Crichton from his office and persona as a servant and perceives him as a human being.

144 *track of commerce*: i.e. commercial shipping routes.

146 S.D. *watching her*: a few minutes earlier Lady Mary was herself watching Crichton as he worked; now the process of observing is reversed. The careful acting of mutual watchfulness is very important in this scene, reflecting the dynamic way in which identities on the island are both discovered and revised. This is reflected in the changes of tone and newly grounded estimates of character in the dialogue.

147 *a good pluckt 'un*: someone with plenty of courage.

167 *unnatural*: this word now carries the full weight of the competing social philosophies at large in the play.

184 S.D. *he is puzzled*: this episode is one of the most difficult in the play to act successfully, though dialogue and action are precisely judged to achieve the intended effect: it is essential that we do *not* see Crichton's seizure of leadership as deliberate and opportunistic, but rather as confirming his own view of natural process responding spontaneously to

circumstances. Crichton's puzzlement is not stupidity or ingenuousness, but a complete and somewhat unwary taking for granted of what nature requires. It is Lady Mary, not Crichton, who perceives convulsion in the switch from one social order to another; for him it is a question of immutable practicalities.

191 *in rows on top of little sticks*: i.e. in a coconut-shy.

199 *All my eye*: all nonsense.

Ginger: 'a mild expletive' (*OED*), as in 'by ginger!'

Nothink: Cockney pronunciation for 'nothing'.

222 S.D. *It is pleasing . . . no coward*: Ernest is to be seen forming the brave reserve strength, prudently guarding the hut, while Crichton and Treherne are in the front line, facing the adversary.

241 S.D. *He is soon busy . . . the hut*: acting editions of the play mark Crichton and Treherne as being off-stage from this point until Crichton is summoned by Lord Loam. However, given a big enough stage area there is no reason why Crichton and Treherne should not be visible working on the hut throughout the ensuing dialogue. This would add comedy and point to the adjustments of rank now in process of being clarified, and especially to Ernest's 'I'm planning out the building of this hut' (l. 328). We are about to see the demise of the dilettante staff officer.

278 *Swiss Family Robinson*: a classic castaway story, by J. D. Wyss (1826).

352 S.D. *in answer to a summons*: acting editions specify that Lady Mary calls 'Crichton' at this point; her tone should be one of accustomed peremptory authority giving an order which she knows to be misguided; hence it is, as usual, Lady Mary (even more than Crichton himself) who *consciously* registers the change of command. Her conscious realization of social process, which is different from and complementary to Crichton's, sets them both apart from all other figures in the play, and places them in intermediate acting roles as *interpreters* of the action as well as participants.

482 *nine-tenths of the scoring*: Treherne as usual draws his metaphors from cricket: he and Crichton have been batting together in an unequal partnership.

501 *take her to the others*: Crichton is concerned for propriety, and he is still anxious not to come between Tweeny and her proper work.

3.1 S.D. *The scene*: *The Admirable Crichton* is, among other things, a satirical version of the *Robinsonade*, or castaway story deriving from *Robinson Crusoe*. The accoutrements of this scene are ingenious examples of 'making do' and creating a fully adequate alternative technology, in the best tradition of this fictional genre.

39 S.D. *in a play we may not*: in the stage directions of a play, however, Barrie is able to specify the presence of an unseen power-house of

authority of which no adequate performance can leave the audience unaware.

48 S.D. *going-away gown*: Tweeny's equivalent of a bridal honeymoon outfit is her best and most practical skirt.

114 S.D. *Parthian shot*: remark made at point of departure, like the arrows shot backwards by Parthian horsemen as they rode from battle.

173 *flying at bigger game*: aiming for a greater prize.

185 *a second eleven sort of chap*: another metaphor from cricket; a person of modest abilities.

206 *walk out with me*: court me. The expression refers to the ceremony of courtship which literally involved walking together, or 'promenading', in designated public places such as the promenades of seaside resorts. The island is comically ill-suited to such decorous conventions.

231 S.D. *A stalwart youth*: although there is satire of the conventional hero-figure, and comic absurdity in Lady Mary's transformation, there is also a genuine physical *élan* in this appearance which is one of many indications that the play is not quite even-handed in its Crichtonian balancing of two social systems: the 'natural' self of the island is unmistakably *more* natural, and more fulfilled, than the 'natural' self of London houses.

247 *I sighted a herd . . . Firefly Grove*: this speech is almost a detachable satire on exaggerated literary conventions, comparable with the satiric presentation of pirates and Red Indians in *Peter Pan*: the practice of mock-literary interpolations within a drama is characteristic of Barrie.

266 *We ran all the way*: again, the novel physical energies of the castaways are both ridiculed and admired.

313 S.D. *Dogs delight . . . bite*: from *Divine Songs for Children* (1715) by Isaac Watts: 'Let dogs delight to bark and bite | For God hath made them so.'

S.D. *tom-tom*: Indian drums.

S.D. *punkah*: a fan, usually made from leaves; in India during the British Raj the punkah was worked by a native servant known as a 'punkah-wallah'.

S.D. £26 *a year*: typical wages for a maid at the time the play was written.

S.D. *oats*: liveliness (especially sexual liveliness, as in 'sowing wild oats').

314 *Clear*: clear soup.

333 *I went across on the rope*: Barrie cannot resist the temptation to make the internal tall story taller still.

360 S.D. *moue*: (Fr.) pout.

363 *like one washing them*: this is a retrospective physical stage direction for Crichton in Act 1, comprising a physical trait of servile deference.

383 *playing the game*: playing fair.

422 *or ever the knightly years . . . Christian slave*: the lines are taken from W. E. Henley's poem 'To W.A.' (*Echoes*, xxxvii). Henley (1849–1903) was a friend of Barrie, and father of the little girl Margaret who suggested to Barrie the name 'Wendy' (see note to *Peter Pan*, I.1.336, on p. 312. Henley was most famous for the poem 'Invictus' ('Out of the night that covers me . . .'). R. D. S. Jack writes: 'The idea of life as a struggle for power is spelt out clearly in the Henley poem which Crichton uses to introduce his proposal to Mary . . . The poem argues out the view of sexual love as a relationship demanding dominance and submission, first depicted by Barrie in *The Little Minister*. It also reminds us that the social inversions we have just witnessed . . . are repeated over and over again, with variations, throughout history' (Jack, *The Road to the Never Land* (1991), 120–1).

426 *hewers of wood and drawers of water*: Joshua 9: 21.

439 *run a goat down*: outrun a goat in hunting it.

567 S.D. *bluejackets*: seamen.

575 S.D. *salt*: rueful.

S.D. *he ceases to be an erect figure*: the play calls for a great deal of skilled physical action, as actors must convey by gradual or sudden changes of physical habit and decorum their altered status in the alternative hierarchies. The mime required of the actor playing Crichton at this point is the most demanding of such moments. He has only two words of dialogue to support the physical expression of the reversionary change from governor to butler, and it is the climactic moment in the intricate body language of the play.

4.1.2 S.D. *the room of the first act*: this was always so in the script, but not in the first production, directed by Dion Boucicault. 'The first and last acts . . . could easily have been played in the same set . . . Not good enough for Boucicault and Frohman and the Duke of York's. Two different rooms must be shown in Lord Loam's London residence, and there was even a time—but somehow the plan fell through—when the family portraits in one of them were to have been painted by Sargent himself. That was the scale of the management's imagination' (Mackail, 333–4).

16 S.D. *frequent use of the word 'furtive'*: Barrie's fun at his own verbal expense is also a comprehensive stage direction for the effects to be achieved in the first part of the scene.

59 S.D. *Crichton having opened the glass case . . . to a retired spot*: another of many points where stage action is tellingly at odds with the social conventions of the dialogue.

84 S.D. *brown study*: reverie.

191 *A mere servant*: the phrase typifies the long series of parallels and inversions which give this last act its light but incessant irony.

206 *she behaved awfully well*: nothing betrays the double standards of Barrie's aristocrats so clearly as their moments of kindness, generosity, and tribute towards their inferiors.

236 S.D. *a better man*: in the closing act the stage directions often dispense with niceties in favour of explicit and unhidden judgements, and in so doing reflect the quality of the dialogue, which by its earlier finesse has earned the right to be unsparing.

299 S.D. *bows, but remains*: Crichton responds only to a direct order. His imperviousness to heavily implied instructions is a complex dramatic signal, indicating on the one hand that his loyalty to the family is not to be confused with general social deference, but on the other that his identification of self with role can no longer be taken for granted, even by them. Not even the admirable Crichton can quite put Humpty together again.

312 *living*: the Church property or benefice held by a rector or vicar.

317 *rather weak . . . turf*: Treherne measures his parish (not metaphorically, this time) by its cricketing amenities. The bowlers in the local team are indifferent, but they have a good pitch.

346 *two of them*: two of the curios, i.e. the servants. Lady Brocklehurst's wit is meant for Lord Loam's discomfiture, but still identifies servants with *things*.

347 S.D. *entrance of Crichton*: with the entrance of Crichton and Tweeny the island party is again complete and, with its social reputation at risk, is again and for the last time in Crichton's power. For the rest of the scene two social hierarchies, two systems of awareness and dependency, are in simultaneous existence.

371 *keep their place*: Crichton carefully omits to specify what the place was, and leaves Lady Brocklehurst to conclude that it must, of course, have been the usual inferior one.

387 S.D. *Vae victis*: (Lat.) woe to the vanquished.

435 *is suited*: has found a satisfactory replacement.

Peter Pan

Dedication

To The Five: the dedication is to the five sons of Arthur and Sylvia Llewelyn Davies, George, Jack, Peter, Michael, and Nicholas (Nico). Arthur Llewelyn Davies died in 1907 and his widow in 1910, after which Barrie adopted the boys and supported them throughout their subsequent education. This family was deeply involved in the genesis of *Peter Pan* both as a story (initially forming part of Barrie's novel *The*

Little White Bird, 1902) and as a play. The Dedication was written at the earliest in 1920, a date established by its reference to *Mary Rose*, and more probably for the 1928 edition. George Llewelyn Davies was killed in the First World War in 1915, and Michael was drowned in 1921, so that when the Dedication was written at least one and probably two of the brothers were already dead.

1 *printing at last*: Peter Pan was first printed in 1928, forming part of the *Collected Plays of J. M. Barrie*. It had been first performed in 1904. The text subsequently underwent numerous revisions, and the printed text as finally prepared by Barrie differs in a number of respects from the production text which was commonly used in the theatre. For the history of the text, and the case for retaining Barrie's 1928 published text, see Introduction, pp. xi–xiii and xv–xviii, and Note on the Text, above.

3 *no recollection of having written it*: Barrie often maintained this, but it must be taken with a pinch of salt. In fact he gave the manuscript to Maude Adams, the actress who first played Peter Pan in America, and it is now in the possession of the Lilly Library of the University of Indiana.

7 *The play of Peter is streaky with you still*: after all the later processes of scripting and production, there remain many traces in the text of the Llewelyn Davies boys and their original games with Barrie which first created the figure of Peter Pan.

10 *Kensington Gardens*: Barrie first met the Llewelyn Davies boys in Kensington Gardens when they were very small children. It was here that he first told them the stories which led eventually to those chapters of *The Little White Bird* which were separately published as *Peter Pan in Kensington Gardens* (1906). Kensington Gardens play an even larger part in earlier drafts and production scripts of the play (see pp. xii–xiii).

11 *killed . . . winded*: Wendy's fate on arrival in the Never Land is thus anticipated in the early fantasies about Peter himself which Barrie devised for the Davies boys.

21 *fit the boards*: become a suitable character for the stage.

23 *a garden at Burpham*: in 1900 the Davies family spent a holiday at Burpham, which was near to the holiday cottage which Barrie's wife had acquired—Black Lake Cottage, near Farnham, Surrey. The subsequent holidays shared by Barrie and the children in Surrey, especially their adventures at Black Lake Cottage, were the source of many ideas and incidents in *Peter Pan*.

24 *No. 4*: throughout the Dedication the numbers refer to the Llewelyn Davies boys in descending order of age.

29 *St Bernard dog*: this was Barrie's St Bernard, Porthos, a great performer who contributed energetically to the games at Black Lake Cottage. In

1902 Porthos died and was replaced by another notable canine character, a Newfoundland called Luath. Luath was the physical model for Nana (closely studied by Arthur Lupino, who first played the part), but the character of Nana was largely derived from Porthos.

31 *The Boy Castaways*: *The Boy Castaways of Black Lake Island* was Barrie's record of the momentous summer holiday of 1901. The book was supposedly written by Peter Llewelyn Davies, then aged 4, and consisted entirely of a Preface and captioned photographs. Two copies only were printed, one of which was given to the boys' father, who (perhaps significantly) lost it.

43 *ploughing woods incarnadine*: causing bloodshed in his progress through the woods.

47 *was begun the writing of the play of Peter*: Roger Lancelyn Green (*Fifty Years of 'Peter Pan'* (1954), 32) dates 'the first real foreshadowing' of *Peter Pan* as a play to Barrie's notebooks for October 1902: '*Play*: "The Happy Boy": Boy who couldn't grow up—runs away from pain and death. . .'

58 *Peter and Wendy*: Barrie's novel for children, retelling the story of the play, was published in 1911.

61 *assay*: undertaking.

63 *Bandelero the Bandit*: this was Barrie's first play, written for the dramatic club at Dumfries Academy when he was a pupil there. A clergyman attacked it in the columns of a local paper as being grossly immoral.

65 *Mr Toole*: J. L. Toole, the actor-manager.

66 *Ibsen's Ghost*: Barrie's first play to be professionally performed, on 30 May 1891.

67 *in front*: in the audience.

68 '*parts*': sections of the complete playscript given to an actor, consisting of his/her own appearances and lines. The term 'part', as in 'the part of X was played by Y' refers to this practice.

79 *another MS, lately made*: probably an oblique reference by Barrie to his compulsive activity as a reviser (not only of *Peter Pan*, but of his plays generally).

89 *in the days when you most admired me*: a characteristic note of wry and amiable bitterness which reflects in part the degree of estrangement in Barrie's later relationship with the surviving Davies children, but chiefly the mere fact that they had grown up; as such, the comment reflects the preoccupation which created *Peter Pan*.

91 *one-and-sixpence*: the equivalent of 7½ p. in decimal coinage, though its actual value was considerably greater.

94 *challenged as collaboration*: this was an enduring joke of Barrie's. The 'legal document' referred to was a formal recognition of Jack Llewelyn

Davies's supposed contribution of one line to *Little Mary*. Later in life he came to a similar agreement with the young Princess Margaret for her 'co-authorship' of *The Boy David*.

102 *gallery boys*: the gallery was the highest tier of audience accommodation, had the cheapest admission prices, and drew the rowdiest theatregoers.

116 *that native place*: Barrie's birthplace, Kirriemuir in Angus, Scotland.

118 *was so hard to reach*: Barrie first went to London in 1885 at the age of 25, 'with nothing but a discouraging letter from an editor to justify the risk' (Mackail, 167). Despite his swift professional success, it was several years more before he had a settled home in the capital.

119 *that great dog*: Barrie's Newfoundland, Luath.

137 *fellow-conspirator Robb*: James Robb, Barrie's childhood friend, who shared his earliest dramatic efforts in the wash-house of the Barries' cottage at Kirriemuir, which became their boyhood theatre.

glengarry bonnets: a type of bonnet worn by some of the Scottish regiments, taking its name from a valley in Inverness-shire.

139 *preens, a bool, or a peerie*: Scottish words: 'preens' are pins or items of small value; 'bools' are balls or marbles; 'peeries' are marbles.

147 *lum hat*: top hat, like a stovepipe hat ('lum'=chimneypot).

151 *wrecked islands*: the islands of Barrie's boyhood reading exerted a lasting hold on his imagination—hence the importance of islands in his plays (see *Peter Pan*, *The Admirable Crichton*, *Mary Rose*). In his Preface to R. M. Ballantyne's *The Coral Island* (1913), he wrote: 'To be born is to be wrecked on an island.'

152 *He buys his sanguinary tales . . . penny numbers*: Barrie as a child was a voracious reader of 'penny dreadfuls'—blood-and-thunder stories in instalments costing a penny each.

153 *Chatterbox*: a magazine for boys founded in 1866 by the Revd J. Erskine Clark in an effort to undermine the influence of 'penny dreadfuls'.

155 *With gloaming*: at twilight.

157 *Pathhead farm*: a farm near Barrie's home at Kirriemuir, where he claimed to have interred his stock of undesirable literature. Mackail warns against taking such reminiscences too literally: 'he frequently has the vaguest ideas of where he actually was' (Mackail, 35).

170 *write with the left hand*: in 1920 Barrie developed severe writer's cramp in his right hand and switched to his left. This was no problem; he was naturally left-handed as a child. He attributed the sinister quality of *Mary Rose* to the fact that 'one thinks more darkly down the left arm'.

200 *Blaikie*: W. B. Blaikie was responsible for printing and binding at Constable's.

225 *lustrum*: strictly a period of five years! Presumably Barrie could not resist inserting a deliberate mistake into the infant Peter's self-satisfied prose.

242 *Wilkinson (his master)*: Wilkinson was headmaster of the preparatory school attended by the Davies boys in London. The unfortunate man was demonized as 'Pilkington' in *The Little White Bird* and was incorporated into Captain Hook (especially in early versions, where Hook is not killed in the Never Land by the crocodile but reappears as a schoolmaster in London).

250 *Seton-Thompson*: Ernest Seton-Thompson (1860–1946), author of *Two Little Savages*. Lord Loam (*The Admirable Crichton*, Act 2) is unable to make fire by rubbing two sticks together, but Seton-Thompson successfully demonstrated the feat to Barrie and the Davies boys.

Reform Club: a London gentlemen's club, closely associated with the Liberal Party, to which Barrie was elected in 1894.

265 *Cocos nucifera*: botanical name for the Coconut Palm.

280 *the hour that best suited the camera*: the time when the light was best for taking photographs.

291 *letterpress*: the contents of an illustrated book apart from the illustrations themselves.

296 *our friend Captain Scott*: Captain R. F. Scott ('Scott of the Antarctic') was a friend of Barrie, and Peter Scott, the explorer's son, was Barrie's godson. The 'strange foreshadowing' refers to Scott's discovery, when his ill-fated party reached the South Pole in 1912, that the Norwegian explorer Amundsen had got there first. In later life, notes Andrew Birkin (*J. M. Barrie and the Lost Boys* (1979), 210), Barrie 'came to regard the explorer as another variation on the Peter Pan theme'.

312 *Psittacidae*: ornithological term for the parrots and closely related species such as lovebirds (Lat. *psittacus*, parrot).

319 *Athos*: one of Dumas's *Three Musketeers*.

326 *Captain Marryat*: Marryat was the author of *Snarleyyow or The Dog Fiend*, from which one of Hook's favourite oaths was derived (see below).

362 *that sly one, the chief figure*: i.e. Barrie himself. The comment is a revealing one. Its strange blend of self-effacement and intrusiveness, of the self-dismissive and the self-assertive, is characteristic of much in Barrie's dramatic practice, both in *Peter Pan* and generally. It is the root of much that is distinctive in his drama, and of the special significance in his case of approved published texts and stage-directions. See Introduction, pp. xvi–xviii.

368 *loyal nurse*: i.e. Mary Hodgson, long-serving nurse to the Davies family.

392 *Mr Crook's delightful music*: John Crook, the composer who was conductor of the orchestra of the Duke of York's Theatre, where *Peter Pan* was first performed. His original music became an integral part of the performance tradition of the play.

393 *a boy whom I favoured*: the boy concerned was Peter Scott.

401 *leading parts . . . youngest children*: this incident suggests much about the theatrical nature of the play and Barrie's attitude to it. On 20 February 1906, because Michael Llewelyn Davies was ill and could not see the London production, scenes from *Peter Pan* were transported to the Davies home in Berkhamsted and performed for him there. Peter Pan was played by Winifred Geoghegan and Mrs Darling by Phyllis Beadon, who were respectively Curly and Second Twin in the production proper. Wendy was played by the diminutive Ela Q. May (the first Liza), who was credited on the first London programme with the authorship of the play. Pauline Chase (Peter Pan 'himself') played the Twin. It is a splendid practical instance of Barrie's taste for satiric topsy-turveydom, which is generally evident in both his chosen themes and his theatrical technique.

421 *as only he and No. 1 could touch me*: Barrie's topsy-turveydom is sometimes satiric (and self-satiric) only in the darkest ways, as here. No. 4 and No. 1, Michael and George, were probably both dead when the Dedication was written (see note to Dedication, p. 307 above). The two were his favourites. There is something peculiarly savage here, in the self-reductive inversion 'End of a tragedian'.

444 *gillie*: servant to hunters, fishermen, etc., in the Scottish Highlands.

1.4 S.D. *Mr Roget*: Peter Roget was a Swiss doctor, the first draft of whose classic dictionary of synonyms, Roget's *Thesaurus*, was completed in 1806. R. D. S. Jack observes: 'One of the truly remarkable gaps in Barrie studies is the failure to see either how closely Roget's life paralleled Barrie's own or to relate Roget's thinking to *Peter Pan*.' For Jack's own discussion of the relationship, see *The Road to the Never Land*, 223–5.

24 S.D. *Never Land*: Peter Pan's island was called the Never, Never, Never Land in the first draft of the play, the Never Never Land in the play as performed (and also in *When Wendy Grew Up*), the Never Land in the play as published, and the Neverland in *Peter and Wendy*.

37 S.D. *pinched*: short of money.

55 S.D. *treasures*: valued servants.

66 S.D. *a most ordinary manner . . . naturalness must be her passion*: this could serve as a direction for the required acting style of the whole play. The language and behaviour of characters constantly involve extravagance and the striking of attitudes, but theatrical mannerisms and overplaying should not be superimposed on what the text itself demands. Rather, the actors should be constantly seeking to convey their sense that these many extravagances and oddities are perfectly natural ways of going about one's daily business.

71 S.D. *'The little less, and how much it is'*: this cryptic motto is Barrie's instruction for underplaying.

79 S.D. *tidying up their minds*: this unactable whimsy is one of the (relatively few) occasions when Barrie's extended stage directions for the published play entirely part company with the theatrical experience. (The passage derives from an unsuccessful section of *Peter and Wendy*.)

89 *we are playing at being you and father*: with the first child-speaker's first remark the play introduces its pattern of intricate role-playing, especially the interchange of pretences between child and adult, adult and child. Secure adulthood is (literally) a no-man's land in the play, though not a no-woman's land. (Mrs Darling is arguably the only adult, the only non-player, in the play.)

139 *A little less noise there*: compare with John's opening speech (1.90) and Peter in Act 4. The phrase is thus common to all three characters who play at fathers in the drama.

175 *his shadow*: Lancelyn Green cites an earlier instance of independent shadows, in Barrie's *Sentimental Tommy*: 'Twice they rushed home for hasty meals and were back so quickly that Tommy's shadow strained a muscle in turning with him' (*Fifty Years of 'Peter Pan'*, 33).

221 *Never mind, father*: another role-reversal, the son adopting fatherly tones for a parent who speaks and acts childishly. The male Darlings are equalized (in childishness) by the subsequent dialogue.

317 S.D. *The nursery darkens*: the technical demands of the play are considerable, and this is the first of many times when Barrie skilfully contrives moments of darkness both for Tinker Bell's appearances and for occasions when characters must be attached to or detached from their wires for flying.

322 *do show me*: after this line there is a lengthy pause, occupied by movement, before Wendy sits up and speaks to Peter. The stage effect of the play is largely achieved by such episodes of wordless movement and tableau, and not only the narrative element of the stage directions, but their precise indications of mood, enable Barrie to achieve in his printed text some of the impact he most sought for in the theatre.

336 *Wendy Moira Angela Darling*: the name 'Wendy' was Barrie's invention. It recalled Margaret Henley, daughter of the poet W. E. Henley, who had died at the age of 5. She had told Barrie that he was her 'friendy' but could not pronounce the letter 'r', and the word became 'fwendy'. 'Moira' is the name of the girl heroine of Barrie's *Little Mary*, a play contemporaneous with *Peter Pan*, and she is another of his 'little mother' figures. 'Angela' was taken from Angela du Maurier, daughter of Gerald du Maurier (the first Captain Hook), and a cousin of the Davies boys.

337 *Peter Pan*: 'Peter' was the third of the Davies boys, and 'Pan' is the goat-footed god of nature in Greek mythology. (All the Davies names were somehow included. Mr Darling is 'George', John is Jack, and Michael is two-in-one, being Michael Nicholas.)

351 *You mustn't touch me*: this line (and accompanying stage direction) was introduced by Barrie in the 1928 text, supposedly for Jean Forbes-Robertson, whom Lancelyn Green describes as 'the most eerie and unearthly of all Peters'. The revision has been generally regretted, though it is hard to see why. A Peter resistant to actual physical contact, always insulated from the mortal, is wholly in keeping with the role and gives ample opportunities for visually effective and meaningful 'close encounters' later in the play.

390 S.D. *gives him her thimble*: cf. *Peter Pan in Kensington Gardens* (the 'Peter Pan' chapters of Barrie's novel *The Little White Bird*), in which Peter and Maimie Mannering (who has erred grievously by staying in the Gardens after Lock-out Time) have the identical misunderstanding.

399 *I want always . . . have fun*: cf. 5.2.135. The child-adult Tommy Sandys, in Barrie's novel *Tommy and Grizel*, plots a story called 'The Wandering Child': 'It is but a reverie about a little boy who was lost. His parents find him in a wood singing joyfully to himself because he thinks he can now be a boy for ever; and he fears that if they catch him they will compel him to grow into a man, so he runs farther from them into the wood and is running still, singing to himself because he is always to be a boy' (*Tommy and Grizel*, 1900 edn., 399).

403 *they are nearly all dead now*: despite the naked appeal to audience feeling when Tink's life is at risk in Act 4, the note of deadpan ruthlessness which is struck here on the subject of death is more essentially characteristic of the play.

436 *You can't be my fairy . . . lady*: this introduces the recurrent theme of Peter's sexual ignorance and imperviousness, and the sexual feeling he arouses in others: a topic much more conspicuous in the play as first drafted and performed (see pp. xi–xii) but still important in the 1928 text.

444 *children who fall out of their prams*: this idea also is taken from *Peter Pan in Kensington Gardens* (where it is associated with death, the stones which mark parish boundaries being fancifully presented as the tombstones of lost children).

482 *a lovely story*: Peter's belief in the literal truth of stories is part of a general concern with the interplay between story and truth and the lack of fixed boundaries between them (so that Wendy in Act 4 narrates the 'truth' about the Darling home as if it were a story, and then constructs an imaginary story from it which accords with her preferred 'truth').

504 S.D. *strikes her colours*: surrenders.

513 S.D. *the maid Liza*: in the first production Liza was played by a child actress, Ela Q. May, who was advertised on the programme as 'author of the play'.

524 S.D. *strange things have been done to them*: i.e. they have been wired up for flying.

548 S.D. *Cave*: beware (Lat. *cavere*).

2.13 S.D. *out pictorially to greet Peter*: the stage direction here reflects the necessary stage effect of an imagined world stirring into life, as Peter and the children (and the audience) approach to quicken it. The shadowy movement of the opening moments of this scene is a theatrical image for imagination's permitted usurpation of reality.

28 S.D. *beached your coracle*: in *Peter Pan in Kensington Gardens* Peter 'did enter his coracle' for his first voyage to Kensington Gardens. His 'coracle' is actually a floating birds' nest, the Thrush's Nest, which has its own counterpart in the play in the Never Bird's nest which allows Peter to escape at the end of Act 3. Thus the vocabulary of Barrie's imaginary voyaging, as in this stage direction, is integral with the theatrical images through which he expressed it on the stage. (A coracle is a wickerwork boat covered with waterproof material.)

88 *a cheque book of my own*: an example of the social satire directed to the adult audience, and plainly incomprehensible to most children. Barrie uses adult voices speaking childishly to create social comedy for children, and children's voices speaking in naïvely adult terms to create social comedy for adults.

94 S.D. *mothers . . . piece of string*: as with death, so motherhood is variously given immense emotional force and treated dismissively as a mere instrument of childhood's heartless expediency. The stage direction is both a Barriesque external comment on the action, and a direction for actors, who must incorporate in the child characters' responses to motherhood this element of negligent and ruthless play.

98 S.D. *Execution Dock*: Execution Dock at Wapping in east London was the place of execution for pirates and others condemned to death by the Admiralty Court.

S.D. *pieces of eight*: Spanish dollars or pesos, valued at 8 reals.

S.D. *Cecco*: named after Cecco Hewlett, son of Barrie's friend, the novelist Maurice Hewlett; Cecco was another of the children Barrie met in Kensington Gardens.

S.D. *Gao*: the imaginary, atmospheric 'Gao' is in the original texts of both *Peter Pan* and *Peter and Wendy*, though reprints of the novel have sometimes emended it to 'Goa', a former Portuguese colony in India. The substitute has slight claims to plausibility: in R. L. Stevenson's *Treasure Island* Silver's parrot 'was at the boarding of the *Viceroy of the Indies* out of Goa'. But there is no real justification for such a change.

S.D. *Guidjo-mo*: a fictitious tropical river.

S.D. *Jukes . . . Flint*: i.e. Jukes received six dozen lashes. The *Walrus* is referred to in *Treasure Island* as 'Flint's old ship', but Jukes is not mentioned by name in the novel.

S.D. *Black Murphy . . . (Morgan's Skylights)*: both Murphy and Morgan were historical pirates.

s.d. *Smee*: Smee is traditionally played as an Irishman, the idea having come from the actor George Shelton, who first played the role. Shelton recalled in his autobiography how Barrie had said to himself and 'Starkey', 'I want you to individualise your two parts'. Shelton replied, 'I'll make an Irishman of mine'.

s.d. *blackavised*: dark-complexioned.

s.d. *prodding them along the plank*: i.e. making his victims 'walk the plank', a form of execution favoured by pirates and featured to bizarre, dancelike effect in Act 5.

s.d. *his public school*: i.e. Eton.

99 *Avast, belay*: Stop and make fast (nautical terms used for comic effect).

140 *odds, bobs, hammer and tongs*: Hook's favourite oath is taken from the sea ballad in Marryat's *Snarleyyow or The Dog Fiend*, ch. 9. A typical stanza ends: 'Odds, bobs, hammer and tongs, long as I've been to sea, | I've fought 'gainst every odds—and I've gained the victory.'

161 s.d. *of one thought compact*: with only one idea in its head.

s.d. *Piccaninny*: 'piccaninny' was the word widely used for the children of black peoples, including Australian aboriginals. Its use here links the Red Indians with children, though Barrie may have just liked the sound of the word.

s.d. *Great Big Little Panther*: Barrie borrowed the name from a character in Ernest Seton-Thompson's *Two Little Savages*.

165 s.d. *invokes Manitou*: 'The Indians (of the forest) believe that everything in Nature—beings, plants, stones, etc.—is inhabited by a mysterious power, which spreads out and influences other beings. The Iroquois call it "Orenda" and the Algonquins "Manitou", and mean by it all magical powers or "medicines" from the lowest to the highest ... According to the Algonquins of the North, the most powerful of all the Manitous is the Kitchki Manitou, the Great Spirit, who is the father of life and was never created ... And it is in his honour that the Indians "smoke the Pipe of Peace" ' (*Larousse Encyclopedia of Mythology* (1959) 436).

174 *look at them through his legs*: the efficacy of this fearsome trick was a cliché of travellers' tales; it provides a fine opportunity for Barrie to produce a mixed stage effect of danger and ridiculous physical comedy.

213 *Omnes*: all.

233 *Wendy is dead*: Peter's line is calculated to produce a very precise effect: '(*He is not so much pained as puzzled*).' Peter does not understand death any more than he understands sex, but the paradoxical quality of brutal innocence in his reaction enables Barrie to present an extreme instance of the 'heartlessness' which the children generally show towards adult emotional investments and priorities.

238 *Oh dastard hand!*: the melodramatic archaic language (and the anticlimax which follows it) are only funny if played seriously, with no overlay of satire on the actors' part.

272 *build a house around her!*: the house, one of Barrie's most spectacular stage effects, is derived from an incident in *Peter Pan in Kensington Gardens* in which the fairies build a house round Maimie Mannering to protect her from the cold.

294 *fetch a doctor*: this incident was not included in the first version of the play. It derives from an episode in the children's play *Bluebell in Fairyland* by Seymour Hicks, a work which Barrie admired and which is reputed to have given him the idea of writing a fairy play for children.

308 *beef tea*: liquid extract of beef, served to invalids.

322 S.D. *In the time she sings this and two other verses*: Wendy's song fills the time gap while the house is going up. Barrie seems to have affected total lack of interest in it. Describing the first version of the play (1903-4), Lancelyn Green notes: 'There is no pirate song—nor are any words given for Wendy and the Lost Boys to sing while the house is being built, though the stage directions give the outline of the song, adding that it will be written when it is discovered how long it takes to build the house' (*Fifty Years of 'Peter Pan'*, 46-7). The full version is, however, included with John Crook's music for the play, published by W. Paxton and Co. Ltd. in 1905, as follows:

WENDY	I wish I had a darling house
	The littlest ever seen,
	With funny little red walls
	And roof of mossy green.
BOYS	With funny little red walls
	And roof of mossy green.
	(Music)
BOYS	We've built the little walls and roof
	And made a lovely door,
	So tell us Mother Wendy,
	What are you wanting more?
WENDY	Oh! really next I think I'd have
	Gay windows all about—
	With roses peeping in, you know,
	And babies peeping out.
BOYS	We've made the roses peeping in,
	The babes are at the door,—
	We cannot make ourselves you know,
	'Cos we've been made before.

(Barrie excised the pun in line 1 from the printed text.)

316

341 *be our mother!*: on stage the melodramatic tableau of this affecting moment ('kneeling, with outstretched arms') physically represents the histrionic falsity which Barrie discerns, and records with cynical humour in the stage direction. ('Now that they know it is pretend . . . '). Exaggerated theatrical expression in Barrie is often the language of his subversive and sceptical detachment.

3.0 *(title) The Mermaids' Lagoon*: this Act was added to the play in its second season. The previous year the play had been in three Acts only, and the scene change from the arrival in Never Land to 'The Home Under the Ground' had occurred in the middle of Act 2. Because the change of set was complicated, it necessitated a 'front-cloth scene' to fill the gap. The 'front-cloth' was a painted scene (in this case of the Redskins' Camp) which provided the backdrop for a front-of-stage scene while masking the main stage area where the change of set was taking place. The front-cloth scene in the first season opened with some peace negotiations between the Lost Boys and the Redskins, and then switched to Hook's entry, carried by the pirates, in a sedan chair called 'Davy Jones's Locker'. Using the sedan chair to conceal a series of disappearances down a stage trap-door, Hook made several re-entries in the guise of various popular actors of the day—Henry Irving, Beerbohm Tree, and Martin Harvey. This elaborate theatrical joke was not appreciated by the critics, and it was dropped for good when the additional Act was introduced.

34 S.D. *before the words . . . meet below*: i.e. Peter reacts to the pirates' approach before the sound of their singing is heard.

35 *Luff, you spalpeen*: bring her into the wind, you rascal ('spalpeen' is Irish slang for a coin of little value).

37 S.D. *To one of her race . . . enough*: this unplayable stage direction, in terms of its specific incommunicable content, is nevertheless both a satiric elaboration by Barrie of the conventions he is using, and a basic instruction to the actress on the dignified impassiveness she must convey by underplaying.

50 S.D. *even the author . . . really Hook*: a subtle piece of interventionist self-characterization on Barrie's part. He feigns to be surprised by intuitions of likeness between Peter and Hook, while actually giving a series of opportunities for their kinship to be powerfully suggested on the stage (e.g. in the 'twinning' of the two characters on Marooners' Rock).

69 *What is a mother?*: the mixture of pathos and absurdity in Smee is summed up in his asking of this question (to which, in fact, no male character in the play is shown to know the answer).

87 *bullies*: mates, friends.

147 S.D. *pinked*: pierced slightly with a sword (cf. *What Every Woman Knows* 4.116).

S.D. *Courteously he waits . . . unfairness is what he never can get used to*: again the stage direction glosses with precision an instruction for performance: Peter combines archaic gestures and attitudes of chivalry with an everyday boyhood morality in which life is a game and 'fairness' is the central moral term.

179 *To die . . . adventure*: in their walks in Kensington Gardens Barrie told the Davies children about the guidance offered by Peter Pan to the dead children whose tombs were supposedly there. Andrew Birkin notes: 'Their initial destiny was some unspecified after-life, later developed into the Never Never Land—a child's paradise, haven of the Lost Boys, abounding in pleasures designed to gratify a boy's appetite for blood. Such visions of delight led George to make the not unnatural declaration, "To die will be an awfully big adventure" ' (*J. M. Barrie and the Lost Boys*, 69).

S.D. *The nest . . . upwards*: when the new Act was first produced in December 1905 Peter drove the bird (a pelican, not the Never Bird) from its nest, and repelled it when it attacked him. This upset the reviewers, and the present episode was substituted for the following season.

4.1.50 S.D. *tappa rolls . . . mammee apples . . . calabashes of poe-poe*: tappa rolls are not edible: they are rolls of unwoven cloth made by Polynesian natives from the Paper Mulberry tree. Mammee apples are the fruit of the Mammee tree of tropical America. Calabashes of poe-poe are gourds containing the Hawaiian food called *poi*, or *poë*. *OED* quotes W. Ellis, *Tour through Hawaii* (1826): 'The house . . . was soon furnished . . . a few calabashes for water and poë'.

55 S.D. *pretend meals . . . gusto*: this whole episode exemplifies the play's various performance opportunities, and indeed requirements, for proficient mime.

111 S.D. '*John Anderson, my Jo*': a song by Robert Burns (1759–96) which idealizes marriage in old age ('jo' is Scots for 'sweetheart').

113 *It is only pretend . . . father?*: between Wendy (the child as proto-adult) and Peter (the child as pretend-adult) a disorientating effect emerges because of their differing modes of child imagination: the disturbing consequence is that forms of dependable truthfulness seem endlessly and saddeningly elusive. The mixture of sexual comedy and tensely exposed innocence can only be achieved if the lines are delivered with sincere earnestness. Barrie's comic fantasy is only theatrically reachable by means of naturalism in the playing.

166 S.D. *The heartless ones*: the quality of amused truthfulness in the stage directions reflects Barrie's endemic neutrality of stance towards childhood and adulthood: belonging to both, and to neither, he is peculiarly able to keep switching sides (like Peter) and present each phase of life disconcertingly from the perspective of the other. The 'tragic' element of the play is present here, however; no feeling which is shown to be

precious to either phase of life is also shown as safe. Thus, the children here depicted as gleefully treacherous will shortly be shown as fearful when they confront the possibility that they too may be betrayed. *Peter Pan*, to achieve these effects, asks for great elasticity and subtlety of playing, often from very young players.

189 *then I flew back*: this incident is drawn from *Peter Pan in Kensington Gardens*.

199 *half-mourning*: in the days of formal mourning, 'half-mourning' was the second stage, in which muted colours such as lavender could be worn to relieve full black.

224 *first Thursdays*: i.e. the first Thursday of the month. This was the date of Mrs Darling's 'At Home', an occasion when her friends in society could call during the afternoon without prior invitation.

239 *like your mothers*: this line is a left-over reference (surviving by dint of its generality) to the 'Beautiful Mothers' scene which was generally felt to be extremely embarrassing and was cut during the play's first run (see Introduction, p. xiii).

S.D. *in mute appeal*: another tableau, combining melodrama with absurdity.

S.D. *Barbicue*: 'Barbecue' was the crew's name for Long John Silver in Stevenson's *Treasure Island*.

S.D. *Alf Mason . . . Chay Turley*: these names did not form part of the original play or production cast-list, but were added by Barrie to decorate the printed text. 'Alf Mason' is Barrie's friend, the novelist A. E. W. Mason; 'Canary Robb' is his childhood friend James Robb (who had recently given him a canary); and Chay Turley is Charles Turley Smith, a writer of school stories.

248 *flannels*: underclothing made of flannel.

278 *If you believe, clap your hands*: the perils of technical disaster here form the climax of Beryl Bainbridge's novel, *An Awfully Big Adventure* (1989), in which a performance of *Peter Pan* is being watched by children from an orphanage. The heroine, Stella, is 'operating Tinker Bell' with a torch: 'Stella dropped the torch and let it roll into the wings as the children brought their palms together to save Tinkerbell. The light swished from the back-cloth. For a moment the clapping continued, rose in volume, then died raggedly away, replaced by a tumult of weeping' (p. 192).

281 S.D. *grig*: grasshopper or cricket.

5.1.6 S.D. *The stage directions . . . Call Hook*: Barrie here includes technical directions for lighting staff, stage-manager, and call-boy, prior to the opening of the scene: theatre jargon is humorously offset against the atmospheric description of the stage effect which follows. Most of the terms concern lighting. The dominant colour is amber, which bathes the pirate ship in a lurid light. The circuit (path from power source to light, via a dimmer) is 'checked' (reduced) to 80 per cent of its power. 'Battens' are lengths of overhead lighting, also reduced in brilliance. 'Perches' are lighting positions, commonly on platforms, on both sides of the stage. The 'prompt' side (where the prompter sits) is stage left—i.e. the left side of the stage as the actor faces the audience. O.P. (or 'opposite prompt') is therefore stage right. A 'flood' is an instrument which controls the spread of light. Arc-lights are positioned to give fixed light on the 'back cloth' or painted scene at the back of the stage. With everything in readiness, the call-boy is instructed to 'call' the actor playing Hook from his dressing-room.

12 S.D. *Mullins*: Darby Mullins, a protégé of Captain Kidd, was hanged at Execution Dock in 1701.

29 S.D. *Long Tom*: Long Tom is the pirates' big gun, which in *Peter and Wendy* is fired at Peter and the Darling children as they fly to the Neverland (ch. 4).

32 *How still the night is*: Lancelyn Green notes: 'At the beginning of the first run Hook had no soliloquy . . . During the run of the play, however, some lines must have been written and inserted and with them Smee's business of tearing the calico . . . Hook's soliloquy continued to grow and develop for some years, even though the rest of the text had achieved almost completely the final wording in use today by the 1905 revival' *Fifty Years of 'Peter Pan'*, 106).

40 *disky*: mischievous, trick-playing.

46 *No little children love me*: Lancelyn Green notes: 'Miss Pauline Chase records (in 1909) that this speech usually produced shouts of "Serve you right!" but also the little girl who remarked loudly when Hook was poisoning Peter's medicine: "I do love that man!" ' (*Fifty Years of 'Peter Pan'*, 114).

77 *Stow this gab*: cease this line of conversation.

85 *King George*: Edward VII was king when the play was first produced in 1904, but George V had succeeded him by the time it was first published.

99 S.D. *Whibbles of the eye patch*: the practical function of this pirate was to detach Peter from his flying wire. Having done his duty, he is thrown overboard. In the 1928 text the character was named after the critic Charles Whibley. Barrie's joke in making Peter's first victim a critic is akin to that of Samuel Beckett, who in *Waiting for Godot* makes 'Critic' the ultimate destructor in a duel of insults.

112 *a touch of the cat*: a flogging with the cat o' nine tails (a vicious nine-thonged whip).

126 S.D. *livid*: leaden-faced.

137 *'Sdeath*: an oath, short for 'God's death'.

145 *I'll swing*: 'I'll be hanged'.

156 *one aboard*: i.e. the devil.

165 S.D. *listen, with arms outstretched*: another still-life tableau, melodramatic in physical portraiture and comic-satirical in effect (especially as it is maintained throughout the children's stealthy movement which releases Wendy).

168 *Jonah*: as in the story of Jonah and the whale. (See Jonah 1: 4–15.)

188 S.D. *buckler*: a small, round shield.

190 S.D. *They measure swords . . . hilts*: this pattern of symmetrical movement, like their earlier symmetrical attitude on Marooner's Rock and their identity of speech, reinforces the undercurrent of suggestion that Hook and Peter are two sides of the same person. See also the final stage direction in this scene.

194 S.D. *quietus*: release from life.

206 *pewling*: R. D. S. Jack notes: ' "Pewling" evokes the cynicism of Jacques in *As You Like It*. In the first of his seven ages of man, that cynic cites the infant "mewling and puking in the nurse's arms". Barrie's coinage combines the two participles' (*The Road to the Never Land*, 234).

207 *road to dusty death*: see *Macbeth* 5.5.23.

208 S.D. *Peter appears with a smoking bomb*: Peter's disappearance on this errand enables the flying-wire to be reattached, so that he can sit in mid-air playing his pipe.

Floreat Etona: Hook's Etonian connections were added to the story for the prose version, *Peter and Wendy*, which was first published in 1911 while the Davies boys were successively going through the school. This line is the school's one major embellishment of the play.

S.D. *The curtain rises*: before the curtain rises it must first fall, as it did immediately after Hook's leap from the ship. In his eagerness to rescue his much-loved Napoleon tableau for the printed text, Barrie overlooked the need for his stage directions to make this clear.

S.D. *Peter a very Napoleon on his ship*: the original production included a tableau which showed Peter posing as Napoleon on the *Bellerophon*, as in a famous painting by Orchardson. The tableau was not liked by the critics, but Barrie clearly remained obstinately fond of it. The brief scene remained in performances for several years, and was retained (or revived, rather) for the 1928 text.

5.2. *Scene 2*: before this scene there is in performance a front-cloth scene which enables the set to be changed. This scene, known as 'Oh miserable Starkey', shows the captive pirate playing his concertina and singing gloomily, changing his words to happy ones only when told he will be scalped if he doesn't. Barrie would never allow the scene to be published, and he is said to have quickly improvised it in the theatre when the need for it became apparent. It is a form of dramatic cadenza which allows great opportunities for inventive actors. However, Barrie's sense of its extraneous nature persists into his 1928 text.

52 S.D. *the sad song of Margaret*: most probably one of the several versions of the ballad 'Fair Margaret and Sweet William', though the ballad of 'Lord Douglas' is also a possibility.

108 *they never come, they never come!*: Barrie characteristically invests his scene with an undercutting sardonic melodrama at the very moment of its supposedly greatest poignancy.

S.D. *The scene changes*: the front-cloth scene which follows allows the main set to be changed for the final Tree Tops scene. The mothering of Slightly by Liza is the one surviving remnant of the otherwise misguided and embarrassing 'Beautiful Mothers' scene (see Introduction, p. xiii.)

135 S.D. *So perhaps he thinks . . . pretend*: in the sustained emotional ambiguity of the play about its contrary time-scheme of life and imagination, time and eternity, home and Never Land, this stage direction is the nearest it comes to a choice and verdict. The degree to which actors and directors decide to press it home will determine the audience's awareness or otherwise of Peter as the 'tragic boy'.

151 S.D. *gripping her for ever*: again, this stage direction is important: for Wendy it is the decisive moment, but the wording is tonally ambiguous, and so should the acting be.

164 S.D. *Mrs Darling closes and bars the window*: in *Peter Pan in Kensington Gardens* Barrie wrote 'there is no second chance, not for most of us. When we reach the window it is Lock-out Time. The iron bars are up for life.' At this moment in *Peter Pan* there is no longer any second chance, to go either in or out. The play is thematically continuous here with Barrie's other work, especially *Dear Brutus*.

When Wendy Grew Up: An Afterthought

See the Introduction, p. vii. This scene was performed once only in Barrie's lifetime, on 22 February 1908. It followed on from the front-cloth scene which ends with the window barred, and was in turn followed by the closing tableau of Tree Tops. This required a long unscheduled interval, since there was of course no front-cloth scene to occupy the time required to reset the stage. However, the scene does itself represent an alternative ending, which can replace the Tree Tops closing scene. The Royal Shakespeare Company has successfully played it in this way, and it seems likely to be generally adopted as the play's most satisfying finale.

1.1 S.D. *Lights in*: i.e. the lamps have been brought in and lit.

S.D. *comes straight to audience, points out to them*: in the most direct, economical, unfussed way possible, Wendy's wordless action signals to the audience the passage of time and her change of status. However, the element of comedy in her complacent adulthood prepares the audience to switch its allegiance for this scene from her to Jane.

120 *Slightly . . . became a lord*: this is Barrie's fun at the expense of the British peerage and its sexist irrationalities. A woman who marries a lord becomes a lady, but a man who marries a lady (i.e. a peeress) does not become a lord.

132 *So did I, mother*: cf. Curly in 4.155 when told that the children flew to the Never Land. Children's ability to convert known fact into speculation and suspense, to replay autobiography as story, is a theme with variations in *Peter Pan*, and is important to its success as children's theatre.

211 S.D. *she lets her hand play with his hair*: there is no question in this 1908 text of Peter's refusing to be touched. But his physical withdrawal when confronted by real and perplexing emotion ('*he shrinks back*') anticipates the later refinement of his physical immunity.

235 S.D. *The lamp flickers*: again scenes of semi-darkness are contrived for flying and the attachment of the flying wires.

258 *so long as children are young and innocent*: the equivalent closing phrase in *Peter and Wendy* is 'gay and innocent and heartless'.

What Every Woman Knows

1.1 S.D. *dambrod*: draught-board.

20 S.D. *merino*: a dress made of merino wool (merino is a Spanish breed of sheep).

22 S.D. *dustcloths*: Barrie's social registration is very precise. The drawing-room is the 'front room' of both Scottish and English working-class and lower middle-class households, containing the best furniture and, except on special occasions, protected from damage by actual use.

24 S.D. *dickey*: a detached shirt-front.

45 S.D. *with a dump*: flopping heavily.

62 S.D. *Contemporary Review*: the *Contemporary Review* was a serious-minded journal in which Barrie himself published a series of critical articles, including pieces on George Meredith, S. Baring-Gould, and Kipling. It is characteristic of Barrie's indirect and mischievous self-mockery—much in evidence in this play—to cite one of his own writing outlets as an example of intimidating self-improvement.

75 S.D. *snell mornings*: bitingly cold mornings.

83 S.D. *in front*: in the audience. Although this comment is clearly addressed to the reader rather than the actor, it neatly exemplifies Barrie's practice in the stage directions for his library editions, which is not to discard but to extend the theatrical experience, to 'freeze-frame' the imagined performance, and to verbalize the hoped-for nuances of playing.

100 S.D. *'lastic sides*: elastic-sided boots.

107 S.D. *wag-at-the-wall clock*: more commonly 'wag-on-the-wall clock'; a design of clock originating in the Black Forest of Germany, with the workings exposed and a short pendulum.

112 *Oh, let the solid ground . . . so sweet*: the verse is from Tennyson's 'Maud', i. 398–401.

121 S.D. *soirée*: evening party.

S.D. *too canny*: too shrewd. James knows that to be alone with a lady places one in instant danger of betrothal.

127 *a kind of a shave*: a close thing.

152 *Galashiels*: a town on the Scottish Borders, near Selkirk.

165 *worked*: embroidered.

170 *Whisht!*: Be quiet!

185 *would make a speech*: was determined to make a speech.

202 *sacket*: 'a pert, impudent person' (*Scottish National Dictionary* (*SND*)).

203 *the want of education*: the lack of education. The high value traditionally placed on education in Scotland is both satirized and implicitly endorsed throughout the play.

213 *brose*: 'A dish made by mixing boiling water or milk with oatmeal or peasemeal, and adding salt and butter' (*SND*).

228 *charm*: sexual attractiveness.

230 *Havering*: talking foolishly.

239 *Ha'e*: here you are.

252 *All of you unsleepy*: the pattern of the 'political' phase of the play is foreshadowed in the opening domestic comedy: a characteristic male behaviour-pattern of ingenuous worldliness, pride, and responsibility is seen by the women for what it is, and treated with affectionate deviousness by them. (But as we realize that Maggie, though lacking charm, is better at this than other women are, we are 'getting near her comedy'.)

283 *carpet bag*: 'a travelling bag, properly one made of carpet' (*OED*).

295 *watch*: wait up.

306 S.D. *incandescent light*: electric light.

310 S.D. *without lifting that piece of coal off the fire*: domestic economy required that unconsumed coal should not be left to burn wastefully after bedtime. Shand's puzzlement here, as indicated by the stage direction,

is virtually unactable, but it exemplifies the habit of watchful social appraisal which is intrinsic to the play's comedy.

S.D. *cockerty bonnet*: 'A boat-shaped cap (the points before and behind) of thick cloth with two ribbons hanging loose behind, the ancestor of the modern Glengarry' (*SND*).

S.D. *His movements . . . staring at him*: the businesslike effrontery of Shand's movements would spring an effective dramatic surprise even if it were supposedly unobserved, but the effect is all the greater because the audience is aware of unseen indignant watchers. The staging of watchfulness is one of Barrie's great strengths, and his elaborations of it for the audience-in-the-book are a natural extension of the theatrical experience.

311 S.D. *hints back*: starts back, draws back with a quick movement. (*SND* cites Barrie, *Margaret Ogilvy*: 'His lithe figure rose and fell as he cast and hinted back from the crystal waters.')

315 *Ticket, please . . . chair comfortable*: each comment combines an estimably restrained touch of indignant malice with nuances of social placement.

320 *Canny, canny*: shrewd. The sheer nerve of Shand's social belligerence in adversity attracts James's admiration in spite of himself.

323 *billie*: fellow (familiar and insulting).

342 *siller*: a question of money ('silver').

349 *Romulus and Remus*: the twins Romulus and Remus were the mythical founders of Rome. Cast out at birth by a wicked great-uncle, they were raised by a she-wolf, and later established the city on the site of their miraculous upbringing. With this contrived allusion to the story, Shand defiantly asserts his status as a classical scholar.

350 *Havers*: what foolish talk.

359 *sit under*: to 'sit under' is to accept the religious authority of a minister. The minister who is the narrator of Barrie's 'Farewell, Miss Julie Logan' reports that his friend Dr John 'sits under Mr Watery, with whom I sometimes niffer [exchange] pulpits'.

371 *maggot . . . in their heads*: bee in their bonnets. (A 'maggot' is a whimsical idea or fancy.)

378 S.D. *chiffy*: i.e. chiffonier, 'a piece of furniture consisting of a small cupboard with the top made so as to form a sideboard' (*OED*).

379 *totaller*: a total abstainer from alcohol, more usually 'teetotaller'. David briskly accepts the pleasant convenience of being 'practically' a teetotaller.

419 *grow a beard*: Maggie is sensitive to the difference in their ages, not insulting about John's appearance.

448 *She's tremendous . . . in a nutshell*: Barrie neatly juxtaposes the comedy of inept lying (James) and the comedy of imprudent candour (David), and

prepares the way for John to show similar comic ineptitudes in more emotionally trying situations later.

466 *went among the English*: the comedy of the Scots 'among the English', a repeated source of self-observing mockery for Barrie, is here introduced. Ostensibly the Scots are innocents abroad, victims of their naïve confidence at the hands of the sophisticated English (and French), but the effect of Barrie's presence in his own dramatic narrative, his control of moments of satiric revelation, is to equalize the national contest and give the dramatist himself a casting vote. (See Introduction, pp. xviii–xx).

508 S.D. *toddy*: whisky (or some other spirit) with hot water and sugar.

515 *better have a legal document*: Maggie is already aligned with John, not with the family voices of honour and romance. (And they say she has no charm!)

520 *if it's not convenient to you*: if you don't have the money readily available.

526 *stepping*: getting on my way.

529 *any orra time*: any spare time when he is not otherwise occupied.

533 *You had better put it twice round*: the stage action encapsulates Maggie's instant assumption of wifely solicitude.

536 *cry in*: call in.

557 *What is it with you . . . I'm ten forty-two*: 'What time do you make it, father?' 'My watch says it's ten forty-two.'

577 *I wonder how some clever writer . . . a whole book about them*: or a whole play! Barrie is again on stage, disingenuously self-linked to the ingenuous James.

2.1.7 S.D. *broadcloth but ill-fitting*: John's career development is precisely signalled by gradual sartorial improvements. Broadcloth is plain-woven black cloth of fine quality.

30 S.D. *teetotum*: a spinning-top.

31 S.D. *determination*: humorous use of the sense recorded in *OED*: 'A tendency or flow of the bodily fluids, now *esp*. of the blood, to a particular part.'

60 *Did you say you had lost, John?*: our attention is skilfully guided to Maggie's world of private stress by a moment of stillness and by the embarrassed apprehension of Alick and David. Maggie's status in the play is repeatedly indicated by episodes when she is insulated from the surrounding action, watching or being watched.

64 S.D. *scrimmage*: confused struggle.

S.D. *a five guinea suit*: this was no small sum for a young man to spend at the turn of the century, and again marks John's advancement.

75 *pump some oxygen into me*: David administers a throat-spray.

89 *This is the House of Commons . . . admiring applause*: Maggie's vision again insulates her from the surrounding action. Her speech is made up of

predictions, accurately borne out by the play, of the particular relationship between herself and John and the general relationship between political man and his wife. It is made up of pride and self-denigration, possessiveness and exclusion, role-play and role-acceptance, public spectatorship and behind-the-scenes alliance. The speech is Maggie's miniature play-within-a-play. It establishes her near-monopoly of conscious humour, provides a neat bridge from domestic to political comedy, and anticipates many of the play's later preoccupations. The *Ladies' Gallery* was that part of the spectators' accommodation overlooking the House of Commons which was reserved for ladies. It was (and is) strictly forbidden for spectators to make any interjections during House of Commons proceedings.

101 *Mon cher Jean . . . un interprète?*: 'My dear John, let me speak in French. Would you like an interpreter?'

103 *Je suis . . . frères écossais*: 'I am the French sister of my two Scottish brothers.'

108 *Mrs John Shand*: Shand's reaction to this proprietorial self-naming is likely to be one of discomfiture.

113 *I'm doubting . . . sit on you*: 'I suspect the baronet would snub you.'

122 *swells*: important people.

129 *a whip and an Honourable*: a whip is an MP responsible for ensuring that members of his party turn up to vote in parliamentary divisions; 'the Honourable' is the title carried by the child of a peer.

145 *prove you*: put you to the test.

156 S.D. *undulate*: sway gracefully from person to person.

S.D. *like a stately ship of Tarsus*: see Milton, *Samson Agonistes*, ll. 710–15:

> 'But who is this, what thing of Sea or Land?
> Female of sex it seems,
> That so bedeckt, ornate and gay,
> Comes this way sailing
> Like a stately Ship
> Of Tarsus . . .'

The Chorus is describing the arrival of Delilah, and Barrie's stage direction is an ironic hint of Lady Sybil's future role.

171 *J'espère . . . Je connais*: [Maggie]: 'I hope that you find this meeting interesting?' [Comtesse]: 'You speak French? But how charming! So, let us have a little talk. Tell me all about this great man, and all the marvellous things he has done.' [Maggie]: 'I—I—I know . . .'

188 S.D. *a weighing-chair*: a form of weighing machine. The 'hairdresser's emporium' serves a more general function as a beauty parlour.

191 *picked up the pin*: the 'pin' is the small and accidental piece of good fortune which comes to every so-called 'self-made man' at the start of

his career, and makes all the difference between success and failure. It does not take the Comtesse long to identify John Shand's 'pin'. At the height of the marital crisis in Act 4, she twice addresses Maggie as 'Miss Pin' (see 4.103 and 108).

225 *a Scotsman on the make*: the character David means this seriously, but the play means it humorously, and the dramatist's voice intrudes upon the character's in delighted self-mockery.

253 *Mary Queen of Scots . . . Bothwell*: Bothwell became the third husband of Mary, Queen of Scots, after the murder of her second husband, Lord Darnley.

271 *they marry young*: Sybil presumably means men of lowly origins, rather than Scotsmen or MPs.

282 *I don't think much of her*: Maggie again objectively dramatizes herself, briefly usurping the dramatist's stance with an almost indistinguishable blend of amusement and self-hurt.

346 *Ah, our hero! . . . Maggie, the ladies are going*: after giving an objective account of herself, Maggie is silent throughout John's exchange with Sybil. Her observational detachment from the others, like her previous self-caricature, is composed from both humour and pain, neat contrivance and vulnerability. The actress has scope for many shades of response.

347 *Are you, then, the Maggie?*: at this point the Uniform Edition of Barrie's plays (1923) abandons speech-prefixes and switches to novelized dialogue, whilst continuing to use stage directions. It is the first of several passages in that edition to do so.

376 *besom*: contemptuous term for a woman of low character.

401 *I would let you off*: Maggie is brought to this unlikely concession by the preceding dialogue, during which John affirms his good faith with a sequence of hurtful bathos ('it's your due'; 'your brothers would insist'; 'Three hundred pounds'; 'respect'; 'a bargain's a bargain'). Every one of these well-meant insensitivities gives the actress opportunities for registering her special form of valour. Yet the exchange is crossed with laughter, precisely because of Shand's emotional idiocy.

415 *Not in Scotsmen*: again the double voice, sincere in the character and satirical in the (only partially concealed) Scots dramatist.

442 *shoon*: shoes (Scottish).

474 *What beats me . . . operation*: here Barrie overplays his hand, and gives his character too imbecile a literalism for the sake of the satiric glance at Scotland.

502 *womanliness*: Maggie exemplifies the ideal of independent femaleness far better than she understands it.

506 *the Pans*: Prestonpans, near Edinburgh.

524 *Give . . . licks*: lit. 'give them a thrashing', hence 'get the better of them'.

536 S.D. *Canute*: the king who commanded the tide to cease advancing, the better to instruct his courtiers on the bounds of kingly power.

552 *My Constituents!*: at the 1906 General Election Barrie followed the electoral fortunes of his friend A. E. W. Mason, who was Liberal candidate for Coventry. In the Liberal landslide Mason gained this safe Conservative seat with a majority of 192, but in the moment of triumph unfortunately lost his voice. Making one last effort to address his electors, he cried: 'My constituents!'

3.1.37 S.D. *the strange days . . . have minds*: *What Every Woman Knows* was first performed in 1908 and first published in 1918. It was a decade of substantial progress for women's rights. Although the Women's Social and Political Union was active in 1908, the years of the Suffragette movement were still to come, after which women played a key role in the First World War. Women over 30 were given the vote for the first time in 1918. The years between stage and print were the years of the gender revolution which the play deals with. If the stage direction is a slightly complacent social comment, Barrie had every excuse for it.

44 S.D. *the woman question*: the play adroitly separates the realities of 'the woman question' (which face Maggie) from the fashionable clichés of political debate.

59 *Tempus fugit*: (Lat.) time flies.

66 *an equal right with men to grow beards*: Barrie scoffs *through* the Countess at the absurdity of egalitarian extremes, but scoffs *at* her for her witty determination to miss the point.

85 *division*: a vote at the end of a parliamentary debate.

108 S.D. *This is evidently . . . admit the visitor*: both public and private politics here take place 'behind closed doors', and Barrie neatly stages the difference between the two.

125 S.D. *sedan chair*: 'a closed vehicle to seat one person, borne on two poles by two bearers, one in front and one behind' (*OED*).

138 *Bosphorus*: the strait joining the Black Sea and the Sea of Marmara. Istanbul lies on its western shore.

140 *Golden Horn*: inlet of the Bosphorus, and the harbour for Istanbul.

141 *caique*: a light rowing-boat or skiff, 'much used on the Bosphorus' (*OED*).

143 *Leander . . . Hero of the Lamp*: Leander swam the Hellespont each night from his home in Abydos to visit his lover Hero, a priestess in the temple of Aphrodite at Sestos. To guide him on his swim Hero held up a torch at the top of the tower where she tended Aphrodite's swans and sparrows. On one night of storm the beacon was extinguished and Leander drowned.

156 *Wiesbaden . . . Homburg*: spa towns in Germany, both near Frankfurt. Moira Loney in Barrie's *Little Mary* observes that in England the best people 'have to go to Homburg and such like places once a year, to be washed out and scraped down'.

166 *he is here for some crafty purpose*: in the following dialogue the Countess is Barrie's 'stand-in', the amused audience for Venables's devious enquiries and Maggie's (seemingly) naïve replies.

189 *session*: the parliamentary year, extending from October or November to July.

258 *And I don't care . . . Government*: this is the moment when Maggie's interventionist role in Shand's career is first publicly exposed, but the playing of the role must prepare the ground for it. The actress playing Maggie has to reveal a combination of personal diffidence with instinctive tactical assurance. Maggie is at once the naïve Scot among the sophisticated English, and the skilled political wife who intuitively understands the power game better than her husband does.

268 *hedge*: equivocate.

310 *excommunicate*: withdraw political favour.

338 *Scotch*: again the Countess is the informed spectator, and from her (and the audience's) position of superior knowledge she uses the word 'Scotch' in a quite different, approving sense from that which Venables intends. In his handling of this dialogue Barrie is (characteristically) both satirizing and celebrating Scotland.

342 *took the horse out of my brougham*: a brougham was a closed horse-drawn carriage. The reference is to the minor acts of civil disorder by which supporters of the women's suffrage movement sought to gain publicity for their cause.

3.2 S.D. *Cupid's flail*: the classical god of love is given an alternative weapon to his usual arrows.

20 *Find her yourself, Comtesse*: evidently John has been emulating Maggie in learning some basic French.

53 S.D. *corduroy*: the material which John wore in his railway-portering days.

106 *take you*: understand the hint.

112 *Tobermory*: a town on the Scottish island of Mull.

124 S.D. *lifting the gage*: accepting the challenge, like a medieval knight picking up the gauntlet thrown down by an adversary.

158 S.D. *lowering*: frowning suspiciously.

211 *There's not one of you could knock John down*: again Barrie causes Maggie to express loyal allegiance to John at a moment when he seems neither to desire nor deserve it. This repeated feature of their particular relationship is one from which the play invites us to generalize, applying it to the norms of relationship between man and woman.

224 S.D. *but we don't hear her*: in an older dramatic tradition this would have been an 'aside', addressed to the audience. As it is, Maggie is speaking to herself, and the audience finds itself momentarily eavesdropping on her private feelings. In this way we are made aware of the gap in attitudes between herself and her male protectors, who certainly 'don't hear her'.

270 S.D. *little old woman who lived in a shoe*: if Maggie is to emulate this nursery-rhyme character, it bodes ill for John and Sybil, for the old woman: 'gave them some broth without any bread; | She whipped them all soundly and sent them to bed.'

291 *rises*: adjourns.

373 *Maggie . . . generous woman*: the situation, now a familiar one, is that of a gullible audience on stage providing amusement for an informed one in the theatre. The stage directions, however much designed to guide a reader rather than a player, are wholly in accord with the appropriate acting style and purposed dramatic effect.

4.7 S.D. *in négligé*: nowadays this would be 'in your dressing-gown'; the term here includes both men and women.

8 S.D. *get the note*: imitate the sound.

20 S.D. *knickerbockers*: loose-fitting breeches gathered in at the knee.

24 S.D. *Sassenach*: Scottish word for 'Englishman' (the Gaelic form of 'Saxon').

91 *'By your leave'*: railway porter's cry as he carries the luggage.

116 S.D. *pinks*: pierces slightly with a sword (as it might be in the imagined duel).

137 S.D. *but lately from the ploughshare*: only recently transferred from agricultural work to domestic duties, and inexperienced in the puzzling ways of countesses.

155 S.D. *Shall we describe Sybil's frock . . . No, let us watch Maggie*: Barrie's conspiratorial stage directions for the reader accurately reflect the theatre audience's rapid sequence of changing attention.

169 S.D. *Caledonia*: Scotland.

178 *my hand . . . lost its cunning*: see Psalm 137: 5.

187 *a fly*: horse-drawn hackney carriage.

246 S.D. *cloth of silver*: tissue of silver threads, interwoven with silk or wool (*OED*).

258 *Give me the dagger*: see *Macbeth* 2.2.53. But the dagger is a paper-knife!

279 *reading of the will*: the reading of a dead person's bequests is not uncommonly the occasion for unpleasant discoveries, and Maggie's ruthless letter has a similar effect.

298 *Arcades ambo*: from Virgil, *Eclogues*, vii. 4; 'both Arcadians', i.e. two of a kind.

334 *womanish*: by this stage in the play this word has lost all currency as a term of self-disparagement. Its indirect effect is to make John (the only person in the theatre to take Maggie literally) the butt of affectionate comedy.

340 S.D. *lost, stolen or strayed*: conventional phrase in advertisements for a missing pet.

360 S.D. *in the black cap*: headgear worn by judges when pronouncing the death sentence.

408 *tragedy . . . found himself out*: as usual Barrie employs this term reductively yet with his own seriousness, to denote a wry and sobering acknowledgement of truth. The narrator of Barrie's 'Farewell, Miss Julie Logan' observes: 'The lad that once I was thought himself a gifted preacher, but the man he became knows better. That is nothing to boast of, for there is naught that houks the spirit from you so much as knowing better.' Much the same could be said of John Shand.

Mary Rose

1.1.9 S.D. *Monna Lisa's*: i.e. the Mona Lisa, the painting by Leonardo da Vinci in the Louvre.

47 S.D. *became such a friendly sound to us*: many Australian troops served with Allied Forces in Europe during the First World War, which had been over for less than eighteen months when *Mary Rose* was first performed on 22 April 1920.

55 *my cabbage*: Harry's literal translation of the French endearment, 'mon chou'.

76 *prodigal . . . done to a turn*: as in the parable of the Prodigal Son (Luke 15: 11–32).

111 *eight-day clock*: i.e. a clock designed to go for a full week without winding (the extra day allowed a margin for forgetfulness!).

125 *favoured parties*: i.e. those who deserve it!

189 *buxom*: in the obsolete sense 'obliging, bright, lively' (*OED*).

204 *stepping*: on your way.

236 S.D. *Then the crafty work begins*: the crafty work is of two kinds. One is technical: Barrie sets and delights in the challenge of effective scene-changing which this moment and its Act 3 reversal demand. The other is the craftiness of time, place, and atmosphere, the elusive power of the supernatural and the disturbing oddity of time's effects. Neat tricks of stagecraft and theatrical illusion are integral with plot and meaning, and calculated scenic effects are interpreted through the stage directions as

precise instructions for the play's adroitly measured blend of disturbance and comfort.

281 S.D. *of full habit*: of ample proportions (habit = bodily make-up).

288 S.D. *magisterial duties*: duties as a magistrate.

291 S.D. *believing it, too*: Barrie's psychology for Mrs Morland is similar to that for Maggie in *What Every Woman Knows*: each exercises an intuitively benign corrective influence on her husband, and settles for a minor public role in the partnership, a form of sexual self-effacement which is the source of a quiet authority. This reading of the approved wifely role may now be dismissed as sentimental, condescending, or fraudulently compensatory for women's actual low status, but it does represent a precise instruction for the playing of what are still eminently playable roles.

314 *going a bust*: spending money daringly.

334 *Gainsborough*: Thomas Gainsborough (1727–88) one of the greatest English artists of the eighteenth century.

370 *machine-made*: many forgeries have been exposed by failures to use hand-made paper of the correct date.

389 *wireless*: i.e. radio. The date of this scene is the early 1890s. Wireless came into use during the last decade of the nineteenth century; the earliest use of the word given by the *OED* is 1894.

397 *more things in heaven and earth . . . philosophy*: see *Hamlet* 1.5.166.

419 *midshipman*: the most junior officer rank in the Royal Navy; sub-lieutenant was the first level of promotion.

421 *tip him*: give him small presents of money. This convention precisely fixes Simon's status, on the borderline between cadet (schoolboy) and officer (adult), and the embarrassing abruptness of transition between the two.

445 S.D. *less fitted . . . tragic role*: but for this very reason more exactly suited for the 'tragic role' in the reductive, ironic, and poignant sense of the term which imaginatively interested Barrie.

497 *freeholds and leaseholds . . . hire system*: freehold is outright ownership of property; leasehold is tenure for a limited period (though often extending beyond a normal lifetime) and usually entails payment of annual ground rent; the hire system is rental. All are, therefore, ways of setting up house independently, which in the event Simon and Mary Rose never actually do. Although practical reasons are supplied for this, it is still a symptom of Mary Rose's ambiguous maturity. Barrie's concern with mundane practicalities is often dramatically suggestive also. (Gravel soil drains well and is held to protect against damp; it still features in advertisements for some preparatory schools.)

547 S.D. *tacking*: changing course.

550 *larky*: mischievous.

577 *people*: parents.

702 *stop the growth . . . blooming*: one of many resemblances which suggest that this play is an autumnal *Peter Pan*.

749 *chaffing*: teasing.

761 S.D. *these two children*: i.e. Mr Morland and Mary Rose.

782 *Honest Injun*: on my honour; derived from Red Indians' assurances of good faith.

806 *nailers*: 'an exceptionally good hand at something' (*OED*). This is what Simon takes Mary Rose to mean by 'good': he assures her that they will be adept at being a loving betrothed couple. However, this is not her meaning exactly. Nor do her words 'Holy' and 'good' refer conventionally to religiously sanctioned virtue. More ominously, she implies a continuing childlike disengagement from the fully adult physicality of courtship and marriage, a strange chastity and innocence produced in her by the other world to which she still belongs. A few lines earlier Simon has similarly misunderstood what she means by 'play'. His boyish manliness seems to be on a par with her innocence, but in reality he is almost adult and entirely of this world, and she is neither.

817 *the little old woman*: an ominous moment of fey abstraction set against the childlike animation of Mary Rose's usual manner: the actress is called upon to brush her playing with shades of 'otherness', clearing the way for the final 'ghost scene' in Act 3. For the play to work effectively the two worlds of Mary Rose's life, though distinct as habitations, must always subtly coexist in her personality, and her childlike quality must always be unnerving as well as charming.

2.1.15 S.D. *whins*: gorse.

27 *Round Pond*: a famous feature of Kensington Gardens, an important place in Barrie's life and in the making of *Peter Pan*.

67 *trumpery*: trivial and worthless.

121 S.D. *gillie*: servant to hunters, fishermen, etc. in the Scottish Highlands.

123 *Iss it the wish . . . land*: Cameron's accent is that of the Highlander, marked chiefly by pronounced sibilances, and in dialect by certain differences in the formulation of tenses. The latter are important in the play because the obvious apparent meaning is not always the correct one. Several instances are noted below as they occur.

130 *There iss one little matter*: relations between the English and the Scots, which provided Barrie with so much comedy at the expense of both, and are a constant preoccupation in *What Every Woman Knows*, are the main source of comedy in this scene. They are, however, integral with the drama, not a mere diversion. The Scottish reverence for education places Cameron on a higher intellectual level than Simon and Mary Rose, but

his discreet superstition about the island ominously overrides Simon's mockery, and invites audience assent to the reason-defying hypothesis of the supernatural island. There may indeed be 'more things in heaven and earth' if the sharp-witted Cameron refuses to discount them, and this diverting comedy is therefore an essential means for Barrie to secure the audience response he wants.

136 *young matron*: young married woman and mother.

149 *the trouts iss now ready . . . humble servants*: a dry and humorous social reproof which indicates to the English couple (had they both ears to hear) their breach of Scottish democratic etiquette.

164 *Prenez garde . . . tellement*: [Mary Rose] 'Be careful, my dear.' [Simon] 'My God! What a funny chap he is!' [Mary Rose] 'But for my part, I like him; he is such a . . .'

167 *coquin*: in this context, 'someone who is amusingly provocative'.

171 *Euripides*: Athenian tragic dramatist, 484–406/7 BC.

191 *a long stay*: the polite enquiry is ironic and inauspicious.

192 *across*: i.e. across to the mainland.

220 *deportment*: behaviour.

230 *crofter*: in Scotland, tenant of a smallholding.

255 *chancey*: lucky, fortunate, safe, but often with a negative: 'not chancey' is 'not to be relied on, dangerous' (*SND*).

311 *a good thing to say*: Cameron says this and finds it good because it is rational; he does not believe it because the island is outside reason's jurisdiction.

318 *will be saying*: not the future but the continuous present tense: 'is in the habit of saying'.

337 *credulous one*: Simon's increasing rudeness is a sign of increasing unease.

341 *ducky*: interesting and quaint.

358 *will be fond of the fishing*: was fond of fishing.

378 *curdling*: blood-curdling.

399 *cold light of remorseless Reason*: this exemplifies Barrie's tendency to personal intervention in his own dialogue. Cameron as a character is represented as being pedantically insistent on his own intellectual rigour, and is wholly serious about it. Barrie gives him the pretentious phrasing in order to scoff affectionately at Scottish solemnity in matters educational, and is adding a personal edge to the scene's international comedy. Yet the distinction that Cameron is so earnestly drawing is wholly vindicated by the play and its outcome. Sometimes, as here, Barrie mistimes or overdoes his fondness for incidental verbal satire. It would be better to let Cameron speak without incurring laughter on a matter which the play as a whole takes very seriously.

406 *Beware, Mr Cameron . . . long cast*: Simon's speech (in contrast with Cameron's) is finely judged by Barrie. Simon is ridiculing Cameron's attitude because it alarms him and he wishes to dismiss it, so much so that it causes a lapse in the English good manners which Cameron so much admires.

462 *Have I been a nice wife to you, Simon?*: this is the kind of language which causes Barrie to be accused of whimsicality and mawkishness, but if played by a sensitive actress it will underscore (with fine dramatic timing) the ominous childlikeness of Mary Rose's speech throughout. It is notable in this scene that Simon's language has matured since Act 1, but Mary Rose's has not.

491 *when a young wife*: i.e. when a young wife tells her husband she is pregnant.

510 *bassinette*: a wickerwork basket used as a child's cradle.

537 *you can tie up marmalade*: Mary Rose protests because Simon (before the advent of screw-top lids) is matter-of-factly putting the cover on the marmalade instead of joyously screaming.

556 S.D. *Something else is happening*: Barrie's 'narrative' stage direction is a very precise orchestration of purposed stage effects. All through, from Mary Rose's first appearance and her parents' first Act recollections, the island magic is ambivalently placed between idyll and menace, a condition personally registered in Mary Rose's enigmatic innocence. The competing notes and voices demanded by Barrie here are a contest in sound which must be played both in musical effect and through Mary Rose's silent responses as obscure and indecisive. The call for Mary Rose which comes at the end of the play must be clearly distinguished in sound quality from the incantation of seductive naming which is heard here, confirming Harry's guess that benevolent supernatural forces have won the battle for Mary Rose's name.

3.1.13 *Punch . . . used to be*: *Punch* was a weekly satirical review which survived into the 1980s; but even in its heyday it was a conversational cliché to say that *Punch* was not 'what it used to be'.

46 *Bradshaw*: then the standard railway timetable and guide.

65 *Turner*: J. M. W. Turner (1775–1851), the greatest landscape painter of his time: both Kirkstall and Rievaulx abbeys were the subjects of major works.

67 *Girtin*: Thomas Girtin (1775–1802), a fine watercolourist who had been a pupil-apprentice to Dayes.

68 *Dayes*: Edward Dayes (1763–1804), a gifted topographical painter who taught both Turner and Girtin.

72 *Kirkstall Abbey*: twelfth-century Cistercian abbey, now part of the city of Leeds.

73 *Rievaulx*: twelfth-century abbey near Helmsley in Yorkshire.

78 *that Copperplate Magazine*: a magazine in which prints of copperplate engravings were reproduced; probably a specific reference to the *Copperplate Magazine, or Monthly Cabinet of Picturesque Prints, Consisting of Views in Great Britain and Ireland*, 5 vols. (Harrison and Co., London, 1792–1802).

81 S.D. *private glass*: personal magnifying glass.

144 *old Adam*: unrepressed natural male characteristics.

155 *blade*: jovial, extrovert man.

168 *jacket suit*: a two-piece dress-suit not including tails (at this period, 'in the evening the tail coat was still essential at all formal functions, but the dinner jacket was increasingly worn at home or when dining at the club'; James Laver, *A Concise History of Costume* (1969), 205).

181 *valley of the shadow*: a reference to Psalm 23.

236 S.D. *sea-dog*: old sailor.

259 *got the Bellerophon*: i.e. been appointed commander of HMS *Bellerophon*.

275 *Avaunt!*: Begone! (commonly, and here with dramatic irony, addressed to devils).

287 *We are all here*: i.e. it cannot be bad news about the family, because the whole family is present. This is a moment of characteristic discreet savagery in Barrie's depiction of the protective oblivion which guards human beings from heartbreak. Mrs Morland has forgotten both her daughter and her grandson. It is not she, but time, that Barrie is castigating.

323 *Mary Rose is coming across the fields*: Something of the eerie, scene-transforming effect of this magnificent line is coincidentally reflected in Philip Larkin's 'Going':

> There is an evening coming in across the fields
> That lights no lamps.
> Silken it seems at a distance,
> But when it is drawn up over the knees and thighs
> It brings no comfort.

334 *They will be saying*: people say that (virtually equivalent to 'the fact is . . .').

336 *she will be thinking*: she thinks.

396 *Cozens*: John Robert Cozens (1752–97), sometimes regarded as a fore-runner of Turner.

461 *allus*: always.

499 *shaver*: lad.

515 *cove*: fellow.

540 *Who is he?*: With this implication (not comic in performance) that even ghosts have fallible stamina of memory, the scene shifts towards potential

release. The impression is at once confirmed with Mary Rose's next speech, with its recessive slipping towards the childlikeness and longing for play from which—if the part is skilfully acted—she is seen never to have fully emerged.

566 *fallen out*: i.e. slipped accidentally back into this world (not 'quarrelled').

579 *The loveliest time of all*: Mary Rose is sitting on Harry's knee. In performance this scene risks sentimental absurdity and places great demands on the players. It needs to communicate the discomfort and eeriness of two worlds momentarily touching, and two time-schemes grazing each other. Although unconscious of Harry's identity, Mary Rose is fulfilling the moment which she once saw as the finale and completion of motherhood. The formal reversal of mother/child roles allows her to reassume the 11-year-old self which was first taken on the island, and her language at once becomes entirely (rather than partly) a child's. Only very tactful performance can produce the effect needed.

609 *mind*: remember.

	Six French Poets of the Nineteenth Century
HONORÉ DE BALZAC	**Cousin Bette**
	Eugénie Grandet
	Père Goriot
CHARLES BAUDELAIRE	**The Flowers of Evil**
	The Prose Poems and **Fanfarlo**
BENJAMIN CONSTANT	**Adolphe**
DENIS DIDEROT	**Jacques the Fatalist**
ALEXANDRE DUMAS (PÈRE)	**The Black Tulip**
	The Count of Monte Cristo
	Louise de la Vallière
	The Man in the Iron Mask
	La Reine Margot
	The Three Musketeers
	Twenty Years After
	The Vicomte de Bragelonne
ALEXANDRE DUMAS (FILS)	**La Dame aux Camélias**
GUSTAVE FLAUBERT	**Madame Bovary**
	A Sentimental Education
	Three Tales
VICTOR HUGO	**Notre-Dame de Paris**
J.-K. HUYSMANS	**Against Nature**
PIERRE CHODERLOS DE LACLOS	**Les Liaisons dangereuses**
MME DE LAFAYETTE	**The Princesse de Clèves**
GUILLAUME DU LORRIS and JEAN DE MEUN	**The Romance of the Rose**

ÉMILE ZOLA

L'Assommoir
The Attack on the Mill
La Bête humaine
La Débâcle
Germinal
The Ladies' Paradise
The Masterpiece
Nana
Pot Luck
Thérèse Raquin

The Oxford World's Classics Website

www.worldsclassics.co.uk

- Information about new titles
- Explore the full range of Oxford World's Classics
- Links to other literary sites and the main OUP webpage
- Imaginative competitions, with bookish prizes
- Peruse the Oxford World's Classics Magazine
- Articles by editors
- Extracts from Introductions
- A forum for discussion and feedback on the series
- Special information for teachers and lecturers

www.worldsclassics.co.uk

American Literature

British and Irish Literature

Children's Literature

Classics and Ancient Literature

Colonial Literature

Eastern Literature

European Literature

History

Medieval Literature

Oxford English Drama

Poetry

Philosophy

Politics

Religion

The Oxford Shakespeare

A complete list of Oxford Paperbacks, including Oxford World's Classics, Oxford Shakespeare, Oxford Drama, and Oxford Paperback Reference, is available in the UK from the Academic Division Publicity Department, Oxford University Press, Great Clarendon Street, Oxford OX2 6DP.

In the USA, complete lists are available from the Paperbacks Marketing Manager, Oxford University Press, 198 Madison Avenue, New York, NY 10016.

Oxford Paperbacks are available from all good bookshops. In case of difficulty, customers in the UK can order direct from Oxford University Press Bookshop, Freepost, 116 High Street, Oxford OX1 4BR, enclosing full payment. Please add 10 per cent of published price for postage and packing.